A Maritime Archaeology
of Ships

A Maritime Archaeology
of Ships

Innovation and Social Change
in Medieval and Early Modern Europe

Jonathan Adams

Oxbow Books
Oxford and Oakville

Published by
Oxbow Books, Oxford, UK

ISBN 978 1 84217 297 1

A CIP record for this book is available from the British Library

This book is available direct from

Oxbow Books, Oxford, UK
(Phone: 01865-241249: Fax: 01865-794449)
and
The David Brown Book Company
PO Box 511, Oakville, CT 06779, USA
(Phone: 860-945-9329; Fax: 860-945-9468)

or from our website
www.oxbowbooks.com

Library of Congress Cataloging-in-Publication Data

Adams, Jonathan, 1951-
  A maritime archaeology of ships : innovation and social change in medieval and early modern
Europe / Jonathan Adams. -- First edition.
       pages cm
  Includes bibliographical references and index.
  ISBN 978-1-84217-297-1
  1. Ships--Europe--History. 2. Ships, Medieval--Europe. 3. Underwater archaeology--Europe.
I. Title.
  VM15.A43 2013
  623.8'121094--dc23
                                    2013042552

Cover: Rear inset: The craft of the medieval shipwright depicted as Noah (after a stained glass
window, Chartres Cathedral); front inset: the post-medieval shipright as professional from Mathew
Baker's *Fragments of Ancient English Shipwrightry, c.* 1572 (Courtesy of the Pepys Library, Magdalene
College Cambridge); Background: the wreck of *Sea Venture* (1609) (the author).

Printed in Great Britain by
Short Run Press, Exeter

Contents

List of Figures and Tables

Acknowledgements

Archaeology is by nature collaborative and interdisciplinary, so any research that brings together material from so many sites inevitably involves large numbers of people, many more alas than I can adequately thank here. In attempting this forlorn task I have broadly divided the following tribute: on one hand are those who have helped in a formative way as teachers, guiding lights and generous supporters, who opened the doors to maritime archaeology and helped me acquire the skills to pursue it. On the other are those who have worked with me in the field, although inevitably there is considerable overlap.

With regard to the subject's *raison d'être* (and to an extent that of this work) it was Seán McGrail who in 1977 first put me on the spot by asking why the *Mary Rose* was important enough to excavate let alone salvage? Having recently joined the project, and as a committed acolyte of Margaret Rule and Keith Muckelroy, I was somewhat taken aback. I assumed its importance was self-evident. Although he was partly playing 'Devil's advocate', later serving on the project's Salvage and Recovery Advisory Committee, the question was a serious one. I have justified both that project and maritime archaeology in various forums since then but I cannot remember my answer on that occasion being very persuasive. I only hope that what follows will convince him that some progress has been made.

Along with Seán the first who directly contributed to that progress was the Mary Rose Project's Archaeological Director Margaret Rule. In those early days, along with Keith Muckelroy and Andrew Fielding, our discussions on the diving support vessels *Roger Grenville* and *Sleipner* were just as focused as seminars I subsequently enjoyed in more stable and less salt-encrusted environments. Together with the practical experience we gained, this was unparalleled postgraduate training. As a director Margaret

routinely asked the impossible of her staff but she made us all believe that we could achieve it. Her constant encouragement was punctuated with various promotions up the supervisory ladder, on every occasion sooner than she needed to. If that were not all, once the *Mary Rose* was safely ashore Margaret was instrumental in getting me involved in the *Sea Venture* project in Bermuda. It was the continuity between these two projects that laid the foundations of this book (in particular chapters 4 and 6). My chief benefactors in Bermuda were the 'Sea Venture Trust', principally Allan 'Smokey' Wingood and Peggy Wingood. The *Sea Venture* lies in less than ten meters of water and as a result I spent more time underwater with Smokey than anyone else. Sadly he is no longer with us but I hope he would approve of the setting that *Sea Venture*, the 'Tempest wreck', has in this book. The other major projects I was lucky enough to join at this time were the excavation of the Roman wreck *St Peter Port* 1, in Guernsey, again through Margaret Rule, and the excavation of the Dutch East Indiaman *Amsterdam*. Under Peter Marsden's Direction I supervised the underwater excavation for him in 1984 then, when he returned to the Museum of London, I co-directed the next two seasons of work with Jerzy Gawronski. He and several other members of the Dutch team still make their annual visits to Hastings, maintaining the momentum of a very special enterprise. Working with Jerzy and the late Bas Kist of the Rijksmuseum was a doubly valuable experience as it also led directly to other things: Firstly, a rescue archaeology project off Rotterdam, where I had the good fortune to work with Thijs Maarleveld and Andre van Holk (and which furnished the material for chapter 7), secondly, my introduction to the astonishing database in the Baltic Sea. This occurred because Carl Olof Cederlund, then of the Swedish National Maritime Museum in Stockholm, spent a month with the

Amsterdam Project in 1984. As a result I visited Sweden the following year to supervise the underwater work on his Bossholmen/Oskarshamn Cog project. He subsequently supervised my doctoral research at Stockholm University and has been a guiding light ever since. Bossholmen was also where I first met Johan Rönnby another of Carl Olof's doctoral students and the person who has been my principal collaborator ever since. Succeeding Carl Olof as Professor in Marine Archaeology at Södertörn University, he has been instrumental in the success of project after project, in particular the 'Kravel', the *Elefanten* and *Mars* (chapter 4). Our investigations of sites in river, lake and sea throughout southern Sweden (in all seasons and all weathers) have furnished not only a series of joint publications and much of the information supporting this work but a store of indelible memories.

In addition to those already named, I have had the privilege of working with many other gifted people. In view of their number as well as the inevitability of omitting someone vital, I ask them to accept a collective salute and an expression of sincere gratitude. However, in terms of human endurance, there are a few whose help has exceeded the bounds of common sense: Christopher Dobbs, Kester Keighley, Charles Pochin and Nick Rule have lent their professionalism (and irrepressible humour) to almost every project encompassed in this book. They, together with Richard Keen, Fred Hocker, Adrian Barak, Colin McKewan, Chris Underwood, Jenny Black, Mats Eriksson, Brendan Foley, Cathy Giangrande, Erik Rönnby, David Parham, Anders Tegnerud and Ray Sutcliffe, have all spent hundreds of hours with me in or on the water, the laboratory, the office and on the road.

Some of those named above have also commented on various drafts of this work. Others who were assaulted with earlier versions of this text, related papers or who have contributed valuable insights in discussion include: Carl Olof Cederlund, Johan Rönnby, Fred Hocker, Richard Barker, Damian Goodburn, Alexzandra Hildred, Gustav Milne, Jerzy Gawronski, Brad Loewen, Brian Lavery, Colin Palmer, Lars Einarsson and David Gibbins. At the Department of Archaeology at Southampton, firstly within the *Centre for Maritime Archaeology*: Lucy Blue, Justin Dix, Fraser Sturt and Seán McGrail; in the Department at large: Tim Champion, Graeme Earl, Clive Gamble, J. D. Hill (now British Museum), David Hinton, Matthew Johnson, Simon Keay, Yvonne Marshall, David Peacock, Jo Sofaer, William Davies and the late Peter Ucko among others have provided a breadth of comment that would be difficult to match elsewhere. In this light I particularly thank Richard Barker who went through an earlier version of the text with a fine-toothed comb not only spotting errors but identifying aspects that needed amendment, further discussion or clarification. This version is considerably sharper as a result of his scholarship and generosity. Errors that remain are of course my responsibility.

Other organisations to which I'm indebted include the Mary Rose Trust; Guernsey Museums & Galleries (in particular Heather Sebire); National Museum of Bermuda (in particular Edward Harris and Robert Steinhoff); Swedish National Maritime Museums; Stockholm County Authority; Kalmar County Museum; the Pepys Library, Magdalene College, Cambridge; The National Maritime Museum, Greenwich (then Brian Lavery, Ian Friel and the late David Lyon); and the Stichting VOC Schip Amsterdam. I am also indebted to Teddy Tucker, the Bermuda Wrecks Authority and, more recently, to Peter Bojakowski and Katie Custer Bojakowski, for the opportunity to work on the *Warwick* (see chapter 6), and to Nigel Boston, Lars Göran Uthberg and Anders Tegnerud who provided research vessels and other equipment for the 'Kravel' project (chapter 4). Philippe and Pia L'Obry, Kenneth and Susanne Lindrooth and Tony Heep, all of Malma Kvarn, generously provided assistance in logistics relating to the 'Kravel' project. To Stolt Comex Seaway who supported three major projects: *Mary Rose*, *Amsterdam* and the 'Kravel', with substantial equipment and technical expertise. Most recently for cutting-edge work in the Baltic, made possible by Marin Mätterknik (Carl Douglas and Ola Oskarsson); Deep Sea Productions (Malcolm Dixelius) and Ocean Discovery (Richard and Ingemar Lundgren).

For the production of this book I first thank David Brown at Oxbow Books for commissioning it, Clare Litt and Julie Gardiner for their patient encouragement, Val and Roger Lamb for everything to do with design, typesetting and proofing. Remaining errors are my responsibility.

Lastly, my thanks also go to students of the subject, both in Sweden and in my own Department, many of whom have also helped on these projects and made valuable comment on the content here. The future of the subject is in good hands.

Jonathan Adams,
University of Southampton 2012

Preface

This book builds on a previous study (2003) in which I focused on major episodes of technological change in northern European shipping between 1450 and 1850. A relatively small print run soon ran dry and a revised version was commissioned. It was David Brown at Oxbow Books who readily agreed to provide the format for a large number of illustrations reproduced at higher quality than seems to be the dismal norm of many academic publications in these digital times. However, the intensity of my involvement in research projects continued unabated as did the remarkable series of discoveries, particularly in the Baltic where much of my research has been carried out. Much of this new material could not be ignored and so simple revision progressively gave way to rewriting and substantial addition. Of the chapters that are recognisable from the earlier book, all have been updated and expanded and several significant new discoveries have been incorporated in the discussion of the social changes that transformed a medieval Europe into a modern, global world. I also bit the bullet and added an entirely new chapter on one of the most controversial subjects of medieval ship archaeology: the much-discussed 'hulk'. This greater volume of material and a considerably expanded time frame of nearly seven hundred years transformed this into a different book and necessitated a new title. The acknowledgements however stand largely unaltered saving the addition of key people whom I have had the good fortune to work with in the last decade. What is a little annoying however is that I know that with every passing year new material will come to light that will need to be considered alongside what is here. Of course this is a condition of all research but it seems that the pace is especially rapid in maritime archaeology at present. For those interested in this field of archaeology and in particular those beginning their studies in the subject, it is an interesting time to be a maritime archaeologist.

1

Pathways and Ideas

Premises

How and why things change (and why they don't)
are central concerns of archaeology, being
imprinted on and variously visible in the material
remains of past human existence: the archaeological
record. As changes in material culture imply
changes in the society that produced it, the
technologies used in its production provide one
of the primary means of analysing the nature of
those changes and their trajectories. In other
words an archaeological study of technology is
necessarily a study of change and indeed of stasis,
both being active processes involving a dynamic
relationship with society. It is however episodes
of change with which this book is chiefly
concerned, and among the myriad forms that
material culture may take, boats and ships were
often the most complex expressions of technology
that societies achieved. The production, use and
disposal of watercraft involved complex patterns
of behaviour and communication within and
between communities. Hence the material
culture of water transport offers one of the best
means of interrogating changes within past
societies, especially considering the 'fine-grained'
nature of the remains preserved in marine,
riverine and lacustrine environments.

Formerly it is debatable how far nautical
research capitalised on these advantages. We
tended to focus on ships as technological
phenomena *per se* rather than relating them to
the contexts of their production. This produced
a database of increasing richness, heavily
augmented by material discovered under water.
But while the database constituted an eloquent
record of change having happened it did not

explain it. On the contrary, technologically
orientated research, especially when entrapped in
simplistic, linear, evolutionist frameworks, has
generated a series of problems that have repeatedly
defied solution. Might these puzzles be more
easily solved when investigated within the social
contexts in which those technologies were
conceived and created? The publications of
synthetic analyses of major projects over the last
decade show how things have progressed but even
these are necessarily focused on individual sites
and vessels.

This book aims to complement this research
by addressing wider but unifying themes through
a series of medieval and post-medieval ships that
represent the major shipbuilding traditions of
northern Europe. Although they are considered
chronologically, this is not a narrative history of
ships but rather the basis for focusing on key
episodes of technological change. Re-examination
of these ships in the contexts both of their
building tradition and of the wider societies in
which they were produced reveals new causal
factors and explanatory relationships.

From the vantage point of the ships themselves
this approach also provides new perspectives on
their respective societies, highlighting aspects that
otherwise remain opaque. The relationship
between social change and its manifestation in
shipping not only reaffirms the role of ships in
the most significant developments of the medieval
and modern worlds but as highly significant
agents in the transition between them. The
strength of this relationship also suggests that the
archaeological boat record is one of the most
potent but as yet under-exploited ways of
investigating prehistory.

Context and scope

A book on the archaeology of ships is in one sense rooted in what Keith Muckelroy defined as '*nautical archaeology*' in that it focuses, at least initially, on ship technology (Muckelroy 1978:4). Yet in line with the stated premises it aims to interpret this technology in a social context, encompassing the ways ships are conceived, designed, constructed, used and disposed of. As the activities of shipbuilding and seafaring constitute social practice, the associated material culture provides an indispensable means for the analysis and interpretation of societies that have utilised water transport and engaged in maritime activity in general. In this sense it goes beyond what Muckelroy saw as the bounding limits for his preferred term *maritime archaeology*, defined by him as '*the scientific study of the material remains of man and his activities on the sea*' (*ibid.*), for it necessarily addresses '*...related objects on the shore*' and '*...coastal communities*', aspects explicitly ruled out of his definition (Muckelroy 1978:6). This book not only addresses those related objects and communities but also social factors that are not necessarily even located on the waterfront. Indeed these include aspects that are immaterial as well as material, and so in another important sense this study ventures beyond what Keith would have regarded as the proper limits of archaeology: '*Of course, archaeological evidence possesses its own inherent weaknesses, notably in being unable to shed light on people's motives or ideas...*' (Muckelroy 1978:216). Most archaeologists now take a more ambitious line, allowing that cognitive and symbolic aspects of past societies can indeed be inferred or 'read' from their material remains, though in what ways and to what degree is hotly debated. In the light of this greater scope and taking Muckelroy's scientific component of archaeology as a given, one might therefore suggest that maritime archaeology is *the study of the remains of past human activities on the seas, interconnected waterways and adjacent locales*.

These differences in perspective are not intended as a negative critique of Muckelroy's definitions or of his general theoretical stance, especially as by the time of his tragic death in 1980 he was already exploring other avenues. The scale of his achievement remains undiminished, and among those who worked with him I am not alone in having wondered, at tricky moments of archaeological decision, what he would have done in the circumstances. So although things he

regarded as limitations are now seen as legitimate challenges for a host of approaches across the archaeological spectrum, much of what follows is still in tune with his general vision for the development of this branch of the discipline.

That being the case, like McGrail (1984:12) who also felt the criteria set by Muckelroy to be too narrow, I nevertheless regard 'maritime archaeology' as the most suitable term for the multiplicity of source material concerned, even when focusing on ship-related research questions (Adams 2002a).

The material presented here is inevitably drawn from past as well as current work, so, although a comprehensive account of the development of maritime archaeology is not within the scope of this book,[1] its theoretical orientation and objectives need to be made explicit in the context of recent thinking. What follows therefore is less a comprehensive historical narrative than a map of approaches and ideas that evaluates some of the key events, factors and people that have contributed to the subject's current state and of the investigative context within which that work was conceived and carried out. This begins with an assessment of early underwater work, firstly because that is where most of the ships with which this book is concerned were found, and secondly, by identifying the formative ideas and theories that drove that work and mapping them onto the general archaeological thinking of the time, we can more clearly understand the nature of the subject as it is currently practiced.

In turn archaeological thinking itself requires some benchmarking, especially as over the period in question, more than half a century, archaeology's theory has been far from static. An added complication is that while it has moved through more or less distinctive phases the trajectory has not been uniform even within the various sectors of the discipline let alone globally. In relation to maritime developments however culture-historical models of the past constructed on the basis of empirical observation and description prevailed, broadly speaking, until the 1960s when, initially in North America and Europe, they were challenged by the New Archaeology, overtly scientific, generalist and processual in its approach (Binford 1972). In its turn the New Archaeology was challenged in the early 1980s by 'post-processual' contextual approaches (Hodder 1986). Some European archaeologists still identify themselves as post-processual but others resist being categorised and today no single perspective dominates although there are international differences in emphasis. The characteristics of these theoretical schools will become clearer below but for a thorough yet digestible analysis the reader is directed to Johnson (1999, 2011).

Foundations

Opinions vary as to who directed the first truly archaeological excavation carried out under water, partly because of the criteria deployed. If it is implicit that the director should have archaeological training, this rules out several notable excavations that occurred before any archaeologist ventured into the water. One that is relevant to subsequent discussion was directed by Carl Ekman, a Swedish naval officer who excavated the Swedish warship *Elefanten* (1564) between 1933 and 1939 (Ekman 1934, 1942). His work was systematic, thorough (especially considering the technology then available to him) and remarkably modern in that it was carried out for predefined reasons of research and heritage preservation rather than casual curiosity or financial gain. His rationale, albeit ideologically coloured by his naval historian's view, was that the remains of ships so significant in Sweden's past and thereby of the 16th-century shipbuilder's art, must be saved and preserved in a museum setting (Cederlund 1983:46, 1994). In this, as will be seen, he was largely successful.

In the late 1950s a French naval officer, Jacques-Yves Cousteau and his Undersea Research Group excavated an amphora mound at Grande Congloué, near Marseilles, using the new *aqualung* he had developed with engineer Emile Gagnan.[2] Cousteau is often credited with being the first to use airlifts for archaeological excavation (e.g. Bass 1966:125; Delgado 1997:22), but Ekman had used them on *Elefanten* in the 1930s (Cederlund 1983:48). Overall the archaeological standards at Grande Congloué were deemed inadequate even for the time. The effects of Cousteau's work were nevertheless far reaching. He had set precedents and demonstrated the potential of the new SCUBA for controlled underwater excavation (Muckelroy 1978:14). But according to Philippe Diole (1954:150–170) this was not the first archaeological work carried out under water in France. In the 1940s Réné Beaucaire was excavating Roman domestic dwellings at Fos-sur-Mer in the Gulf of Saint-Gervais. Much of the site is now underwater so he literally followed it into the sea. In the relatively shallow waters some work was possible but opinions vary as to its extent and also on how much was achieved. It is interesting that neither Cousteau nor Beaucaire are celebrated as true pioneers of underwater archaeology in France. That accolade goes to Philippe Taillez, head of the French Navy Diving School at Toulon (Elisabeth Veyrat pers. comm.). He had worked with Cousteau at Grand Congloué but there the similarity ends, for in his excavation of a Roman wreck on the Titan Reef in 1952, he demonstrated an attitude towards underwater archaeological material that was ahead of its time (Du Plat Taylor 1967; Muckelroy 1978:14).

Other work that constituted a real advance was the excavation, also of a Roman wreck, at Albenga, by the Italian archaeologist Nino Lamboglia. He himself did not dive, nor apparently would he permit his archaeological assistants to do so, something that puzzled another of the subject's pioneers, Peter Throckmorton, when he visited the site (Throckmorton 1987:22). Lamboglia relied on photography and what his non-archaeologist, professional divers told him, clearly a limitation. In contrast, the benefits of first hand observation were already being demonstrated by Honor Frost. With archaeological training and able to dive, she had worked with or knew many of these Mediterranean pioneers. She undertook various projects, some of them with Frédéric Dumas, an enlightened collaborator of Cousteau's at Grande Congloué, others with Throckmorton, a visionary whose general contribution to the development of this new field was considerable. At this stage her work was more orientated to survey and recording than to excavation (Frost 1963) but among other things, she was establishing the true nature of features erroneously described by divers to the Jesuit priest Pierre André Poidebard (Frost 1972:97, 107). His excellent survey work of Levantine harbours in the 1930s using aerial photography was pioneering but in this instance had been compromised by the same limitation accepted by Lamboglia.

Perhaps the first example of a comprehensive, professionally directed underwater excavation that would satisfy any professional code of conduct today was carried out on the Bronze Age wreck at Cape Gelidonya, directed by George Bass in 1960. The conceptual difference that marks this out from earlier projects was Bass's realisation that, although at a depth of 30m each person's work would be limited to twenty or thirty minutes at a time, there was no reason for it not to conform to the minimum standards expected on land. As Muckelroy put it, this excavation '... *allowed few if any concessions to the fact of being underwater...*' (Muckelroy 1978:15). The corollary of this was the requirement for a team that was recruited on the basis of skills relevant to archaeology rather than to diving (Bass 1966:18–19). Frost had thought it impossible for anyone to be both a professional archaeologist and a professional diver, so that if archaeology was to be successfully carried out under water, archaeologists would have to work closely with professional divers (Frost 1963:xi). Bass realised, as the major oil field diving companies were to, that it is easier to teach someone with a professional skill to dive than the other way round. This reversed the previous mode in which the archaeologist was seen as an adjunct to the team of 'real' divers. Of course there need be no difference and today many professional archaeologists are also professionally qualified divers. But whether they are or not, the principle is that archaeology whether on land or under water should be done by archaeologists, at least in the sense of controlling strategy and procedure,[3] and this is what was done at Gelidonya.

The late 1950s and early 1960s was one of the key developmental periods in the theory and practice of this new field. Momentum had been building in various countries and several highly significant events occurred at much the same time. Not long after the Gelidonya excavation, Ulrich Ruoff was demonstrating the wholesale application of archaeological method on submerged prehistoric sites in the Swiss lakes (Ruoff 1972). Similarly painstaking excavation of the remains of five Viking ships found in Roskilde Fjord, Denmark, was taking place under Olaf Olsen and Ole Crumlin-Pedersen (Olsen and Crumlin-Pedersen 1967; Crumlin-Pedersen and Olsen 2002). Although it had begun as an underwater investigation in 1957, it was then converted to a land excavation by the installation of a cofferdam. Even further north, in 1961 the salvage of the Swedish warship *Vasa* (1628) from Stockholm Harbour (Franzén 1967) set in motion an enormous archaeological investigation carried out by a team of eleven archaeologists under Per Lundström (Lundström 1962; Cederlund and

Hocker 2006). The following year further dramatic ship finds were made: a medieval cog discovered in the River Weser at Bremen in Germany, and on the other side of the world the wreck of the VOC ship *Batavia* was discovered in Western Australia. Just as in Sweden and Denmark, these sites would play a significant part in the development of maritime archaeology in their respective countries. *Batavia* was excavated under water (Green 1975), but as with the Swedish and Danish finds, the archaeology of the Bremen cog, was largely carried out after the wreck had been recovered. They were nevertheless part of the growing corpus of potent 'underwater' archaeological finds.

Britain and Ireland's tentative moves into this new field were characterised not by a single large scale project but by a flurry of shipwreck investigations from the Scillies to the Shetlands. Of note were a series of Armada wreck excavations directed by Colin Martin (Martin 1975; Martin and Parker 1988), in whose team was the young Keith Muckelroy. In parallel with these, several wrecks of Dutch East India Company ships were investigated including the *Kennemerland* (1664). It was on this site among others that Keith Muckelroy developed many of the ideas that underpinned his various seminal publications (Muckelroy 1975, 1977, 1978). In contrast to the substantial structures discovered in Germany and Scandinavia, *Kennemerland*'s hull was long gone. The ship survived only in the form of its guns, ballast and widely dispersed, largely fragmentary artefacts. Yet for maritime archaeology it proved fertile ground. This was just as well, for in 1967/68 Alexander McKee's team had discovered the Tudor warship *Mary Rose* at Spithead, off Portsmouth, England. The ship itself was not seen until 1971 (Rule 1982:57) but by the mid 1970s the project was steadily gaining momentum. It drew on the experience of all the European and Scandinavian ship projects, in particular that of *Vasa* which was seen as the closest logistic (and ideological) parallel. Unlike them however, the entire excavation of the *Mary Rose* was to be carried out underwater prior to salvage. Because of this the project became a focus for methodological development in northern European waters. Published estimates vary, but it is clear that nearly 600 people completed some 30,000 dives, the equivalent of fourteen working years under-water.[4]

The momentum generated by all these projects was considerable and to a very real extent is ongoing, especially now that substantive reports have been published. The series of publications emanating from Roskilde established a new benchmark for such work (e.g. Crumlin-Pedersen and Olsen 2002), followed by the first Serçe Limani volume (Bass et al. 2004), the first of the *Vasa* volumes (Cederlund and Hocker 2006) and all five volumes of the report on the Red Bay Basque whaler (Grenier et al. 2007). 2011 saw the publication of the fifth and final *Mary Rose* volume (Marsden 2003; Jones 2003; Gardiner 2005; Marsden 2009; Hildred 2011). Quite apart from these directly related aspects, such high-profile projects have significance for the discipline and society at large that extends beyond the intrinsic archaeological and historical value of the finds themselves. But despite these signal advances, these projects were still haunted by others that went under the banners of 'marine' or 'nautical' archaeology, etc. but which were nothing of the kind. So it is not surprising that, in terms of research strategy, there was little if any cohesion, even in regional terms let alone internationally. Momentum was increasing but often by unevenly lurching from one discovery to the next. In this sense the early years of the application of 'archaeology' in rivers, lakes and seas, as distinct from what Margaret Rule has dubbed 'antiqueology',[5] was inevitably reactive in nature. In this environment it is not surprising that there was a lack of any coherent body of theory and practice. By the 1970s, if there was any identifiable paradigm, in a Kuhnian sense, it concerned methodology. The assumption was that there is a link between field techniques designed to ensure the successful collection of data and subsequent analysis and interpretation. In other words the only basis on which the new 'sub-discipline' could successfully contribute to archaeology as a whole, breaking free of association with antiquarianism and outright treasure salvage, was to develop an appropriate methodology. This was not confined to the art of digging neat holes in the seabed, but embraced every aspect of strategy, excavation procedure, recording, post-excavation analysis and conservation of the recovered material. This was the prevailing ethos on the *Mary Rose* project in the late 1970s. In a very real sense many of those who were involved in this and other excavations at that time were conscious of the need to 'catch up' with land archaeology and demonstrate credibility through controlled excavation and recording, and the acquisition of high quality

data. This was assumed to be the passport to academic acceptance of archaeology under water as valid research, rather than simple object recovery. This method-centred approach was a positive side of what was otherwise a somewhat rudderless progress though it can be argued that this was an inevitable and even necessary stage in terms of the subject's general development. Gosden (1999:33–61) has made a similar point with reference to the development of archaeology itself, citing the work of Pitt-Rivers, and of anthropology through the fieldwork of Malinowski.

This preoccupation was one reason why, when the juggernaut of the New Archaeology hove into view, attended by aggressive debate between its proponents and 'traditionalists', the underwater community took relatively little notice. While methodology and theory are undoubtedly linked, the mistaken assumption was that method provided theoretical self-sufficiency. Not that conscious theorising had much significance to many of those who were practising at the time in any case. As recently as 1990 Gibbins referred to: '*...the relative scarcity in this field of scholars who are strongly conversant with prevailing archaeological method and theory*' (Gibbins 1990:383). Lenihan (1983:39) put it more poetically in observing that the demands of the environment surrounding shipwreck sites have perhaps tended to stir men of action more than men of contemplation. Though Lenihan was speaking figuratively, it is worth noting that in the UK the gender bias in the practice of this new area of archaeology was less than it was in the discipline as a whole.[6] The fact remains that there has long been a perceived dichotomy between 'dirt archaeologists' and theoreticians and, in the light of the explicit emphasis on method and technique, many underwater workers felt they belonged in the 'dirt' category even though such views were intrinsically theoretical. Though this dichotomy has become less marked, Hodder noted that it was still evident in land archaeology in the 1990s (Hodder 1992:1). Similar views were also evident internationally. At a subsequent *European Association of Archaeologists* conference in Gothenburg a number of those present who were contract archaeologists – 'diggers' – were generally unreceptive or even disparaging of views expounded by the more overtly theoretical speakers.

Another factor for the archaeology being practised under water in the 1970s was that some of its chief practitioners were not archaeologists by training but had moved into the subject from various backgrounds. Of twenty-one contributing authors to the 1972 UNESCO publication *Archaeology Underwater, a Nascent Discipline*, less than a quarter were archaeologists of any description by academic training. They were far outnumbered by scientists and engineers. This is not surprising for a field that was so new and in some ways it was an advantage. As a group they were more entrepreneurial, assumed nothing was impossible and had developed autonomous trusts and raised private funding in a way that mainstream archaeology was not to do for another ten years. Archaeologically, they strenuously attempted to produce results of a professional standard in terms of what they understood archaeology to be, essentially a normative culture-history. In this they modelled their work on those in the field who were archaeologically trained, many of whom were classicists (cf. Bass 1967; Casson 1971; Basch 1972).

The other obvious area of influence was medieval archaeology as so much of what was being discovered underwater was from that period or later. As Matthew Johnson has observed, medieval archaeology even in the early 1980s was still 'pre-processual' (Johnson 1996:xii). Under both influences nautical publications tended to be largely descriptive and such discussion as there was focused on method, technology and typologies. This is an observation rather than a criticism, for there were also other factors operating that related to the problems faced by a new field of study. As a parallel to a necessary emphasis on methodology suggested above, Bass (1983:97) has argued that the emphasis on data collection and classification is both inevitable and necessary for a new area of enquiry assembling its database. Nor is any academic snobbery intended in pointing to the non-archaeological background of practitioners. Firstly, some became leaders in the field in every respect. Secondly, entrepreneurial figures were often the public face of projects that had a solid academic stature.[7] The difficulty in judging the character of academic enquiry on the basis of publications is raised below. It remains true that the underwater and nautical communities were an eclectic blend possessed of remarkable energies. A disadvantage was that they were often peripheral to the archaeological mainstream. Forming societies, launching journals and holding their own conferences, while laudable

initiatives in themselves, reinforced the segregation promoted by the differences in their working environment and methods. Only a few underwater practitioners went to general archaeological conferences and similarly, few 'dry' professionals came to underwater conferences. The result was that to much of the European and American academic community, 'underwater archaeology' was variously seen as synonymous with treasure hunting, the lunatic fringe or at best a somewhat esoteric pursuit of little interest to central archaeological research. George Bass came up against the latter in the difficulties he had obtaining funding (Bass 1983:91). A happier situation prevailed in some places such as Sweden and Denmark perhaps due to the quality of the material being found and the evident scientific footing on which its recovery was based. Alas this did not promote recognition of the wider potential of the subject, probably due to ignorance about underwater environments, particularly the marine. This was assumed to be utterly destructive for any cultural material lost in it. Even if something were to survive, its recovery was not seen as the province of archaeology but of wreck exploration and engineering. If the succession of impressive things recovered by treasure hunters and 'antiqueologists' (as well as those recovered by the UNESCO contributors) steadily eroded the misapprehension about the preservative properties of the environment, they did little to promote the realisation that this was first and foremost an archaeological resource. Even those 'dry' archaeologists and museum curators who began to realise the extraordinary nature of submerged archaeological sites found it difficult to accept that their investigation could be anything other than fiendishly difficult. For a long time this tacit assumption meant that second-rate work was applauded as an achievement, and worse, that treasure hunting continued to masquerade as archaeology. Although Bass, Ruoff and others had demonstrated it was possible to carry out controlled archaeological work under water, it took a surprisingly long time for the ethical corollary of this to be acknowledged: if, on a particular site, it proved impossible to maintain appropriate standards, then it should not be excavated at all unless it was under threat.

Continued segregation and erroneous stereotyping were therefore effective impediments to the acceptance of underwater research by the archaeological mainstream. So even in the late

1970s, if asked what they thought of the New Archaeology, few underwater practitioners would have been able to give a considered reply and many would have assumed it to refer to the new 'underwater' archaeology that they themselves were doing.

Archaeology or anthropology?

In contrast to most of Europe and Australia, some North American scholars involved in the archaeology of shipwrecks enthusiastically embraced the New Archaeology. This was eloquently manifested in the proceedings of a symposium on shipwrecks as anthropological phenomena entitled 'Shipwreck Anthropology' (Gould 1983). As the title implies, the majority of the contributors advocated generalist, anthropological approaches and, in tune with the times, nomothetic goals: approaches that sought to discover general or 'covering' laws of human behaviour applicable cross-culturally. In the process a robust critique was directed at the particularist nature of then recent and current research. Contributors included some prominent names such as Mark Leone, Patty Jo Watson and of course the volume's editor Richard Gould. Watson (1983:27) maintained that, as in any other variant of archaeology, shipwreck research can be specific or general in the questions that it addresses. She cited various publications that represented the former specific or idiographic emphasis from Marsden (1967) and Fenwick (1978), which she labelled '*rather minutely particularistic*', to others including Bass (1967) which she termed 'broader historiography'.

> ...*but all are characterized by a primary emphasis on the particular wreck or set of wrecks rather than on a general question or problem to which the wrecks were thought to be relevant.*

She then noted that there were no good published examples of the second nomothetic emphasis, though she acknowledged that this was doubtless because the field was so young and because in this early phase so many wrecks had been found by accident.

The most conspicuous dissenter among the volume's contributors was that of George Bass who argued that there was a place for particularistic study and questioned many of the taken-for-granteds of processual anthropology such as formal research designs (Bass 1983:100). With the benefit of hindsight it is interesting to consider

the advocacy of generalist approaches embodied in the comments by Watson. In criticising idiographic (particularist) work she outlines a generalist research programme centred around the Bronze Age wreck excavated by Bass and his team at Cape Gelidonya. Summarising the new insight that the excavation gave to our understanding of later second millennium BC trade, she says that, while fascinating to ancient historians, these details are also of interest to the anthropological generalist concerned with long distance trade, with technological innovation and diffusion, or with the expression of ethnicity in the material goods. Her suggested research design for the 'anthropological generalist' would require data from the cargoes of several other eastern Mediterranean ships, especially information on metals and metallurgy, that pre- and post-dated the Gelidonya wreck which could then be compared with the evidence from terrestrial sites in the same geographic region, etc. (Watson *ibid.*). Admittedly, at the time, many people working underwater would not have conceived a project in such broad terms (though Toby Parker's work for one used specific sites to address broader themes of trade and exchange (Parker 1984, 1992). But much of this research design was already encompassed within Bass's historiographic approach, such as: 'detailed knowledge' of several wrecks, etc. As to the wider issues, it was Bass's concern with long distance trade and exchange networks that is evident in the published work on Gelidonya. Bass and his team were already looking for other Bronze Age wrecks, and indeed discovered the even more dramatic wreck at Uluburun (Bass 1987, Pulak 1998). It was the aggregate expression of ethnicity in the Gelidonya assemblage that led Bass to suggest a Canaanite origin for the vessel and crew, at a time when it was assumed that maritime trade would have been dominated by the Mycenaeans.

Watson rightly concludes that the logical response to the debate between the generalists and the particularists is that both emphases are essential and inseparable (Watson 1983:31), and while a '*direct historical approach*' and other narrowly particularistic techniques are necessary, they are not ends in themselves. Instead

> *carefully designed and executed particularistic studies can be employed in the pursuit of broadly conceived questions about processes generalizable to many human societies, regardless of their placement in time or space (ibid.:33).*

The degree to which social processes can truly be generalized across cultures became a focus for much subsequent theoretical debate but it could nevertheless be questioned how concrete or significant the distinction drawn between generalist and particularist stances really is. Watson argued that generalist questions can only be answered after the acquisition of 'detailed' information. Bass's recording of the Gelidonya site, the structural remains and the ship's cargo facilitated not only a reconstruction of that particular vessel, its crew, its contents and its last voyage, but a reappraisal of early 2nd millennium BC eastern Mediterranean trade and potentially all the aspects included in Watson's suggested research design.

This raises the question as to what particularism really is. In a sense it is not really a theoretical perspective at all but an aspect of empirical observation and data collection. As such it is a phase through which every archaeological field project must pass: from a starting point of both general and specific research questions to detailed observation and recording of the archaeological source material, then to reconstructing and understanding specific aspects of that site, and finally to answering more general questions and interpreting the site in wider social and environmental contexts. Hence the 'perennial archaeological dilemma' to be faced by Watson's hypothetical generalist: i.e. whether the excavator is *'justified in extracting only the information required for the specific research design being implemented'*, is less a dilemma than an inherent part of defining and executing research aims. This is especially so in today's environment where relatively few sites are excavated *in toto*, even under the constraints of developer funding and rescue. So selection during excavation is unavoidable both in terms of strategy and procedure and in terms of the researcher's socially situated preconceptions in interrogating the record. As Watson points out, excavation involves destruction. Thus responsible excavation must aim at dismantling deposits in such a way that both specific and general questions can be addressed, and which minimises destabilisation of any parts of the site left unexcavated (Adams 1986a, 2002b).

If detailed observation and recording of the data can be regarded as a particularistic phase of a research programme, so the mode of enquiry of several projects at a broadly comparable stage of development might appear to characterise an entire area of the archaeological discipline. Therein lies the root of many of the criticisms in Lenihan's contribution to 'Shipwreck Anthropology'.

> *The questions the marine historians and marine architects ask of shipwrecks are different from, but every bit as valid as, those an anthropologist would ask. What has been unfortunate is the fact that rarely is there an understanding by the former that major non-renewable resources are being destroyed for only highly focused data returns.* (Lenihan 1983:43).

Like Watson, Lenihan's substantive paper was also concerned with the perceived dichotomy between the general and the particular, taking his particularist cousins across the water to task, especially those in what he referred to as the 'British School of Nautical Archaeology' (Lenihan *ibid.*). In many respects these criticisms were justified but even at the time they deserved some qualification in the context of the subject's developmental stage, not only with regard to the method-centred priorities described above but to the types of site being investigated.

Damned with faint praise, the 'British School' was acknowledged to have an approach to excavation and interpretation as responsible and professional as that of some of the classical marine archaeologists. Their work however, was *'almost totally descriptive and oriented toward historic particularism.'* [though he refers to one 'major exception' by which he means Keith Muckelroy]... *Demonstrating little interest for the most part, in human behavioural problems, they operate almost totally without benefit of any demonstrable, explicit research designs, much like the classical archaeologists* (*ibid.*).

He then summarises the content of volumes of the *International Journal of Nautical Archaeology and Underwater Exploration* (IJNA) for the years 1978 and 1979, in which he observes: *'the concepts 'research design', 'research strategy', and 'theory' were never even prominently mentioned, let alone addressed.'* (Lenihan *ibid.*)

Admittedly there is a great deal of validity in this criticism (and he stresses it is a criticism). However, as indicated above there are mitigating factors to be taken into account when drawing attention to the influence of classical and medieval archaeology. Firstly, in terms of data collection and analysis, let alone synthesis and interpretation, the majority of projects were still at very early stages. Secondly, given the intentional and necessary emphasis on field technique, it was inevitable that authors would discuss methods, especially as in many cases they were being used for the first time.

A significant factor in the underwater work at the time was that the predominant site-type being excavated was shipwrecks. Outside the Mediterranean most of these were post-medieval. This was partly due to their visibility on the seabed, many having been discovered, as Watson noted, by divers and fishermen (Watson 1983:28). The level of preservation meant that on many of these sites there were vast amounts of surviving material, hence a potentially high return of new information. Any project involving excavation might face the recovery of hundreds, if not thousands of artefacts and all the attendant recording that necessarily went with it. This kind of work can quite easily appear to be frenzied data collection of an overtly particularistic kind. It also predisposes interim publications to be predominantly descriptive in their treatment.

Another factor is time. Even modestly scaled projects run over several years. Hence it is not surprising that in 1978 and 1979 the majority of papers published in the IJNA were of a descriptive nature, simply because they were 'initial', 'preliminary' or 'interim'. Indeed these adjectives occur eight times in titles during these years with several other titles using wording that implies a periodical rather than interpretative report. For example Colin Martin's paper on the *Dartmouth* (Martin 1978) was number 5 of a series. In such reports authors often emphasised the preliminary nature of the paper:

> *It is far too early, both in the course of excavation and in preliminary research, to attempt answers to numerous questions raised by the 1977 campaign at Serçe Liman.* (Bass and van Doorninck 1978:131).

It was twenty-six years too early in fact, not an unusual interval for large excavations, and answers were duly provided in the first volume of the subsequent final report (Bass et al. 2004).

The Journal was also intended to carry 'Technical Communications'. These, by definition, are usually concerned with method rather than the research for which they are being employed. They range in the volumes concerned from historical research (Ahlström 1979) to navigational control of surveys (Mazel and Reiss 1979). Others are concerned with specific artefact types, e.g. Spanish Armada pottery (Martin 1979). Lastly, several other papers, not to mention editorials, are clearly addressing issues of protection and management, the importance of which Lenihan acknowledges (Lenihan 1983:47).

That the term 'research design' was not prominent is therefore hardly surprising but its total absence is admittedly odd. Of course at that time it was a relatively recent term in academia, so even those authors who were formally trained were probably unfamiliar with it. An interesting anecdote in this context is one told by the Swedish archaeologist Mats Malmer, fieldworker, theoretician and one time Head of Archaeology at Stockholm University. He had counted the use of the words 'theory' or 'theoretical' 16 times in the first half page of a paper written by one of his colleagues. '*...on the other hand I searched in vain for the word in my own doctoral thesis.*' (Malmer 1997:9). Hence fashionable terminology does not necessarily relate to substance. An example of an IJNA paper in the cited issues in which research questions are outlined together with possible strategies with which to address them is Richard Bradley's paper on the interpretation of bronzes from rivers (Bradley 1979). Others such as Bass, did not care for formal research designs in any case, finding them proscriptive (Bass 1983:100). In this regard his comments were prophetic. The concept of a formal research design was integral to Hempelian philosophy and hypothetico-deductive approaches embedded in the New Archaeology. These days research designs incorporate a more flexible approach in the realisation that at every step new information modifies, in a series of feedback loops, the hermeneutic relationship between the investigator, the data and interpretation.

A reiteration of Lenihan's criticism of the published work in this field (e.g. *History of Seafaring*, Bass (ed.) 1972) centres on the complete lack of any '*that directly contribute to the anthropological database in a nomothetic sense.*' By then of course many archaeologists were beginning to regard 'covering law' as a mirage. Yet if these comments are not to be mere apologies for an emergent subject, a survey of the IJNA content since 1979 should show an increase in articles of interpretative nature or which clearly outline long term, multi-disciplinary research.

There have certainly been papers of an overtly theoretical nature since that time. However, heavily particularistic papers still feature which could be viewed as adding substance to Lenihan's criticisms. Furthermore no considered reply to the gauntlet thrown down in 'Shipwreck Anthropology' was ever made in print. The comments here are too late for that and, critique aside, the volume was something of a milestone in the development of the subject and is now much sought after (being long out of print). By bringing together Leone and Watson with those who worked on underwater sites such as Bass, Lenihan and Murphy, Gould facilitated the sort of intra-disciplinary discussion that has happily become more common (Adams 2006:2). Many years later at a conference on deep water archaeology at MIT, several land archaeologists participated, Patty Jo Watson among them. Her paper on the archaeology of marginal environments (in her case 'dark zone' caves) was of impressive breadth and perception, dealing with the archaeology of place, social context and the different levels of meaning these places have for us in the present and for those who used them in antiquity, issues of importance to the interpretation of any sites, including ships (Watson 1999).

There is one final observation to make on the reasons why processual, adaptationist approaches to understanding past societies had so little immediate impact even on those who appreciated what the New Archaeology and its agenda involved. It has been noted elsewhere that most New Archaeologists were prehistorians (Renfrew and Bahn 1991:406), while much shipwreck archaeology in the UK and northern Europe was being carried out on well preserved, post-medieval sites. The point has already been made that recording complex structures and recovering thousands of objects can appear to be an orgy of particularistic data collection. But in such circumstances it is a little difficult to focus on generalist approaches if you are up to your neck in the 'particulars' of history. One is literally within the physical context of past events and it is difficult (and unnecessary) to deny what Barker (1977:259) referred to as the 'frisson of discovery' especially when so much of it is new.

The middle range

Ironically, where the more rigorous approach of the New Archaeology did have an influence was partly born of the attempts to come to grips with the sheer volume and complexity of material being discovered in maritime sites. Above water, McGrail, influenced by David Clarke, advocated rigorous recording of ancient watercraft in order to reconstruct, test and analyse what he called 'floating hypotheses' (McGrail 1992). His work and that of Basil Greenhill, Eric McKee and others sought to develop new standards in the recording and analysis of both archaeological and ethnographic subjects in parallel with similar trends in Scandinavia (e.g. Olsen and Crumlin-Pedersen 1967; Christensen 1985; Cederlund 1978). Underwater, overtly scientific applications were brought to the examination of site formation processes. The chief exponent was Keith Muckelroy who had studied at Cambridge under David Clarke. In practice Muckelroy was as fascinated by specific circumstances as he was by general trends and his work on formation processes served both ends. In contrast to systems theory and covering laws, the importance of formation processes and their implications for interpretation seemed to most underwater workers to be intuitively obvious. If we did not understand how the site came to be as we found it, any subsequent conclusions might be seriously flawed. On several shipwreck excavations such as the Mary Rose Project, understanding the formation processes both modified excavation procedure and demonstrably improved the subsequent understanding of the ship and its contents. Hence the ideas of Schiffer (1976, 1987), Muckelroy (1975, 1978) and where stratification was concerned, Harris (1979, 1989), sat comfortably alongside the developments in underwater excavation technique. To an extent the study of site formation processes, often erroneously understood to be synonymous with the broader issues encompassed within 'middle range' research, is still a prominent feature of underwater work. This is partly a continuation of methodological concerns and partly because on many underwater sites a greater proportion of the deposits are formed through natural processes and are therefore understandable through physical modelling. To an extent one can view this as a positivist phase of underwater archaeology in Britain, involving strenuous attempts to understand site formation, together with methodologies designed to extract 'quantifiable' data for reconstruction and analysis. Yet in general, in contrast to the New Archaeology, this was resolutely pursued within historical approaches.

In this, aspects of maritime research might with hindsight be claimed to have anticipated subsequent developments. For as early as 1972, incidentally, the same year that Lewis Binford published 'An Archaeological Perspective', the Swedish maritime ethnologist Olof Hasslöf had recalled the discredited attempts of 19th- and 20th-century positivist historians like von Ranke to establish history as a scientific discipline and show 'how it really was' in the past (Hasslöf 1972a:10). Exactly the same criticisms were subsequently levelled at the New Archaeologists and the 'logical positivist empiricism' that characterised so much of their work (e.g. Hodder 1986; Gibbon 1989). In considering the nature of facts, Hasslöf used E. H. Carr's analogy of fish swimming about in the ocean, where what researchers catch will depend partly on chance but mainly on where they decide to fish and with what tackle, both in turn being determined by what kind of fish are being sought (Hasslöf *ibid.*). Just as 'history meant interpretation' for Carr, so did the research of living traditions and maritime material culture for Hasslöf. Like Carr, Hasslöf recognised that the information he was recording was not self-evidently the whole truth but was, on one level related to the ideas behind the material culture and on another, dependent on his context as a researcher. In this, as well as his analyses of fundamental aspects of shipbuilding (see chapter 4), Hasslöf was ahead of the game.

Shifting sands

Ironically, a year before 'Shipwreck Anthropology' appeared, Ian Hodder had published 'Symbols in Action' and 'Symbolic and Structural Archaeology' (Hodder 1982a; 1982b). They marked the beginning of a concerted challenge to the overtly nomothetic stance of the New Archaeology. If the traditional vs processual debate had largely gone unnoticed by the underwater community, Hodder's views were more enthusiastically received. Perhaps by then there was also a greater mutual awareness between the discipline as a whole and those working under water. By the mid 1980s underwater archaeology was becoming a more focused and respectable area of research. Since the mid 1970s there had been a steady trickle of people coming into the subject with a university training and therefore a larger proportion of the community who felt themselves to be archaeologists who happened to work under water rather than some sort of separate breed implied by the term 'underwater archaeologist'. It was almost as though having gone underwater in bewilderment at the New Archaeology, we surfaced in the mid 1980s and found that a concern with the historical and the specific event were legitimate after all. Not only that but, as many had always felt, successful archaeological interpretation needed to consider both the specific and the general, just as Watson (1981:31) had said. A re-assertion of the role of the individual in the past and of archaeology's links with history was greeted with sighs of relief. The proposed 'symbolic' or 'contextual' archaeology, or at least its more direct, bullish clarion calls, resonated much more with the general profile of underwater research. The assertion that material culture was not simply functional, a passive reflection of the past, or 'fossilised action' (Hodder 1982b:4) but was 'meaningfully constituted', active and possessed of more than one meaning depending on context (echoes of Hasslöf), fitted very well with the contextually rich assemblages which are so often found in shipwrecks which are discussed in the next chapter. It also anticipated more recent discussion on the nature of materiality, agency (of people and things) and the networks of relationships between them (Latour 2005; Miller 2005, 2010; Ingold 2007; Dolwick 2008, 2009).

This was fine, but as with the processual New Archaeology, this 'post-processual' phase was a mixed bag. Many found some if its ideas hard to swallow, in particular the rather depressing implication that we were doomed to a weightless environment of relativism where any handhold on 'real' or factual data was illusory. Ten years later Hodder observed that post-processual theory had not significantly impacted the way archaeology was actually practised (Hodder 1992:171), and at the time this was just as true for most of those working under water. Perhaps in both spheres this was another manifestation of dirt vs theory. Since then however there have been a growing number of research projects that have sought to bring variously contextual and reflexive approaches to bear on the process of field investigation, notably by Hodder himself at Çatalhöyük in Turkey (Hodder 2000). Here an explicit attempt was made to integrate post-processual theory into the way the site was excavated, recorded and made accessible. Similar approaches involving multi-vocality and community archaeology have been applied at the excavations of the Roman and Islamic ports at Myos Hormos/Quseir al-Qadim in Egypt (Moser 2003; Peacock and Blue 2006) and at Portus, the ancient port of Rome (Keay 2011; Keay and Paroli 2012).

From method to management

While archaeology's theoretical pendulum has oscillated violently over the last few decades, maritime archaeology has quietly profited. Although often perceived to be lagging behind, it nevertheless generated its own approaches as well as selectively adapting elements from the wider discipline and beyond. There have been distinct shifts in the subject's priorities or at least in the relative emphasis placed on certain themes. Over time there has been a gradual lessening of focus on method as an end in itself and a reduction in the dominance of ship-related research This has not been because the archaeology of ships and seafaring is no longer regarded as important but because the potential of other aspects of the maritime past have become increasingly apparent. As a result the generally dislocated and reactive character of the subject has become more cohesive, pro-active, and area-orientated, encompassing not only ships but other submerged structures, landscapes and maritime communities ashore and afloat. This has resulted from a number of interrelated developments: growing collaboration between researchers (wet and dry); improving theoretical maturity; changes in the management of underwater and coastal zone archaeology, and new educational initiatives at all levels. Nor is this a specifically British perspective. Many of these aspects of management have been in place to varying degrees, elsewhere in Scandinavia in particular but also in Australia, Canada, Holland and France to name a few.

None of these developments happen in a vacuum for, as with all other disciplines, the context of archaeological practice is society – the ultimate beneficiary. Alongside the strategic academic factors of formulating research and generating output are others that both constrain and enable. These have particular significance for the maritime archaeology of ships.

Money, policy, law and ethics

Ucko (1995:2) pointed out that the nature of the available funding mechanisms has a profound effect upon the overall complexion of the archaeology practised and this has certainly been visible in the work done along coasts and under water. The private, philanthropic, entrepreneurial style of funding particularly of underwater projects tended to promote site-specific investigation

rather than broader research programmes. Now, with greater interdisciplinary collaborations along with the establishment of inventories, not just of shipwrecks but all maritime sites, as well as a modest but significant presence in universities, maritime archaeological research has begun to adopt broader and longer term perspectives manifested in various regional suveys (e.g. McElearn et al. 2002; Hampshire and Wight Trust for Maritime Archaeology 2010), regional research frameworks (Williams and Brown 2010) and national research frameworks (Ransley et al. 2013).

Of course the ability to develop and execute long term strategies implies the existence of a certain level of policy and some sort of legislative and management infrastructure. A detailed analysis is not relevant here except to stress that that inadequacies of heritage management whether national or international have severely impacted on the preservation of maritime sites particularly shipwrecks. This is because in most countries the need to protect the underwater cultural heritage either did not exist or was not recognised until the second half of the 20th century. This meant that while protection and management of the historic environment on land was often long-established and in some cases relatively comprehensive, there was little or no provision for what might lie under water. To regulate activities in an environment that was increasingly accessible, some countries passed entirely new law, for example Australia's Historic Shipwrecks Act (1976, no. 190). Others such as Sweden simply augmented their existing ancient monuments legislation (Ancient Monuments Act 1942) to protect marine sites (Act no. 77, 1967). Others, including the UK, assembled composite systems of management largely from existing statutory instruments or their parts. Expedient this may have been, but managing cultural heritage with legislation never intended for that purpose is problematic, especially where the legislation enshrines principles that are incompatible with heritage protection, as in the case of salvage law.

The other limitation was that all these approaches were largely adopted for protection and control of sites lying within state territorial seas, out to 12 nautical miles. In the zones beyond, the degree of protection and control progressively reduces, something that has become alarmingly evident with the increasing impact of industry but also with the discovery and commercial exploitation of wrecks in deep water (Adams 2007).

Partly in response to the variability in national controls and to its virtual absence in international waters, UNESCO adopted its *Convention on the Protection of the Underwater Cultural Heritage* in 2001. Its proposal met determined opposition from the salvage industry, and from treasure hunters. At first the rate of ratification was slow, especially as most of the larger maritime powers including the USA and the UK had abstained. However, the Convention passed into law in 2009 and since then the number of states ratifying or adopting the Convention has more than doubled (Evans et al. 2011). Encouragingly several other maritime powers including France, have stated their intention to ratify while in others, such as Australia, it is under serious consideration. The UK, while not minded to ratify at present, has nevertheless stated in Parliament that it endorses the principles set out in the Annex to the Convention (Hansard 2008).

Knowing what is there

There are therefore grounds for cautious optimism, especially as heritage managers around the world are becoming increasingly aware of the importance of their intertidal and sub-tidal areas. Some countries may not have the resources to do much at the moment but awareness of a problem necessarily precedes action to address it. The key to any subsequent measures taken to protect and manage cultural heritage is gaining some idea of its nature and extent. The establishment of digital inventories of the historic environment is therefore crucial as they not only build sophisticated archives but are powerful tools for active management as well as research (Herrera et al. 2010). Assisting the construction of these databases is the new generation of marine survey technologies, in particular seismic reflection systems. Though not originally developed for archaeology, the utility of these systems for imaging archaeological material on and under the substrate has opened up new opportunities for the discipline (Quinn et al. 1997; Plets et al. 2006, 2008, 2009; Bates et al. 2011; Eriksson and Rönnby 2012). These systems have not only become indispensable for the purposes of quantifying the resource, but are also the means of rapid and efficient monitoring and where necessary optimising diver intervention (Quinn et al. 1998). They are also indispensable in larger scale interdisciplinary research projects such as the recent surveys of Doggerland (Gaffney et al. 2007, 2009) and deepwater surveys of wreck sites in Greece (Foley et al. 2011) or the Baltic (Eriksson and Rönnby 2012). A current initiative involving twenty-six states is the research network on the *Submerged Prehistoric Archaeology of the Continental Shelf* (SPLASHCOS) funded through the European Union's COST Scheme (Bailey and Sakellariou 2012). Investigation on this scale would not be possible without the new technologies. Furthermore because these technologies are generic across the marine sectors, data collected by offshore industry have become available for heritage management and archaeological research (Flemming 2005; Eriksson and Rönnby 2012; Sturt and Nilsson forthcoming).

This is a partial and admittedly personal perspective on the current complexion of maritime archaeology. A complementary analysis of the subject and its theoretical development on a global scale and from a Latin American perspective has been undertaken by Jorge Herrera (2009, and in preparation). Both, I believe, reveal a subject which is facing severe challenges but which has also achieved substantive development in recent years manifested in increased interdisciplinary investigations into past human activity represented by all forms of evidence preserved in the subsea, intertidal and coastal zones. This of course includes watercraft, as they will always remain one of the most significant entities of the maritime past, and it in no way detracts from the best investigations to date to argue that we have by no means exhausted their potential.

Notes

1   For a broad introductory overview, see Blot 1996.

2   Self-contained underwater breathing apparatus (SCUBA) was not in itself new but Cousteau and Gagnan's 'aqualung' was far more practical, easier to use and capitalised on modern high pressure cylinder technology.

3   Project teams of course often include students and, as the subject is by definition multi-disciplinary, volunteers and avocationals can provide an invaluable contribution, especially as they are often professional in a relevant skill. Through educational initiatives such as the *Nautical Archaeology Society Training Programme* they can also become highly knowledgeable about the subject as a whole as well as skilful practitioners.

4   Total of all dives including inspection dives divided into 7.5 hr days. Figures published elsewhere vary according to what is counted as a dive and the number of hours in the working day.

5   An unpublished paper given at a conference in Brighton, 1983. Margaret Rule was referring to the often well-intentioned and carefully re-searched salvage of shipwrecks by object-focused wreck investigators. Objects, often of intrinsic value, are seen as the goal of research, rather than as material culture constituting part of an archaeological assemblage that entrains wider meanings.

6   If one includes the nautical as well as underwater archaeological sites, women filled many positions of responsibility from the outset: Honor Frost's work in the Mediterranean has already been mentioned and Joan Du Plat Taylor, who was also with Bass at Gelidonya, was the founder editor of the *International Journal of Nautical Archaeology and Underwater Exploration* (IJNA). Margaret Rule directed the excavation of the *Mary Rose*, the largest underwater excavation ever done, Valerie Fenwick chaired the *Council for British Archaeology Sub-Committee on Underwater Archaeology*, was instrumental in the excavation of the Graveney Boat, edited its publication, and has also edited the IJNA. The subsequent editor was Paula Martin, who has recently handed over to Miranda Richardson. Angela Care-Evans of the British Museum was also central to the Graveney excavation and that at Sutton-Hoo. Gillian Hutchinson is the only diving archaeologist currently at the National Maritime Museum, Greenwich. Alexzandra Hildred is one of two diving archaeologists at the *Mary Rose Trust*. Lucy Blue, Helen Farr and Jesse Ransley lecture in maritime archaeology at the University of Southampton.

7   For example the chapter in the UNESCO volume on the *Vasa* was contributed by Anders Franzén, the technician who was responsible for the ship's rediscovery and instrumental in its salvage, although the archaeological excavation of the ship had been done by eleven archaeologists recruited at the time of the salvage in 1961. Together with new museum staff, and ethnographic and nautical historians, they formed an academic community who saw themselves as pioneers in a new field. In this, Sweden and Denmark, also recruiting a team around the Skuldelev project, were in advance of most of Europe.

2

Watercraft

Communication, subsistence, trade and exchange

For people living on or near the shore, bodies of water have always constituted both a cultural and an environmental paradox. In the age of the combustion engine and air travel we tend to think of water as a barrier, a natural perimeter, the limit to where we may go unimpeded and in safety. So too in the past, bodies of water constituted barriers, being seen as a natural delimitation of range or territory and forming natural defences. But, more importantly, the waters of the world have connected rather than divided communities and from the earliest times water transport has been of vital importance to society. To acknowledge this is now rather a cliché, a mandatory observation in any introductory course on maritime archaeology, yet the reasons it has become so remain valid, particularly as the indirect evidence for seafaring is repeatedly shifting to earlier probable dates.

The first sefarers?

Until relatively recently a date of *c.* 40,000 years was accepted for the arrival of modern humans in Greater Australia via the Wallacea Archipelago and was thought to be the earliest evidence for colonization that must have involved crossing significant bodies of water. New evidence from various sites in Australia, supported by a range of dating techniques, has pushed this back considerably. For example Thorne et al. (1999) calculated a date of 62,500 ± 6,000 BP for anatomically modern human skeletal material found at Lake Mungo, New South Wales. This

and other dates have been vigorously debated largely because of the difficulties in demonstrating association between the fossil remains and the material being dated or with aspects of the dating methods themselves (McGrail 2001:281). However, although there has been some scepticism about the oldest proposed dates, an increasing number of scholars now put the arrival of people in Australia around 50–60,000 BP: 'by at least 48,000 BP' (Bird et al. 2004) or 56,000 ± 4,000 (Roberts et al. 2001:1888).

In the Mediterranean it has long been known that people were voyaging to the island of Melos, a distance of nearly 120km (possibly broken into shorter legs by islets), because the obsidian they went to collect there has been found in stratified deposits on the Greek mainland at Franchthi cave dating to the 11th millennium BC (Renfrew and Aspinall 1990). We also know that people had reached Cyprus, an impressive unbroken distance of 65km from Anatolia, not long afterwards and probably many of the other islands in the process of maritime exploration (Broodbank 2006: 208–9). Going back in time, colonization may have resulted in early crossings to Sicily as early as 30,000 years ago (Broodbank 2006:206). But as Farr (2010:179) points out, although sea level at this period may have necessitated crossing water, the complex interrelated processes of eustasy, isostasy and tectonics mean this cannot be assumed. More certain is the crossing of *c.* 33km between the Italian peninsula and the island of Corsardinia 15,000 years ago (Broodbank 2006:206). From the end of the Pleistocene *c.* 12,000 years ago the incidence of seafaring progressively increases and we begin to see evidence for routine seafaring rather than occasional sea crossings, for example in the ways that Mesolithic seal hunters exploited the rich archipelagic seascapes of Scandinavia ten thousand years ago (Rönnby 2007).

Taken together this evidence suggests that voyaging was one of the many strategies for which the abilities of *Homo Sapiens* were well suited in terms of their command of appropriate technologies, as well as their abilities to acquire knowledge and skill. Indeed it has been argued that such abilities were the province of anatomically modern humans dating from *c.* 60,000 years ago (Davidson and Noble 1992). However, recent evidence, if confirmed by further work, suggests otherwise. Recently discovered lithic assemblages on Crete suggest that hominins had reached there by at least 130,000 years ago, far earlier than previously believed (Strasser et al. 2010). The evidence is still being considered but if the Palaeolithic attribution of the lithic assemblages is correct this material can only have got there over water, Crete having been an island for around 5 million years. From Africa this was a distance of at least 200km, though routes from mainland Greece or Anatolia would have involved shorter island-hopping legs of up to 24km. But even this pales against recent evidence from Mata Menge on Flores, an island between Timor and Java. Here a tool assemblage has been found associated not with modern humans but possibly with *Homo Erectus,* dated by fission-track analysis to 0.8–0.9 million years ago (Morwood et al. 1998, 2005; Brown et al. 2004; Morwood 2001). Further work on a nearby site has pushed this back to over 1millions years ago(Brumm et al. 2010). At present it is believed that even at the lowest glacially induced sea levels, a crossing of *c.* 20km would have been necessary to get there (Duller 2001:271). The implication then is that *Homo Sapiens* was not the first seafarer, although the same cautions that were noted above in respect of modelling sea levels that long ago also apply here.

What the incidence of these early sea crossings was at these remote times is impossible to say, except that colonising new lands does not mean the accidental survival of individuals but the intentional movement of viable populations (Irwin 1992: 18–30; McGrail 2001: 282; Broodbank 2006), just as it did with the movement of people and animals into the British Isles at the beginning of the Neolithic. The ability to do this implies an adequate technology and a considerable level of knowledge and skill (Farr

2006). It also implies an exploitation of the coastal zone, perhaps associated with movement through it during colonisation and migration (Westley and Dix 2006). Since then maritime activity in general has been a prominent component of both hunter-gatherer and sedentary populations and in terms of the material record of that activity, ships and boats are the most prominent class. Their remains must therefore constitute a primary source of archaeological evidence. Their importance stems from the processes involved in their conception, design, construction, use and disposal, for these were dynamically linked to society as a whole. For this reason they cannot be seen simply as interesting technological phenomena or merely as passive 'reflections' of a society or, for that matter, a segregated 'maritime' community. Watercraft often had a prominent symbolic profile associated with their involvement in social mechanisms, such as trade and exchange, industry, warfare, projection of personal status and political legitimization. Ships and boats are therefore directly or indirectly implicated in almost all strata of society.

It might be assumed that these considerations are only valid for those communities situated on the coast, and even for only those that were directly involved in maritime activity of some sort. However, for moving people and things long distances, water transport was far more efficient than travel over land. Hence this was not simply a matter of transport across bodies of water or along coastlines. Both long distance deep water seafaring and coastal traffic often formed part of water transport networks reaching considerable distances inland via estuaries, navigable rivers and lakes (Westerdahl 1992). Nor did such networks require continuity. Long before the cutting of canals, boats were sometimes transferred from one body of water to another, a process known as portage, extending the range over which people and goods could be transported. A major motive for doing this was of course communication and exchange; hence it was often by water that the most extensive networks were developed.

As well as trading activities and transport, water was important as a means of subsistence. At least as early as the Upper Palaeolithic period, societies have utilised or even depended on the water as part of their subsistence strategy. Archaeological evidence of these communities has been found in coastal environments (Andersen 1987), in estuarine areas (Wright 1990;

McGrail 1996a) and in lakes (Ruoff 1972; Morrison 1980; Dixon 2004; Henderson 2007). In many cases dietary and other evidence indicates that exploitation of resources was not exclusively aquatic (Andersen 1987:267), so we cannot see them as entirely maritime-dependent societies. However, among some island communities, a relationship with the sea can be seen in almost every aspect of surviving material culture.

For these reasons one can conclude that most societies exploited water or used water transport of some description, or were part of a communication network facilitated by water. In the past therefore water was the means of many forms of communication and contact rather than division and isolation. This being the case, any attempts to understand past societies need to take account of their maritime aspects including water transport and interrelated social factors. For archaeological research the remains of boats and ships will therefore be a primary class of evidence. This is not simply because millions have been constructed but also because ever since people set out on the water there have been steady losses, both of the vessels themselves and their unfortunate crews. Even today, as accident statistics show, travelling over any body of water is a hazardous undertaking. Prior to modern navigational aids, satellite communications and other life-preserving technologies, things were far less safe. So due to an unending catalogue of disaster we have a huge wreck database of material to investigate, augmented by craft that were abandoned or ritually disposed of in various ways.

Preservation

In addition to any intrinsic value of boat and ship remains as archaeological assemblages, there are also naturally fortuitous qualities which enhance that value. The same hazardous environmental elements that for millennia have caused a steady sequence of contextually rich accidental losses often conspire to preserve those losses in extraordinary condition. This is particularly the case for cultural material that is assimilated into the anaerobic sediments of sea-, lake- and riverbeds. The differences in preservation between dry and wet environments has become increasingly apparent in a series of wetlands excavations (e.g. Coles and Coles 1989; Prior 1991) as well as those of submerged settlement sites (Ruoff 1972; Dixon 1982) and of course shipwrecks. Essentially it is characterised by

dramatically better preservation of organic materials, diagrammatically illustrated in Coles and Lawson (1987) and Dean et al. (1992:31). However, other materials such as metals, particularly some alloys, often do not survive as well, especially in salt water environments. This differential preservation means that material found in waterlogged and aquatic environments is often complementary to that found on land sites, promoting the value of research that addresses questions relating to land and submerged material in an integrated way.

Failure or success?

It has been argued that the wreck database is biased towards failure, in that it inevitably accounts for poorly maintained, old and rotten vessels and the generally less successful designs (e.g. Hasslöf 1963:163). If this is true it could undermine the claims being made here that boats and ships provide high quality information about the past and generally have a high archaeological potential. As already pointed out, all voyaging is hazardous to a degree. These days 'risk-assessment' has become an administrative formality for every aspect of corporate or institutional activity. But it is only the term that is an invention of modern bureaucracies. Measuring risk is a human constant, and has certainly always been so for seafarers. Every voyage begins with a risk-assessment of sorts, involving judgements of the various environmental, human and technological factors. Individual voyages involve a different balance of risk factors but where the vessel itself is concerned, as it gets older, the risk-assessment takes progressively more account of its condition until at some point the owner and/or the crew decide discretion is the better part of valour. However, various motives such as gain or imperatives such as defence have often persuaded people to continue using their ships well beyond their safe working lives.

One of the strongest and insidious pressures to do so has arisen in trading activity (as opposed to the obligations of exchange). If anything the imperatives of commerce have been felt most sharply in the modern age of capitalism. Hardly a month goes by without some vessel being impounded by safety inspectors who pronounce it to be a miracle that it is still afloat. In many cases such vessels founder and have done so throughout history. The behavioural blend of calculated risk and negligence that promotes such wreckings is expressed in Larry Murphy's 'one more voyage' hypothesis: This argues that many wrecks are the result of an erroneous judgement that the vessel in question would be good for 'one more voyage' (Murphy 1983:75). This is a self-perpetuating tendency, for if the vessel did return, the natural temptation would be to see it as fit for yet another voyage. If this process continues, at some point the vessel's loss proves the judgement erroneous. Of course elderly and unseaworthy ships can successfully complete a voyage while a new and far more seaworthy vessel is overwhelmed by environmental forces. As Muckelroy (1978:232) pointed out, vessels in either condition can also be lost due to human error quite independent of their suitability for a particular task. It is therefore incorrect to assume that the ships that sink are the less successful designs. Certainly there have been documented instances of spectacular loss on a maiden voyage, most famously of the Swedish warship *Vasa* in 1628. However, relatively few wrecks are the result of quirkish design. Even in the case of the *Vasa*, the fundamental aspects of the imported Dutch shipbuilding tradition were not at fault. The widely accepted explanation, summarised by Soop (1992:15), was that the builders were compelled by the king (Gustavus Adolphus II Vasa) to alter the specifications after construction had started, resulting in an inherently unstable vessel. But recent re-evaluation of the evidence suggests that insufficient ballasting of a narrow hull, compounded by human error, was the cause (Cederlund and Hocker 2006:44–46). In other cases boats or ships are repeatedly modified throughout their lives in ways the original designers and builders could not have foreseen or intended. The cumulative effects of this often make them less seaworthy. One could put another famous royal warship in this category. The *Mary Rose,* built in 1510, was fairly old by the time she sank in 1545. Reputedly fast and manoeuvrable in her first campaigns of 1512, a long life punctuated by successive repairs and alterations progressively changed her fundamental characteristics. A substantial rebuilding programme, probably beginning around 1536, involved structural strengthening that was almost certainly associated with the increased weight of ordnance she subsequently carried. In this configuration she was to prove drastically less stable.

The fact remains that in the majority of cases wrecking occurs as the result of a combination of forces, including human error, but relatively rarely is this directly attributable to an unsuccessful design. Most wrecks therefore can be viewed as the result of misfortune or misjudgement with respect to their final voyage. In another sense, where their use has extended over many voyages and sometimes over many decades, they are a measure of success, both of the individual vessels and of the building traditions within which they were created.

Ritual deposition and abandonment

As well as negligence, accident, violence or sheer bad luck, watercraft also enter the archaeological record due to other forms of social action. The most obvious is the use of ships in burials, as containers for a body and grave goods, and as a symbolic component of funerary ritual. Grave finds such as those at Oseberg and Gokstad in Norway, at Sutton Hoo in Suffolk, England, and in the tomb of Khufu in Egypt, have provided nautical archaeology with some of its finest 'type sites'. The fact that ships were used in this way is one of the prime indicators of the high symbolic profile they achieved in their respective societies (Varenius 1992; Ellmers 1995), but until recently this aspect, together with the significance of those persons buried, has been considered rather less than the ships themselves as technological entities (Dommasnes 1992; Ingstad 1995; Warmind 1995). As well as these patently high-status burials, small boats were also used in many other societies as coffins. How limited their use was related to purely functional utility, as opposed to social attitudes to death, the deceased's occupation or ethnicity, has been the subject of considerable discussion (Carver 1995; Crumlin-Pedersen 1995; Müller-Wille 1995; Skaarup 1995).

Other forms of ritual deposition are perhaps best characterised by finds such as those at Hjortspring, Nydam, Illerup and Vimose in Denmark, and Kvalsund in Norway. In all these cases vessels seem to have been placed in bogs or small swampy lakes as votive offerings. Bog finds of boats or boat elements occur all over Scandinavia, many of them in peat (Rieck 1995). The reasons for their deposition are probably as varied as the theories offered to explain them. Some deposits are interpreted as primarily functional: e.g. the use of old boats as navigational blockages or the storage of boat elements or partly completed boats in water for better preservation.

Nevertheless it must be presumed that even functional blockages could have huge symbolic significance connected to access, power and protection, etc. Others, such as those at Hjortspring and Nydam are undoubtedly ritual deposits with complex relationships to warfare and social organisation (Randsborg 1995; Rieck 1994:45, 1995:127; Jørgensen 2003:15).

Just as many other types of material culture are discarded when broken or worn out, so too are boats and ships. At one extreme this may simply be the abandonment of aged and rotten craft, a practice evident today throughout the estuaries and creeks where hulked vessels slowly decay in the mud (Milne et al. 1998). One of the best known assemblages of this type is the remains of some twenty five medieval and post-medieval vessels found in the former medieval harbour at Kalmar in Sweden (Åkerlund 1951), some of which are referred to below. Of course the way in which old vessels are disposed of reveals a great deal about social attitudes to them and the mechanisms of which they were part: Where are they abandoned? What equipment is left on them? To what extent are materials removed for recycling? In some cases they may simply be dumped, but often there is a great deal more involved. In some societies boats are seen as possessing souls and are afforded mortuary rites at the end of their useful lives (e.g. Layard 1942:470–2). Even towards the more utilitarian end of the spectrum, boats may be methodically dismembered, burnt or intentionally sunk as part of a decommissioning ceremony. A medieval cog found in shallow water off the island of Bossholmen in Sweden (Cederlund 1990, 2001) was found to have had its keel half cut through with an axe. The cut was made from one side only and must have been done with the vessel heeled over on land, yet it was still the most inaccessible place to get to, let alone swing an axe. Wood for fuel or any other purpose would have been far more easily removed from elsewhere. This sea-going vessel had clearly been abandoned in the sense of no longer being needed or fit for a certain context of use, and a possible explanation is that a severing of the keel was designed to make it uneconomic to repair thus ensuring it never sailed in anyone else's service. Alternatively, it may have been as much a symbolic drawing to a close as a functional one. If this seems far-fetched one does not have to look beyond our own era to find far more highly charged events. A recent example in our supposedly cynical Western world was the scuttling of the Royal Navy's 74 gun ship *Implacable*. Built as the *Douguay Trouin*, she was captured from the French at Trafalgar and had remained afloat in Portsmouth Harbour for nearly a century and a half. In this she had outlasted even Nelson's Flagship *Victory* (1765) which was dry-docked permanently in 1928. At last, in 1949, judged too rotten to be kept any longer, *Implacable* was towed out into the channel to be sunk. Explosive charges were detonated in the bilges but after two and a half hours they had failed to sink her and tugs tried to finish the job. The seeming reluctance of the ship to sink only served to heighten emotions among those who watched. That she went to her grave flying the White Ensign *and* the French Tricolour, to the sounds of a gunnery salute and a bugler playing the 'last post', demonstrate the symbolic significance of the ship, the historical events in which it had been involved, and not least the ritual nature of its disposal. It was the fate of this venerable old hulk that led directly to saving the famous tea clipper *Cutty Sark* from a similar end. Appalled by what happened to the *Implacable*, Frank Carr, then of the National Maritime Museum at Greenwich, formed the *World Ship Trust* who's motto was to be 'Never again'.

Contexts and meanings

Some years ago a graffito that was fashionable on lavatory walls in many departments of archaeology stated: 'archaeology is rubbish' referring to the fact that on many land sites, much of the material we excavate has been intentionally abandoned, destroyed, robbed out, discarded, re-used or built upon. Of course this is not always the case, obvious examples being graves or tombs. In burials that have escaped the attentions of tomb-robbers, the ways that the dead are treated and the ways grave goods have been selected and placed according to funerary ritual, in turn derived from that society's ideas about death, status, the afterlife, ancestors, etc. Other forms of ritual deposition, discard and re-use, also relate to specific people, materials, locations, procedures or occasions. See for example, J. D. Hill's analysis of structured deposition in the Iron Age in Wessex (Hill 1992). In catastrophe sites (one way of categorising shipwrecks), there are distinct differences in the character of their assemblages compared to those found on most land sites. This is primarily based on the fact that until the recent phenomenon of insurance fraud, no one intentionally set out to become the victim of shipwreck. Derived from this accidental nature, two principal qualities have been highlighted: the absence of 'purposeful selection' and 'contemporaneity' (Gibbins 1990:377). Both need to be qualified as their acceptance at face value can lead to dangerously simplistic views of wreck assemblages.

Time capsules?

The tantalisingly graphic images of the past provided by well preserved underwater sites and shipwrecks in particular have led to the repeated use of the term 'time-capsule', the popular equivalent of the archaeological term 'closed find' or 'closed context'. How apt a description this really is for any particular site partly depends on the circumstances of loss and the wrecking process, the site environment and the subsequent formation processes. However, the number of wreck sites where the appellation is valid, at least to a degree, has been recognised by many. Gibbins (1990:377), using Binford's term, referred to them as 'fine grained' assemblages, by which is meant that they have vastly more 'relative contextual complexities' (Binford 1981:20). In other words they can give us a high-resolution image of past activity, not only in the individual well preserved material objects but in their relationships and other immaterial though discernible attributes. If the objects survive in a context of use, we have a much better chance of being able to discern relationships between individual objects, between assemblages of objects and between these assemblages and the structures within which they were stored or used. As Gibbins put it (1990:377) they have a higher 'inferential status'. These relationships often reveal symbolic attributes and different levels of meaning to a degree that is difficult to derive from other types of site. Of course this is only the case where the coherence and integrity of assemblages can be demonstrated archaeologically. But the contemporaneity of a wreck strictly refers to the wrecking event and not necessarily to the assemblages of material carried aboard. The wrecking locates, in time and space, all the constituent materials of the vessel and its contents in the context of that event, but it does not follow that the materials present were necessarily in use at the same time or that they are bonded by uniformly strong

relationships. Many vessels reached a considerable age before they sank or were abandoned. As noted, they were often substantially rebuilt and might also have had their role and modes of use changed. Of the materials present at wrecking, some may have been on board a matter of hours, some for decades. As Gibbins and Adams (2001:279–291) have observed, the operation of ships generally militates against the accumulation of redundant material, so the majority will comprise assemblages related in various ways to each other, the ship and to the people aboard. In contrast, other items and residual materials may have no direct relationships to that voyage bar that of physical association, i.e. by simply being on board. In effect, a ship arrives at its place of wrecking with an onboard stratigraphy, for as Harris' work has demonstrated, units of archaeological stratigraphy include structures as well as deposited sediments together with any associated features of use that have sequential and contextual relationships (Harris 1979 *passim*). The hull structure, its ballast, the residues of previous cargoes, fixtures and fittings, together with all other assemblages actually in use constitute a stratigraphic sequence that in some cases may extend to a century or more. So not only might a ship have considerably more time depth than commonly thought but, in terms of its biography as a social and technological entity, its use life can be positively kaleidoscopic. While some craft were constructed for specific purposes, the uses to which a vessel was put could and often did change. The ownership of a vessel often changed through sale, gift or by force, and this might happen more than once. As Murphy pointed out (1983:74), this also might involve transfer between ethnic groups or nationalities. Nor does it end there, for depending on where it sinks, a wreck may be exploited by other societies than the ones that sailed it. Evidence of their activities of salvage or fishing will also enter the archaeological record. Hence the simplistic notion that a wreck is a 'single event phenomenon' is a dangerous one that can blind the investigator to many aspects of the vessel's past. Of course these provisos do not detract from the 'closed find' value of those assemblages that are related through use at the time of sinking. On the contrary it can be argued that they extend the general contextual benefit of the wreck as an archaeological entity, opening it up to diachronic analysis rather than a synchronous 'freeze-frame' approach.

Selection

It was noted that the degree to which a site is regarded as a 'closed find' is often related to wrecking and formation processes, where well-preserved, coherent wreck assemblages, designated 'continuous' by Muckelroy (1978: 182–195), are easily regarded and treated as 'time-capsules' while scattered 'discontinuous' wreck sites are not. However, many of the interlinked component processes of site formation are natural (Schiffer's 'N Transforms', see Schiffer 1987:7) and can be modelled and deciphered. Even cultural activities ('C Transforms') such as salvage that impact the wreck on the seabed may leave traces that can be recognised through stratigraphic excavation just as other events are. Of course not all these activities are 'readable'. As Ferrari has shown, even well preserved wrecks may betray no evidence of cultural behaviour that has selectively removed material from the assemblage, and which was integral to its function (Ferrari 1995). However, the fact remains that the degree to which a ship's contents are scattered and reorganised by these processes does not in itself change their status as a related assemblage, only our ability to read and understand them as such. Through analysis of formation processes, relationships between component objects, assemblages and structures and their varying qualities of contemporaneity and selection can be recovered, thus preserving 'closed find' advantages on even the most dynamic of sites (see for example Tomalin et al. 2000).

As Muckelroy put it, a shipwreck: 'is the event by which a highly organised and dynamic assemblage of artefacts is transformed into a static and disorganised state...' (Muckelroy 1978:157). This definition implies a short term and dramatic event, and in terms of selection it is true that little socially structured selection would occur (apart from jettisoning objects in an attempt to stay afloat). But the process whereby the organisation of the vessel breaks down, culminating in wrecking, may begin hours, if not days before the vessel actually sinks (the example of the *Sea Venture* is outlined in chapter 6). The crew of a vessel in trouble will make strenuous efforts to avert disaster and these activities can radically alter the ship as a machine, as well as what it carries aboard and the way it is organised and used. In violent weather the rig may be substantially altered or cut away. Cargo, equipment, fixtures and fittings may be jettisoned in addition to any items lost involuntarily.

Stowage of materials carried aboard may be reorganised and various emergency alterations or repairs made to the vessel. In these cases the assemblage deposited on the seabed in the event of wrecking is not the same as it would have been had the vessel unexpectedly foundered or sunk due to naval action or piracy.

In quite another sense the very fact of putting to sea constitutes an exercise in cultural selection. It not only requires the construction of an appropriate vessel, but activities of subsistence, industry, trade or warfare will involve a variety of materials and artefacts specific to the enterprise. These may be more or less specialised for maritime use. Of course this could be a reason to question the usefulness of shipboard material to inform about aspects of wider society, but all material culture is variously 'specialised' in relation to the reasons for its production and contexts of use. The nature of that specialisation is another of archaeology's central concerns. Even where material culture is specialised for shipboard use, assemblages can reveal unsuspected aspects of society, beginning with the very way chosen to organise and execute maritime and water transport. The degree of specialisation is also variable. Much of the material culture used on boats in prehistoric periods was far less specialised than it came to be in historical times, particularly in post-medieval Europe. Even in the latter period, only part of shipboard assemblages were specific to shipboard life and enterprise. In both mercantile and naval activity, everyday possessions would comprise a substantial proportion of the objects found on board. This was more so on voyages of discovery or colonisation.

Aggregate value

In spite of the manifest value of ship finds, there is an important proviso which is related to site formation and which therefore affects what might be inferred from various classes of evidence found aboard. There is of course no necessary direct relationship between the wrecking location and the vessel's home port or intended destination. Certainly, in many cases, evidence from any combination of hull structure, rig, fittings and the contents, especially cargo, can indicate where the ship came from and often where it was going, so contributing to a knowledge of the patterns of communication or details of ancient trade and exchange networks in which it was involved. Even so, inference on the basis of any one wreck's location can be problematic, even when the relationship between the vessel's wrecking location and its function seem intuitively obvious. A perfect example of this was the collier bark *Charles Kerr* that left Shields (near Newcastle, England) in 1852 bound for a coaling depot at Aden in the Persian Gulf. Caught in a heavy gale in the North Sea, the Master tried running for shelter but was driven in different directions as the winds repeatedly shifted. After nearly coming to grief several times the ship eventually grounded near Cuxhaven in the river Elbe. In the event, the ship was rescued in the nick of time by a steam tug. But had it sunk with its cargo of coal, maritime archaeologists might reasonably have believed that she was bound for Cuxhaven or one of the other nearby ports. For at the time coal was being shipped there in similar vessels and from the very same port (Adams et al. 1990). A vivid account of these events in the form of a letter written by the Master, George Sargent, to his brother is reproduced in Appendix 1.

Of course the lack of a direct, functional connection between the ship and the locale where it wrecks will not detract from other archaeological qualities of the assemblage. There is also the chance that this information can be combined with that from other sites and it is just this sort of aggregate data from many wrecks that have occurred over time, that can reliably demonstrate trends. The classic work where this is concerned is Toby Parker's study of Mediterranean trade, particularly of the Roman period (Parker 1992). The patterns that emerged indicate the transport of various commodities along certain routes and between specific locations, together with the fluctuations in intensity of that traffic over time. The clarity with which this can be demonstrated exceeds anything that could be achieved on the basis of material from land sites alone. Similar benefits can be gained from the analysis of material in harbours accumulated over time. Although individual finds may be unstratified and usually impossible to relate to specific events, the whole assemblage in effect logs the changing intensity of activity at that place over time, indicating the nature of its role within wider networks.

While these points usefully temper any naive assumptions of pristine time-capsules in which the past is perfect and self-evident, it can still be maintained that in shipwreck assemblages we often observe a broader cross-section of material culture that is contextually related. What are these contemporaneous assemblages with their multiple relationships and meanings telling us about? In a word: society. What ships are as material culture, what they are used for and how they are used, reveal aspects of society, both in terms of the people on board, and also of the wider society of which they are a part.

Ships as things

Muckelroy observed that: '*In any pre-industrial society, from the upper palaeolithic to the nineteenth century A.D., a boat or (later) a ship was the largest and most complex machine produced.*' (Muckelroy 1978:3). In some ways this claim still holds true in the space age, for ships are still the largest moving objects made by far. They are also the most complex. A nuclear submarine comfortably exceeds the now retired space shuttle in terms of the volume and the complexity of the systems it utilises, both in its construction and its operation. As both vehicles and machines, ships represented an enormous investment in resources, requiring a synthesis of the skills of many different crafts. Shipbuilding was therefore a complex social activity involving organisation, co-operation and investment in the long term, so there is a strong time dimension here. Ships, through the economic, social and political mechanisms of which they were part, therefore deeply pervaded society. From being linked to society in such complex ways, their material remains can potentially reveal aspects of society from perspectives unavailable from land sites or other classes of evidence.

Functionally watercraft can be platforms, vehicles, homes, tools, weapons, containers and machines. They are used for transport, warfare, trade, industry, communication, accommodation and leisure. Muckelroy rationalized these into three ways in which ships can be understood and which are still a useful basis for analysis: The ship as a machine; as an element in a military or economic system; as a closed community (Muckelroy 1978:216). Gawronski (1991:83) for example, rationalised the VOC ship *Amsterdam* in a similar way but extended Muckelroy's three categories to five. However, going beyond functional and systems analyses to achieve fuller explanations of the roles of ships in a broader social context necessitates invoking the ship as a symbol, as floating ideology and the expression of social ideas, including those of the tradition within which the craft is constructed. For it is these aspects that influence many of the choices made in the process of production as well as modes of use. In reality of course each of Muckelroy's and Gawronski's aspects necessarily incorporates symbolic meaning as well as, or rather as an inherent part of, various functions and configurations. As well as analysing specific aspects of ships, with regard to their wide-ranging functions and associated social implications, ships can be viewed as manifestations of the maritime needs and aspirations of society, produced within a series of constraints that are both physical and metaphysical. In a sense they represent the combined agency of both social and environmental factors and are represented in Figure 2.1. The balance and relative strength of the interconnect-ions between the

various constraints vary with type, function and social context. The Swedish naval architect Fredrik Henrik af Chapman observed that every ship built was an attempt to achieve an elusive balance, appropriate to specific tasks, between the opposing nature of various criteria (Chapman 1768 (1971):76). Chapman was concerned with their functionality but looking at ships in their widest sense, one can define each vessel as the product of a dynamic tension between, on the one hand the stimuli behind the building, expressed as need and aspiration and, on the other; the various constraints whether, environmental, ideological, technical or economic. Each ship is a resolution of this dialectic relationship between infinitely variable factors.

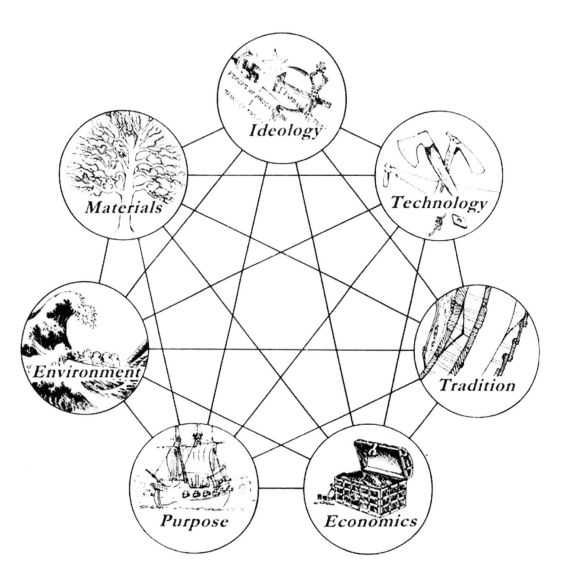

Figure 2.1 Interrelated constraints on the form, structural characteristics, appearance and use of watercraft. An alternative caption à la Magritte might be: This is not a model! Although it is similar in appearance to various systemic models and although geometric black lines on white paper imply rigidity and certainty, the diagram represents infinite fluidity (J. Adams).

Reading ships

Every vessel therefore has the potential to reveal these aspects that underlie its creation, and through them the related aspects of the society that used it. In considering the various constraints shown in the diagram:

Purpose refers to the intended function(s) of the vessel and directly relates to society's maritime needs, whether providing various forms of communication and trade, subsistence or industry such as fishing, military purposes or leisure. Many vessels were intentionally built for general use and so may not exhibit design and construction features related to specific functions. Other vessels exhibit a high degree of specialisation and this imposes constraints on the size, form, layout, adornment and use. The degree of specialisation of an individual vessel can also indicate the complexity of the water transport system within which it operates, though complex systems may include very simple forms such as rafts. Examples of some of the most specialized, yet rarely considered, forms of watercraft include various ingenious dredging machines that populated the estuaries and ports throughout the medieval period and the equally ingenious camels used in Holland. Dredgers imply the existence of watercraft whose draft exceeds local depths of water, and therefore a pressing need to provide for their passage. Camels were also connected to the available depth of water but were used over distances where dredging was out of the question. Dutch shipping was constrained by the depth of water between ports like Amsterdam and the open sea. Unaided, their largest ships had too deep a draught and camels were the means of reducing it. Shaped to conform to ship hulls, they were rigged, semi-flooded, either side of large East Indiamen or warships. Once rigged in position they were pumped out, increasing the combined buoyancy and thus reducing the draft. The whole assembly was towed to the open sea whereupon the camels were re-flooded, disengaged and attached to an inbound ship. Both types are a response to environmental constraints, where social needs stimulate enormous effort to overcome them.

Technology is the development, application and control of processes through which raw materials are acquired, converted, refined, worked and fashioned to form new materials or things, including the production of tools to assist these processes. To develop and use technology, whether by discovery and/or experiment and design implies intentionality, knowledge and skill driven by aspirational goals. As with any artefacts the construction and use of watercraft are related to the technologies available. Whereas a simple boat might be made even where sophisticated materials and tools existed, the reverse is not possible. For example, if these are limited to stone tools, fire and cordage for fastening, then this will constrain the size and nature of the vessel that can be constructed. However, within the constraints of a society's technological envelope, archaeology reveals that the uses for which watercraft were needed gave rise to extraordinary ingenuity and complexity. This was partly physical in that as structures, boats, and ships in particular, have to resist far more complex forces than stationary buildings. This is one reason behind Muckelroy's observation that shipbuilding often represented the technological cutting edge of a society, simply because nothing else faced such great demands. The other side of the coin is that a boat or a ship was important in many ways other than utility and these stimulated extraordinary effort and craft in shaping its qualities whether functional, symbolic or aesthetic.

The technology visible in ships is therefore one of the most potent means of discerning the motivations, needs and priorities of past societies. As the making of watercraft manifests social aspiration, whether of specific communities, groups or individuals, understanding the development and use of the technologies involved is a means of understanding the processes of innovation and change related to wider society.

Tradition is the craft tradition within which the vessel is constructed. It will embody a system of ideas about what boats and ships are and how they should be designed and constructed. This will impose constraints in terms of design parameters on the practice of construction. Obviously our perception of particular craft traditions of the past can only be based on the sum of their surviving products and any other related source materials. In that incomplete database we observe similarity and difference in physical features, period and geographic region. Hence in an important sense, as McGrail has pointed out, what we identify as a 'tradition' is 'our' construct, which as a classification system is 'an abstraction from reality' (McGrail 1995:139). In another sense, people who built watercraft in the past were aware of the specific rules and conventions that governed their work, even if only at the level of 'we always do it this way' – that infuriatingly simple yet honest response to inquisitive ethnographers. Craft traditions therefore constituted social practice and, motivated action. They were therefore constructs in the minds of their practitioners too.

Hence from both ends of the telescope so to speak, ours and 'theirs', a tradition may be regarded as an array of material, technological, aesthetic, and symbolic characteristics, none of which are necessarily diagnostic or exclusive individually, but which together characterise a coherent assemblage in time and space. How much correlation there may be between our perception of this material and that of the people who produced it in the past is yet another of the central concerns and challenges of archaeology.

Until recently it was the significance of the physical traits – the typological characteristics of building traditions – that were the primary focus of most attention. While inevitable in research that was rapidly building its database, this approach only utilises one half of archaeology's double hermeneutic: what this material means to us now. The significance and meanings these assemblages had for those who built and used them has been less explored. This is a dichotomy that has also been an issue in archaeology in general. Sørensen (1997) addresses just this dilemma: Either typologies are viewed as arbitrary in their relationship to the societies that produced them or as having some correlation with past meaning on the basis that the observed similarities and differences are the result of motivated human action (Sørensen 1997:181). In this sense boat and shipbuilding traditions, treated as complex typologies, have operated as a sort of nautical archaeologist's equivalent to 'archaeological cultures' (where artefact typologies and distributions were seen as representing real 'peoples'). But whereas the concept of the archaeological culture has proved to be, in Shennan's words: a complex and unsatisfactory explanatory edifice (Shennan 1989:5), boat building traditions have more validity and potential. Perhaps this is more by accident than design but the way building traditions develop and interact is much more akin to the way real societies behave because they are often overlapping and interactive. Certainly medieval and post-medieval European ship-

building traditions were not bounded and sealed entities. Like the real societies in which boat and shipbuilding was practised, traditions were interconnected and synaptic, and it is in this cross fertilisation of ideas and technique that many aspects of change are initiated. It could therefore be argued that building traditions, as interfaces between societies and their seafaring, have great potential as a means with which to infiltrate the past.

As social practice boat and ship production inevitably incorporates symbolic and ideological constructs designed to safeguard best practice. In this sense traditions embody a paradox where, like any craft tradition, the protection of 'traditional' values tends to suppress alternative methods and innovation. Yet at the same time, as noted above, boats and ships often represented a society's most advanced technology. The reason is that there is always a dialectic interplay within the corpus of traditional practice, and between the tradition's practitioners and wider society. Ideological barriers are never impervious and are under constant bombardment from external influences and the human tendency to refine or innovate. It is this constant dialectic tension that leads to change.

Materials are the natural or manufactured materials available for construction and use. As observed under technology, availability will strongly influence the vessels that can be built. In some situations the environment will limit the choice. In more bountiful regions, choice may indicate cultural attitudes and preferences or be related to the technological capability to exploit them. Long-established shipbuilding industry, like agriculture, can have a permanent effect on the landscape both through exploitation of a resource, like timber or its managed production through forestry. At a large scale therefore the activity is manifested socially and environmentally. Within the craft tradition the materials themselves have qualities that exert influence beyond their technical roles Working with materials produces characteristic sounds, smells, patterns, colours and tactile experiences that become part of the craft tradition along with formal techniques, procedures and ritual. The embedded nature of the relationship between workers, tools and materials therefore contributes to the longevity of tradition and of preferences for some materials over others (that might function as well if not better). Some of these characteristics remain evident in the finished product: the smell of cedar furniture, the touch of oak timbers dubbed with an adze, the optical qualities of hand-made glass, the sound of musical instruments, etc. In boat-building the affinity between the builder and the vessel under construction is paralleled by that between the boat and user, for the materials of construction are as much a part of its fundamental identity and character as its function: English references to 'hearts of oak' and 'wooden walls', evoked all that was seen as positive in wooden warships well into the era of iron and steam. Modern builders who work in wood express similar sentiments (perhaps with more technical justification, for with the rising cost of plastics and with modern glues and preservatives, sustainable and 'carbon-neutral' wood is enjoying something of a revival). For archaeologists, sensitivity to the 'materiality' of objects, both in its more literal sense, i.e. to the nature of component materials, their conversion and the ways they are worked, and to the active role things play in society, is therefore fundamental to understanding artefacts, their purposes and the social relations in which they are implicit (Olsen 2003:87; Jones 2004; Ingold 2007:9).

Economy refers to the resources in terms of labour and/or wealth required to produce the vessel. At the level of subsistence economies the ability to allocate labour for example to the cutting of suitable trees and reducing them to produce logboats, would have depended on a social organisation and subsistence strategy successful enough to make that labour available for the required time. Where logboats were concerned this was routinely achieved by Mesolithic societies in Europe and Scandinavia who were thus able to transport and exchange commodities over long distances via coasts and river systems. Danish finds demonstrate that their production, together with associated fishing equipment and paddles, etc. constituted a major proportion of their material culture and was of considerable complexity (Andersen 1986, 1987, 1994).

In complex societies resources are often directly related to political and military policy as well as depending on economic capacity. The economics of shipbuilding on a large scale required access to materials, often acquired and protected militarily, as well as a considerable labour force, thus creating large infrastructures involving a number of satellite industries and crafts. In modern societies, surplus wealth has also created a considerable leisure market in the use of boats. On the other hand downturns in the economic cycle have a marked effect on maritime communities, including the leisure industry but also more traditional industries such as fishing with the resultant drastic reduction in boat numbers, and of course shipbuilding.

Environment is the intended operating environment of the vessel. Obviously if a boat is built for use in sheltered coastal waters or lakes it does not need the same characteristics of stability and robust construction as a vessel intended for the open sea. The characteristics of the operating environment therefore exert powerful practical and mechanical constraints on the possible ways in which a vessel can be made. Where cultural requirements override or stretch these parameters, for example in the construction of ceremonial craft not intended for the rigours of long distance voyaging, the resulting vessel will often be severely restricted in its use. Sometimes an uneasy compromise becomes deeply entrenched in practice. A good example from the period of interest here is the protracted attempts of northern European navies to incorporate the manoeuvrability of oar-powered vessels in their fleets even though they were generically unsuited to the prevailing conditions. The French maintained a galley base at Rouen for over a hundred years, primarily to counter the English who also had their galleys or later derivatives: barges and balingers. The latter name is derived from the Old French word for a whaling boat (Friel 1995:147) and its use in England for what were often large warships suggests that their builders were seeking to improve an essentially Mediterranean form with the sea-keeping characteristics of an open rowing boat designed for the Atlantic. This was a worthwhile aim while sailing ships were still single-masted but once their capabilities advanced through a two- and then three-masted rig, combined with the development of shipboard gunnery, the obsolescence of oared warships for all but very specialised tasks was inevitable. Nevertheless their use endured for a surprisingly long period. The Clos des Galées at Rouen may have been closed in 1418 but galleys were present in the French fleet that sailed against England in 1545. The day the two fleets met at Spithead on July 19th is remembered because *Mary Rose*, Henry VIII's vice-flagship, capsized and sunk. Engaged against her on the French side were galleys. Henry's fleet also had its squadron of oared vessels: galleasses and the smaller row-barges. They were hybrids of oar and sail power and like galleys duly vanished as distinct types but not without influencing subsequent developments in ship-building (discussed in chapter 6). In the Baltic, galleys endured until the end of the 18th century, where among the more sheltered archipelagos, the fleets of Sweden and Russia used large squadrons of them in the fleet actions at Viborg and Svensksund in 1790 (Derry 1979: 189). The partial successes of combining oar and sail power in the Henrican fleet of the 16th century had reached its apogee in Henrik af Chapman's designs for galleys that were propelled by banks of oarsmen but in which, by ingenious engineering, broadside gunnery was possible. But these proved a developmental dead end. The dogged use of oared warships in the north demonstrates a dialectic tussle between pragmatic design of ships for the prevailing environment and a durable norm: the perceived and potential advantages of having oared warships.

In considering the interrelated way in which all these constraints operate, one can rationalise change in the ways boats and ships are produced as being due to one or more of these constraints operating in different ways or at different levels of intensity. That we can, at least to an extent, read these changes in the materiality of watercraft allows us to relate observed technological change to its environmental and social causes. Usually of course, changes in the environment at large operate over longer cycles than the duration of all but the longest-lived boatbuilding traditions. Hence it is with social change that we may more often find mutually explanatory relationships and this is very much interrelated with the final constraint represented.

Ideology in its widest sense refers to the conceptual and ideological context that governs what ships are understood to be and how they are used. This includes the ideas of those who need ships for various purposes, as well as the ideas of the builders and this is related to the concept of 'tradition' discussed above. Both may impose constraints on the form of vessels that are as proscriptive as any of the material and functional constraints. This aspect also includes the whole symbolic profile of ships as they are perceived, not just by their builders, owners and

users but by society in general, for whom many of the external aspects of appearance are specifically designed. It is through the richness of meanings with which watercraft are imbued that they transcend technology, assuming important roles in social negotiation. As complex objects in which so much is invested, and which often have use-lives broadly similar to a human lifespan, their production, use and disposal can readily be understood in terms of biography, a concept usefully applied to other artefacts (Gosden and Marshall 1999). Although archaeology has only recently developed this idea as a way of understanding the accruing social meanings of objects over their use-life (see Kopytoff 1986), ships have been conceived as having a life history for some time. An example is a series of 18th-century engravings by Sieuwert van der Meulen entitled *Navigiorum Aedificatio*. It depicts the life history of ships in a series of sixteen prints (see de Groot and Voorstman 1980: prints 138–153). It is easy to draw a human analogy from each stage: Like an embryo, the ship slowly takes form in the womb of the shipyard. Released down the launchways, it is named and born into the water. Nurtured to maturity in the dockyard by being painted, rigged, equipped and provisioned, the ship then leaves its home port to make its way in the world's oceans. The rigours of ocean life are reflected in battle honours, voyages of discovery or successful trading enterprise and safe homecoming. Life's trials and tribulations are storm-tossed seas, causing fatigue, stress and injury all necessitating repair. Unlucky accident may see the ship's life cut short through wrecking, but otherwise, having survived into old age, the ship is 'retired' into a less demanding occupation. Commonly for the sort of ship depicted by van der Meulen, it is in the hospice of the breaker's yard that the ship meets its demise, perhaps bequeathing some of its heartwood for use in a new vessel and maybe even its name, and so the cycle begins anew.

Other ways in which ships end their 'lives', often specifically as part of funerary ritual have already been discussed above. No wonder then that ships are one of the few artefacts that are commonly given names (along with swords, guns, bells, and more recently other vehicles, e.g., *Flying Scotsman*). In having life, ships are also almost always gendered. Interestingly, irrespective of whether their names are male (*Nelson*), female (*Demeter*), neuter (*Bulwark*), celestial (*Polaris*), meteorological (*Boreas*) zoological (*Tiger*), mythical (*Griffin*), religious (*Holy Ghost*), qualitative (*Illustrious*), etc., their gender is almost always female. There are intriguing exceptions such as when a ship's identity is not known, and others where gender is clearly fluid (Maginley 1989:97). Admittedly this may be a relatively modern construct, possibly gaining widespread use in the medieval period for linguistic reasons (Conway 1989:96). By contrast in prehistory, maleness has been postulated for Scandinavian Bronze Age rock carved images of boats, e.g. Tilley (1991). The figures carved in or in proximity to the boats are predominantly male but many interpretations are possible, and indeed span the mundane to the cosmological. This is revisited in chapter 9.

Certainly cosmology is often involved and in many societies boats are associated in various ways with deities (Blue et al. 1997). In relation to these sorts of associations they may also be consciously afforded persona. In many instances their names may refer to an owner, an owner's relative or another significant person. As will be seen, they are often designed, adorned and named specifically to project selected aspects of their owner's persona, functioning as a kind of complex alter ego. Again though, even where the person concerned is male, the ship essentially remains 'she'. In some societies, Polynesia for example, canoes are understood to assume the identity of their owners to the extent they are afforded funeral rites at the end of their 'life' (Layard 1942). Hence it is in the social life surrounding the production and use of ships that these ideologies are played out and become most visible. Specific examples are now considered in the context of shipboard communities and their relationships with wider society.

Ships as society

Looking more closely at Muckelroy's term 'closed community': certainly shipboard societies are closed for the duration of the voyage but the term implies a more fundamental segregation from wider society. Muckelroy noted that there were often distinct differences between land and seafaring communities and correlated differences in the associated material culture. However, his assumptions about the nature of seafaring and shipboard communities seem to presume various constants based on what we believe to have been common practice in historical times, and that, inevitably, from a predominantly Western

perspective. In that context it is true that most shipboard communities had a rigid hierarchy with one person in command, and that most crews have been all or at least predominantly male. It is also the case that a highly specialised and male-dominated system of seafaring has arisen in other parts of the world at different times, for example among the island societies of Polynesia or the coastal communities of India, but there is no evidence to suggest that these are universals. Just as there are mixed crews now, so may there have been in various cultures in the past. Even on ships in the heyday of sail there were women masquerading as male sailors (Dugaw 1996; Stark 1996) perhaps the best known being Mary Lacy who ran away to sea and served aboard a naval vessel then subsequently worked as a shipwright in Portsmouth dockyard (Lincoln 2008). We know so much about her through her memiors (Lacy 1773) but there were others like her. Very occasionally these women's true sex was successfully concealed as was apparently the case with Mary Lacy who went by the name of William Chandler but in others it was more of an open secret, where their presence was tolerated because they agreed to conform to the gendered norm of seafaring as practised in that time and place (Creighton and Norling 1996). In effect they agreed to become men in the sense of conforming to expectations of dress, behaviour and work. In other situations female presence was official, although this varied according to the trade or to the nationality of the ship. This ranged from rigidly codified circumstances in which wives of captains, masters or mates would travel aboard, often having official roles (Weibust 1968:421), to river and canal craft where whole families lived aboard (van Holk 1997).

Within the widespread domain of piracy in the early modern world there were other interesting inversions of gendered norms, also not necessarily related to sexuality. Pirate crews of the Caribbean practised a form of democracy in which all members of the crew could be included. For women and for ethnic minorities, black sailors in particular, this was in stark contrast to much of wider society. Through this process women like Anne Bonny and Mary Read became prominent members of pirate crews (Cordingly 1996: 57–65). Male pirates on the other hand, at first sight the epitome of machismo, adopted forms of dress, hairstyle and adornment both for themselves and their weapons, using ribbons, sashes, ornaments, etc., that in other social contexts would have been seen as inappropriately feminine (Harker 2002). In this context however, it was a form of ostentatious display of difference that in its subversive defiance of social norms has some similarity to expressions of identity seen in modern subcultures such as punk and Goth (Gelder 2007).

Of course where it is evident that seafaring has developed as a male-dominated practice, as in post-medieval Europe, the mechanisms of genuine segregation or the covert acceptance of female presence, invites questions of gender roles and power relations in wider society. Historical and ethnographic studies, in addressing power relations between the sexes within the fishing industry for example, suggest that gender bias in one area is counterbalanced in another (Thompson 1983, 1985).

Just such a dynamic has been demonstrated within many areas of 19th-century shipping. For example, while men were commonly masters of ships, women were often the managing owners, i.e., the owner or part owner who was responsible for the running of the business. Women also, far more frequently than might be assumed, ran shipyards both for merchant and warship construction. In many instances this seems to have occurred after the death of a husband but while it might not have been the norm it was certainly not unusual (Doe 2009).

While such research into maritime aspects of society is becoming more common, Muckelroy's observation (1978:221) that little analysis of any sort had been carried out on shipboard communities is still partly true (though see Creighton and Norling 1996 and Ransley 2011). Formerly, where this aspect of seafaring was addressed on the basis of archaeological data somewhat simplistic comparisons or analogies tended to be drawn. Shipboard societies were referred to as 'mirror images' of society at large or as microcosms of wider society in the sense of societies in miniature, etc., whereas in most cases, as Muckelroy recognised, they are liable to be radically different. Even where all the components of wider society were apparently present, such as on Dutch inland shipping, Van Holk (1997:254–259) has detected differentiation of shipboard families according to class, influenced by Dutch social developments from *c.* 1550. In the many other Western contexts where crews were officially all or predominantly male, shipboard societies were therefore atypical by definition. In rigidly hierarchical systems such as post-medieval naval ships, the tiered system of rank is more a realisation of the ideology of those in power than a direct reflection of wider society. Rönnby and Adams (1994:67–68) have pointed out that rather than reflecting wider society as it was, many ship communities indicated how those in power thought society 'should' be. This applies to many of the ships discussed below, particularly those of the 16th century dealt with in chapter 4.

Of course the use of the ship as a metaphor for society goes back at least as far as Plato's '*The Republic*', written around 360 BC, in which he draws a direct analogy between a ship and a democratic city state. Thereafter it reappears frequently, both in the service of political justification and in literature:

> *Thou, too, sail on, O Ship of State!*
> *Sail on, O Union, strong and great!*
> (Henry Wadsworth Longfellow 1850).

But few expressions of the analogy are as detailed and ideologically explicit as that of the Swedish nobleman Axel Oxenstierna: In propounding his view of the Swedish state and society, he likened it to a ship upon the ocean, steered by the firm hand of the king. Society was seen as a pyramidal hierarchy with the king, then the aristocracy at the top. The warship was organised on similar lines with the nobleman Admiral at the top, with officers, other ranks and crew below. The internal arrangement and allocation of space reflected this division of social rank very clearly, a characteristic of naval ships into the modern age. So as Rönnby put it, when summarising the significance of the wreck of the *Riksäpplet* (1667), it is not just the remains of an English-designed warship from Sweden's 'great power period' lying on the seabed, it is also a 17th-century concept of how society should function (Rönnby and Adams 1994:68) (Fig. 2.2 and Plate 1). The physical counterpart of this construct reached its apogee in the stern carvings of vessels such as the Swedish warship *Vasa*. Here the illustrious king Gustav II Adolph Vasa is set above gods, mythical heroes and biblical leaders alike. Thus the way in which these ships were constructed and operated embodied ideology in such wholesale fashion as to include all three types proposed by Giddens (1979:193–6, 1984). It firstly promoted and represented the interests of the vested power as universal. It also suppressed contradictions or tensions between the different social elements (ranks) that comprised the ship's company, and it naturalised and reified shipboard life and social organisation.

Figure 2.2 Social structure? The timbers of *Riksäpplet* (1667) thrust up into the water like the bones of some vast dinosaur. The wreck, near Dalarö, Sweden, was dynamited by 'black oak' hunters in the 1930s (Cederlund 1983:37) but the general arrangement of the vessel as warship and organised space can still be discerned. (J. Adams).

See also Plate 1

Hence the hierarchy of a commanding elite who literally had the 'whip-hand' and the power of life and death over a subordinate crew was the natural order of things, often to a degree that exceeded the day to day control of the ruling classes over the populace in contemporary society at large. As noted above, the way in which this system is still assumed to have been a universal norm demonstrates how successful this propaganda was. Of course it can be argued that the hazardous nature of seafaring necessitates a hierarchical chain of command to maximise safety and to an extent this is true, though more so in naval and military contexts. By contrast, shipboard societies based in rural communities and in pursuit of more mercantile objectives could have a more egalitarian organisation than the contemporary hierarchical social structure on land, such as feudalism or even the bonded agricultural labour systems typical of much of post-medieval Europe.

In spite of this one model that has been applied to the study of merchant ship crews is Erving Goffman's concept of the 'total institution' (Goffman 1961). At first sight naval crews might seem to be better examples of a total institution: an organisation that is both part of and separate

from society at large, '*a place of residence and work where a large number of like-situated individuals cut off from wider society...lead an enclosed, formally administered round of life.*' (Goffman 1961:11) Here '*all aspects of life are conducted in the same place and under the same authority...the day's activities are tightly scheduled...the whole sequence of events being imposed from above by a system of explicit, formal ruling and a body of officials.*', in which the various enforced activities are carried out in order to realise the aims of the institution (Goffman 1961:17). For Goffman, principal examples are asylums and other institutions such as prisons. However, he also discusses other institutions including the armed forces, private schools, lumber camps or monasteries and while they all conform to his definition, they vary markedly in their degree of openness, i.e., the freedom with which one may join and leave voluntarily, as well as the purpose for which the institution exists. The primary difference between Goffman's asylum or a prison and going to sea is that the latter is usually voluntary. The privation, discipline and structured order of time, space and social relations on board are accepted as a way of life. Of course there are exceptions, either when parts of a crew were slaves or when European powers used various forms of arrest and impressment of ships and their crews or the forced enlistment of individuals by the infamous press-gangs of the Napoleonic era. Here too there is a distinction however, in that the same crew would comprise both pressed men and those serving voluntarily, all subject to the same rules. For the pressed men it was initially akin to Goffman's totalitarian regime but for volunteers it was a way of life which was a natural order of things. Even pressed men with no skills whatsoever had far greater potential mobility than the prisoner or the patient. Initially rated 'ordinary', once a certain level of skill had been acquired they might be rated 'able', and thence move to progressively more specialised and senior roles. In some instances, those from 'before the mast' became officers.

For Goffman the total institution was also fundamentally incompatible with what he described as another crucial element of our society: that of the family. He saw a stark contrast between family living and what he called 'batch living', where fellow workers eat, sleep and work together but who can 'hardly sustain meaningful domestic existence' (Goffman 1961:22). But perhaps the naval shipboard structure in which the crew were divided into numbered messes, typically of six to twelve men, challenges this. In the sailing navy a member of a mess would often have a 'tie-mate' and younger crewmen had their 'sea daddies', all creating a familial sense of belonging in which the bond between 'messmates' was stronger than that with the crew at large. Death was also related to the mess, a crew member who had died was said to have 'lost the number of his mess'.

There are problems then in both distinguishing between different forms of total institution and applying them to the complexities of shipboard life. Even more so to merchant crews, especially in view of the greater variety of their constitution and which often includes members of the same family. The crews of whalers are an example in which the command structure was far less rigid than in other contemporary merchant vessels let alone warships. Salary was based on shares, in turn dictated by the success of the voyage. This practice survives in the crewing of some fisheries today, particularly the more hazardous forms such as the crab boats of the Bering Sea, an occupation that according to the US Bureau of Employment is currently one of the world's most dangerous occupations (*US Department of Labor* 2005). In

such crews, status might be accrued on the basis of age, experience and to an extent be dependent on the skill in which a particular person has specialised, rather than social class, wealth or kinship. Of course status on board may accrue from a combination of these. Ownership of sizeable merchant vessels was often beyond the means of one person and thus shared ownership became common, often in multiples of two. Hence half, quarter and, particularly in the case of larger vessels, one-eighth shares and progressively smaller fractions were common. Such shares were not necessarily equally divided and the greater the share one owned brought with it corresponding influence on the use of the ship (e.g. see Peterson 1988 on the ownership of the *Sea Venture* of 1609). Where kinship is concerned there are many examples of seafaring families who have not only been engaged in the same activity for generations, such as fishing (or indeed, building boats and ships), but who have also had specific roles in their use, such as coxswain or navigator. In many cases these survive as surnames of medieval origin such as Mariner, Fisher, Boatwright, Cleaver, Boarder, Holder and Boatswain, along with their continental counterparts, and indeed their land equivalents such as Smith, Mason, Baker, Tailor, Shepherd, Carpenter, Thatcher, etc., showing that this is not an exclusively maritime characteristic.

So in terms of relating social aspects of shipboard life to those of wider society on the basis of the archaeological remains, there are distinct dangers in simplistic analogies but at the same time considerable potential. Much of it is embedded in the qualities of ship structure, internal arrangement and disposition of equipment. The spatial division of the vessel indicates both functional and social aspects and the related divisions of labour, power and status. The organisation of space also reveals attitudes towards such things as health, death, property and privacy, etc., in terms of where the related activities are located in the vessel and the amount of space afforded them. In turn, these are related in various ways to the organisation and activities of wider society, not as passive reflections from which one can 'read off' what wider society must have been like, but as translations of social attitudes to a shipboard situation in pursuit of those aims and needs that underpinned the construction of the vessel in the first place.

There is clearly potential here for the analysis of ships and society, the way they develop and the relations between them. Just as funerary practice has been used to infer the way society was organised, so can the construction, internal compartmentalisation, access and decoration of ships and boats. But whereas Barrett (1988) has shown there are knotty problems in any attempt to discern generalities on the basis of specific mortuary practices, perhaps the finer grained qualities of ships as structures and their often highly preserved remains from aquatic contexts may harbour greater potential.

3

Sources, Theories and Practice

The central case studies in this book draw on a variety of sources related to shipbuilding and seafaring and, although the primary data are from shipwrecks, use is also made of ships that were abandoned rather than wrecked as well as those that were intentionally deposited. In constructing explanations as to why as well as how things changed some reference is also made to ethnographic material and surviving historic vessels. Importantly, these episodes of change fall in the medieval and historical periods, so use has been made of contemporary manuscripts as well as iconography and models. The nature of these sources and relationships between them therefore require some consideration before arriving at the case studies themselves. So too do the data collected and the factors affecting the ways this was done.

As the starting point for much of this research is the technologies of shipbuilding and seafaring, data acquisition has involved extensive recording of the hull remains. Some of the data have been generated specifically for this work while other data-sets were extant. In some cases many different people collected data over periods of time varying between days and years. Recording techniques included conventional tape measurement and hand plotting, although extensive use has been made of photography and video and the majority of spatial data have been processed with various computer applications.

Images and altered perception

Archaeologists who work in rivers, lakes and seas obviously have to do so within the constraints imposed by those environments, but, because these are so variable, the common assumption that it is always more difficult to do archaeology under water is mistaken. Indeed as Muckelroy (1978:49) pointed out, some things are actually easier. There are however, some differences that are inescapable and one of these concerns perception, for all the senses are affected to some extent by being under water and so alter our perception of what we are trying to understand. The primacy of the visual sense in Western thinking and the associated correlations between seeing and knowing have been the subject of considerable analysis (e.g. Merleau-Ponty 1962; Jenks 1995) but although we can investigate an underwater site without taste, smell, hearing or even direct touch, to do so without seeing, though not impossible, is challenging to say the least and certainly much slower. Underwater vision is the primary sense although paradoxically no-one familiar with recording underwater is ever likely to assume that 'seeing is knowing' (or believing). For even when one can see one does so in a medium that affects the way light behaves. Water attenuates the spectrum of light visible to the human eye. This, together with refraction and suspended particulate material, means we do not see the site as we would in air. As a result we cannot see as far, so that in all but the smallest sites or the clearest water we cannot see a site in its entirety. This is why, to assist in the process of recording as well as generating its output, various forms of illustration including drawings and paintings have been used to convey or evoke qualities of some of the underwater sites and ship remains discussed in this book.

The attrition of time

Another reason for these illustrations arose during the course of research in the Baltic. It became increasingly apparent that, in spite of the extraordinary preservative properties of this sea and the generally more enlightened attitude of Scandinavian divers in comparison to some of their counterparts elsewhere, these sites were more fragile and less stable than was commonly believed. They are subject to decay, albeit slower than in most other environments, but at a rate that was noticeable even within the space of a few years. The paintings and drawings therefore document the state of preservation of these Baltic wrecks, initially between 1990 and 1992, then at intervals thereafter. Since 1992 a series of events have demonstrated just how vulnerable these apparently robust, well preserved structures are to mechanical damage. This is thought to be caused sometimes by the movement of ice flows during the spring thaw, at other times by the injudicious anchoring of boats and, on the more popular dive sites, a general and inevitable impact on the more fragile structure by passing divers. It was certainly a boat anchor that ripped out the foremost surviving upper deck beam of the *Anna Maria* (1709) in Dalarö (Fig. 3.1). The event was seen as an outrage and featured in the broadsheets. Together with graffiti found carved into a beam (by an overseas diver if the name was any indication), this was enough for the county administration to close the site to diving, an anomaly in Sweden that has championed an enlightened policy of unrestricted access to almost all historic wreck sites as long as certain protocols are observed.

Another example of the sort of change that can occur was seen in the wreck of the brig *Margareta* (Rönnby and Adams 1994:132–141). Though the stern opened where she dragged onto the rocks one winter storm in 1898, much of the foredeck is in place. On it stands the windlass with the anchor chain still passing around the windlass barrel and down into the chain locker. Heeled to starboard the ship lies in the seabed sediments to a level that approximates to a light waterline. Viewed from forward in good visibility, with the bowsprit still raking up into the water, the ship gave every appearance of being in motion. Sometime between 1992 and August 1997, the bowsprit and associated timbers collapsed, the bow framing opening slightly in the process. Figures 3.2a and 3.2b are underwater sketches that illustrate before and after the collapse. As if to press the point that these well-preserved 'Tintin' wrecks could not be taken for granted, shortly afterwards the bow of another well-loved wreck in the vicinity, *Fäderneslandet*, also collapsed. Neither of these events may have had anything to do with diver traffic but the Älvsnabben wreck, originally excavated in the 1970s (Cederlund 1981) and now identified as the *Concordia* of 1754 (Ahlström 1997), was damaged by divers who removed the windlass, leaving or dropping it on the seabed some distance from the wreck (Fig. 3.3). The motive is unclear and, although it has since been replaced by staff from Sweden's National Maritime Museum, it was an unwelcome and uncharacteristic event in

Figure 3.1 'Saltskutan' (the salt ship) now known to be *Anna Maria* (1709) depicted prior to the damage that ripped out the upper deck beam aft of the stump of the foremast. (J. Adams)

See also Plate 2

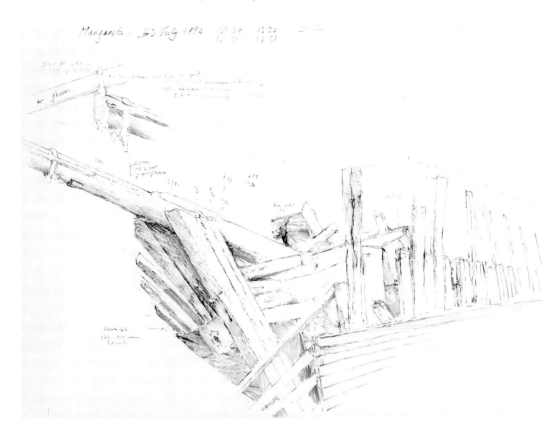

Figure 3.2a Underwater sketches of the wreck *Margareta* (1898) drawn in 1992.

Figure 3.2b *Margareta* drawn from a similar position in 1999 after the bowsprit had collapsed (J. Adams).

16·8·97

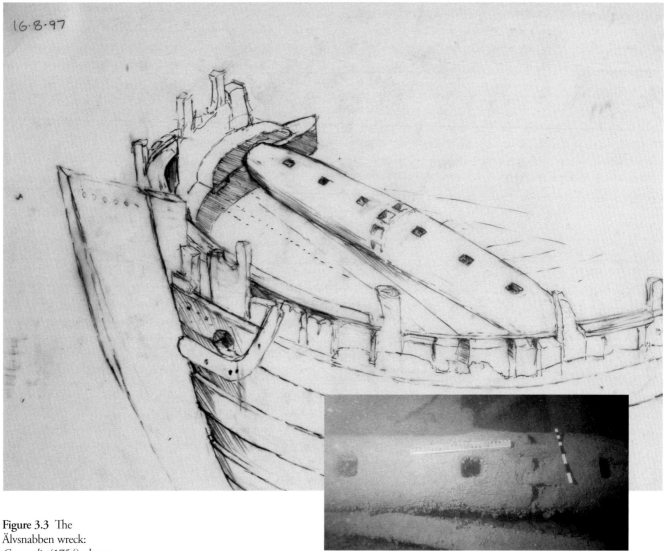

Figure 3.3 The Älvsnabben wreck: *Concordia* (1754), drawn in 1997 with the windlass in place (Sketch: J. Adams, photo: K. Keighley).

view of the way the Swedish diver population normally treat their heritage (though there is no indication of the nationality of the culprits).

Discovery, management and access

From these examples it is not hard to understand the dilemma facing those charged with the protection and management of such sites. Whereas until recently, the authorities generally employed a 'hands-off' approach, these events have prompted a reassessment of the existing predominantly passive management policies. The urgency of such a review has been precipitated by developments in marine geophysical systems and robotic technology as well as advances in diving technology. The dramatic increase in our

ability to image features both on and under the seabed and with markedly increased graphic resolution (e.g. Plets et al. 2009), and for recreational and scientific divers to go far deeper than before, has led to a flush of new discoveries. If anyone had assumed that the shipwrecks in Baltic waters must all have been discovered by now, recent events show that this is far from true. In 1998 the Swedish navy discovered the wreck of a complete snow-rigged vessel in 105m of water. Sitting upright on in the seabed there was no obvious reason for its sinking but its gunports and snow rig suggest it may be a naval sloop. In spite of recent surveys in 2008 and 2009, its nationality is not certain so it is simply known eponymously after its striking figurehead of a seahorse (*Sjöhästen*) (Fig. 3.4). While the video

Figure 3.4 *Sjöhästen* (The Seahorse) discovered at 128m in the Baltic by the Swedish navy (Courtesy of Swedish National Maritime Museum, Stockholm).

recordings present us with an astonishing and immediate view of the 19th-century maritime world, we have ships of that era still afloat. The implication was clear however: these anoxic environments must preserve wrecks of earlier periods and it was not long before they began to be found.

Ships of trade

In 2003 the survey company Marin Mätteknik (MMT) was conducting a search for the Swedish government during which it detected a typical sonar indication of a wreck in 128m of water off Gotland. The sidescan image suggested something extraordinary and when the ROV was deployed the cameras revealed an almost complete 17th-century flute (Dutch *fluit*) ship in a similar state of preservation as the Seahorse. Its main and foremasts remained standing, the deck was littered with rigging elements, the anchor was still catted over the gunwale (Plate 3) and the hull was still adorned with many of its carvings (Fig. 3.5). As the ROV passed along the deck one had the feeling that the crew had not long gone, an impression heightened by the sculpted knight-heads abaft the main mast. Their supplicant faces raised towards the surface

looked so real that the ship was immediately dubbed the 'Ghost wreck'. The ROV surveys using multibeam bathymetry and video have already furnished the sort of high-resolution data unobtainable anywhere else and have stimulated new avenues of research into the social and spatial organisation on smaller merchant flutes (Eriksson and Rönnby 2012). Being some way offshore however these two sites, although a concern, were perhaps not so pressing a management problem as they would be if they lay in coastal waters. This was just the situation created by the discovery of two more well preserved wrecks.

In 2003 MMT made another discovery when their survey vessel *Franklin* was testing some new sidescan equipment which detected a typical wreck-like anomaly in 30m of water. What was surprising was that it lay within the archipelago near Dalarö, a coastal town where several wrecks have been discovered and excavated and where diving had been frequent (Cederlund 1971, 1983; Rönnby and Adams 1994). A group of local divers were informed and they duly investigated. What they discovered was the wreck of a ship from around the third quarter of the 17th century. Two of the three masts were in place, a gun still mounted on its carriage stood on deck. Both pump tubes, the capstan and a windlass remained in position above a largely intact main deck pierced by a hatch complete with its combing. The figurehead of what appears to be a lion rampant lay amid the components of a galleon bow (Figs 3.5–3.7). The diving group carried out a preliminary survey and reported the find to the Swedish National Maritime Museum. The discovery had not yet been made public and required some swift decision making. To do nothing was not an option and simply to prohibit the site to divers was judged too negative a strategy for a public increasingly well informed about its maritime past, especially with the means available for visualising such sites that are now available. The museum therefore decided to mount its own survey. In the summers of 2007 and 2008 a comprehensive structural survey programme was carried out. The methods integrated conventional structural survey techniques with video as well as close visual inspection by a team of diving archaeologists specialised in the archaeology of ships. At this stage the strategy was not to excavate but to leave the site as unaltered as possible. In

tune with that rationale the output of the project was envisaged as much in visual terms as anything, and this was conceived in ways that would make the site as accessible to as wide a public as possible. To that end a camera was mounted on the site to relay video live via the internet (Fig. 3.8). As the survey work continued (Fig. 3.9), its archaeological and historical significance began to become apparent. Firstly, it provides new information on a little known period of ship development and secondly, it manifests a key period of growth in the political and economic environment of northern Europe (Eriksson and Rönnby 2012). As a small but fast, armed vessel, it could have operated as a carrier of high value goods, a privateer or as a naval vessel. Although the ship may have been under Swedish ownership, structural characteristics, dendrochronological analysis and some artefacts suggest it might be English or at least English-built. Other artefacts suggest it might have been involved in trade between England, the Continent and the Baltic.

Barely had the second season of work been completed on the Dalarö wreck than the discovery

Figure 3.5 Anoxic preservation in the Baltic: The 'Ghost Ship', discovered in 128m of water (Photo courtesy of MMT).

of yet another well preserved 17th-century ship was announced to the press. This one also lay within the diving range, and although it was only a little deeper at 47m, its preservation rivalled that of the 'Ghost Wreck' lying in anoxic conditions at 128m. Dating to around the mid 17th century, all three masts remain standing and the hull retains much of its carved adornment. It bears the usual scatter of rigging elements on deck and silt lies thick inside the hull obscuring its doubtless well-preserved contents. This ship also bears a lion but in this case atop the rudder, facing aft. For this reason the wreck is now known as the Lion Wreck and, like the Ghost ship, is a *fluit*. It lies in an area of the archipelago that is rather more enclosed than at Dalarö and the silty seabed suggests there is relatively little water movement. These factors may provide semi-anoxic conditions and, together with the additional depth, have perhaps contributed to the better state of preservation than at Dalarö, especially the much less abraded surfaces of the wood.

With news of yet another *fluit* discovered in deep water (still to be surveyed) the full import of these remarkable finds was clear: treating them as a series of discrete investigations would simply delay the process of unlocking their archaeological potential. To that end their investigation has been integrated under a single collaborative research programme based at Södertörn, focusing not just on new discoveries but on key examples already known (Eriksson 2012; Adams and Rönnby 2013). Not only will this optimise the study of these sites but in terms of research strategy they contribute to a rebalancing of maritime archaeological study of Baltic shipping that was first called for by Carl Olof Cederlund in the 1990s. In spite of being one of the team of archaeologists who excavated *Vasa* (Cederlund and Hocker 2006), he regarded Swedish maritime archaeology (and to an extent that of many other countries) as being too focused on the remains of prestige warships (Cederlund 1994). Much of his subsequent work directly addressed that imbalance through his own focus on merchant ships (e.g. Cederlund 1980, 1981, 1990). But Cederlund would be the first to stress that it is not a case of 'either, or'. The same integrative strategy should

Figure 3.6 The Dalarö wreck, looking aft past the capstan and (inset) the carved lion head from the figurehead (Photos: Jens Linström)

See also Plate 4

Figure 3.7 Left: A gun on its carriage. Right: a museum archaeologist hovering just below the combing of the main hatch (Photos: Jens Linström).

See also Plate 5

Figure 3.8 Images downloaded from video transmitted live over the Internet from the webcam set up on the wreck. (Sjöhistoriska Museum / J. Giddins).

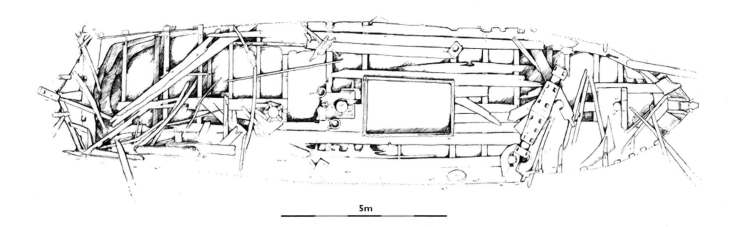

5m

be applied across all facets of the maritime system and here too the opportunities to do this have advanced dramatically.

Ships of war

Dramatic though finds such as the Ghost ship are, interest in medieval and post-medieval warships, especially those of Sweden's great power period, has remained strong at least since Ekman's work on *Elefanten* in the 1930s (chapter 1). The high profile of these vessels prompted a series of protracted searches, leading not only to the rediscovery of the *Vasa* (Cederlund and Hocker 2006:115, 172) but others such as *Kronan* (Johansson 1985). Others proved elusive however, and this only served to heighten their mythical status. But with the advent of modern digital survey systems and technical diving, several of the wrecks that were hunted for so long by Anders Franzén and others have just been discovered. Within days, two major discoveries were announced in 2011, the first was the 16th-century warship *Mars*, the second was the 17th-century warship *Svärdet* (the *Sword*).

The first of these losses occurred in 1564 during the Nordic Seven Years' War (1563–70) when the Swedes met a combined Danish-Lübeck fleet off Öland. At first superior firepower gave the Swedes the upper hand. As flagship, under the command of Admiral Jacob Bagge, *Mars* was one of the largest ships of its time and heavily armed. It succeeded in sinking one of the principal enemy ships *Lange Barken* (the *Long Bark*, now the subject of search itself), an unusual

achievement especially at this early period of stand-off gunnery. Fortunes were reversed the next day when the Danes, realising that with their advantage of numbers, their best chance lay in old-fashioned boarding actions, succeeded in closing with *Mars*. After a bloody fight, with ship on fire, Bagge surrendered and was taken prisoner. Then at some point the powder magazine exploded taking the ship and a thousand men to the bottom. In spite of its violent end the remains of the ship now lie on its side in 70m of water with a large amount of coherent stern and starboard side structure (Fig. 3.10; Plates 6 and 7). The significance of the ship in the context of northern European development is discussed in chapter 4.

The loss of the *Sword* in 1676 during the second Battle of Öland in the Scanian War (1675–79) was no less dramatic. As Vice-flagship she was commanded by Admiral Claes Uggla. But the Swedes suffered a damaging defeat against a Danish-Dutch fleet under the overall command of the renowned Cornelis Tromp. Early in the action, through misadventure, the Swedish flagship *Kronan* capsized and blew up (Einarsson 1990). In the ensuing confusion the allies pressed home their advantage and four ships including the Dutch and Danish flagships surrounded *Sword*. Uggla put up heroic resistance for two hours before surrendering but a Dutch fireship, apparently not realising the action was over, struck the *Sword* and set it ablaze. The powder magazine exploded and Uggla died with several hundred of his crew. The remains of *Sword* now lie in 90m of water and although the explosion

Figure 3.9 Preliminary plan of the Dalarö wreck at deck level. Drawn using a DSM survey as control (J. Adams / N. Eriksson).

ripped apart the midships and stern, the bow half of the structure sits upright and substantially intact (Fig. 3.11; Plate 8).

Both ships therefore have iconic status, not only as they were among the largest warships of their time and therefore symbolically as well as militarily important, but because they were both commanded by national heroes, especially Uggla, who died after a valiant struggle against the odds not unlike Grenville on the *Revenge* in 1591.

At the time of writing the series of discoveries shows no sign of slackening. Another elusive wreck *Resande Mannen* (*The Travelling Man*) (1660), another target of Anders Franzén and many others over the last 40 years was discovered in 2012 (Eriksson et al. 2012). Yet another, though first discovered some years ago, has been revisited and tentatively identified as the Danish warship *Gripshunden* (1495). Investigation is still at an early stage but if its identity is confirmed this is one of the most important of all wreck sites in terms of northern European ship development.

The Baltic finds presented here, although reflecting a Swedish research focus, nevertheless include ships that are Danish, Dutch and possibly English. To these we could add several other discoveries from the waters of all the states that surround the Baltic including several well

preserved wrecks in Finnish waters for example *St Michael* (Ahlström 1997) and *Vrouw Maria* (Leino and Klemelä 2003). Together they considerably increase our capacity to understand and interpret the interrelated maritime pasts of all the states that surrounded this sea as well as those whose maritime strategies depended on it. With respect to Sweden and the case studies discussed in chapter 4, these new discoveries have provided us with a sequence of wrecks that materially punctuate the story of modern Sweden's emergence as a nation state, from its late medieval gestation (Adams and Rönnby 2013a) through its competitive struggle with the other Baltic powers, to the point where it became for a time the dominant power in the north with the most powerful and professional army in Europe (Glete 2002: 174–186). Returning to Cederlund's aims of balanced enquiry, alongside the sequence of naval wrecks we now have a similarly informative series that reveal the mercantile element in which communication and trade facilitated the socio-political agendas that dynasty, diplomacy, military and naval power sought to implement. In other words the database now facilitates more integrated research into groups of vessels, both temporally and spatially, rather than as isolated phenomena and this aspect will be addressed further in chapters 4, 6 and 7.

Figure 3.10 Diver inspecting one of the many bronze guns of the warship *Mars* (Photo: Ingemar Lundgren/ Ocean Discovery).

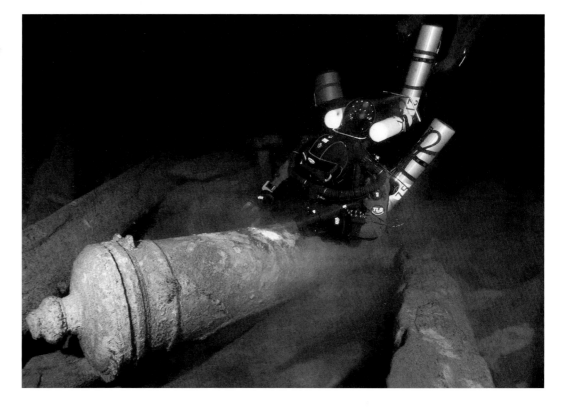

Figure 3.11 A gun still in place on the wreck of *Svärdet* ('the Sword') (Photos: Jonas Dahm/ Deep Sea Productions).

See also Plate 8

Art or science?

These discoveries bring to mind something that the polymath Salomon Reinach once observed, that the greatest museum of antiquities was the seabed of the Mediterranean. Had he known about the Baltic he might have said 'one of the greatest'. Reinach's observations were based on artefacts recovered from the sea in various ways, at a time when the seabed was inaccessible to all but a few. Even though this is no longer the case, it is still a minority who enter the sea as divers or in submersibles. For this reason the visualisation of what is there has become an increasingly important component of archaeological research both in terms of methodology and of output (Smiles and Moser 2005). Within maritime archaeology it was one of the three principal themes: 'Visualization, Monitoring and Safeguarding' of the recent MoSS Project (Cederlund 2004; Leino et al. 2004). What forms this takes and the means with which images are created are many and varied, significantly augmented in recent years by computer-aided technologies. So in this light the use of drawings and paintings that are freehand rather than measured projections might seem oddly out of place in a digital world and therefore need some explanation. They have no direct parallel in land

archaeology, perhaps the nearest being the well-established tradition of the 'artist's reconstruction'. Classic examples of this form are the paintings of Alan Sorrel (e.g. Sorrell 1978) but the drawings used here, as well as those done by other maritime archaeologists such as Henry Forsell, Harry Alopaeus and more recently Niklas Eriksson and Tiina Miettinen (Eriksson and Rönnby 2012; Adams and Rönnby 2013) do not really fall into that category for they depict the sites as they are, not as they were.

In some ways they have more affinity with conventional archaeological illustration where specific characteristics of the site or object are enhanced or emphasised, albeit using accepted conventions. Even though these drawing are not necessarily projections based on Cartesian coordinates as in the case of plans or find drawings they nevertheless select, emphasise and clarify. The important distinction is that this does not involve exaggerating what is there or replacing what is no longer present. The artist's brush merely delineates those surfaces, seams and joints obscured by marine growth or sediment and restores contrast, tone and hue muted by underwater optics.

The procedure begins with an orientation dive around the site to gain an idea of its extent and general characteristics. These days video and still photographs are valuable, especially as the advent of digital technology has made it far easier to get good results, but it is often the sketches that are more useful for establishing physical relationships. This may be because they can incorporate more than is ever visible at one time and clarify what can remain frustratingly obscure even with photographs taken in clear water. Interestingly, the process of drawing also embeds what one sees into memory far more effectively than any amount of purely visual inspection. Perhaps this is because if you can draw it you can understand it, and memorising something you understand is easier than recalling an unintelligible jumble. The sketches therefore form the basis of the subsequent recording strategy as well as being potential illustrations. Another interesting aspect is that they reveal how one sees and thinks, manifesting the hermeneutic process in which impressions are successively refined with each phase of recording and analysis. Initially this tends to focus on characteristics relating to dating evidence, constructional aspects, and the vessel as a functional object. But they are also addressed within a framework of pre-defined research questions as well as others that are generated as the work progresses. While this is a cognitive process that any archaeologist will go through, on land it is continuous and often subconscious. In contrast, unless one is working in a particularly benign and shallow site that allows long dives, working underwater is more episodic. The process is therefore iterative rather than continuous and becomes a more conscious one.

In a way the drawn images document this process but they also have another function. As most people will never visit these sites, the paintings created from them attempt to convey an impression of the sites as a way of sharing the experience of being there. For the way these wrecks are now derives from the way they were as ships in use and what has happened to them since. From that perspective seeing the images is relevant to what is said about them in subsequent description, analysis and interpretation. This is why some of the illustrations that appear in black and white within the text are also reproduced as colour plates.

For these reasons, producing these images is far more than resorting to making a sketch when we cannot get a decent photograph. Instead it is a case of using the cognitive processes of observation and visual analysis involved in drawing as a foundation for subsequent understanding and interpretation. That is why, although we might afford them artistic status, they also take their place in a scientific approach to archaeology, a discipline that perhaps more explicitly than any other seeks to integrate the fundamental principles of enquiry that drive both the arts and the sciences (Jones 2002). Indeed it is perhaps in visualising archaeological sites and materials that we break down cumbersome notions of the arts, craft, engineering and science as mutually exclusive domains and this bears on the ways in which we have built maritime archaeological theory.

Theory and practice

It has been observed that some archaeologists simply want to get on with digging rather than grapple with theory (Hodder 1992:5) and, as noted in chapter 1, this could certainly apply to many who have wrestled with the investigation of underwater sites. McGuire (1992:5) has noted that others have tried to avoid the limitations of any given perspective by constructing theory drawn from many different sources. At least in this case there is an active selection of conceptual and interpretative tools that is far better than attempting to maintain an atheoretical stance (by definition impossible in any case). For McGuire, '... *eclecticism would be defensible if a conscious effort was made to apply one coherent approach to a specific problem or area and another approach to a different area.*' (*ibid.*). Indeed it might be argued that a degree of eclecticism is inevitable unless one is subscribing to grand theory of everything. Certainly this research does not fall naturally into a single theoretical arena. If I have tended towards eclecticism (partly stimulated by the temporal and spatial spread of the source material) rather than dogmatic adherence to one perspective or another, so too has archaeology as a whole, at least since the 1980s. For archaeology is perhaps the ultimate 'multidiscipline' having imported much of its theory, as well as its methods from so many others. Although some have argued that archaeology needs to develop its own theory (Dunnell 1989: Hodder 1986; Yoffee 1993), Julian Thomas (1995:345) has noted that 'Theory is nomadic', meaning that in its transference and utilisation it is inevitably transformed to a greater or lesser degree by the context in which it is deployed. Hence perspectives applied to analyse and interpret new aspects of archaeological material inevitably mutate. If this is so then in a sense archaeology *de facto* has its own theory, though in its scope it is certainly not unitary. By the 1990s it had something of the appearance of a patchwork quilt. Some were seeing signs of a coalescing of ideas leading to suggestions that a coherent 'grand theory' was again becoming possible (Renfrew and Zubrow 1994), though others (Hodder and Preucel 1996:13), while agreeing that there seemed to be more common ground, denied the possibility of grand theory in archaeology due to its double hermeneutic, i.e. its two frames of meaning, that of the investigators and that of the people being studied.

For maritime research, which after all is archaeology first, and 'maritime' only in the sense of environment, context and methodology, there is a choice: Whether to consciously adopt available theory, assuming that, following Thomas's 1995 observation, it will to an extent become 'maritimized' through its application, or actively to seek to develop theory specific to maritime aspects of culture. To a degree, the former is inevitable, as maritime researchers will call upon what they know and this is certainly happening at the moment. Work containing identifiable theoretical stances nevertheless shows a certain amount of eclecticism as well as the intentional melding of various perspectives (cf. Kist 1992; Cederlund 1993; Westerdahl 1992, 1994; Crumlin-Pedersen and Munch-Thye 1995; Rönnby 1995; Gawronski 1997; Gibbins and Adams 2001; Adams 2002; Flatman 2004; Dellino-Musgrave; 2006; Rönnby 2008; Herrera 2008). But the real challenge must be to develop theoretical perspectives that capitalise on the strengths of the classes of information and the characteristics of preservation common in maritime contexts. Not in the sense of developing a separate maritime archaeological theory, but enhanced perspectives on archaeological material in general, arising out of the opportunities to relate maritime pasts with the present. This work aims to link together aspects of various case studies of the maritime record. Although in most cases they were originally planned and executed as independent projects, they have nevertheless pointed the way towards some unifying perspectives on the past, not in terms of providing 'grand' or even general theories applicable to all pasts but in terms of using a series of specific 'thick' studies to discern trends and underlying causal relationships. This distances it from post-structuralist views that would deny the possibility of tying down causes in the first place, especially as much of the data are analysed from an explicitly materialist and historiographic standpoint. Yet their interpretation attempts to discern and deal with social factors that are not quantifiable in a Cartesian/XYZ sense as well as those that are. This is also attempted in the light of a critical approach where my situation as a researcher is acknowledged to have a bearing on the choice of questions and the ways they have been addressed. However, I would reject any implication that this locks constructed pasts in the present or that the data are necessarily imprisoned by vested interest rather than being (relatively) autonomous. Although archaeological practice is subject to the ideologies of the present, as some of the material discussed below shows, this does not mean it cannot reveal those of the past. This brings into focus the fundamental differences between various stances that have been drafted into archaeological service over the last three decades.

Technological particulars or social trends?

In the 1980s and 1990s much of the theoretical debate in archaeology seemed to be polarised in the claims and counter claims of materialist and idealist philosophies, applied, as though through the barrel of a shotgun, to all archaeological data in all circumstances (and at some conferences one had the feeling that had shotguns been available they would have been used). Those who invoked science in the analysis and reconstruction of the past were labelled as positivists by those who denied any possibility of being objective and factual about the archaeological record. The advocates of processual, generalist approaches on the other hand saw many of the perspectives grouped within 'post-processual' archaeology as 'hopelessly relativist' or as Binford put it, moving 'from science to séance' (Binford 1989). In practice most archaeologists fell somewhere between the two and for many the polarization between these two positions has lessened. Binford, a champion of the hypothetico-deductive approach, along with Sabloff (Binford and Sabloff 1982:138) admitted theories are not testable *per se*. Tilley (1991a:14), on the other hand, has argued that, contrary to common assumptions, there is a strong materialist thread running through post-processual thinking, and

Hodder (1992:156), has *'...accepted the need for scientific rigour in field methods, generalisation and theory-building.'* Nevertheless, many texts on archaeological theory seemed to find it obligatory to develop a detailed critique of the perspective(s) they despised, effectively establishing either a materialist or idealist position. Yet the material described here resists confinement within either. Ships and boats are material culture created for various purposes. They are conceived and designed to answer specific social needs. They are constructed using specific technologies, fabricated from various materials and are built to operate in specific environments. They are used and ultimately disposed of in various intentional ways or lost through accident. There are therefore aspects of boats and ships as artefacts that are undeniably quantifiable and testable in terms of physical laws. Equally there are those aspects of their form, arrangement and of their modes of use that are dictated by symbolic association, aesthetics, ideology and ritual, none of which can necessarily be correlated with environmental conditions or predicted and modelled in the same way. So whereas the technical characteristics of a boat as it was actually built can be quantified and analysed, the reasons that people made it that way rather than another are also related to the customs, ideology and traditions that comprise the local social context. In other words, we can measure thousands of component dimensions of an ancient hull. We can then reconstruct it on paper or with computers, enabling us to calculate capacity, waterlines, tonnage and aspects of performance such as stability. Alternatively we can build physical models and even reconstruct a full-size 'floating hypothesis', but none of these will provide an objective reason why certain decoration was applied, why voyages where made at unsuitable times of year, why certain rituals were enacted that had no apparent 'functional' relevance to the vessel's security or the intended voyage.

Good examples of this apparent duality are provided by recent ethnographic research in India (Blue et al. 1997), in particular the Patia, a fishing boat of Orissa. The initial focus of study was its 'reverse-clinker' construction, thought by some to have been a characteristic of the 'hulk', a medieval ship type (see chapter 5). However, as well as providing invaluable new technological information on the use of this construction technique, the investigators witnessed a rich overlay of cultural behaviour relating to the decoration and use of the boat. Most importantly boats are regarded by the fishermen as living spirits that provide them with their livelihood and protect them from danger (*ibid.*:201). In itself, this is not unusual, being similar to the way boats are afforded personality in Oceania (e.g. Layard 1942). Depending on the region in which they are used, patia boats are associated with a goddess: Mangala or Kali. A representation of her face is carved on the stem and a cruder, more schematic full-figure inboard amidships. Both are decorated, the latter covered in vermilion, into which incense sticks are placed at the start of each fishing trip (Blue et al. *ibid.*). To western eyes the adornment and the ritual can be separated from the construction and functionality of the boat respectively, yet to their crew they are inseparable – the burning of the incense stick being just as much a part of using the boat as hoisting a sail. In another study, by the same group, the Vattai, a type of fishing boat used in Tamil Nadu, is built with a high gracefully formed prow (Blue et al. 1998). Originally this may have been connected with safe launching in surf but high prows have become valued for aesthetic reasons linked to status and identity, at the expense of handling – a clear example of a cul-tural factor overriding a techno-functional consideration.

The social aspects of the production and use of water craft must therefore require other analytical and interpretative instruments. Otherwise, interpretations of vessels and their use are limited to analyses of form and function, cargo capacity and stability, constructional technique and anatomy. These may of course be the stated research goals, leading logically towards reconstruction. But however satisfying in themselves, reconstructions are produced as the basis for subsequent testing or interpretation in which links can be made between the material as recorded and its wider meanings. If, as is argued above, ships provide some of the contextually richest examples of specific events in the past, they are also located within and are part of longer historical trajectories. As they embody investment, evidence for changes in the ways they were conceived, created and used may become archaeologically visible as a result of events, but by definition they also invoke longer term trends. The analysis of ships within the context of maritime society must therefore address the general and the particular, as well as the metaphysical and the material.

Data, facts and objectivity

All the principal vessels discussed here have been examined and recorded in various ways, and this raises certain questions of epistemology and inference. It has been indicated above that wreck sites are the result of interacting physical, chemical and biological processes, some of which are cultural and some natural. These processes of site formation are often referred to as middle range data (Raab and Goodyear 1984; Gibbins 1990:377). The natural processes involved are often cyclical and predictable and in this sense can be modelled and used to explain aspects of the observed archaeological distribution. Cultural activity, while it may be predictable to a degree, cannot be modelled in the same way. For example, salvage activity on a wreck may be entirely predictable in the sense that if the wreck is accessible, people will seize the opportunity it presents, but the ways in which they will do it are less so. The evidence for it occurring and its partial reorganising of the deposited materials can only be derived from the archaeological record where it has left traces. Sediment transport, on the other hand will obey certain physical laws and archaeological material embedded in various deposits must have arrived there by certain natural processes and in a certain sequence. Much of the material can be empirically observed and treated as factual. This is not however, to claim objectivity for the resulting database.

Even if we accept that the choices of what to measure are theory-laden, as are our interpretations of the resulting data, the existence of factual information itself has been challenged. Shanks and Tilley (1987:47) in critiquing positivism, nevertheless imply 'facts' and 'objectivity' are synonymous, or at least that they are regarded as such by archaeologists who misguidedly apply 'rational method', their shorthand for the positivist/empiricist discourse (*ibid.*) where

> ...*the observed immediate appearance of the object is taken as being real, something existing independently of its investigation. So it is objective facts which count; knowledge depends on them; they are, after all, considered to be hard physical reality.* (ibid.).

But do data not have characteristics that can be accepted as factual without invoking the spectre of positivism and without implying objectivity in their collection? Hodder, moving towards a realist position, is now of the opinion that: '*The data might not be objective but they are real, existing outside our observations of them*' (Hodder 1992:89). In other words our datasets are not objective because their compilation is theory-dependent and contextually situated but they nevertheless contain factual information. The data are 'real' and exist whether we dig them up or not but this is different from treating them as self-evident truths. Hodder goes further, and in noting the successful reinterpretation of old datasets by new researchers, acknowledged: '...*that the relative autonomy of theory and observation was important in the attempt to break out of a relativist position.*' (Hodder 1992:172).

The position taken here is that shipwrecks as material culture can be observed empirically but the recorded datasets are necessarily the product of a situated research agenda. No absolute objectivity is therefore assumed, only that the resulting interpretations are rooted in material reality, the realm of the 'actual' in realist terms.

Archaeological historical synthesis

There is another aspect to the theoretical potential of the sites discussed here and that relates to their place in time. In spite of the arguments advanced in the previous chapter for the superiority of ship finds as archaeological source material, there naturally remain substantial difficulties in any attempts at interpretation. In some ways the problems associated with the case studies discussed below are distinctive because they all come from historical periods. This raises key issues related to specific bodies of theory that have been advocated for historical sites, as well as (or rather including) the ways in which we attempt to synthesise source materials of different types, dissolving disciplinary boundaries in the process. Exactly how one goes about this has perhaps been of more concern in the domain of 'old world' historical archaeology (e.g. Muckelroy 1976; Ahlström 1995; Gamble 2001:167–170) than the issues which will be discussed later in relation to the new domain of North American historical archaeology.

Undoubtedly, the archaeological data presented in the following chapters can be augmented by, compared with, tested against or even used to verify documentary, iconographic and epigraphic forms of evidence. However, the immense opportunities this brings are accompanied by dangers. In attempts to combine source materials, all too often it has been the historical sources that have been assumed to have primacy or superiority over the material evidence, irrespective of their relative quality. In this situation the historical sources steer the research and to an extent control or even predetermine the archaeological interpretation (Adams and Rönnby 1996:86). In a maritime research context a typical such marriage of convenience is where information from a wreck is used to identify it in the historical sources. This can be very productive but often the assumption seems to be that until an identification is made the archaeological material is somehow sterile, like a floating chronology, of no use until it is anchored to an absolute date. From this perspective, once identified, the wreck material simply becomes the physical illustration of the 'real' written history. The structure, the equipment, the personal possessions, etc., are confined to being curiosities rather than being recognised as things that have their own interpretative value. Perversely, even where an identification of the vessel is made, the majority of its constituent materials and contents are still likely to remain anonymous. Yet it is exactly these things that constitute so much of the contextually rich character and 'inferential status' of shipwrecks. Much of this inference derives from the relationships preserved in the juxtaposition of objects and assemblages. It is in their location relative to each other, within containers, compartments and within the ship, that we see evidence of use, ownership, status, organisation, and other behavioural traits and attitudes that in turn articulate with wider concerns. These attributes are not necessarily intrinsic to the objects themselves and may only be visible or otherwise evident in their contexts of use. It is these contextual relationships that remain unsuspected and indeed which are lost for ever when objects are recovered without proper recording. So the relegation of archaeology to an illustrative role, or as others have put it, to being the 'handmaiden' or 'academic maid-servant of history' (Corbishley 2011:83; Muckelroy 1978:6) is not only wholly unnecessary, it is effectively ignoring the interpretative potential of the archaeological material. These wrecks are all laden with information about the societies that built and used them. Their remains carry meaning in ways that both complement and add to historical texts and are of far more interpretative value than the identification labels in an old-fashioned museum case. A far better strategy is an approach that seeks to capitalise on the source materials in a more integrated way. An archaeological/historical study where the source materials are combined can not only produce new insight, it can lead to a greater understanding than is possible when the two classes of source material remain discreet. Ahlström has aptly described it as reuniting what was part of an original whole (Ahlström 1997:212).

An attempt to employ just this sort of holism was made in the research into the Dutch East Indiaman *Amsterdam* (1749). The Dutch East India company (VOC) is one of the best documented of all maritime enterprises, while the remains of the ship in Bulverhythe beach constitute the best preserved East Indiaman so far known. It was felt that our understanding of the historical and the archaeological sources would be far greater if they were interrogated concurrently in an integrated way, rather than being seen as distinct entities to be consulted at different stages of the research process (Kist 1992). Normally archival sources are used prior to, and after fieldwork. In this way each source material sequentially generates questions for which answers are then sought in the other, but there is no real integration. In a more dialectic approach the resulting insights are far greater than the sum of the parts, for they include the answers to questions that would never have been asked without the juxtaposition of the sources in the first place. Specific aspects of this synergy are discussed in the overview of carvel building in chapter 8. Similar benefits were found in applying this approach to the wreck of a 16th-century carvel ship in the Baltic, discussed in chapter 4.

Exactly this sort of synergy has been noted by James Deetz of the excavations at Flowerdew Hundred and Great Island (Deetz 1999:48). This is where there is considerable articulation between the concerns just outlined and the distinctive identity of North American historical archaeology. Throughout the Americas a sharper dichotomy is perceived between prehistoric and historical archaeology as fields of study. This is hardly surprising as there is a more abrupt transition between the archaeology of regionally delimited cultures unattested by the written record and the global archaeology of the colonial period after the arrival of literate Europeans in the 15th century. This is one reason why an explicit body of theory has been generated for an 'historical archaeology' that has become a distinct branch of the discipline with its own conferences and learned journals.

Deetz has summarised historical archaeology as: '*the archaeology of the spread of European Cultures throughout the world since the fifteenth century, and their impact on and interaction with the cultures of indigenous peoples.*' (Deetz 1999:5). It is the phrase 'throughout the world' that he highlights as being significant for it is the global nature and interconnectedness of human existence from the 15th century onwards that is one of the principal building blocks of historical archaeology theory. For Orser (1996:15) '*the modern era incorporates important disjunctions with what came before, particularly prehistory.*' These disjunctions make the historical world (for Orser, after around 1492) 'a vastly different place' from its prehistoric progenitor (*ibid.* 16). Hence this requires a concomitantly global focus in research to take account of the changed nature of human interaction characterised by what he terms the 'four haunts of historical archaeology': colonialism, Eurocentrism, capitalism and modernity (*ibid.*22). As so much maritime and nautical research of the last forty years has been of ships and sites that were built and founded in the modern period these ideas have obvious relevance. Within such a global context the maritime nature of social interconnectedness is implicit, yet this is not an aspect that is as prominent in the literature as one might expect.

For in its theorizing about diaspora, modernity and globalism, historical archaeology has shown little consideration of the maritime strategies, practices and environments through which these processes occurred. These concerns have been addressed within explicitly maritime research frameworks, for example by McGhee (1997) and Staniforth (Staniforth and Nash 1998) among others, but now there are signs that a more integrated approach is entering the discipline at large (Adams 2006, and, for an example of an archaeologist who is not 'maritime' in terms of specialism but who integrates maritime perspectives, see Johnson 2006).

In acknowledging the pervading presence of Orser's 'haunts', this means that as processes their roles in social change in the modern world must be part of the analysis of associated archaeological material. However, human action takes place within a context created by previous events and actions, so anything that happened after 1492 happened because of what happened before 1492. The fundamental changes in European shipping for example, dealt with in the following chapter,

straddle this proposed watershed, for the ships concerned span more than seven centuries. And while the specific episodes of change under analysis can be related to Orser's 'four haunts', their genesis is rooted in a past before modernity. But rather than see this as a theoretical problem, instead it serves to focus even more attention on the processes of change that generated this modern, global world.

Technology, innovation and social change

Change, and technological change in particular, are acknowledged to be central concerns within archaeology (Ucko 1989:x). As assemblages of unusually high resolution, changes in the way ships are produced within the array of constraints discussed in chapter 2: as technology; as social practice; as expressions of maritime enterprise and of social need, offer ways of explaining aspects of change in past societies. Changes in the observable technology of ships are the results of, and answers to, changes in society at large, and as such cannot be understood in isolation. This study is therefore based in the observation and analysis of ship finds, leading firstly to their interpretation in the context of the societies in which they were conceived, designed, built, used and disposed of.

In the light of comments in chapter 1 about new areas of enquiry establishing their database, it is perhaps not surprising that until relatively recently much of the enquiry into the development of medieval and post-medieval ships focused on their technological and functional characteristics and distinguishing features. To an extent this may still be the case because we are still finding 'wonderful things' and their description is undoubtedly part of what needs to be done. But with the database having reached healthier proportions and its classification having become usefully sophisticated (McGrail 1995:139), the balance has shifted towards perspectives that are better suited to discerning reasons why change occurred and the processes involved.

A similar trajectory is discernible in maritime ethnography. Crumlin-Pedersen for example, was concerned with '*...just how a new material or a change in technique gains a footing in such a trade as boatbuilding.*' (Crumlin-Pedersen 1972:216). Perhaps this was more typical of Scandinavia where ethnographic techniques have been woven more seamlessly into archaeological research than elsewhere (e.g. Humbla 1935; Hasslöf 1958a and b, 1972; Christensen 1972; Westerdahl 1992). The closest parallels in British nautical research include Greenhill (1978), who closely collaborated with Scandinavian researchers, McKee (1983), and Osler (1983). Another notable ethnographic study within the same time period was that of Prins (1986). Even within this area of study, research questions have generally remained close to the realms of form and function, and to the characteristics of building traditions. However, as noted, recent research driven by McGrail and Blue (Blue, et al. 1997; 1998) has begun addressing cross-cultural issues including the parallel development of technological solutions to boatbuilding in apparently unconected cultural and environmental contexts. Shipwreck research often retained a predominantly functionalist approach in projects focused around single vessels. This has tended to restrict ability to address issues of change for which examination of more than one vessel is a prerequisite. The ability to do this in a structured manner takes time and resources so it is no coincidence that it is the long-lived programmes such as those centred in the Mediterranean, Scandinavia and Australia have provided the necessary context. More recently the longer established projects built around single sites or vessels have also tended to develop more expansive research programmes that reach beyond technology, form and function (e.g. Cederlund and Hocker 2006).

The reasons to do so are fundamental. While evidence for change remains central to any form of analysis, the underlying reasons for change and the mechanisms by which it has occurred, although implicit in the observed technological characteristics, are unlikely to be self evident. As a general observation, in focusing on technology, much nautical research has, for the last century at least, consciously or unconsciously adopted this broadly functionalist approach allied to notions of cultural evolution, notably those that employ analogies between cultural and biological change. This is manifested in the importance attached to discerning evolutionary progressions and links between different boat and shipbuilding traditions on the basis of observed physical traits. The assumption, stated or implied, is that there must be linear progressions between antecedent and descendent types. There often are, but an assumption that the nature of the development and its causes will become clear if only the missing links in the chain can be found is erroneous.

Developmental sequences that appear analogous to biological evolution undeniably exist, in which the iterative selection of characteristics in response to various stimuli such as threat or competition produces a series of increasingly efficient ('successful') watercraft ('phenotypes'). But, as the fundamental mechanisms of biological evolution and cultural selection are different, how useful this similarity is in explicating the whole process of social change is widely debated (Dunnell 1989; Maschner 1996; Cullen 1993, 1996; Preucel and Hodder 1997:205; Miller 2010:45; Shennan 2011). As the collected wisdom of the ages has expressed in so many ways, and as the cases in this book suggest, 'there's nowt so queer as folk'. An example is referred to in the next chapter, where a technological progression is clearly indicated by the archaeological evidence but in a rather more variable and multilinear way than at first thought. This emphasises the problem: to show that change has occurred is one thing; to explain it is quite another. From experience this partly stems from the richness of well preserved finds that appear to be self-explanatory. The plethora of technological details observed in ship structure, like the data referred to by Lewis Binford (1972:5), stored in his professor James Griffin's filing cabinets, scream forth self-evident truths: 'This is how I am. This is how it was.' But as to why? – the perfectly preserved tool marks, the joints, the fastenings, the moss caulking, however painstakingly described, often remain frustratingly mute.

As well as a lack of explanatory power, there are also dangers in applying cultural evolution models where change is seen in terms of inevitable 'progress' from one increasingly sophisticated type to another. Of course things can and do get better, more sophisticated, more useful (Adams and Rönnby 1996:10, 85) but there are also examples of a technology being abandoned or of a simpler procedure being re-adopted in place of the more 'modern' one (Sarsfield 1991:137–145). In the context of ship technology, Cederlund (1984:174) and McGrail (1987:1, 4) have warned of the dangers of such teleological assumptions. So too have others with regard to the whole issue of 'innovation' and the component processes involved (Ucko, 1989: ix–xiv; van der Leeuw and Torrence 1989:1).

Unfortunately a technologically based analysis of ship finds tends to promote simplistic evolutionary analogy. Paradoxically, this tends to be synchronic rather than diachronic. Two types of vessel, the one deriving from or superseding the other, are effectively studied as two static situations rather than as the products of a social continuum. Pursued in isolation, this path is inevitably frustrated by lack of evidence. For as change is not necessarily linear, and as it is influenced by many factors other than technological sophistication, it tends to leave lacunae that fail to be bridged however many subsequent cases are added to the database. Ironically then, a functionalist approach, while presenting detailed evidence of change, often leaves the questions of 'how?' and 'why?' unanswered.

The case studies in the following chapters attempt to work outwards from the hull remains towards explanations that encompass the technological developments in a social context. This is not to downplay the importance of physical and technical analysis in the understanding of specific vessels and their use. Nor have functional aspects of explanation been eliminated from what follows but an attempt has been made to augment this by exploring the underlying, interrelated causes of change and the mechanisms by which changes have come about. The archaeological research of ships is therefore far more than a study of a building tradition, of the shipwright's art and of their technological products. It attempts to understand the context in which they worked, the socio-economic needs that drove that work as well as the motives and ideas of the people who used them and controlled them. A careful distinction is made here. No claims are made for being able to get 'inside the heads' of historical figures and know their thoughts (although we are trying to come as close to that as possible). But ideas, aspirations, opinions and mood-swings they certainly had, and what it is possible to understand is some of the origins, causal factors and contexts of those ideas. In so doing we understand the material reality that they created and the events in which they played a part in greater depth than if they remain represented only through description and technical detail.

4

From Medieval to Modern: Ships of State

When Henry VIII ascended the throne of England in 1509 he inherited a naval infrastructure that, while vestigial, had at least set some precedents, and in terms of dockyard facilities and administation pointed the way for what was to come (Loades 2002:55). What then occured was a substantial programme of building, repair and arms manufacture, although he may have been considerably involved or even the prime mover in these initiatives as heir apparent. Although naval investment had fluctuated, and would continue to fluctuate depending on perceived threat, foreign policy and the state of the economy, what was notable about this episode was that it consolidated the Crown's irrevocable commitment to a new technology for the building of its 'great ships'. These new vessels were designed to carry a greater weight of heavy ordnance than their predecessors and this necessitated new designs and different construction. Unlike most earlier English vessels their hulls were no longer clinker-built, the method that had been dominant in England since the Saxon period. New needs and circumstances had stimulated a change to a new way of building ships known as 'carvel'.

Terminology

Here the terms 'clinker' and 'clinker-built' refer to ships built within the wider Nordic tradition, often called 'keels' (*ceol, köl, køl, kjøl:* Anglo-Saxon, Swedish, Danish, Norwegian respectively) suggesting an etymological root in the primary element of construction, and surviving in the names of several clinker-built vernacular forms such as the Tyne keel (McKee 1980:72). The word clinker is Germanic in origin and relates to the process of assembly in which the hull was generally constructed from radially split oak planks, though other woods and other methods of conversion were used. These cleft or cloven planks were overlapped and fastened to each other through the overlaps, forming an integral 'shell'. In some regions the fastenings were treenails (Marsden 1994:141–153; Litwin 1995:19), or sewing (Cederlund 1978), though by the period under discussion the most widespread were iron nails. The planks were drilled through the overlap with an auger, the nail was then passed through the hole and 'clenched' (bent or otherwise deformed) usually over a washer called a rove, in effect riveting the planks together (Fig. 4.1). The precursors of the modern words clinker, clinch and clench are seen in the terms like 'clynche- or 'clench-nail' found in medieval building accounts and in descriptions of such vessels as 'clenchers' or being clench-built.

In classic clinker construction the framing system was secondary, in the sense that it did not control hull form and was inserted after the plank shell had taken shape. For more detailed discussions of origins, characteristics and regional variations see for example Christensen (1972:235–259), Crumlin-Pedersen (1972:208–234), Hasslöf (1972:27–72), McGrail (1987:102, 2001:223–232).

The word 'carvel' believed to derive from the Portuguese *caravella* has generated considerable discussion. Greenhill (1995:60) distrusted the term enough to abandon it completely, but it is used here for two reasons. Firstly, it has gained general currency among researchers and much of

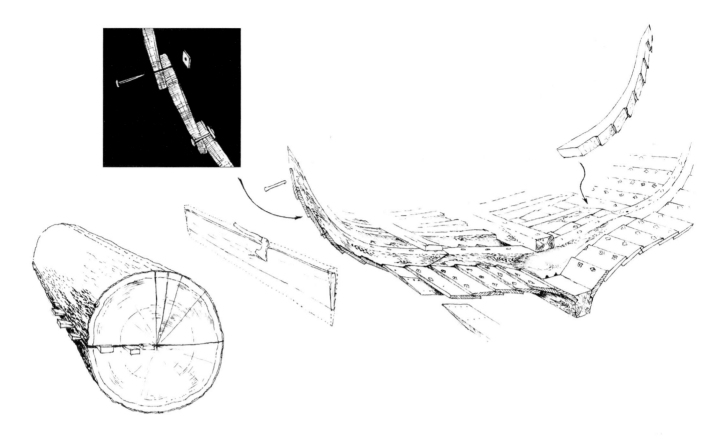

Figure 4.1 Typical late Nordic clinker construction. The planks are converted from the log by radial splitting, then dressed to the shape required with an axe. They are overlapped and fastened to each other through the overlap, in this case with roved nails. Frame timbers were then fitted into the plank shell and fastened with treenails (J. Adams).

the misunderstanding associated with the term has been dispelled, not least by the explanatory writings of Greenhill himself. Secondly, it is the term that was widely used at the time to describe the ships themselves and was clearly related to the way they were constructed. 'Carvel' in this sense therefore refers to a hull construction that is 'frame-orientated' or 'frame-led' because it is the frame elements rather than the planking that lead and control the process of forming of the hull. The hull planks were sawn rather than cleft, laid flush and fastened to the frames, not to each other (Fig. 4.2). The ships that comprise the principal case studies in this book are the product of this building tradition.

The first of Henry VIII's new English ships, the *Mary Rose* and the *Peter Pomegranate*, were probably laid down in 1509, while the *Sovereign* of 1488 was completely rebuilt the same year. What are believed to be her remains were revealed in 1912 by building development at Roff's Wharf in Woolwich. The frame timbers had originally been joggled (notched) to accommodate clinker planks but at some point these had been stripped away and the joggles worked back sufficiently to accommodate flush-laid, carvel planks (Anderson 1926:132; Salisbury 1961; Rule 1982:22; Friel

1995:175) (Fig. 4.3). Irrespective of whether this occurred as part of the 1509 rebuilding as has always been assumed, to those not versed in ship technology this does not sound particularly radical. As will be argued, in a way it was not, for changes had occurred in the framing systems of large clinker-built ships that would have allowed such a conversion to take place relatively easily. More fundamental were the changes in maritime needs and therefore the roles of ships built to fulfil them. The measures initiated by Henry VII and continued by his son were manifestations of the changes sweeping through the whole of European shipbuilding, effectively setting it on a trajectory from which it did not deviate in major respects until the end of the wooden ship era in the late 19th century. Perhaps because these changes can be seen as a technical watershed, the end of one era and the beginning of another, few episodes in the field of nautical research have generated so much discussion as the appearance in northern Europe of so-called 'skeleton-built' or 'carvel' ships. It is not so much that a new form appeared, but how it did so, and the way in which it eventually supplanted, for some purposes at least, ships built in the long-established clinker tradition.

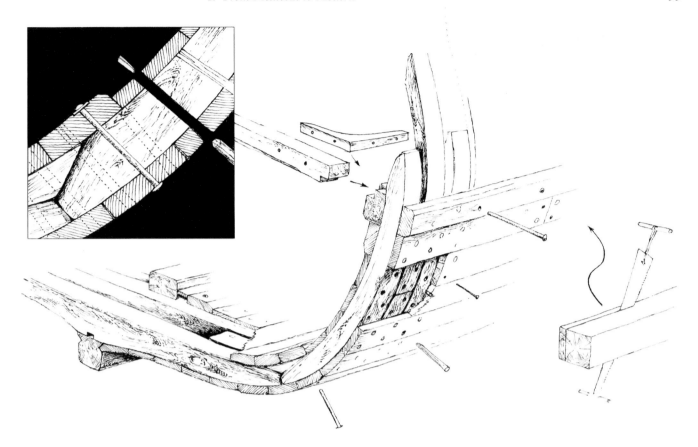

Technological precedents

Much of the interest generated by this episode of change is due to the fact that it has seemed so hard to explain satisfactorily. We have indisputable evidence that the change occurred but its causes and the mechanisms by which it was effected proved elusive. Attempts to explain it as a transition from one construction method to another concluded that it was both a technological and conceptual revolution with mysterious origins. This perhaps derived from Hornell's impression that there could have been no smooth transition between the two and that '*the pre-erection of transverse frames* (was) *clearly an act of invention...*' (Hornell 1946:194). This view was reiterated by Eskeröd (1956:72), though it was effectively dispelled by Olof Hasslöf (1958). Indeed ideas that anticipate Hasslöf's treatment can be seen in the work of Philibert Humbla, an archaeologist and ethnographer who Hasslöf worked with extensively (Humbla 1934). This episode of change has nevertheless retained its mysterious and revolutionary status and is repeatedly referred to in those terms. Sarsfield referred to the origins of carvel building as '*One of the most curious mysteries in the history of naval architecture.*' Sarsfield 1991:137). Greenhill, having done more than most to elucidate it, still described it as a 'complex technical revolution' (Greenhill 1995:256). Though the aura of mystery surrounding these events has been somewhat dispelled by new archaeological evidence, the mechanisms involved continue to be seen as problematic. Certainly changes in aspects of shipping in general at this period were 'revolutionary', but to adopt this as an explanatory label for an enduring gap in our understanding is unsatisfactory. The case made here is that from different perspectives the process can be seen in a new light and connections drawn between various contributory and interrelated factors. In that light it also becomes clear that such complex change cannot be attributed to a single, primary cause such as warfare or the gun (e.g. McKee 1968:148, 1973:22; Marsden 1997:80).

Firstly, these developments in the building and use of ships were linked to widespread and profound changes occurring across the whole socio-political spectrum in Europe. In that light, as will be seen, the clinker to carvel transition appears rather less dramatic. Secondly, even on technological grounds there are various precedents that undermine the idea of 'revolution' in the

Figure 4.2 Typical carvel construction based on English finds *c.* late 17th century. Planks are sawn then treenail-fastened to the frames. The plank butts are additionally secured with a blind bolt or spike. Major structural elements such as keel, keelson, stringers and knees, etc., are also bolted (J. Adams).

Figure 4.3 The 'Woolwich ship'. Drawing from a photograph of the ship found at Roff's Wharf in 1912, believed to be Henry VII's *Sovereign*, built in 1488. The underside of the floors retain a series of shallow notches which are the remains of the joggles for clinker planks, removed for the fitting of flush-laid 'carvel' planking (J. Adams).

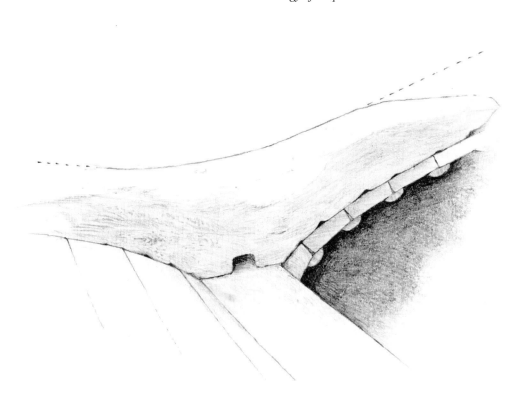

sense of a sudden overturning of previous tradition and ideology: In northern Europe, alongside the methods of fabricating watercraft through the joining of overlapping planks, there have been others that involved flush-laid planks, fastened not to each other but to frames.

In the construction of cogs, a medieval shipbuilding tradition distinct from keels, we see the two approaches used together (Fig. 4.4) (Reinders 1985; Hocker and Vlierman 1996). In turn, plank on frame Romano-Celtic boats have been proposed as ancestral to cogs (Ellmers 1985:81, 1994: 34; McGrail 1995:139). So the concept of a vessel built this way was by no means alien. But it is the terms 'shell-built' and 'skeleton-built' that embody the conceptual gulf perceived to exist between the two approaches. In principle, skeleton construction requires a pre-conceived design that is difficult to alter or adapt once construction has started, whereas builders of clinker boats advance plank by plank, controlling the shape as they go (Christensen 1972:239; Greenhill 1976:73). However, in view of the relative simplicity of early carvel design criteria it is debatable how limited the builder's ability to adapt really was, at least in the crucial early stages. It must also be asked, how free-form the clinker approach was in many cases. At its simplest a carvel boat can be built on the basis of a desired keel length, with everything else

derived from it by proportion. Conversely, clinker boats were often not entirely built by eye. Their form was also regulated by various types of guide, such as ells or control levels, or even with moulds and templates (McGrail 1987:98–103). Although Christensen (1972:252) argues that moulds are later borrowings from the carvel tradition, McGrail (1987 *ibid.*) suggests that some means of controlling the final form are likely. Determining whether any such aids were used for regulating hull form in early clinker building relies on finding them in an archaeological context and this is perhaps unlikely (McGrail 1987:102). Although guides and more recent types of template might not have been necessary for skilled builders of smaller craft, questions hang over the construction of the larger Nordic vessels. The largest examples reached such a size that it is difficult to believe that such enormous investments would have been entrusted entirely to the shipwright's optical judgement.

Any idea of conceptual incompatibility is also eroded by various instances of a practical merging of the two methods. In the Baltic it was not uncommon to repair or consolidate a clinker-built vessel by adding a layer of flush-laid planks onto the clinker hull (Hasslöf 1972:58). In some cases they may even have been built this way. The Maasilinn wreck in Estonia, for which

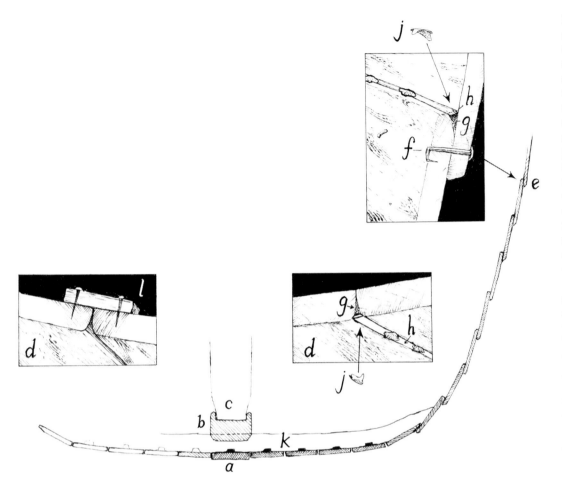

Figure 4.4 Generic cross section of a medieval cog. The centreline usually comprised a keel plank (a) and a keelson (b), often expanded to accommodate a mast step (c). The bottom planks are flush and not edge-joined (d), whereas the side planks are overlapped (e) and clenched with turned nails (f). Both bottom and side seams are caulked with moss (g) retained by oak laths (h), in turn secured by sintels (j) (a flat iron staple holding the lath tight to the seam). Heavy frames are treenailed (k) to the planks. See Reinders (1985) for other characteristics of cog-like vessels found in the Dutch Polders, Adams and Rönnby (2002) for Swedish finds of various origins, Hocker (forthcoming) for a corpus of all cog finds (J. Adams).

dendrochronology dates fall between 1543–1546, has a heavy layer of flush planks laid over the clinker shell (Arens 1987:47; Mäss 1994). In recent years several other examples have been discovered in southern Scandinavia, mostly in the Baltic (Grundvad 2011). One of them, discovered near Preow, Germany (designated FPL 77), dated to *c.* 1590, was converted after a period of sustained use. This was a conclusion supported by the dendrochronological evidence which indicated an origin in the Lübeck area for the added flush planking as opposed to the Øresund region for the framing and clinker planks (Auer et al. 2009:13). Although the method continued into the modern era, several, including the two examples mentioned here, are from the 16th and 17th century. Their appearance shortly after the introduction of carvel technology to the Baltic cannot be a coincidence. Local shipwrights realised that this was both a good way of strengthening a ship and an expedient way of achieving many of the advantages of a carvel hull such as increased strength and ease of repair. It may also be significant that these 'new' carvel-like hulls could also be built with existing knowledge.

Whether built this way or converted, this is not too dissimilar to the expedient adopted in Tudor England, purportedly in the case of the *Sovereign* referred to above but certainly with other vessels such as the *Great Bark* built clinker in 1515 and rebuilt carvel as the *Great Galley* in 1523 (Anderson 1962:62). Further variations have involved combinations of the two approaches during initial building. Hasslöf (1972:58) describes the 'half-carvel' building of Baltic galleasses, having a clinker-built lower hull with carvel construction above the bilge. Some examples are known from the 18th and 19th centuries but he thought that this principle evidently went back to the 17th century, and quite possibly earlier, perhaps to the very period of change under discussion. Indeed in 1994 the remains of a half-carvel ship were found near Sundsvall, Sweden (Holmkvist 2000). Known as the Åkroken-wreck, extensive surviving structure was recorded by the Swedish National Maritime Museum in 2006 (Eriksson 2008).

Figure 4.5 Dutch ship construction. Detail from No. 2 in a series of 16 engravings by Sieuwert van der Meulen (de Groot and Voorstman 1980:139).

Some of its timbers had waney edges right out to the last growth ring allowing them to be dated by dendrochronology to the summer of 1577 (Eriksson 2008:5). Generically similar to the later examples, the Åkroken ship represents an approach already established by the late 16th century.

This and the other procedures described demonstrate that shipwrights through time have had no conceptual problems in adapting their procedures in the face of various stimuli, even though it may involve overriding ideological objections and preferences. Another example from this period that involved the merging of existing ideas with new needs is the method used in Holland. Dutch carvel hulls were begun, in a sense, shell-first, with temporary formers or cleats holding the bottom planks in place prior to insertion of frame elements (Fig. 4.5). This technique has a long history and is also evident in the lower hull construction of some cogs (Figs 4.4d, 4.5 and 4.6) (see Van der Moortel 1991; Adams 1995:59; Hocker and Vlierman 1996). It is so similar that it is presumably one and the same technique simply adapted for the construction of completely flush-planked hulls. Even outside Holland, as will be demonstrated in the following chapters, the building of relatively

large carvel hulls was not always simply a matter of applying planks to a previously erected skeleton of frames. In many cases particularly in early carvel building, framing and planking advanced together based on the erection of a few control frames, the intervening timbers being controlled by ribbands (see chapters 4, 6, and Glossary).

Another factor is the development of the Nordic clinker tradition. The ship of the so-called Viking Age manifested itself in a variety of forms (Crumlin-Pedersen 1967, 1997, 2002) but as that period drew to a close, these vessels did not disappear. They continued to be built in an ever wider variety of shapes and sizes, founded on the same plank-orientated principle. The enduring adaptability of the tradition is attested by the range of clinker vessels found at Kalmar Slott in the 1930s (Åkerlund 1951) and more recently elsewhere (Bill 1999; Bill et al. 1989). Not only could the Nordic tradition produce vessels very similar in form to cogs, e.g. Kalmar II which is entirely clinker-built, but evidence from Bergen (Christensen 1985; Crumlin-Pedersen 1994:70), the Polders (Reinders and Oosting 1989), Guernsey (Adams and Black 2004), Sandwich (Milne 2004), and Newport (Roberts 2004; Nayling and Jones 2012, Nayling and Jones forthcoming), demon-

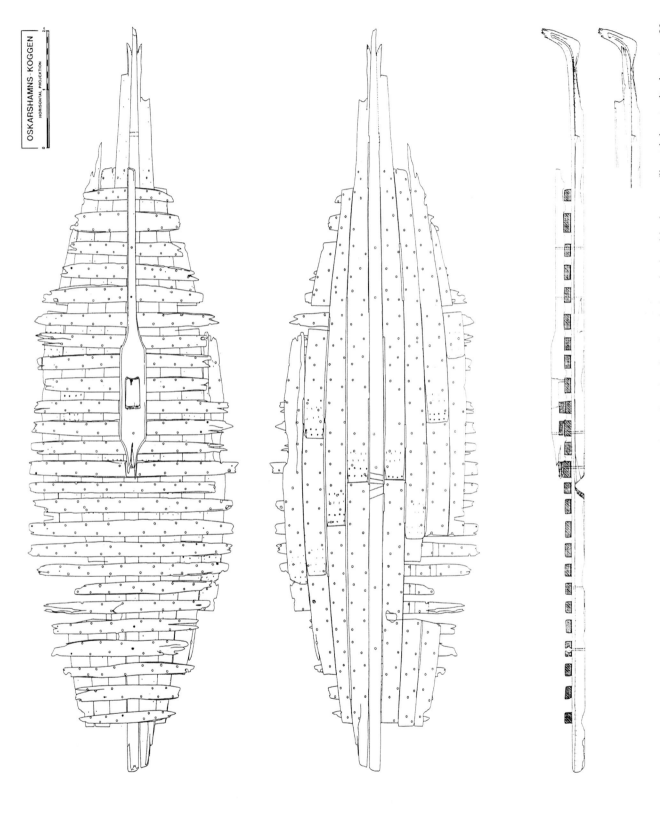

Figure 4.6 The cog found off the island of Bossholmen, near Oskarshamn, Sweden. Inboard and outboard plans; keel and keelson profile with longitudinal section. Unusual for this type is the deep keel (J. Adams).

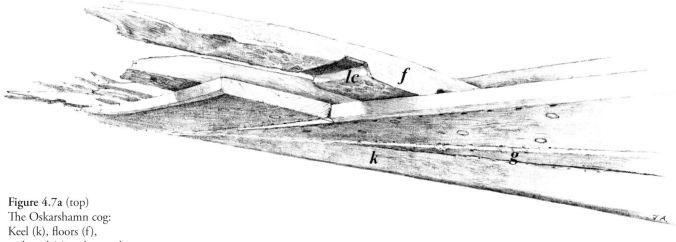

Figure 4.7a (top) The Oskarshamn cog: Keel (k), floors (f), garboard (g) and second strake, limber channels (lc) cut into the floor, the caulking bevel in the outer planks and the laths and sintels retaining the moss caulking (refer to Fig. 4.4d). The sintels were spaced approximately 110mm apart. Note the bevel countersinks the laths and sintels so they are flush with the plank surface (J. Adams).

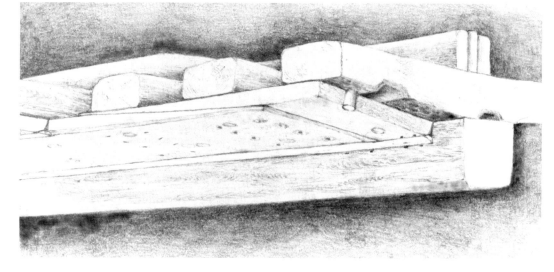

4.7b Oskarshamn cog end-to-end plank joints fastened with turned nails, driven inboard across the aft, lower end of the joint (1) and outwards at the forward end (2) (J. Adams).

strates some of them were also extremely large. So, at the time when large carvel-built carracks were beginning to appear in the waters of northern Europe, there were clinker vessels in existence that were nearly as big.

An aspect of these late medieval clinker ships which may be implicated in the introduction of carvel technology rests in the correlation between their increasing size and their framing systems. The larger the hull, the harder it was to produce a coherent shell of planks simply because of the limitations of the materials. In response, a greater proportion of hull strength was invested in the framing system rather than the planking. This would have been exacerbated by any reduction in the quality and size of available timber. The database of Nordic ship remains generally shows a progressive reduction in the length and width of the planks used to build them (Crumlin-Pedersen 1986, 1989;

Goodburn 1992). This reflects a reduction in the size of trees available, for a cleft board cannot be much more than a third of the parent tree's diameter (Fig. 4.1). Both increased vessel size and smaller planks forced a shift in emphasis to the frame elements, which became much heavier relative to the planking, more closely spaced, and further reinforced with more systematic arrangements of stringers and other internal strength members. This also prompted remedies for other weaknesses arising from increased size. The method of locking beams by rebating their projecting heads into the hull planks, worked well in vessels the size of Kalmar 1 (Fig. 4.8), but exerted considerable stress on the hull planking in larger vessels. A remedy seen in the relatively large 15th-century, clinker-built, Aber Wrac'h 1, was to reinforce the plank rebates for the head of the beam with an additional layer of timber (L'Hour and Veyrat 1989:293; 1994:174).

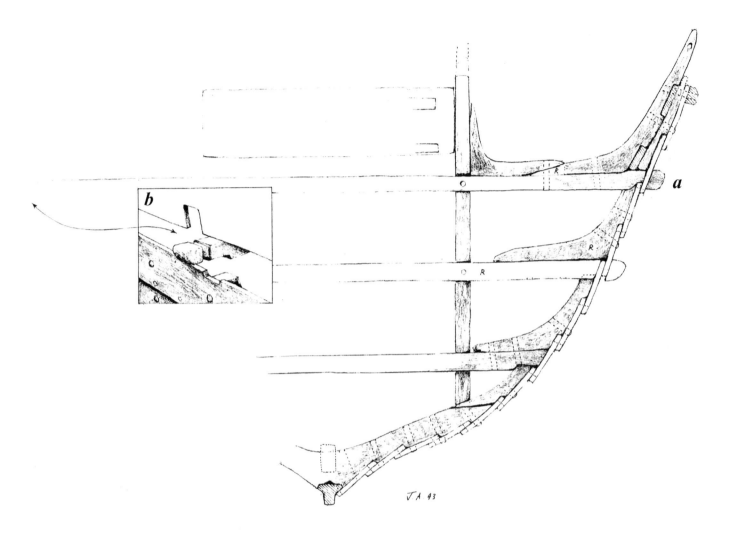

The builders of another clinker built vessel, the so-called 'copper wreck' found in Gdansk used a similar system (Litwin 1981). Other vessels show an alternative, internal beam-locking method that was possibly developed from the way beams needed to be secured at or below the waterline. Parts of a heavily built clinker ship found in St Peter Port harbour, Guernsey (Adams and Black 2004) have a sturdy beamshelf arrangement together with fastenings and rebate positions that indicate substantial lodging knees (Fig. 4.9a). This system not only provided secure fastening for the beams but removed the need for them to pierce the hull planking. A further advantage was that the beam ends no longer needed to be protected from impact by the cone-shaped fenders illustrated in many manuscript illuminations and seen for the first time in an archaeological context on the Aber Wrac'h 1 (L'Hour and Veyrat 1994:176). The result was a more coherent internal structure, very similar in fact to the framing systems of equivalent sized vessels built in the carvel manner. From a purely practical point of view this would have made it a relatively simple matter to change their edge-joined clinker planking to flush carvel planks (Fig. 4.9b). Attempts by English builders to retain the clinker-built shell as the main repository of hull strength in ever larger ships gave rise to the triple-layered planking seen in the *Grace Dieu* of 1418 (Anderson 1934; Hutchinson 1994:24). This vessel and (possibly) others built in a similar manner represent the most extreme expression of the wider Nordic tradition. But while *Grace Dieu* was admired in her time as an astonishing structure, nothing like

Figure 4.8 Kalmar 1, drawing of the cross-section on display in the Sjöhistoriska Museum, Stockholm. The planks are clenched with roved nails in the lower hull but with turned nails in the upper planks. The beams protrude through the hull (a) and are rebated to lock with the planks (b) (J. Adams).

Figure 4.9a
St Peter Port 3: a section of heavily built clinker hull found in St Peter Port harbour, Guernsey, in 1985, showing the clamp and knee arrangement connecting the beam to the hull.

Figure 4.9b
An imaginary conversion of St Peter Port 3 to carvel. This was not done until much later but would have been possible in heavily built and relatively coherent framing systems like this one (Drawings: J. Adams).

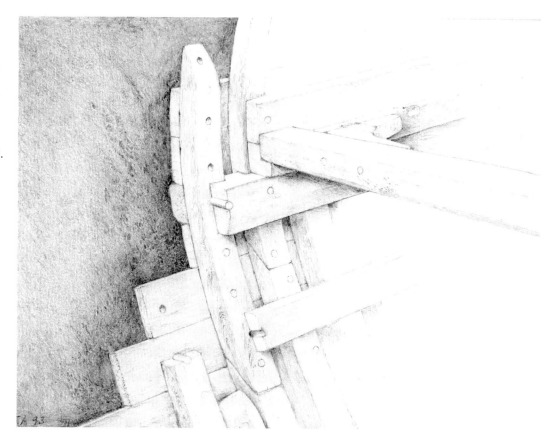

her was attempted again. Less than 50 years after she had burned and sunk at her moorings in 1439 in the Hamble river, the English Crown seems to have embraced a more viable method of constructing the largest seagoing ships.

Innovation and change

These findings break down modern perceptions of insurmountable difficulties in effecting technological change, but identifying, let alone understanding the network of interrelated causes requires both a consideration of the context in which that change occurred and the way in which it came about. In this case the context of change is broadly 15th-century Europe, though the origins extend back many centuries into the shipbuilding traditions of northern Europe and the Mediterranean. The causes relate to the fundamental trajectories of medieval and early modern society in those regions. The innovations that occurred in the 15th and 16th centuries must therefore be set in the context of the broader development of northern and southern European maritime enterprise and this involves summarising the way in which their two distinct approaches to shipbuilding developed.

Northern Europe

McGrail (1987:5) has outlined various classes of watercraft based on their fundamental characteristics of construction which can be defined as floats, rafts, and boats. It is the developmental trajectory of boats that is relevant here, and plank boats in particular. It is widely believed that the origins of many plank-built boats and ships have their roots in logboats (Humbla 1937; Eskeröd 1956; Ellmers 1996:15; Greenhill 1995:101). This is based on extensive archaeological and ethnographic evidence for the various ways in which the basic logboat can be extended and/or expanded to increase its capacity and improve its stability (Crumlin-Pedersen 1972; McGrail 1987:67). It is in the methods of extension/ expansion that the fundamental concepts underlying the construction of planked craft are thought to be seen. It certainly seems a logical step that having extended a dugout structure, such as by adding wash strakes, as appears to have been done with the second of the Neolithic dugouts found at Åmose in Denmark (Ellmers 1996:22), subsequent increases in size can be achieved by the addition of further planks. Once a craft of a certain size is envisaged by its designer

and progressively more effort is invested in the extension elements, the labour-intensive procedure involved in fabricating the logboat base becomes increasingly redundant. It effectively forms a basal, keel-like element of the enlarged craft. One can certainly postulate a neat evolution from logboat to plank boat using an archaeological example for every stage. The problem is that the archaeological record does not provide these 'stages' in the right order. Many extended logboats are fairly recent and are predated by complex plank boats and ships by thousands of years. The development of watercraft occurred in different ways at different times in different places depending on local environmental and social circumstances. Logboats may have provided the root for some types of plank boat but this does not preclude the possibility that other types may have derived from other forms such as rafts, skin boats, bundle rafts or bark boats (e.g. see Greenhill 1995:78–116). Logboats, though highly varied in themselves, have endured for thousands of years and are still produced in some regions today. In answering simple water transport needs, they have provided a continuum alongside which more complex forms serving concomitantly more ambitious and more precarious socio-political agendas have come and gone.

The earliest known plank boats outside Egypt have been found in Britain. A series of finds from around the coast show that sophisticated, relatively large plank-built boats were being constructed in Britain for much if not all of the Bronze Age. The discovery of a boat plank at Kilnsea (Van de Noort et al. 1999) and the recent re-dating of other plank boat finds from Ferriby (Wright 2004) suggest that we are dealing with a well-established building tradition that must have originated prior to the second millennium BC, i.e. the early Bronze Age. Although water transport was important in the British Neolithic, and planks were produced for some structures, the available technology suggests logboats and skin boats would be more likely forms. Unfortunately skin boats are less likely to be preserved but the relatively numerous logboat finds from the Mesolithic and Neolithic periods suggest that they achieved ubiquity soon after there were available trees to convert. The oldest known so far are from Pesse in Holland: *c.* 7920–6470 BC (Gro-486) and Noyen-sur-Seine in France: *c.* 7190–6540 BC (Gif-6559). So it may be that in looking at boats of the Ferriby type we are looking at an approach to producing watercraft that developed with Bronze Age culture itself and its increasing use of metal tools.

Although these Bronze Age finds have strong generic similarities, there are differences of detail which seem to correspond to date. McGrail (1996a:36) has therefore suggested a provisional chronological classification: Group A includes Ferriby 1, 2 and 3 (Wright 1990), recently re-dated through AMS to *c.* 1780 BC, *c.* 1830 BC and *c.* 1900 BC respectively (Wright 2004), Kilnsea dates to 1870–1670 BC (OxA-6939, 6940) (Van de Noort et al. 1999), Caldicot 1 to *c.* 1600 BC (McGrail 2004:190) and Dover to 1575–1520 Cal BC (Bayliss et al. 2004:254). Group B includes Caldicot 2, *c.* 1100 BC (McGrail 2001:188); Goldcliff, *c.* 1000 BC (McGrail 2001:190), Brigg 2, *c.* 800 BC (Q-1255), (McGrail 2001:187) and possibly Ferriby 5, *c.* 380 BC (McGrail 2001:187).

How long this tradition survived into the British Iron Age or how it might relate to continental or Scandinavian traditions, if at all, is not clear as there is so little information. Of two further finds at Ferriby, Ferriby 4 is an element of alder whereas the other finds are of oak. It may or may not be part of a boat of this type (McGrail 1996:a36; Wright 1990:78). Ferriby 5, dated to *c.* 380 BC, consists of part of a cleat and may be part of a craft similar to the Brigg 'raft' (McGrail 2001:187). McGrail places the Danish Hjortspring boat (*c.* 350 BC) in group C, on the basis of strong affinities with the British group.

Technological similarities alone provide uncertain grounds to postulate a common root, still less continuity between building characteristics separated in time and place. However, the exchange of prestige materials in the Bronze Age was certainly extensive enough to have brought people from these regions into contact throughout the period under discussion (van de Noort 2011). Ferriby 5 apart, at present the British finds of this type are confined to the Bronze Age. In the Iron Age there have been several significant boat finds, e.g. at Poole, Hasholme, Holme Pierrepont and Clifton but these are all logboats, demonstrating the continuity of their production and use. It is several centuries before we see the collective evidence of another distinctive, plank-based building tradition, represented by shipfinds at Blackfriars and New Guy's House in London (Marsden 1994:33–96), St Peter Port in Guernsey (Rule and Monaghan 1993), and the Barland's Farm boat (Nayling and McGrail 2004). These seagoing/estuarine vessels exhibit certain similarities to continental finds such as Bevaix (Arnold 1975), Bruges (Marsden 1976) and Mainz (Rupprecht 1985:81). Both groups are currently classified as 'Romano-Celtic' as all the finds so far associated fall within the Roman period and within the geographic region populated by Celtic peoples (McGrail 1995: 139). However, McGrail (pers. comm.) has expressed the view that the European finds may exhibit more disparity than can be accommodated within a single building tradition. They are certainly overdue for a comprehensive, collective assessment. As for relationships between them and their early Iron Age and Bronze Age antecedents, if any, and how these relate to the population movements and social changes of those periods may become clearer with new finds. Arnold's attempt to plot such relationships shows how difficult this is to do on technological grounds alone (Arnold 1999).

The plank boatbuilding tradition that was to become dominant in northern Europe for nearly two millennia is first seen with any clarity in the early Scandinavian Iron Age. The earliest find we have was the ritual deposit, referred to in chapter 2, placed in a bog at Hjortspring on the island of Als in Denmark, dated to *c.* 350 BC. It is too sophisticated to be an ingenious 'one-off'. This being the case, it strongly suggests that the origins of its building tradition must extend back into the Scandinavian Bronze Age. This is also suggested by the striking resemblance of the Hjortspring boat to many of the images in Scandinavian Bronze Age rock carvings. It has been exhaustively debated as to whether these images represent boats as opposed to sledges, and if boats, whether they were skin, log, bark, plank boats or all of these (Brøgger and Shetelig 1950; Eskeröd 1956; Marstrander 1963; Crumlin-Pedersen 1972; Roberts 1978; Ellmers 1984, 1996:11–23; McGrail 1981; Tilley 1994). Modern scholarship accepts them as boats and some, for example Kaul (1998:87–112) and Kristiansen (2004) have attempted to establish a typology and regionality of the forms represented, although the difficulty of dating individual carved images limits the precision achievable (though see Coles 2008). There certainly are differences however: many of the boat-like motifs from rock art sites in Norway and central Sweden resemble skin boats not unlike the umiak or 'family boat' of the Innuit. In more southerly areas such as Östergötland, Uppland, Bohuslän and Skåne in southern Sweden, images that resemble Hjortspring predominate. So perhaps we are seeing a record of the boat types that were specific to different regions and their associated environments, reflecting the materials available for their construction: colder, northerly and more exposed waters to which skin boats are demonstrably suited, and the more temperate, sheltered waters of the southern Baltic archipelagos. That some images resembling skin boats appear in the south and a few that seem similar to southern forms are found as far north as Alta in Norway, suggests that people were moving between these regions.

Whatever the reality, many structural characteristics of the Hjortspring boat apparently endure. A Swedish find from Hille known as the Björke boat has been dated to around 100 AD (Humbla 1949). Another Danish bog find, at Nydam, is a virtually complete boat from the Iron Age, dated to around 320 AD (Rieck 1994). Both are similar to the Hjortspring find in some constructional details and demonstrate that the concepts of building plank boats had become widely embedded in Scandinavian culture. Thereafter an increasing number of Scandinavian finds, and the distinctive but clearly related Saxon burial ship of Sutton Hoo, Suffolk, England (Evans and Bruce-Mitford 1975; Carver 1998), attest to a widespread and highly developed form of northern European plank boat. McGrail uses the term 'Nordic', subdividing it into 'Early' (including Hjortspring, Nydam and Sutton Hoo), 'Classic', denoting craft associated with the Viking Iron Age, and 'Late' encompassing late Viking and medieval vessels. It is this tradition that became the most widespread for the construction of watercraft of all sizes, although it was by no means the only one. Logboats as noted above, as well as rafts have continued to be constructed throughout the world and remain in use in many regions today.

In terms of plank-built boats it was however, the Romano-Celtic tradition that, for a time at least, represented an alternative approach to the early Nordic forms. Although at present we have no vessels of the Romano-Celtic tradition later than the 4th century AD, it is very possible that there is a continuity, archaeologically invisible at present, between them and the type we know as the cog, illustrated in Figures 4.4 and 4.5. The reasons that vessels of this type are identified as cogs are discussed in chapter 5 but they start to appear in the historical and possibly iconographic sources around the 9th century and seem to have

been developed in the region of north Germany, Denmark and the Low Countries. Ellmers has postulated an association with the Frisians and their move to urbanism that prompted development of their flat bottomed inland waterway craft into larger coastal merchant vessels (Ellmers 1985:87, 1994:34). Of all the peoples on the maritime fringes of the Carolingian Empire they were probably the most prominent traders (Hodges 1989:87) and the development of suitable craft in which to prosecute that trade from types already existing in the region is certainly possible. So far the earliest archaeological examples come from southern Jutland, (Hocker and Dokkedal 2001; Adams and Rönnby 2002). This is on the fringes of the Frisian region and so may be related, perhaps being where larger seagoing cogs were first developed before variants appeared elsewhere along the southern North Sea and Baltic coasts.

Irrespective of regional differences, generically, cogs were constructed in a way sufficiently different from Nordic vessels that they must be the product of a different set of social and environmental circumstances and as such are recognised as a quite distinct building tradition. As to whether they could be descendents of Romano-Celtic vessels, parallels for such long survival of boat building traditions are not hard to find. Many centuries after their larger forms passed out of use, both Nordic ships and cogs survived in the form of smaller regional craft. The clinker-built Shetland yoal for example (Osler 1983) is only one example of a plethora of Nordic boats still in use. Likewise, other vernacular craft may be continuations of the cog-building tradition. Very similar in form are a group of vernacular craft known as flatners ('flatties') from the West of England, particularly the Somerset turf boats and withy boats, suggested by Greenhill (1995:28) to be '…*probably the oldest in design and structure of any in use in twentieth-century Britain.*' (McKee 1983:108–9; Greenhill 1995:28–29). Whether there is any continuity between these simple boats and the medieval cog is not known but similarly intriguing connections exist elsewhere. Boats still used into the second half of the 20th century on the Vistula Lagoon in Poland are very like small cogs, having the same primary constructional features and still being fastened and caulked in exactly the same way (Litwin 1991:120). It is therefore quite possible that the Romano-Celtic tradition endured in the Low Countries in the form of smaller coastal, river and lake vessels and if so they could have provided some of the bases for the development of cogs. There are certainly constructional features of cogs that are strongly reminiscent of many of the vessels currently designated Romano-Celtic, in particular their flush laid, non edge-joined bottom planks and the so-called 'twice-bent' 'cog nails', turned back in to effect a secure fastening in a similar way to the spikes used to join the planks to frames in Romano-Celtic construction (McGrail 1995). In cogs these were used to secure the end-to-end scarf joints of the flush-laid bottom planks and to clench the overlaps of the side planking (Fig. 4.7a, b) (Reinders 1985:17; Adams 1995:59).

As the high Middle Ages drew to a close in the 14th century it is these two traditions, Nordic ships and cogs, that were the dominant forms and which provide the maritime technological canvas onto which the impending changes were applied. (For detailed treatment of the boats and ships of northern Europe see Friel 1994; Hutchinson 1994; Greenhill 1995; McGrail 1998, 2001; Crumlin-Pedersen 1997, 2010.)

The Mediterranean region

In the period that Ellmers (1996:11) is postulating the use of skin boats for river transport in northern Europe, it was noted in chapter 2 that obsidian was already being obtained by sea from the island of Melos in the Aegean. We have no evidence for the sort of craft involved but, as in the north, skin boats are a possibility and, in this region, bundle rafts. The earliest material evidence for boats of any sort in the Mediterranean comes from various representational forms from the Cyclades dating to the third millennium BC. These take the form of lead and ceramic models and depictions on ceramic objects: the so-called 'frying pans' (Johnstone 1980:64; Broodbank 1989:326; Morrison 1995:134). The earliest evidence from Egypt is in the form of rock paintings and images on ceramics dating from the fourth millennium BC (Johnstone 1980:76; Casson 1994:14).

It is on the Nile that many of the technological precedents may have been set, and various authors have discussed the factors that may have played a part, for example in the development of the sail (e.g. McGrail 2001; Casson 1994:13). Although early forms of Nile watercraft were bundle rafts, it seems that plank boats were produced in a

similar form. What is certain is that by the early third millennium a sophisticated plank boat technology had developed, using a very different approach to those of the north. The frequency with which boats were portrayed, and the presence of both model boats and occasionally the boats themselves in tombs demonstrate that they pervaded all aspects of Egyptian society from royal and religious affairs including funerary ritual, to day to day transport, warfare and industry such as fishing.

One of the most remarkable features of these early plank-built vessels is the use of mortise and tenon joints for locking the planks edge-to-edge. This technique had a role in technological change thousands of years later. The technique has been described and illustrated in detail elsewhere (e.g. Greenhill 1976, 1995; Steffy 1994), and has very early origins. It is also found in some items of Egyptian wooden construction including furniture at this period so there may have been a transfer to/from boatbuilding. It has also been suggested the technique might have arisen as a way of connecting planks of native acacia wood which is only obtainable in short lengths. If so the technique became so well established that it continued to be used even after longer lengths of timber were imported from elsewhere. Its first known appearance in shipbuilding is also Egypt's most impressive: the Royal ship of Khufu (Cheops) was discovered in 1954 sealed in a rock-cut 'boat pit' beside the Great Pyramid at Giza and dates to *c.* 2,600 BC (Lipke 1984:1). The hull planks of imported cedar were located edge to edge with hardwood tenons and held together with a system of transverse lashing (Lipke 1984: fig. 48). The remains of even earlier Egyptian boat finds, though much less well preserved have been made at Abydos, 300 miles south of Cairo. Dated to around 2,900 BC they are therefore the earliest plank boats known so far. Like the Khufu find, they were also boat burials and appear to have been perfectly viable for actual use. Whether their planks were locked with tenons or not awaits further excavation (Ward, pers. comm.) but they were certainly lashed together through channels cut into the plank edges (Ward 2003:20). A similar fastening solution is seen in the planks of the Dashur boats, also tomb finds from Egypt and dated to around 1,850 BC. They were locked with tenons in a similar way to the Khufu find but the tenons were much larger. Today the planks are also connected with dovetail clamps. However,

Cheryl Ward (1993: 224) suggests that these were added during museum reconstruction, some possibly being cut into the eroded channels that would have originally held lashing.

Not all Egypt's early boat finds are from funerary contexts. Timbers found at Lisht are probably from Nile working boats dated to *c.* 1,950 BC. They were heavily built from planks of local tamarisk and acacia and would have been securely lashed with woven straps of grass fibre (Ward 2000:107). Missing until recently were any remains of seagoing vessels but recent finds from two sites, Ayn Sokhna near Suez and Wadi Gawasis on Egypt's Red Sea coast have provided impressive evidence of the extent and complexity of ancient Egypt's maritime infrastructure. At Wadi Gawasis timbers of cedar as well as various fittings, most dating to the Middle Kingdom (1956–1650 BC) are believed to result from ship breaking. They are generically similar to the river finds but are even more robustly constructed than those represented by the Lisht timbers (Ward and Zazzaro 2010).

Beyond Egypt the mortise and tenon technique became widely used but with significant differences. The Bronze Age vessel, possibly of Levantine origin, that wrecked at Uluburun around 1305 BC exhibits mortise and tenon fastenings but is also the earliest example so far of small dowels being used to lock the tenons in place (Steffy 1994:37; Pulak 1998). From discoveries like the late 4th-century BC Kyrenia ship (Steffy 1994:42–58) and the 2nd-century BC Roman ship found at Madrague de Giens (Pomey 1978) we know that tenons locked in this way remained an established method of hull construction throughout the Classical, Hellenistic and Roman periods.

Subsequently, underwater finds from the 1970s onwards began to show that the technique persisted throughout the Byzantine and into the medieval periods but with significant changes. The wreck of a small 4th-century AD merchant ship found at Yassi Ada (Yassi Ada B) in Turkey, has mortise and tenon joints that were smaller and more widely spaced than those of the Classical period (Steffy 1991:1). Those of Port-Vendres A, *c.* 400 AD, are also widely spaced, though not so much as Yassi Ada B (Parker 1992:330). Lazzaretto, 4th century AD, has tenoned lower planks but the alignment of a large number of nails suggests the upper planks may have been plank-on-frame (Riccardi 1994). Another wreck from Yassi Ada (Yassi Ada A) dated to around 625 AD suggests a continuing trend as it has even fewer mortise and tenon fastenings. In addition these joints were only found in the lower strakes. Above the turn of the bilge the planks were simply nailed to pre-erected frames. This seems to be a transitional stage from the earlier shell-built, mortise and tenon technique towards a non edge-joined method. Both the Pantano Longarini ship dated to 600–650 AD (Throckmorton and Kapitan 1968; Parker 1992:303), and St Gervais 2 (Parker 1992: no.1001) also show similar transitional characteristics. This sequence of wreck evidence is completed by the medieval wreck from Serçe Liman dated to the 11th century AD (Steffy 1991) and a wreck found at Pelagós in Greece dated to the mid 12th century AD (Parker 1992:306). In neither of these vessels were there mortise and tenon joints and they were effectively a 'skeleton-built' or rather, frame-orientated construction (Steffy, *ibid.*).

Interesting corroborative evidence from Roman Britain is the County Hall ship. The ship was built of oak and dendrochronological analysis shows that this vessel was built in southern England around the end of the 3rd century AD. The mortise and tenon joints were not as closely spaced as those of Madrague de Giens or Kyrenia and the intervals varied between *c.* 0.15m for those locking the keel and garboard, and nearly 1m elsewhere (Marsden 1994: fig. 106). They were also irregular, and the tenons were not as large relative to the planks as in earlier Mediterranean examples.

All the above indicate a conveniently progressive change from shell-built, mortise and tenon construction, via transitional forms to a fully frame-orientated approach. However, still more recent finds indicate that this development may not have been quite so comfortably linear as it first seemed. An apparently frame-led vessel has been discovered in the Tantura Lagoon (Tantura A), Israel, dated between the 5th and 6th centuries AD (Waschmann 1996; McGrail 2001:162). Another fascinating find has been made on the west coast of France. It is incomplete, lacking elements of the lower hull, so some questions remain but Port Berteau II, analysed by Eric Rieth, seems to be frame-orientated or as Rieth says: 'proto skeleton first' (Rieth 2000:228). Dendrochronological analysis indicates a late 6th/early 7th century AD date for its construction. Perhaps the move towards frame-led building occurred in small boats early on whereas it took longer for the constructional sequence to be worked out for larger vessels. The Charente river is also not far in seafaring terms from the waters navigated by frame-orientated vessels of the Roman world such as St Peter Port I and Barland's Farm. The latter is not so dissimilar in size or date from Port Berteau II, and the two vessels operated in similar estuarine and coastal environments. Perhaps frame-orientated boatbuilding, once established in the Iron Age, never entirely disappeared. If so this raises questions about the relationships between the Atlantic seaboard and the Mediterranean and the wider development of plank-on-frame constructions.

Another factor that confounds any idea of a tidy three thousand-year 'rise and fall' of mortise and tenon technology is the use of cordage for connecting structural elements. First seen in Egypt, it was undoubtedly used in the construction of far earlier forms including reed bundle rafts and skin boats. It remained in use throughout the mortise and tenon period and is clearly implicated in the ways in which this developed. In general it seems that mortise and tenon construction superseded sewn construction but the ways this was achieved as well as where and when it happened all varied considerably. Archaeological finds have provided a range of examples usefully summarised by McGrail (2001:134–137). Some, such as the Bon Porté wreck found off the south coast of France and dated to *c.* 530 BC (Pomey 1997) and a small fishing vessel from the Place Jules-Verne in Marseilles dating to the end of the 6th century BC (Pomey 1995), show sewn construction as the principal fastening method. Others show the two techniques in the same vessel. Another wreck found at the Place Jules-Verne has its main hull planks fastened with locked mortise and tenons but the plank ends are sewn to the posts at bow and stern (Pomey 2005). A very similar combination is seen in the Ma'agan Mickael wreck found near Haifa which dates from a hundred years later (Kahanov 1996; Parker 1992, no. 612).

All this provides a cautionary example of the dangers in explaining technological and social change through simplistic analogy with biological evolution, or related ideas of teleological development inherent in various models of technological determinism (e.g. see MacKenzie and Wajcman 1999:5). Only a few years ago we had a series of archaeological finds that suggested a logical 'evolution' of one method of building

out of another, commonly represented by a diagram of progressively reducing mortise and tenons (Steffy 1994). While the finds were irrefutable in themselves, their apparent linear sequence was an artefact of discovery and the small size of the sample at that time. Subsequent finds have not filled in the gaps but have (pending full analysis) disrupted the time line. That there was a general move towards 'skeleton' construction is certain but the interplay of constraints discussed in chapter 2, especially when operating over such a large geographic region, is likely to have forged a more complex development. Environment, intended function, size of vessels and the social circumstances of the builders and users will all have had their influence. As for what drove the process, it has been suggested that the primary cause was economic (Casson 1994:107). The mortise and tenon shipbuilding of the Classical period has been described as being more 'cabinetry than carpentry'. It was certainly labour intensive. Hence factors such as availability of materials, skilled labour, and associated costs are implicated in the change. Related to this is the decline of the Western Roman Empire which would have progressively reduced the availability of slave labour. After the break-up of the Roman Empire, changed trading patterns are also implicated, with less centralisation and more small scale shipping enterprises needing more flexible vessels that were cheaper to build.

Of course ships need to be propelled and the other major changes we see in Late Antiquity (*c.* 3rd–8th centuries AD), is in their rig, notably the development of settee and lateen sails used fore and aft in preference to the square sail of antiquity. Evidence for these changes is sparse but recent analysis by Whitewright (2008, 2009) suggests that they too manifest the political and socio-economic factors that resulted in fundamental changes in the patterns of maritime affairs throughout the Mediterranean and beyond.

While analysis of this process is relatively new, in the light of recent finds, a single cause for the demise of mortise and tenon joinery or the adoption of the lateen sail is scarcely credible in a process of change that occurred at different rates in different regions over so long a period. Whatever the reasons, by the medieval period both the oar-powered warships and the merchant sailing vessels of the Mediterranean were probably frame-orientated in their construction. By the

13th century this had progressed to what can justifiably be called full 'skeleton' construction, in the sense of a framing system that was a coherent structure in its own right. Such vessels are exemplified by the Contarina ship (Bonino 1978; Prior 1994) and the Logo Novo boats 1 and 2, all found in the Po Delta region of Italy (Prior *ibid.*). Along with their skeleton-built hulls, medieval Mediterranean ships of all types carried a lateen rig on one or more masts depending on size, and were steered by side rudders. Merchant vessels seem also to have had a fairly full hull form giving rise to the term 'round ship' (Prior 1994), though how ubiquitous this was we do have not enough evidence to say. It is however these characteristics of the Mediterranean medieval merchant ship that are significant in subsequent developments that occur on a European scale.

Cultural transmission

It was around this time, the late 13th or early 14th century, that a remarkable exchange and fusion of northern and southern technologies took place. From around the 12th century AD documentary sources indicate that northern European cogs had been sailing into the Mediterranean and by the 13th century 'coggones' are mentioned in Mediterranean sources. It is thought that their single square sail, and hulls with a relatively sharp entry and fine run to a stern rudder, made them superior sailors in some circumstances to the round ships of the south. By the early 14th century it appears that Mediterranean ship builders were adopting aspects of the northern technology. The Florentine chronicler Giovanni Villani writes that Basque 'pirates' sailed their cogs into the Mediterranean and that local shipwrights started to copy them in 1304 (Friel 1994:78; Hutchinson 1994:41). Villani specifically states that cogs were adopted in preference to the lateen-rigged ships for reasons of cost (probably related to a smaller crew size). Recorded events of this nature must be treated cautiously, often being merely the first time a practice that started some time before has entered the written record. Cogs had apparently been used in the Mediterranean as transports during the crusades. Scammel (1981:77) notes the use of German cogs in the rescue of Christian prisoners from Beirut in 1197. Hutchinson (1994:41) cites the case of a '*navis sive cocha*' (ship or cocha) owned by a Bayonne (Basque) merchant

in partnership with two Genoese, shipping alum to Flanders in 1286. However, in corroboration of Villani's writings, 1312 is apparently when the name 'cocha' first appears in Venetian documents (Balard 1991:119, in Hutchinson *ibid.*). Whether the word 'cocha' at that stage referred to cogs, as the similarity in sound suggests, we cannot be certain, but it is soon afterwards being applied to Italian-built ships that combined some of the features of northern ships with those of Mediterranean vessels. The earliest known illustrations of 'coche' are also the earliest illustrations of a two-masted form of these vessels and show how it was configured. From a distance the most obvious feature would have been the northern-style square sail on the main mast, apparently absent from the Mediterranean for centuries, but with a lateen-rigged mizzen mast (Friel 1994:79). The other major change was the adoption of the stern rudder. Significantly however, these vessels retained their Mediterranean frame-orientated hull construction.

Until now the nature of what must be one of the most intriguing episodes of technological exchange has been interpreted predominantly from a northern perspective because of the imbalance in archaeological evidence. One might ask why it is cogs that seem to be implicated instead of (or as well as) the far more numerous clinker-built keels? They were ubiquitous throughout northern Europe and were regular traders up and down the Atlantic coast, including to the Biscayan ports where Villani's pirates came from. So it would seem odd if none ever ventured into the Mediterranean. The recent discovery off Barcelona of a clinker-built vessel from the 15th century (Pujol i Hamelink 2012) not only shows they did but raises the question of what the term 'cog' as used by Villani and other medieval writers meant. Perhaps all northern ships carrying a square sail on a single mast were generically referred to as 'cog/cocha', irrespective of their construction just as others used ship/navis. The distinction might not have been regarded as important even had it been apparent. In any event the features adopted by Mediterranean shipbuilders, the square sail and the stern rudder, were of course carried by both keels and cogs.

Cocha – Carrack

Just as northern vessels had traded in the Mediterranean, the southern coche traded north where the large ones seem to have been called 'carakes'. Friel suggests the name might have a connection with the Arab word *Karaque* denoting a small vessel. However, the name was also current in 13th-century Spain and Spanish sailors are known to have been involved in coche voyages to England (van der Merwe 1983:125). However the term originated, to date the first known mention of a two-masted ship in England is in 1410. A Genoese carrack '*Sancta Maria & Sancta Brigida*', captured by pirates the year before, was taken over by the Crown. Thereafter it was simply known as *Le Carake* (Friel 1994:80). Soon afterwards, in 1416–17, the English captured six, large, two-masted Genoese carracks that had been hired by the French. It appears that this may be an instance when a specific event stimulated a technological adaptation, for between 1416 and 1420 six English ships were fitted with a two-masted rig. By 1420 this second mast was called 'mesan' (Friel 1994:80). At this stage, however, English ships were still clinker-built, apparently to the extent that foreign shipwrights had to be hired to maintain the frame-orientated carracks. Perhaps significantly, the Venetians who were hired to do this requested permission to employ Portuguese and Catalans as well (Friel 1983a:).

When and where a third mast was first fitted is not known but a Catalan document believed to date from 1406 shows a detailed sketch of a three-masted ship. Certainly within a few years of the adoption of a two-masted rig in England, there followed a third, and by the mid 15th century a three-masted square rig was in use throughout northern and southern Europe.

From carrack to carvel

It is only at this time 'carvels' are first mentioned in English sources. The word itself is presumed to derive from 'caravela', first recorded in Portuguese in the 13th century as a type of fishing boat (Hasslöf 1972:56). Phillips postulates a relationship with the 'Caravo', an Arab craft used in north west Africa and the Iberian Peninsula well into the 15th century (Phillips 1994:91). By this time the caravela or caravel was a frame-orientated, lateen-rigged small ship noted for its speed and manoeuvrability. By the 1430s they were beginning to appear in northern Europe and it appears that their name became a generic term for ships constructed in their manner, though as Friel points out, skeleton-built carracks had been sailing to England by then for nearly a

century (Friel 1994:80). It may have something to do with the fact that it was caravels, rather than carracks that first transferred to merchant ownership in any numbers, and through the necessities of routine repair, became more familiar to local shipwrights. From the late 1430s there are references to 'carvels' being built in northern Europe and to the presence at least of several of them in England from the 1440s. Friel also makes the point that it may have been a more viable prospect for English builders to begin carvel construction of something akin to a 50 ton caravel rather than a 500 ton carrack. The earliest documented record of a carvel ship being built in England was between 1463 and 1466, in Ipswich for Sir John Howard (Friel 1995:164) but it is quite possible that others were built earlier still. There are references to carvels being built on the continent by the 1430s, and before long some of them were of equal size to their Mediterranean predecessors. Nevertheless there was quite an interval between the first English experiments and the decision by the English Crown to build some of its large vessels in the new way. By implication the first occurrence of a new building in carvel, rather than a rebuilding, may have been 1487. This was occasioned by the regime change that marked the end of the Wars of the Roses when Henry Tudor fought and deposed Richard III in 1485. Having gained the crown, one of the many ways in which the new king Henry VII could establish his regime and consolidate power was to build 'great ships'. Before his return to England Henry had been much impressed by the French ship *Columbe* and directed that his new great ship should be built like her. Whether the *Columbe* was a carvel is not known but by this date it is quite possible. What we are told is that the *Regent* of around 1,000 tons was of 'novel' construction (in Carr Laughton 1960:251). Interestingly, her accounts, compiled by Thomas Roger, Henry's 'Clerk of the Ships' state that 'carvell nayles' were used (Oppenheim 1896b:228). Significantly they also omit the 'roff and clynche nayles' (rove and clinch) that appear in the building accounts for the smaller clinker-built *Sweepstake* and *Mary Fortune* (Howard 1978:21). What exactly carvel nails were is uncertain but they were clearly distinct from clench nails and were also more expensive so presumably larger. Oppenheim says they were 'long tie nails', but the term may refer to the large spikes used to retain the butt ends of flush-laid planks (Fig. 4.2) and which were not needed in the end to end scarfed joints of clinker planks (Fig. 4.9a). On balance therefore, the evidence suggests that the *Regent* was carvel-built. If so, it raises the question as to why the 800 ton *Sovereign* would have been clinker-built the following year. Although some royal ships were subsequently built in the traditional clinker fashion, it would seem odd if this prestige vessel had been. Loades (1992:39) comments on the dire economic situation when Henry VII came to the throne in 1485, and as many aspects of clinker building had become progressively more expensive, the *Sovereign* is unlikely to have been built clinker to keep down costs. One way of doing this was by reusing timber, a relatively common expedient and this raises the question of the *Sovereign*'s 1509 rebuild when, as has been noted, it is widely accepted that the hull was converted from clinker to carvel. Another possibility is that the adaptation of these timbers to take carvel planks occurred at her original building in 1488. In fact Thomas Roger's accounts imply as much for he records that the *Grace Dieu* (of 1449) was handed over to Sir Reginald Bray to be broken up for the '*makyng of his Ship cald the Souveraigne*' (Oppenheim 1896b: xxi, 47). While this does not prove that the framing was used for the corresponding timbers of the new hull, it is likely. It may also be significant that 'roff and clynche nayles' are absent from the accounts for the *Sovereign* just as they are for the *Regent* (Howard 1978:21).

Even if the English Crown had tentatively begun carvel building in the 1480s, it was by no means at the forefront of the trend. Danish records mention a 'royal kravel' in 1474 as well as the *Gripshunden* of 1480. Large merchant-owned carvel ships were clearly being constructed in France and Holland by then, including the *Peter of La Rochelle*. Other powers bought carvel ships as they needed them, such as the emergent Swedish monarchy under Gustav Eriksson Vasa who bought several ships including 'kravels' from the city of Lübeck in the 1520s, one of which is discussed in detail below. By the second quarter of the 16th century most European powers were committed to more or less extensive carvel building programmes. Henry VIII, continuing the initiative started by his father, saw the building of the *Mary Rose* and the *Peter Pomegranate* through to completion in 1511 and by 1512 had ordered nine other new buildings, two rebuildings and had captured or purchased ten others. In 1514 he built the largest of them all, the 1,000 ton *Henry Grace à Dieu* known as the *Great Harry*.

Among the nations who were building such vessels at this time there developed one fascinating exception. In contrast to what might be called the Iberian model of carvel construction, was that developed by the Dutch. What Dutch shipwrights seem to have done is graft the carvel, frame-orientated approach onto a method that had been established centuries, if not millennia, earlier. In cog construction as shown in Figure 4.4, there was a distinction between the assembly of the flush-laid, non edge-joined, bottom planking and the edge-joined, clinker side planks. As the procedures by which such ships were produced are neither frame-led yet not entirely shell-first either, the term 'bottom-based' has been advanced (Arnold 1991:22; Hocker and Vlierman 1996:12). This method with its natural differenti-ation between the bottom and side, provided Dutch builders with a platform (quite literally) from which to develop frame-orientated con-struction. The technique that resulted has been termed 'Dutch-flush' by Maarleveld (Maarleveld 1994; Maarleveld et al. 1994). In this method the bottom planks are positioned and held in place with temporary cleats (visible in Figure 4.5) which are then removed as the floors are installed, just as they were in many cogs. Hocker (Hocker and Vlierman 1996:76) suggests that this expedient measure gave Holland a head start in carvel production, although this may have been less an instant reaction to an opportunity than a different long term strategy.

The first 'karviel' constructed in Holland is believed to have been built, not by a Dutchman, but by a Breton, at Zierikzee in 1459–60 (cf. Unger 1978:32) although others were built at Hoorn from 1460 (Sleeswyk 1998:223). In fact there are references to others being built in the region well before that. A 'caravel' type was built at Sluis in 1438–1440 (Unger *ibid.*:189) and another two were built in Brussels in 1439 by Portuguese shipwright Jehan Perhouse for Philip, Duke of Burgundy (Sleeswyk 1998:226). Philip was also Count of Flanders and the connection with Portugal was through his marriage to Isabella.

In other words the earliest carvels seem to have been built by itinerant or specially commissioned shipwrights who presumably worked to the Iberian model. The Dutch developments would after all have needed some period of gestation. In developing Hocker's idea one can point to the other significant difference of emphasis in the Dutch developments – for while in most states early carvel building was quickly appropriated for the construction of prestige warships, the Dutch, quite literally on the basis of cog building, directed much of theirs to the construction of merchant vessels. It was the superiority of these types as efficient cargo carriers across the spectrum of trade that played a key role in the 'golden century', that unprecedented economic boom in the 17th century when Holland was the leading mercantile trading nation. The newly discovered *fluits* referred to in Chapter 2 are impressive examples of the Baltic vessels involved.

Holland is something of a special case, while France, central though its northern shipwrights were in this formative period, is relatively impoverished in evidence so far. So it is on England and the Baltic Sea area, particularly Sweden. that the rest of this chapter will focus, for it is in their waters that so much of the archaeological evidence has been found.

In Sweden we have the remains of both an early carvel ship purchased as a ready-made addition to a royal fleet and two built by the same administration a generation later. In England there are the remains of the best preserved of all early 16th-century naval ships, the warship *Mary Rose*. These two powers also illustrate the socio-political changes that were underway throughout Europe at the same time.

Mary Rose

The warship *Mary Rose* is of considerable historical and symbolic significance not only by virtue of being a flagship of one of England's more charismatic (and infamous) kings, Henry VIII, but also through having sunk in action against a traditional foe, the French in 1545. Quite apart from its historical profile it also had considerable allure from an archaeological point of view. As a ship, it was built before shipwrights began leaving us plans and drawings to demonstrate how they did what they did. It was also an embodiment of the rapidly changing technology of the time, not only in terms of structure but of the equipment and other instrumentation it was designed to carry. These developments not only enhanced its capabilities as a naval ship but its potency as a symbolic projection of royal power. Archaeologically, in addition to the information related to its naval functions, the discovery provided a highly detailed cross section of Tudor material culture, an era when shipboard life was less differentiated or distinct from society on land than it later became. As an assemblage it not only comprised a large volume of well preserved material but, being relatively undisturbed, it was rich in the contextual relationships of the type of closed find discussed in chapter 2.

As a structure the *Mary Rose* was large, though by the standards of the time not the largest by any means. The tonnage stated at her building was 600, but after a major rebuilding some time around 1536 this had increased to 700 tons.

What were the differences between *Mary Rose* and her precursors? Apart from the carvel method of construction (in which she was not the first) *Mary Rose* carried a greater weight of ordnance than vessels of a comparable size. The inventories of earlier vessels listed significantly more guns but these were relatively light, mounted and fired from the weather deck or the castle decks. The number and total weight of guns were obviously limited by their combined effect on stability. *Mary Rose* marked a radical step forward, for the heavier pieces were mounted on specially designed trucked carriages and were fired through lidded gunports on the main deck – the solution to carrying heavy ordnance without unduly raising the centre of gravity. The benefits can be seen in the inventories of the ordnance assigned to ships. Even in her original configuration *Mary Rose* carried relatively fewer guns than other ships of a comparable size but they comprised a significantly greater total weight. This was still the case after the 1530s rebuild (Blackmore 1979) and on the day she was lost, although there were several other vessels of similar size, *Mary Rose* was the most heavily armed ship in the fleet except the Flagship *Henry Grace à Dieu*, some three hundred tons larger (Hildred 2011:13). It was the rapid increase in the number and size of guns carried aboard ships that represents a fundamental change in the concept of naval warfare, for they were carried with the express intention of bombarding an enemy vessel from a distance, at least in the initial stages of an engagement, reducing its fighting capability as much as possible prior to closing and boarding. Although boarding actions remained one of the ways ship to ship engagements would be decided throughout the era of the sailing navies, this was a decisive step away from the use of ships simply as floating platforms for hand to hand combat between soldiers,

Almost from the first day the timbers of the *Mary Rose* were seen by modern eyes in 1971, information began to flow that both repudiated established ideas and shed entirely new light on Tudor seafaring. In terms of the hull design and construction technique, perhaps the greatest surprise for nautical historians was its length to breadth ratio. Predictions that it would be a beamy vessel were proved utterly wrong. In the years since the hull has been raised, it has continued to provide new insights into the building methods and procedures of the time. A significant discovery arose from work by Brad Loewen and Richard Barker on behalf of the Mary Rose Trust (Loewen pers. comm.). They have demonstrated that the method used to develop the hull form in the design process was a three-arc system, little different in principle to those still in use in English shipyards over two hundred years later. This is the earliest evidence we have for English design methods and extends what we knew from documentary sources back by half a century. As the *Mary Rose* represents an early phase of large carvel shipbuilding in England it raises the questions of how and where the method developed. The extent of Venetian influence still remains in question, for although we know Venetian shipwrights worked in England, Italian documentary sources seem to indicate quite different methods of hull design (Lane 1934:24–49). Although northern European carvel building (as opposed to Dutch bottom-based versions) were ultimately derived from the Mediterranean, the technique was transmitted via the Iberian peninsula. It will become apparent below that there were strong similarities between aspects of design and constructional features of Iberian and English practice. So it seems possible that some of the fundamental principles of constructing frame-orientated ships for north Atlantic sea conditions arrived from Iberia and integrated with local skills. But if the construction of the first carvels in England occurred not long after the mid 15th century, this does not leave much time for a distinctively English adaptation to have developed in time for the building of large warships like *Mary Rose*. Or were large clinker-built vessels of the Nordic tradition also being designed according to geometric principles by the end of the 15th century?

While the building of clinker boats can be done by eye with the form controlled and adjusted by the builder throughout the process (e.g. Christensen 1972), it has never been ascertained whether this was done for very large ships. Perhaps the evidence of the *Mary Rose* gives us a clue. While it is possible that the three-arc method of hull design was developed in England specifically for the building of the first carvel ships, it seems more likely that it is an adaptation of a procedure that had been around considerably longer. Crumlin-Pedersen (1984:145) has identified a system of geometric control involving interrelated circles used for defining the stem pieces of 'Viking Age' Nordic vessels. In turn the stem piece had a determining influence on the shape of the vessel as a whole. The notion of controlling the form and proportion of boats with geometry is much older than northern European carvel shipbuilding and had probably been embedded in the Nordic tradition for centuries. This is not to argue that anything like a three-arc method was used to form the body shape of vessels such as those found at Roskilde, but the concept of geometric proportion had been present in every other field of the arts and architecture for millennia (Pacey 1992:47). As the problems of building increasingly large vessels within the Nordic tradition were addressed, ensuring proportion and symmetry through commonly understood geometric principles seems plausible, more so perhaps than a 35m or 40m long ship being built entirely by eye. An intriguing piece of documentary evidence in this context concerns a very large ship being built in Bayonne (then English territory) for Henry V in 1419 (Manwaring 1922:376). To be called the

Dieulagarde, it was apparently never finished or at least never delivered, for Henry died in August 1422, but references to its construction mention the width of the main deck at three points. Such specifications imply some degree of control and, as well as raising the question of how this was applied in what was presumably clinker construction, it also implies that the process meant something to those negotiating the contract from England. It would if geometric control of large ships was normal practice. A further intriguing possibility emerges here, for Bayonne is in the Basque region, the shipbuilding of which was to have such a great influence on subsequent carvel design and construction. Within the Basque tradition much of the control of hull form was dependent on three key body sections. The most important was the midship section. Fore and aft of this were frame stations at the points where the relatively straight, main body of the hull began curving towards the stem and stern. Could the proximity of the English to them on land as well as through maritime activity be a factor in the marked similarity of design elements and constructional features such as square sterns.

Hull structure

With the recent publication of the *Mary Rose* volumes including analysis of the hull, only a broad summary is necessary here, primarily to highlight those characteristics to be explored in subsequent discussion. Figure 4.10 is an isometric drawing of the structural assemblage raised in 1982.

The hull structure is primarily built of oak. Exceptions include parts of the keel, some deck timbers that may be repairs, and other upper structural components. The keel is formed from three pieces, scarfed together with vertically tabled joints. The stem, together with the foremost bow structure had collapsed into the scour pit that had formed around the bow. This section is not fully articulated and not as well preserved as the main assemblage of the hull salvaged in 1982. At that stage therefore the decision was taken to leave it in the seabed (Rule 1982:70). However, when it became apparent that a realigned and enlarged channel required for projected Royal Navy aircraft carriers due to enter service in 2012 (now 2016) would involve dredging very close to the site, the decision was made to excavate the most important sections remaining on the seabed. The stem, other hull elements and an anchor were duly recovered

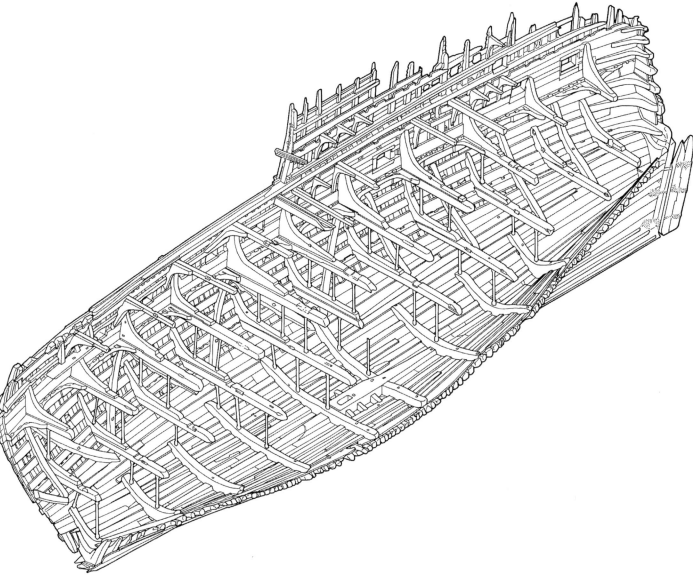

during three seasons of work between 2003 and 2005 and have enhanced our understanding of the complete hull form.

The stern assembly consists of a stern post, a false or inner post, fashion pieces, transoms, transom knees and diagonal stern planking. The floors and futtocks of the framing system are of reasonably high quality. There is some sapwood in places but in general the timbers are well finished. The outer planking is also oak, averaging 100mm in thickness in the lower hull. Above the waterline there are wales corresponding to the main deck beam shelf, the gunport sill timbers and the upper deck beam shelf. Inboard, the ceiling consisted of 75mm thick planks alternated with heavy stringers. A three-piece keelson is

expanded to accommodate the main mast step and this is given additional support by a series of buttresses. The beams of the orlop deck and main deck are of very heavy scantling reflecting their importance as both struts and tie-beams as well as for load-bearing. They were interset with carlings and half-beams, though in the central area of both decks, removable decking gave access to companionways. The deck beams are strongly attached to the frames with grown knees, bolted through to the frames. Within the hull, a series of heavy floor riders are set below the orlop deck beams. Pillars or stanchions are mortised into them and provide additional support to the beams. In addition a series of diagonal futtock riders or braces run from the hold to just below

Figure 4.10 Internal structure of the *Mary Rose* 1545. Note the diagonal bracing that dendrochronological research shows was added post 1536 (Dobbs and Bridge 2000). Together with the paired lodging knees between the main deck beams and the heavy standards above them, the result is a well integrated system of reinforcement (Courtesy of the Mary Rose Trust).

See also Plate 9.

the main deck. Towards the stern these are set vertically between the beam stations. Fastenings are predominantly treenails with iron bolts connecting major elements such as knees, wales and beam shelves.

Principles of construction sequence

Building sequences are discussed in more detail in chapters 6 and 7 in the context of development and the long term trajectory of carvel building. To summarise briefly from what can be inferred from the structure at this point: The building sequence began with the assembly and setting of the keel, followed by the raising of the stem and stern assemblies. Framing was probably based on the partial erection of control frames. These were set up at key stations along the keel including the midship section, and carefully shaped to conform to the design. The intervening frame timbers were controlled by ribbands. On the basis of what can be seen of the framing between the decks, although many of the timbers meet in various forms of butt, overlap or simple scarfs, very few of them are actually fastened to each other. This implies that framing and planking advanced in an alternating fashion, with the futtocks between the control frames being raised, positioned and faired individually. As will become apparent, this was a far more common method than has often been assumed.

In principle, outer planking could be applied at any time after the floor timbers of the control frames were in place. From the evidence of later periods, it was often started at different heights in the hull at the same time. The advantage in larger ships was that a few runs of plank provided a more stable armature against which to fair the intermediate timbers than the ribbands alone.

Once all the floors were in position the keelson could be fastened in place. This was bolted at intervals through to the keel, although treenails were used as well. Once the framing advanced far enough some of the internal stringers and ceiling could be laid. As the ceiling was relatively thick and depending on the run of the timber it could have required a great deal of force to apply. Some form of wrain stave might have been used but often much of it could be left until after the first beams and knees were in, allowing the necessary leverage to be applied with temporary struts.

From this stage on there are many possibilities as to the order in which the rest of structure was assembled.

Form and adaptations

By design, the majority of the *Mary Rose* hull surface is curved, as opposed to other vessel types that had flat floors or large areas of relatively straight sides. Ideally a rounded hull required the individual frame elements to be cut from timber of matching curvature (later termed 'compass timber'). This appears to have been done, so although the scantlings are not excessively large for a ship of this size, the quality of the timbers contribute to a very strong structure. Another crucial factor is the pattern or system in which the frame elements are arranged. The joints between the various elements are disposed so that they fall evenly throughout the hull rather than being concentrated at specific heights, as they have to be in other examples discussed below. Avoiding lines of weakness in this way also contributes to overall hull integrity.

Aft of the main body, the hull reduces to a relatively fine run to a square stern. Forward, although reasonably full, there is still a pronounced hollow. This relatively fine hull form may account both for the euphoric accounts of her sailing qualities in 1512 as well as her ultimate fate in 1545, though analysis of stability and performance is still ongoing.

In addition to the obvious difference between clinker versus carvel planking, it is when looking at the arrangement of timbers around the gunports of *Mary Rose* that the differences between these new carvel vessels and their predecessors is emphasised. Figure 4.10 shows the *Mary Rose* internal structure with deck planks and partitioning removed for clarity. This configuration is the result of rebuilding carried out later in the life of the vessel. It has not yet been ascertained which timbers are original but dendrochronological analysis has demonstrated that the riders, including the large diagonal braces, are part of the strengthening work carried out from around 1536 and intermittently thereafter (Dobbs and Bridge 2000). These caused considerable surprise when first revealed, for diagonal reinforcement in this manner was not thought to have been introduced until Sir Robert Seppings devised his 'trussed frame' presented to the Royal Society in 1814 (Fincham 1852:201–202). As in many other technical expedients, it may have been adopted either in construction or for remedial purposes in various places at various times. The other change that resulted from the *c.* 1536 rebuilding phase was an effective, albeit modest increase in the orlop and main deck heights. This was probably more a product of increasing the size of the beams and associated timbers rather than a calculated decision to raise them. Nevertheless, together with the additional guns, this would have further raised the centre of gravity and while the ship was still inherently stable, it was less so than before the rebuild.

On July 19th, 1545, various references tell us that there were many additional people on board. The often quoted 700 is almost certainly an exaggeration but fighting close to home in front of the king, and carrying the Vice Admiral Sir George Carew, were all circumstances in which there were very likely to have been more than the normal complement of 410. The reference to there being a hundred mariners on board, 'the worst of them being able to be master of the best ship in the realm', sounds like a recipe for disaster. Indeed we are told in the same account that with the ship evidently heeling badly, Sir George shouted across to is uncle, Sir Gawain Carew aboard the *Matthew Gonson*, '*I have the sort of knaves I cannot rule*'. The author of this version of events was Sir Peter Carew, Sir George's brother, so it is unlikely to be impartial and

probably contains an element of exoneration in view of what happened. Even so the two observations complement each other and an unruly crew might suggest that the mariners, professional seamen as opposed to the gentlemen of rank, realised the ship was now unsafe because of the way it was handling.

Unfortunately predictive stability calculations were still two centuries away and the consequences of overloading and mishandling on this occasion were to prove fatal. However, the structural implications of mounting heavy guns on the main deck appear to have been better understood. It has often been implied that cutting gunports in an existing hull was a relatively simple affair but this is not so. It was certainly more feasible in carvel hulls than in clinker but it was by no means as simple as cutting away frames and planks and fitting a port lid. The main deck structure of the *Mary Rose* is a good example of the integrated way in which the deck timbers that were to carry the weight of the guns, and the hull timbers to which they were attached had to be arranged (Fig. 4.11). The arrangement of grown knees and multi-directional bracing shows an appreciation (born of experience?) of

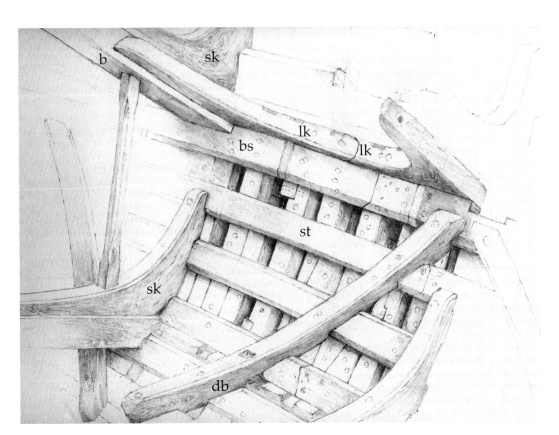

Figure 4.11 'Timber engineering' for the carriage of heavy guns in *Mary Rose* area O3. The main deck beams (b) are set in a heavy beam shelf (bs) and are braced by a system of paired lodging knees (lk) that runs the length of the ship. Large standing knees (sk) rise from both the main and orlop beams. Heavy stringers (st) are in turn clamped by the diagonal braces (db) (and riders further down). The varied forms of framing joints are evident between the stringers, some of which are probably due to repair and alteration (J. Adams).

the stresses that carrying and firing such guns would impose on the hull, especially as it seems likely at this period they were lashed firmly against the hull and fired without free-recoil. While it may have been possible to carry this weight of ordnance on an equivalent sized clinker-built vessel, on the evidence of inventories and contemporary iconography this does not seem to have been done. As clinker construction is plank-orientated, a greater proportion of hull strength is invested in the shell. Incorporating gunports would compromise longitudinal strength to a greater degree than in a carvel hull and this may have presented a more complex task of strengthening than was thought worthwhile. Even without gunports, contemporaries clearly regarded clinker construction as being weaker than carvel in any case. In 1545, John Dudley, then Viscount Lisle and Lord Admiral, stated as much in correspondence to the Secretary of State, Sir William Paget, in which he describes 'clenchers' as *'ships which cannot abide the boarding with another ship without danger of perishing'* (State papers Henry VIII R. O. St. P., i. 801). In the same correspondence, concerning the acquisition of ships for royal service he refers to 11 arrested 'hulks' of which

he had chosen only two being *'carvilles of 250 and 300 tons, as very meet to serve, if the King pleases'*. The others he rejected because they were *'clenchers, feeble and old fashioned.'* (State Papers R. O. St. P., i. 804.).

So while clinker ships could certainly have been fitted with watertight lidded gunports, the fact they weren't suggests that as well as social and economic reasons there were also inescapable functional realities. For even after the introduction of heavy guns, if a ship to ship action ended in boarding, the perception (and very likely the reality) was clearly that the clinker-built vessel would come off worst.

Does this mean that it was it the use of guns at sea that is the primary stimulus for the building of carvel ships in England, and indeed the rest of Europe? Guns were certainly a major factor in their development, specifically in the service of the emergent royal navies of the time, but the simplistic idea that it was the gun alone that initiated the transition from clinker to carvel construction does not stand up to scrutiny. The process of innovation in the Baltic makes this clearer, in particular the historical events that surround the wreck of another early carvel-built ship discovered near Stockholm.

The Kravel: key to a kingdom

Gustav Vasa and the Swedish State

In some ways the exploits of the Swedish Crown parallel those of England, yet events here provide a clearer explanatory framework partly because developments occurred over a shorter time period. In a way, in spite of differences in the Swedish situation, they stand as a metaphor for social change throughout Europe.

Since 1397 Denmark, Sweden and Norway had been effectively one political unit under the Kalmar Union. By the second half of the 15th century the bonds of union were becoming increasingly strained not least because of a growing awareness of national identity in Sweden and a concomitant desire for self government. Exacerbated by the political and economic interests of surrounding states, as well as mercantile cities like Lübeck, armed conflict was probably inevitable.

It is in this cauldron of increasing tension that some of the early uses of carvel ships in the Baltic can be seen. A few found their way into the fleets of the Sture family who, as the first Swedish noble family, were leading the struggle for independence from Denmark. Carvels also figured in the fleet of their adversaries, the Oldenburgs of Denmark. For these families and others like them were ship owners, using them for mercantile and political ends both on their own account as well as in volatile alliances with others. The role of ships in this particular struggle was seen most clearly when events came to a head in the 1520s. The Swedish regent, Sten Sture the Younger, had won consecutive victories against Christian II of Denmark in 1517 and 1518, after which the Danish king had little choice but to agree to a truce. Six members of the Swedish nobility, the young Gustav Eriksson Vasa among them, were sent to wait with the Danish fleet pending negotiations but were instead taken as hostages back to Denmark. In the event their presence proved no disincentive to Sten Sture and the armed struggle was resumed. Gustav Vasa, knowing his position would become increasingly delicate, absconded to the Hanseatic city of Lübeck, later quietly making his way back to Sweden. Swedish success was finally halted by a heavy defeat in 1520 in which Sten Sture was mortally wounded. Christian took Stockholm and had himself crowned hereditary king of Sweden (thereby sweeping away any pretence at maintaining the elective monarchy of the Union) and, in what proved to be a badly misjudged attempt to secure control, had more than eighty Swedish nobles and administrators massacred in what became known as the 'Stockholm Bloodbath'. Although Gustav Vasa was by then back in Sweden, he was one of the few who avoided this fate and soon assumed the mantle of leadership.

Almost from the start Gustav Vasa's military campaigns were successful but he realised the necessity of sea power to gain ultimate success. He turned to his friends in Lübeck whose vested interests were threatened by Christian's ambitions. Wary of growing Danish power and Dutch mercantile competition, they effectively provided him with a fleet on a 'fight now – pay later' basis. The flagship was the great carvel *Lybska Svan*, (*Swan of Lübeck*). At 7,600 marks she was more than two and a half times the cost of any other vessel in the fleet. Gustav Vasa took possession of the ships in the spring of 1522 and in June 1523, little more than a year later, lifted the siege of Stockholm, effectively breaking Danish power over Sweden (Roberts 1968:22). In doing so Gustav Vasa took the first steps to becoming the first dynastic monarch of modern Sweden and subsequently gained the sobriquet 'Landsfather'. Among Sweden's variously famous monarchs he still has pre-eminent iconic status.

Discovery

In December 1990, a wreck was discovered in the Nämdöfjärd (Nämdö fjord) area of the Stockholm Archipelago, lying below an exposed skerry known as Franska Stenarna (the French Stones) (Fig. 4.12). The find caused frenzied excitement in the media because it was initially identified as *Lybska Svan*. It was found exactly where Anders Franzén, (discoverer of the *Vasa* of 1628) had marked it on a map he had published showing the locations of Sweden's most significant wrecks (Franzén 1961:19). Not only was the *Swan* the flagship of Gustav Vasa but it was the ship upon which the Danish Admiral signed the document of surrender in 1523. This immediately elevated the wreck and what might be done with it to an unusually highly-charged ideological and emotional plane (Cederlund, 1994). Alas (for the press at least) the bubble of euphoria was about to be pricked by archaeology. In Cederlund's words, the swan was about to become a duck (Cederlund 1995).

Inspection confirmed that this was certainly a vessel from the first half of the 16th century.

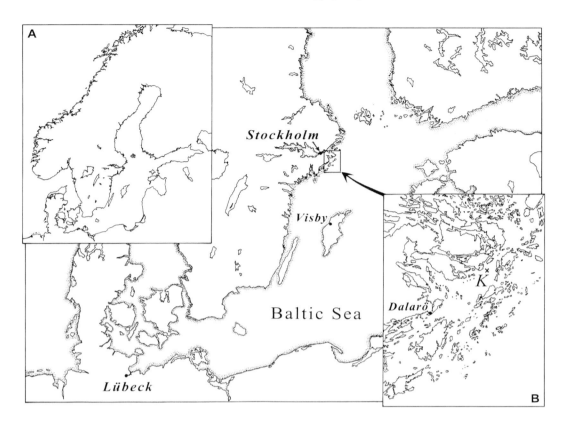

Figure 4.12 Map showing the location of the 'Kravel' (J. Adams).

Its carvel hull, artefact typologies and armament were all consistent with a date of 1524 when the Swan was lost. However, the ship seemed far too small to be Gustav Vasa's flagship. (Adams, Rönnby and Norman 1992; Rönnby and Adams 1996). In fact the identity of the ship shown on Franzén's map as the Swan had been challenged in the 1960s by Bertil Daggfeldt (Daggfeldt 1963; Cederlund 1995) and it was in this light that the archaeological investigation proceeded, the wreck simply being referred to as 'the Kravel' (Adams and Rönnby 1996). Irrespective of whether the ship's actual identity could be determined and whether it had any connection with Gustav Vasa and the early Swedish State (which was highly probable), the wreck was nevertheless of an early carvel ship from a key developmental period in European history and as such a highly important find.

Whichever ship it was, its wrecking had obviously been violent and perhaps unexpected, as the stones would have been almost invisible in rough weather. Some wreckage lies in shallow water to the East of the stones but the majority is on the West side between 30m and 56m, depth. The main concentration lies between 30m and 35m precariously perched on a ledge that interrupts the steeply sloping rock and clay that

run from the surface all the way to the seabed proper (Fig. 4.13). The hull lies on its port side, held in place under many tons of limestone ballast which had shifted as the hull sank and crashed down the slope (Fig. 4.14).

Hull structure

A detailed description of the structure as well as the objects and materials aboard has been given elsewhere (Adams and Rönnby 2013) but a summary is provided here relevant to its wider significance.

On initial inspection, in terms of its general oak, plank treenailed to frame construction, the timbers of the ship seemed to be relatively light. Even in the dark waters of the Nämdöfjärd, this together with the relatively thin planks was an early indication that the ship could hardly be the *Swan*. In uneroded locations the planks are around 45–50mm thick in the lower hull, compared to 95–100mm for those in a similar position in the *Mary Rose*. However, typical of early carvel ships, the builders were able to make extensive use of grown timber including floors and knees as well as using relatively wide planks. This is characteristic of early carvel building where the timber resource was being expoited in an entirely more profligate way.

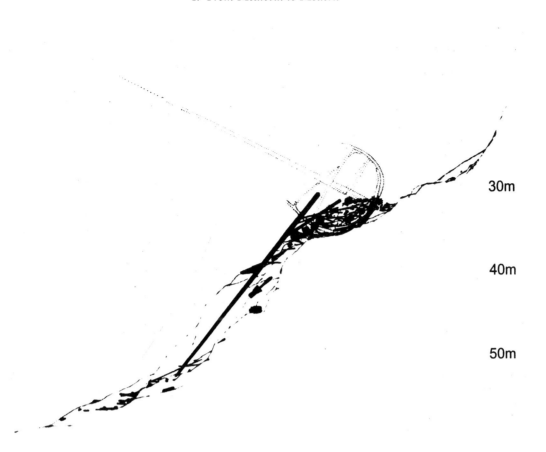

Figure 4.13 The main assemblage of the 'Kravel' wreck site lying on a break in the steep slope at 30–35m. (J. Adams).

30m

40m

50m

Figure 4.14 Plan of the main surviving hull structure of the Nämdöfjärd Kravel (J. Adams).

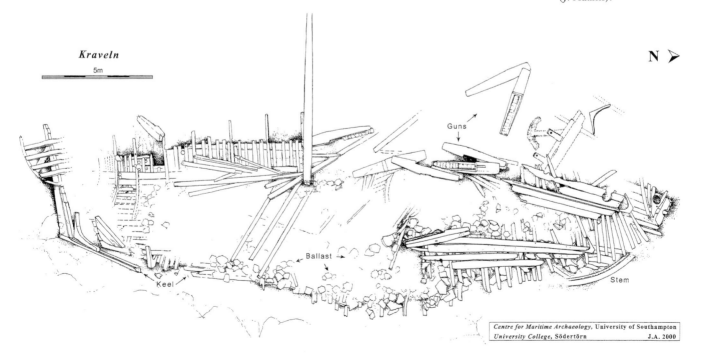

Kraveln

5m

N ⟩

Guns

Ballast

Keel

Stem

Centre for Maritime Archaeology, University of Southampton
University College, Södertörn   J.A. 2000

Other structural elements include several large deck beams that lead down the slope from the main wreck assemblage, The only one accessible so far is 6.25m in length. Forward, a 4m-long section of the stem lies still approximately in position, though no longer attached to any other structure. It is very similar to the lower stem element of the ship thought to be the *San Juan* (1565), a Basque vessel found at Red Bay, Labrador (Grenier, et al. 1994:138). The collapsed starboard planking includes a wale which, instead of simply butting against the stem, turned forward and continued to the forward edge of the stem, a feature seen in contemporary illustrations including the well known engraving of a Mediterranean carrack by 'WA' *c.* 1470 (Sleeswyk 1990:347) and in engravings of various carrack-like vessels by Frans Huys in the 1560s after paintings by Peter Bruegel the Elder, (e.g.

de Groot and Vorstman 1980: plate 5). The method was still in use nearly two centuries later and is seen on the recent wreck find at Dalarö, described above in chapter 3.

Parts of the stern structure are also well preserved. The keel fractured a few metres forward of the sternpost allowing the whole stern assembly to fall away from the rest of the hull. It now lies as a dislocated but coherent unit (Fig. 4.15). Its transoms, curved fashion pieces and diagonal outer planks show it to be square sterned, similar in many respects to the Red Bay wreck (Grenier et al. 1994: 138; Grenier et al. 2007) and to the much larger *Mary Rose* (Rule 1983:104).

Rig

The majority of the rigging is now widely scattered over the site but the principal element,

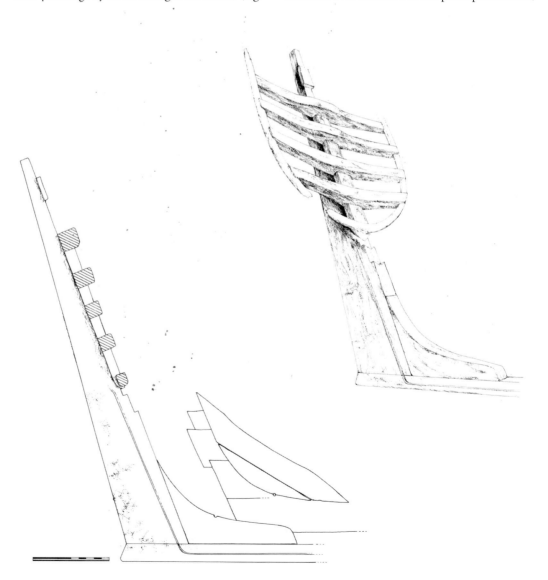

Figure 4.15 The stern structure of the 'Kravel' in elevation and perspective (J. Adams).

the main mast, still lies approximately in position. It is a large single trunk of pine, 450mm in diameter at its foot and around 18–19m in length (Fig. 4.14). Whether this piece is a central spindle that would originally have been braced with oak baulks is not known though if so the baulks should lie below this part of the site. The 1587 *Instrucción Náutica para Navegar* by Diego García de Palacio, states that the main mast should be the same length as the keel and rake, though recommends it be somewhat less. The foremast should be the same as the keel, and the mizzen four fifths the length of the foremast. Most illustrations depict mizzen masts considerably shorter than this and main masts of similar length to the keel, and this is probably the case here.

Fittings

Of the ship's fittings, a capstan was found that had probably been mounted aft the mast. Its drum and spindle are cut from one piece of oak and in general shape it resembles the capstan found on the wreck of the Basque galleon in Red Bay (Grenier 1988:78), also believed to have been mounted on the upper deck just aft of the main mast (*ibid.*).

Towards the bow lies the massive bitt-beam, 0.5m square, with two 250mm square bitts mortised into it at rightangles around which the anchor cable was secured (Fig. 4.14). In shape it resembles those in many illustrations of early carracks and also in the Mataro model, a votive ship from the Catalan monastery of San Simon de Mataro dated to around 1450.

Ordnance

Undoubtedly, one of the most significant assemblages on the wreck in terms of its identity and role is the collection of wrought iron guns. These are not exactly rare and can be found in many arsenals and museums around the world but until recently they were poorly understood. The assumption was that they were primitive, more dangerous to their users than to the enemy and generally indicative of a medieval date or an impoverished society. It is only since these guns have begun to be found associated with closely dated 16th-century shipwrecks, that their long-lived role as components of the integrated naval weapons systems of the time has begun to be appreciated.

Sites with assemblages comparable to that from the 'Kravel' are rare though and do not comprise as many pieces still attached to their wooden carriages. From this point of view, the collections that are most relevant are those of the *Mary Rose* (Hildred 2011); Villefranche Sur Mer, tentatively identified as the *Lomellina*, 1516 (Gerout et al. 1989), and of the wreck found at Anholt in Denmark (*c.* 1400).

On the *Mary Rose*, several wrought iron guns were found detached from their original location but seven were recovered still attached to their carriages, some of these still being on their carriage wheels. There were 15 wrought iron guns in the wreck at Villefranche, but only one was still on its carriage (Gerout et al. 1989). At Anholt, five guns were found on their carriages (Howard 1986: 445).

The Kravel's guns have been described in detail elsewhere (Adams and Rönnby 2013) but in summary it was realised that the 14 guns seen so far that are still on their carriages fall into two groups. The first comprises the largest guns which were clearly being transported, being stowed in the hold lying fore and aft. The other group of smaller calibres were disposed around the ship and represent its own armament (Fig. 4.16, 4.17).

The large guns are around 3.5m in overall length, their barrels being between 1.5 and 1.7m in length and their chambers between .7m and .8m. Concretion makes it difficult to measure the bore but they are approximately 200m and they would have fired stone shot. The largest of the guns that appear to have been deployed around the ship were 3m in length and with a smaller bore. There are also two pieces that are presumably swivel guns, having beds that taper into a long tiller with which the gun could be pointed.

Dating and identification

So in the Namdöfjärd Kravel we have a small but well-armed ship in which the structure and objects carried aboard all indicate an early 16th century date. A further indication was a tree-ring date of 1512 obtained from a sample including sapwood from one of the oak hull planks. 'One date is no date' as the saying goes but it closely matched the north Polish reference chronology and given the sapwood allowance for this region, the felling date is likely to have been soon afterwards and so is consistent with a vessel built around 1520 (Bråthen, pers. comm.).

This ship was evidently not the *Swan* so why had Franzén thought it would be? He had probably drawn this conclusion on the basis of

Figure 4.16a
A generic wrought-iron gun from the 'Kravel', compared to one from the *Mary Rose* (below) (J. Adams).

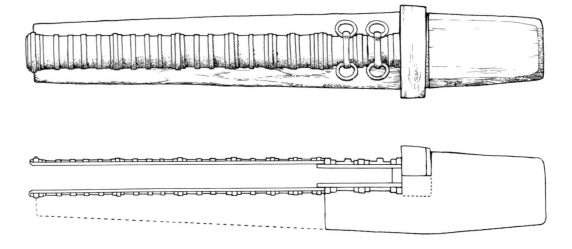

Figure 4.16b
A port piece recovered from the *Mary Rose*: gun 81A2604.
The larger 'Kravel' guns are very similar, though their carriages extend to the end of the muzzle (as do the carriages for the slings on *Mary Rose*) (J. Adams).

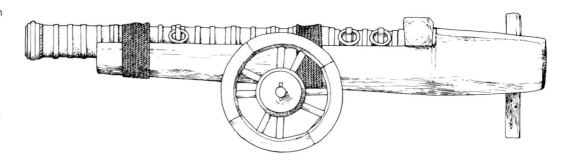

Axel Zettersten's Svenska Flottans Historia, 1, 1522–1634, written in 1890. It was Dagfeld (1963), who suggested that Zettersten had misinterpreted the admittedly confusing contemporary accounts.

In reviewing what the two sources closest to events actually say, it becomes clear that the Swan did not wreck on Franska Stenarna. The first of these was Peder Swart, Gustav Vasa's biographer, who was writing of his King's heroic exploits in 1561–2. He is probably the source of the confusion because in one instance he writes that *Swan* was abandoned in a badly leaking condition at Horn on Öland. Subsequently however, he says it sank in 20 fathoms of water but does not say where. The other source is Clement Renzel who was writing between 1536 and 1538. In 1524 Gustav Vasa had dispatched a fleet to Gotland to evict Sören Norby. Norby had commanded the Danish navy for Christian II and was regarded as too dangerous a threat to

leave at large. Renzel commanded one of the ships in the fleet and later wrote an account of his life at sea including the events of 1524. He writes that on the way back from Gotland in heavy weather the *Lybska Swan* began to leak badly. So the captain, Staffan Sasse, had to turn back and beach the ship on Öland, saving the crew and allowing the guns to be later removed. Renzel also says that a year later in 1525, after another bloody campaign in Kalmar, Gustav Vasa dispatched one of his *beste kraffwell* (best carvels) back to Stockholm with guns and other equipment retrieved from the *Swan*. It was this ship that wrecked: '...*i Swenske skären emillon Dalerna och Diurehamn...25 famnars djup*' (in the Swedish Archipelago between Dalarö and Djurshamn in 25 fathoms). In spite of strenuous efforts it proved impossible to salvage '...*och thet ligger thet ther än i thenna dag*' (and it lies there to this day). This area includes the Nämdöfjärd and the fact it was carrying guns from the Swan might explain

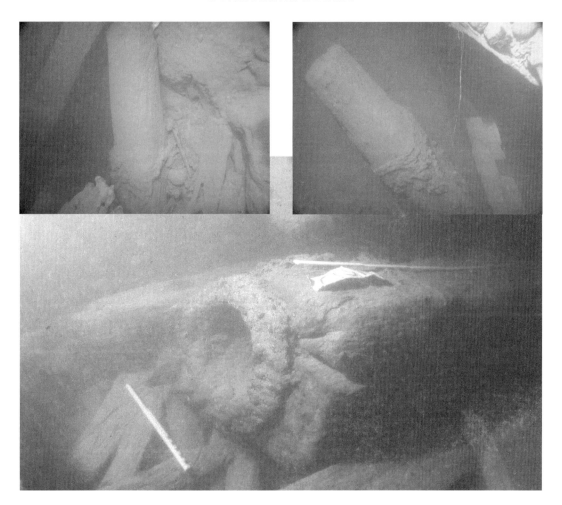

Figure 4.17
Upper: two of the ship's own guns still mounted on the their carriages that have fallen out of the sterncastle.

Lower: the muzzle of one of the large wrought iron guns lying on the ballast. Its carriage extends to the forward end of the barrel (J. Adams).

Swart's confusion. Renzel does not name the ship but it could be one called '*Kort Konig's kravel*'. Kort Konig was a Lübeck merchant from whom Vasa bought ships between 1522 and 1524. In 1525 Gustav Vasa ordered one of his carvels from Finland to Kalmar. Finland may be the source of the limestone ballast aboard (Johansson pers. comm.). At this time there were not many carvels in the fleet and so it is possible that this was also the one formerly owned by Kort Konig.

In the light of historical sources, the archaeological evidence strongly indicates that this is the vessel lost on the return voyage from Kalmar in 1525. The ship is too small to have been the *Swan*, but it is from the right period and is of a carvel-built ship. At this date carvel hulls were still relatively rare and prestigious, so it is consistent with a description as 'one of His Majesty's best carvels'. As noted, the larger pieces of ordnance were stowed in the hold rather than deployed around the vessel. Although ships often transported their own armament in this way if it was not required to be at immediate readiness,

these guns are larger and more numerous than one would expect for a vessel of this size, particularly as there are almost certainly others on the site below the area recorded so far. Nor do any of them have their chambers fitted. While some could have fallen out in wrecking, the fact that none are present in the guns so far seen suggests they were stowed elsewhere, reinforcing the impression the collection was cargo (Fig. 4.17 lower). Significantly, the smaller guns deployed around the vessel all have their chambers fitted ready for use (e.g. Fig. 4.17 upper). The location of the wreck is also consistent with Renzel's description of where the 'Kravel' was lost: '*between Dalarö and Djurshamn*'. So too does the depth of 25 fathoms, which is approximately 45m. Finally, the dendrochronological date is consistent with a vessel built and lost in the early 16th century. Though the date in itself is not diagnostic, a north Polish origin is plausible as Gustav Vasa is known to have acquired several vessels from Gdansk, Lübeck and other north German cities.

Ship type and origin

In its construction, the vessel in the Nämdöfjärd exhibits various characteristics that indicate Mediterranean and Iberian influences in the development of northern European ships. With regard to size, the keel was in the region of 17–19m long. It is difficult to be more precise at this stage as both the stem and the aft section of keel are disarticulated and the main section of the keel is partly inaccessible. Large carracks had length to breadth ratios of around 2.5:1 but proportions recorded in the Venetian 'Timbotta manuscript' indicate that the smaller vessels became progressively narrower in proportion to their length (Friel 1994:82). This document may be of dubious relevance to a vessel built somewhat later in a different region, but it illustrates that at this period the parameters, even for fundamental criteria, were fairly wide. The Kravel's main breadth according to these proportions would have been around 6.5–7m with a depth in hold of about 3–3.5m. According to English formulae in use some half a century later, capacity would have been around 120–150 tons. However, tonnage formulae and keel to breadth ratios only give a crude indication of size at this time. Swedish läster (lasts) were a measure of weight approximately equal to two tons but at this period they varied slightly according to the commodity concerned (Ekman 1946:216). Carracks and their derivatives also had long raking stems and the radius of the Kravel's surviving stem timber is consistent with this. Long curving stems of this nature had the effect of extending the main body of the hull, producing a hull shape that was much finer than the keel to breadth ratio might suggest. The *Mary Rose* for example, had a keel to beam ratio of 2.8:1, which with its rake of stem gave a relatively fine hull. Grenier made a similar observation about the *San Juan* that had a keel of only 14.75m (less than twice the breadth) but was 22m long at the weather deck (Grenier 1988:72).

Whatever the true figures, the 'Kravel' is a product of the process of development that produced the northern European three-masted ship around the second quarter of the 15th century, fusing aspects of northern and southern technology. This vessel is a carrack derivative, in that it was a northern-built ship incorporating features developed in Mediterranean carracks and the galleons and naos of the Atlantic coast. However, in view of the region of origin indicated by dendrochronological analysis, and as the term 'carrack' was apparently not used in Sweden, it is perhaps more appropriate to stick to the name used at the time: 'Kravel'. In view of the elasticity with which many ship names have been applied throughout history this might seem unsatisfactory and there are certainly problems in identifying the various types that appear alongside the kravels in the ship inventories of the period. The most apposite examples are the annual lists of Gustav Eriksson's own fleet. Each vessel is listed by type such as 'holc' (hulk), 'krejer' (krayer), 'bark' (barque), 'jakt' (yacht) or simply 'skepp' (ship) etc., (Glete 1977:29). These names were clearly interchangeable because each vessel is listed in enough detail, including the capacity, rig, armament and the name of the master, to be able to identify them in sequential lists. What is clearly the same ship might be called a kreyer in one and a holc in the next. The implication is that all these are clinker-built ships, the names having more to do with hull form and/or function with considerable overlap between them. By contrast, in those same documents it is just as evident that a kravel was always a kravel. The term was clearly specific, having a generic relationship to construction.

What is also clear that by this time the idea of a carvel ship as the appropriate vessel to form the core of a battle fleet was becoming established. And while acquiring these prestige vessels ready-made had been expedient, the logical next step for Gustav Vasa, just as for his contemporaries, was the construction of purpose-built warships.

Figure 4.18 The underwater remains of Gustav Vasa's *Elefanten* (1559–64) (J. Adams 1990).

See also Plate 10

Symbols of Power

The Elephant

Acquiring power was one thing but to hold on to it was quite another and for the first few years of his reign Gustav Vasa's position was far from secure. If a navy had been the key to the kingdom, it was also the talisman needed to keep it, but even though he was now master of his own realm and its natural resources, it was a few years before he was able to generate a sustained building programme. The first large carvel warships he built in the 1530s were simply known as 'Stora Kravel' (Great Carvel) and 'Lilla Kravel' (Little Carvel). No remains of either are known to have survived but *Stora Kravel* was large even by the standards of the time and was his equivalent of Henry VIII's *Henry Grace à Dieu* (1514) and the Scottish *Great Michael* of 1511 (Anderson 1913a). After his initial burst of energy in building large ships, for a time Gustav Vasa seems to have concentrated on smaller vessels. Interestingly, in England too, not all Henry VIII's investment was being directed towards the large heavily armed sailing ship. Around the same time several smaller carvel ships were built or acquired and numerous rowbarges and galleases were built (discussed in chapter 2 in the context of operating environments). Then towards the end of his reign Gustav Vasa resurrected his building programme of large prestige warships. One that survives from this phase is *Elefanten*, built in 1559. It was a capital ship in every sense of the word and might have ultimately been a success. Its status within the Swedish fleet is indicated by the fact that Gustav Vasa's son Erik who succeeded to the throne in 1560 intended to sail in *Elefanten* to England in an attempt to gain Queen Elizabeth's hand in marriage. Unfortunately for Erik the ship was to have neither diplomatic nor naval success. In 1564, after being damaged, it was towed in for repair but accidentally sank only a few hundred metres short of the shipyard at Björkenäs near Kalmar. Strenuous efforts to salvage it were unsuccessful and, apparently for fear that it might be salvaged by the arch-enemy Denmark, it was entombed under hundreds of tons of large boulders and remains there to this day. Even though it lies in only six metres of water, the majority of the lower hull together with beams and other internal elements still survive under the mountain of protective stone (Fig. 4.18, Plate 10). This is the vessel on which Carl Ekman (1934, 1942) lavished so much attention in the 1930s (chapter 1) and a large section of the stern was salvaged, part of which is displayed in the Sjöhistoriska Museum in Stockholm (Fig. 4.19).

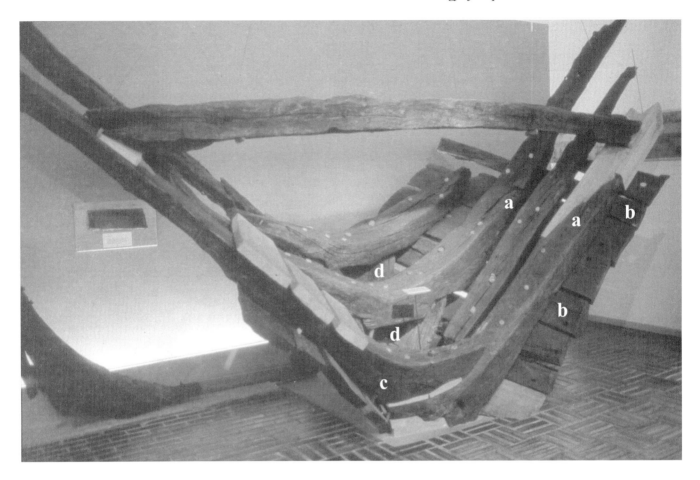

Figure 4.19 Part of *Elefanten's* stern structure slavaged by Carl Ekman and now on display in the Sjöhistoriska Museum, Stockholm. Note the scarf joints (a), wales (b), the overlapped half-floors (c) and the V-shaped crook timbers below the two aftmost floors (d) (Photo, J. Adams).

Naval enterprise and novel solutions

Apart from its age and historical associations, *Elefanten* represents an early phase of carvel building before many of the procedures were perfected and standardised. While the adoption of carvel technology was rapid and widespread across northern Europe, its execution, as we have seen, was anything but standard. In *Elefanten* there are indications of local Swedish solutions being developed to answer problems generic to wooden ship construction. For example, being fairly close in date to the English *Mary Rose*, it is not surprising that *Elefanten's* hull exhibits some similarities. However, other features are very different. In both ships the hull planking is fastened to the frames with treenails while iron bolts fasten the main structural elements such as clamps and knees. *Elefanten's* framing, like the *Mary Rose,* is of relatively high quality curved timber that is well squared. Unlike the *Mary Rose,* many of the end-to-end joints of the futtocks are scarfed in a fairly uniform fashion. Indeed the whole framing system is more regular than its English parallel, perhaps in part because it never

reached the point of needing major repair or rebuilding. Other elements the two vessels have in common include the huge grown knees, and the thickness of the sawn hull planking, ceiling and stringers. These are all joined and fastened in similar ways, illustrative of ships built before any serious economies were enforced by timber shortage or cost. An example of this is the system used for the floor timbers as they rise towards the stern. In later periods, for vessels with pronounced hollow runs, this 'V'-shaped part of the hull was partly filled with solid deadwood, into which floors or half floors were rebated. In *Elefanten,* although it would have been impossible to find single timbers for the floors aft of a certain point, the floor was made from two pieces. Either in the form of overlapping half floors (Fig. 4.19 c), or as a lower crooked piece set on the keel providing the lower part of the 'V', with a timber laid across and fastened to it for the upper part (Fig. 4.19 d). In the smaller 'ravel', the builders were able to use V-shaped, 'crooked' floors all the way aft to the stern knee. In the *Mary Rose,* crooked floors are also used further aft than would have been the case in later periods. However, this part of the *Mary Rose*'s hull is still intact so the details of construction are largely inaccessible and the presence of some deadwood cannot be ruled out.

Incorporated in the outer planking of both vessels are a series of heavy wales through-bolted to riders and knees. In *Elefanten* they are used every third strake all the way down to within three planks of the keel. This gives the outer hull a distinctly ribbed surface (an advantage in ice?). In *Mary Rose*, three heavy wales reinforce the hull in the region of the main gun deck, the lower wale corresponding with the main deck clamp and the upper two running above and below the main deck gun ports. Below the lowest wale the planking is flush all the way to the keel. The planking is not entirely smooth however, and therein lies a difference in the methods used in attempting to achieve the impossible: keeping the hulls watertight. In the *Mary Rose*, substantial seam battens, 110mm wide × 45mm thick, were nailed over the outer plank seams in the lower hull, retaining the caulking in that part of the hull it would be difficult to reach without dry-docking. In *Elefanten*, rectangular blocks of wood were placed behind the seam inboard and at least partly held in place by being locked into small rebates cut into the sides of the frames. Published sketches make it appear as though these blocks are highly regular and tightly fitted, which meant the only way they could have been placed is during construction or during plank replacement (Fig. 4.20). Recent examination of examples on the accessible section of hull still lying underwater has shown some of them to be fairly loose. The rebates were big enough to allow the blocks to be inserted by sliding them all the way into one, then back into the other to be retained under both frame timbers. Erosion notwithstanding, this raised the question of whether they could they have been fitted as a remedial measure to reduce leakage after the ship was afloat. Some could be remedial but others lie under stringers or adjacent to knees, etc., so the lack of access would have made cutting the rebates impossible. But the fact that they are not present throughout the hull suggests they were fitted only where deemed necessary. Perhaps they became so after being at sea, in which case repair involving the replacement of only some of the planks could explain their partial distribution. It is not known if this was done but even though *Elefanten*'s working life was relatively brief the necessity of

some plank replacement over five years is quite likely. Another possibility is that they were only fitted in those areas of the structure where it would be impossible to stop leakage if it occurred, hence their location under stringers, etc., in the lower hull. Over-particularistic concerns? Maybe, but discovering the rationale for these seam backing pieces bears upon the way in which a newly adopted tradition was bedding in. Both this method and the outer capping pieces seen in the *Mary Rose* are characteristic of early carvel building when, despite the thickness of the planking, leakage was a greater problem. This seems to have been because the technique of caulking had not been perfected. The observation has been made that the edges of early carvel planks were not finished with the supposedly vital 'caulking bevel' on the outer edge of the planks. As a result the caulking medium could not be jammed in so tightly, necessitating the capping of seams. However, this is an oversimplification resulting from assuming the text-book techniques of the 19th century had either always been the norm or that no alternatives were possible. Recent

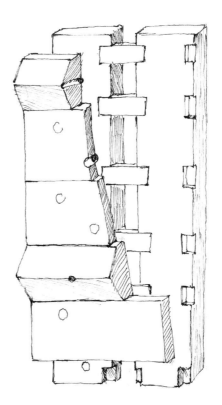

Figure 4.20 The ectangular fillets or backing pieces let in to the outer face of the frames behind the seams to retain caulking and slow leakage. After a sketch by Carl Ekman (1942:94). A tidied-up version was also published by Sam Svensson (1963:98). One still in situ is shown in the centre of Figure 4.15 (J. Adams).

finds have shown that the outer hull planks of some 19th-century vessels had no caulking bevel either (Adams et al. 1990:82). The critical factor is how closely and how evenly the plank edges are faired to each other and this involves careful attention especially over the most curved areas of the hull. The resulting seam not only needs to be an optimum width but it must be consistent or the caulking materials will be more difficult to insert evenly. Early carvel builders were probably not as skilled as their later counterparts. If the seam is too wide or irregular the hull will 'spew' its oakum as the ship flexes when underway, hence the measures taken to cap the seams inboard and out seen in the *Elefanten* and *Mary Rose* respectively. *Mary Rose* shipwrights seem to have largely achieved a fairing of the planks in which the inboard edges met flush with enough space to introduce caulking which in the lower hull they then capped. In *Elefanten*, where many of the planks do not seem to meet as tightly, the backing pieces would have allowed the caulkers to ram the caulking in as hard as possible without fear of it being driven right through.

Mars

Until recently it was not known whether the *Elefanten*'s structural peculiarities were unique, perhaps the result of expedient problem-solving in a single royal dockyard or whether it was characteristic of a Swedish form of early carvel building, or indeed a Baltic one. Then in 2011 came the remarkable discovery noted in chapter 2. The company Ocean Discovery were running a sidescan survey in 70m of water some 12mm east of the island of Öland and passed over what was obviously a large wooden wreck. Diver inspection showed that it was several centuries old and, although much of the hull was fractured and collapsed, a large section of the aft half hull and stern was substantially intact. The find was reported to the authorities and on viewing the video footage it became obvious that this could only be the warship *Mars* built in 1564. Bigger even than *Elefanten*, indeed the biggest ship in the Baltic at the time, a wreck of this size ruled out most other possibilities especially as *Mars* had gone down in this very area after blowing up in battle against a Danish/Lübeck fleet in 1564.

A preliminary survey was carried out in 2012 resulting in the plan shown in Figure 4.21 and a high-definition photomosaic (Plate 11).

The materials carried aboard that have been recorded so far are all of the right period, including its many bronze guns. Structurally diagnostic were various features that had been spotted on the video: the same scarfed joints in the framing as in *Elefanten* and also the paired rebates to take the same kind of seam backing pieces. Further work in 2013 has allowed detailed inspection of these features (Fig. 4.22). One might expect that they would not be used above the waterline but they are clearly visible in places well above the main deck gunports. As *Mars* was a new ship it now seems unlikely that the method was used to progressively waterproof a working hull and the fact that both ships exhibit this feature increases the likelihood that it is a local variant in building procedure associated with the retention of caulking. Perhaps not surprisingly in a ship that blew up, none of the actual backing pieces have yet been seen *in situ* on *Mars*, but one wonders how effective they were in any case. If the battens were only loosely located as some of *Elefanten*'s seem to be, then caulking could progressively shift with the working of the hull. If they were tightly fastened down it would make locating and remedying points of leakage even harder than it normally was. The fact that the technique did not last suggests it was either ineffective, (*Elefanten* proved unable to stay afloat after all) or it became redundant once the art of caulking was perfected. Neither method has yet been seen on the 'Kravel', probably built in what was Germany at the time (modern Poland) but in this smaller ship fairing planks may have been less of a challenge. Both English and Swedish methods illustrate the greater elasticity in practice following the adoption of a new technology. In a sense we are looking at the formation of a northern European tradition of carvel building involving the creative search for new solutions to achieve the desired ends.

Those ends were of course connected with the wider socio-political trajectory. Together with the 'Kravel' these two extraordinary Swedish ships enhance our understanding of how Gustav Vasa and his heirs built Sweden as a maritime power in the volatile world of the 16th- and 17th-century Baltic. In chapter 2 it was observed that this sequence of ship finds, including *Vasa* (1618) and *Kronan* (1676), manifest the process by which Sweden became a nation state, but, along with their parallels elsewhere, they also manifest medieval Europe becoming modern.

10m

Figure 4.21 (above) Preliminary plan of the main concentration of coherent structure of the warship *Mars* (Niklass Eriksson).

Figure 4.22 Details of the frames of the warship *Mars*, showing the same type of scarfed joints between futtocks and the same paired rebates as are seen in *Elefanten* (J. Adams).

A social context

In looking at these two different national situations in which a similar process of change occurred, the underlying causes begin to become a little clearer. That carvel building was able to be adopted relatively expediently is due to two sets of related circumstances, one technical, which until recently was the aspect that had most absorbed researchers, and the other social. As technological change is a product of people's intentions and actions it makes sense to examine what was happening in society at the time.

In this case something of a social revolution was occurring too. Profound changes had taken place, not least resulting from the Black Death (Brown 1988:21), and the subsequent, interrelated phenomena that can be referred to collectively under the terms Renaissance and Reformation. One of the lasting legacies of successive plague epidemics was an irreversible effect on demography. Incredibly, by 1420 some estimates put the population of Europe at about one third of what it had been a century earlier (Herlihy 1997:17). In turn this had marked effects on the availability of skilled labour and the social changes that were set in train by so severe and enduring a condition are responsible for many of the fundamental characteristics of Western society today (Platt 1997:viii). Such profound effects on population and labour were also linked to cultural changes. To what extent the Renaissance is regarded as a definitive period, a phase of transition, or merely a collective label is debatable (Brown 1988:1), but few aspects of European society were left untouched by the concepts engendered in this period, firstly rooted in Renaissance thinking itself, and also in the variously traumatic religious reformations.

Throughout Renaissance Europe new outlooks are evident in every aspect of the State, both at the centres of power and those related classes of society otherwise invested with power through kinship, status or alliance. A key aspect of this was an increase in the scale of state as increasingly powerful dynastic monarchies arose out of the former plethora of dukedoms and elective monarchies. This was assisted by the system of dynastic allegiance which tended to aggregate power over time. We see the process reflected in the 14th- and 15th-century political map of Europe which progressively looks less and less like a patchwork quilt as larger polities established borders nearer to those of today. These larger and eventually more stable entities were the 'nation states' to be and the increase in scale created a fundamental reality: their larger geographic regions all had coastlines and this meant that affairs of state and relations between them were increasingly maritime. Another aspect of this increase in scale was that it highlighted the inadequacy of much of the existing, essentially feudal system of government. New secular administrative councils and assemblies were devised, in the process appropriating some of the former responsibilities of the Church, not to mention many of their rights and possessions. These developments are to an extent implicated in Renaissance thinking that had fostered a new approach to the arts, architecture, philosophy and political thought. 'Man' was seen as a central figure, rooted in a natural, ordered universe. Such ideas were propagated by the dramatic spread of knowledge following the invention of printing. New texts as well as new interpretations of the old became available to all who could read or listen – the fuel of reformation.

Connected to the general increase in the size of these emergent nation states and the much larger geographic regions over which they now attempted to exercise control were interrelated shifts in wealth, population, and mobility between centres of production and consumption. As Platt summarises: '*...as labour learnt its strength and flexed its muscles, most of the ties of feudal bondage fell away.*' (Platt 1997:viii). Along with the decay of feudalism and associated changes in agriculture there was an inexorable rise of capitalism. The nature of this change is an area of perennial and vigorous debate (Dobb, 1963; Johnson 1996:5–10). It is certainly of a complexity which is impossible to thumbnail but most commentators point to a complex shift from a service-based economy to an entrepreneurial, employment-based, money economy (Herlihy 1997:39–57). Labour (and time) were commodified, changing the socio-economic value of things and the ways they were produced and consumed. In the context of trade and shipping there was a rapid growth of a mercantile business class, more independent of direct authority, concentrated in the towns and ports. This in turn sharpened the focus on maritime resources, chief among which in a technological sense, as well as in other ways, were ships. How far technological development may be initiated by specific social or economic developments, and conversely, whether technology drives history is a matter for discussion (cf. Smith and Marx (eds) 1994; Unger 1991) but the increasingly international character of Europe certainly provided a context in which new and innovative uses of ships were beneficial. Throughout Europe this was also the age of discovery. Control of overseas resources and trade routes, and the potential economic benefits were the fuel of colonial energy. The increasingly international environment tended to sharpen perceptions of political cohesion, if not of ethnicity, for by this time few if any European states were homogeneous entities with a common language (Clarke 1966:19). International communication and trade also meant competition. Just as trade was conducted in increasing volume, over greater distances and was therefore increasingly 'maritime' so too was warfare – part and parcel of obtaining these trading opportunities and safeguarding them.

Principal agents

Although Gustav Vasa was 'elected' king in 1523 his coronation effectively marked the foundation of a dynasty. His regime ultimately incorporated the Lutheran Church (a direct product of reformation) and his administration was heavily influenced by Renaissance thought. It is not known whether he himself had one of the manuscript copies of Niccolo Machiavelli's '*The Prince*', then circulating throughout Europe (it was not printed until 1532), but judging by the way he conducted himself it is very possible. His enemy Christian II of Denmark certainly did. In any event, either from his time in Denmark or from his teachers, Vasa is unlikely not to have been aware of this handbook on the techniques of political success. Machiavelli aspired to a united Italy free from foreign rule. For him, the means, however ruthless, were justified by the ends (though these were vested in the state not the prince). There are strong parallels here in Gustav Vasa's vision of a united Sweden free of Danish control, and in how he went about attaining it, especially as he personified the *principe nuovo*, the 'new prince', with whom Machiavelli was principally concerned, carving out his power base rather than simply ascending to a hereditary position. His political acumen in cultivating and manipulating the maritime muscle of Lübeck, his subsequent acquisition and consolidation of power were all in accord with the tenets advocated by Machiavelli. Indeed, Gustav Eriksson Vasa was a far more successful exponent of Machiavelli's

teaching than Cesare Borgia, whom Machiavelli cited as a perfect example of a 'new prince' come to power through his own 'virtù' and 'fortuna'. Cesare Borgia lost power after a relatively short time, whereas Gustav Vasa not only held on to his crown but, in passing it on to his three sons, laid the foundations of Sweden's period of 'great power' in the following century.

Integral to Vasa's strategy from the beginning was the possession of a fleet. That he was well aware of its importance in maintaining and consolidating his position is evident in the campaigns he undertook immediately after gaining power and in his subsequent building programme. Not surprisingly this included the construction of large 'carvel' warships.

What of the Tudors? Gustav's contemporary Henry VIII was no less a renaissance man than his Swedish counterpart, and in Henry's shipbuilding activities, and his appropriation of ecclesiastical administration, albeit for different reasons, one sees strong parallels. Both men, like those they fought against, militarily or otherwise had a clear view of statehood and Henry was no less Machiavellian in pursuit of his aims.

Innovation

In this light we can now return to the appearance of 'carvel-built' vessels in northern Europe and to the questions of how and why the transition occurred. To an extent one can focus on the Baltic, as many of the component factors, both of the context in which the change took place, and of the mechanisms of change themselves are clearer there.

Documentary evidence indicates that the increased maritime activity included trade between the Mediterranean, northern Europe and the Baltic. Mediterranean carracks were probably fairly regular visitors to the Baltic by the mid-15th century if not earlier and Baltic shipbuilders would have seen these foreign ships alongside their own. The episode often implicated in the spread of carvel shipbuilding into the Baltic concerns the 'Great Carvel' *Peter of La Rochelle* which was left in the port of Gdansk in 1462 after a dispute. Local shipwrights are said to have learned the techniques of carvel shipbuilding from it (Friel 1994:80). Litwin (1995:23) considers the *Peter of La Rochelle* incident was not a factor in the adoption of a tradition of skeleton building by the shipwrights of Gdansk, pointing out that they appear to have continued building in the Nordic tradition until much later. Certainly it may be too simplistic to attribute the adoption, in effect overnight, of another approach to shipbuilding or any other technical process to a chance encounter with one example. A case of significant change that does seem to have come about as a result of a specific incident was noted above: the English adoption of a two-masted rig soon after capturing six Genoese two-masted carracks. However, rig is something that proved fairly flexible in subsequent periods, a variety of rigs being used on the same hull in different circumstances (Adams et al. 1990:126). Hull construction, not to mention the processes of design that precede it, took a little longer.

Why would Polish shipwrights consider the careful examination of a foreign built vessel to be valuable? Perhaps if they were already familiar with the type and recognised that its characteristics of form, construction, capacity, handling and even armament potential gave it certain advantages over local types. In this sense the recorded event could be seen in the context of a long period of demonstrations carried out by foreign crews. Another possibility is that the story of the *Peter of La Rochelle* is a compression of other instances where similar opportunities were taken. It would seem unlikely that, over a period of time, this was the only occasion where a large carvel-built ship had become available for inspection. Some of the attributes of these vessels must have been becoming increasingly well known to local shipbuilders every time one of them needed repair that could not be carried out with the ship's own resources.

Whether we can pin down the introduction of carvel shipbuilding into northern Europe to specific events or not, it is clear that we are not dealing with invention. Nor, given the speed at which it happens, is it the sort of complex, iterative process discussed for the Mediterranean and the Atlantic. It was a form of diffusion. In accordance with the terminology proposed by van der Leeuw and Torrence (1989:3) to describe the whole process of innovation and its components, this is an instance of 'adoption'. In the Baltic, and northern Europe generally, facilitated by increasing maritime interaction with the south, social change provided the context for technological change. Certainly functional considerations are part of the equation. Available materials and labour-intensive techniques made it economically difficult to build Nordic vessels

of the sizes increasingly demanded by long distance trade and warfare. But these factors have to be set alongside the social, which is where the stimulus for change was generated. In this context, perhaps the ideology and symbolic associations of the long established Nordic building tradition were steadily altered and augmented through repeated exposure to foreign vessels, effectively changing northern ideas and perceptions of the nature of ships and what they could achieve. The anthropologist Robert Layton has pointed to similar mechanisms in the adoption of new methods and technology in agriculture. Farmers of one region were '*repeatedly made aware*' of the appearance of new breeding techniques, new crop varieties and new machinery (Layton 1973:34). Layton's analysis highlights the role of individuals as central to the whole process, their social status being a crucial factor in whether new methods and technologies were accepted or rejected. He also stresses the interplay between internal and external factors, as well as between technological and social factors, all of which finds resonance in more interpretative archaeological approaches: '*the ability of individuals to create change and to create their culture as an active social process*' (Hodder 1986:157).

Viewed in these perspectives the causes and mechanisms of change in 15th and 16th century shipping become clearer. For, as Renfrew (1986:146) has pointed out in connection with the development of new commodities, '*the decisive innovation…is generally social rather than technical. Often the technology is already there*'.

The Nordic tradition, long established and widespread, cross-cut many cultural and ethnic groups. Given the breadth of form and function it had achieved, and in the light of various precedents discussed above, the acceptance throughout Europe of a 'skeleton' approach was not conceptually or technologically as problematic as might be thought, especially as the construction of clinker vessels in the Nordic tradition continued long after the adoption of carvel building. Any ideological objections of shipbuilders were probably eroded through frequent contact and a growing realisation of the manifest functional, economic and prestige advantages that carvel ships offered for specific purposes. Not least of these were the political and military ambitions of new rulers like Henry Tudor, Francis I, Gustav Vasa, and the merchants, bishops and nobles with whom they collaborated or competed. For them a positive advocacy of carvel shipbuilding very soon became explicit. Similarly, as already noted, in English sources there are derisive references to clinker vessels being 'both feeble, olde, and out of fashion' (Oppenheim 1896a:54). In Sweden, not only are references to 'kravels' in the inventories always specific to carvel-built ships, but by the 1530s the term 'kravel' has become synonymous with 'örlogskepp' (warship). As such they were clearly prestige vessels and their perceived status affected how they were deployed. One wonders whether there was any functional reason for Gustav Vasa to transport so many major pieces of ordnance back to Stockholm on his ill-fated '*beste kraffwell*'. No doubt the captain of such an important ship would have been one of the more experienced. However, one also suspects that Gustav Vasa chose to use a prestige vessel. In terms of capacity and the weight involved there must have been many of his 'holcs' or 'krejers' that were quite big enough.

Floating Castles: architectural analogies

Indications of the way these ships were seen is implicit in much of their architecture and nomenclature. For centuries, seats of power had been fortified buildings – castles. In feudal society, these were multi-functional, being far more than the fortified stronghold of monarchs and barons. Generalisations, particularly on a European scale are dangerous, but castles wherever they were, by their very presence, were statements of potentially coercive power. In England, however, coercion (as opposed to defence) was a lesser function. Castles embodied the link between land-holding and military service that was part and parcel of Norman feudalism (Hinton 1990:113). They also acted as administrative centres. Castles therefore promoted and literally set in stone the social order and with them the position of the élite. Recent research into castles has justifiably rejected the traditional interpretation of them as an inexorably improving sequence of military installations (Stocker 1992). However, in many cases they were expressly sited to provide defence and in some cases, their construction in towns may have been, at least initially, coercive (Hinton 1990:115). As real concentrations of power as well as its symbolic projection, they facilitated regional control even if that was not a primary function. They regulated access and passage. This multi-faceted role embodied an enormous symbolic profile linked to, though different from, that of the Church. Operationally, the sheer size necessitated by the various functions of castles made them pre-eminent among standing buildings alongside cathedrals. Integrated in their defensive design, a similar progression of architectural styles can be discerned over time broadly spanning a period from the eleventh to the 15th centuries. By the end of this period changes in society and in technology were having an irrevocable effect on the idea of the castle, as well as the physical entity and its administration. By this time castles had become progressively less important as concentrations of military power and as defensive fortresses. As political power became increasingly centralised and more secure, the need for regional strongholds with which to project control through local representatives (feudal barons) was reduced. Fortified strongholds, if they were needed, were increasingly built to counter external threats. Pounds (1990) has drawn a distinction between castles and forts in which the former are integrated into their social and economic setting, while forts are divorced from it, staffed by a professional garrison. Good examples of the latter in this context are the shore forts built by Henry VIII along the south coast, as opposed to the castles in the border country built by Edward I to control Wales. It is this distinction that was becoming sharper as time went on and to a degree it was spurred by the technology of the gun. By the 14th century the days of the castle as a virtually impregnable refuge were numbered. Castles were still built in the 15th century but had become more residential homes than military strongholds and administrative centres. They were now the estates of those who had power and wealth rather than their military means of maintaining it. However, just as socio-political change and military technology undermined the monolithic nature of the castle, these same factors were promoting the development of another type of structure in which the same multi-functional aspects of power were vested: the ship.

In medieval England, while military power had been vested in castles, there was no equivalent permanent embodiment of power at sea. The Crown from time to time built very large prestige vessels but these did not constitute a standing navy. Navies were temporary mobilisations to answer a specific need in which only a minority of ships might actually be owned by the Crown. As David Loades put it, the navy of the 13th and 14th centuries was more an event than an institution (Loades 1992:11). This was feasible because ships could be switched between mercantile and naval roles with minor, temporary alterations. The greater part of such fleets, whether a 'navy royal' for an enterprise like an invasion of France, or smaller flotillas mobilised seasonally to 'keep the seas', were assembled principally through two mechanisms: 'Ship service', was where a specified number of ships were provided by each port for an agreed time. 'Commissions of impressment' was the compulsory requisitioning of ships at a fixed rate based on their tonnage (Loades *ibid.*:12).

It is probably no coincidence that the early 15th century is when the first really large vessels are built or procured for the crown. Ships like the *Holy Ghost* (1416) of 760 tons, the *Jesus* (1417) of 1,000 tons and the enormous *Grace Dieu* (1418) of 1,400 tons, involved huge investment on a scale that only a national agenda could justify and only royal coffers could finance. In the context of the time the *Grace Dieu* must have embodied royal power as effectively as any flagship before or since. In fact that is all she did as she never saw action. Although there is no direct reference to the ship being unseaworthy she may well have been very difficult to handle. Her crew mutinied after the one and only voyage she ever made (off the Isle of Wight), but the cause seems to have been political rather than trepidation. So in a very real sense her symbolic value was the crown's only return, for although justifying the construction of the vessel would not have been made in economic terms, clinker construction on this scale did not occur again (Friel 1995). For the rest of the century, the building of royal vessels was sporadic, not least as the political situation was highly fluid. With the accession of Henry VII in 1485 came greater stability, and with it a more international outlook that in turn necessitated attention to the maritime. It is in this context that Henry immediately ordered his two great ships, *Regent* and *Sovereign*. While the Crown had owned ships this size and larger before, Loades (1992:39) makes the point that they had been constructed for particular wars and, like the *Grace Dieu*, had become redundant once the events for which they were built had passed. Henry VII's great ships were not built in response to a war but to establish

a high profile naval presence and through it symbolic as well as practical authority at sea. An underlying reason is that ever since the loss of Normandy in 1204, the Channel had progressively become less a highway between English lands and more a frontier between competing powers. But the speed with which these vessels were ordered, as well as the cost in relation to the weakened finances of the new regime, suggest that this was done as much for prestige and legitimisation of power, as to provide a core of naval force for future use. The implications of such a strategy were far-reaching, especially in view of the Crown's ownership of several other ships as well, for the *ad hoc* arrangements for maintenance and repair were found to be inadequate. By 1495 Henry was building a new dock at Portsmouth, which together with ancillary facilities and associated fortifications to the harbour constituted the first stage of the town's development as a permanent royal naval base. In turn this required a concomitant increase in the administrative infrastructure. So although Henry VIII is often credited with being the founder of the Royal Navy it is clear that the foundations were laid by his father. It is certainly true however that it was under Henry VIII that a standing navy in the modern sense was formalised. The embryonic beginnings at Portsmouth grew into a network of docks and stores servicing a fleet that was centrally administered through the institutional framework of government. It was the building programme begun in 1509, producing the *Mary Rose* among others, that took the ships of this bourgeoning institution to new levels of sophistication and power.

Dynasty over Deity

These were the new floating castles. Their design and nomenclature makes this clear. Where castles had been the principal architectural expression of power in the medieval period, now at the dawn of the modern age, ships could perform a similar function. Sails were emblazoned with heraldic devices – symbols of lineage, the legitimisation of the new dynastic power. Commensurate with their importance to the regime, their command was delegated not to professional seamen (though these were vital to their operation), but to privileged noblemen of high rank. Whereas the names of Henry V's great ships had been predominantly ecclesiastical: *Holy Ghost, Trinity,*

Jesus, Grace Dieu, those of the Tudors were not only more secular but often explicitly dynastic: *Regent, Sovereign, Mary Rose, Peter Pomegranate* (the latter referring both to the orb of state and to its emblem in the coat of arms of Catherine of Aragon, Henry's first wife). Like many of his predecessors, Henry VIII had a *Grace Dieu* but his was *Henry Grace à Dieu* commonly referred to as *Great Harry*.

Ships also had the advantage of being mobile. Whereas a castle on a remote border could only execute its administrative, military and propaganda functions in that region, a ship could convey royal power and prestige across the seas. The analogous links between castles and ships were therefore manifested in many ways in addition to the functionality of their guns, principally in nomenclature and display. The upper works of the *Mary Rose* and contemporary vessels utilized the architectural motifs of palace architecture. So although the 'sterncastle' and 'forecastle' were certainly functional structures in terms of the intended mode of naval engagement, they were also metaphors for power in its widest sense. The Tudor rose, heraldic pennants and the porticoed mouldings reminiscent of the most sophisticated Italian renaissance buildings, transmitted the status and prestige underpinning the building of the ship. This conspicuous display was as much a part of the functionality of these vessels as the row of guns protruding from the hull. This aspect of ships was progressively developed until a century later one sees an even more sophisticated and explicit symbolic language used for the same projection and legitimisation of power, now transmitted through carefully arranged tiers of carved images. This was the ship as 'floating ideology' par excellence (Rönnby and Adams 1994:68) and typified by the ill-fated flagship *Vasa* of Gustav Adolph II Vasa (Soop 1992). Throughout 17th-century Europe, states competitively adorned their ships for the same reason. In England they are typified by the ships of the Stuart period such as *Sovereign of the Seas* (1637), known to the Dutch as the 'Golden Devil', and by the Restoration period vessels so well depicted by the van de Veldes.

Guns or barricas?

Analogies with castles raises a question about the use of guns, for it has often been stated or implied that they provided the principal spur to the development of the three-masted carvel sailing ship. This is a maritime equivalent of White's (1962) ingenious argument that feudal society stemmed from the development of the stirrup and needs qualification in similar ways. Certainly the gun was a primary factor in the way warship design and construction subsequently developed. However, in this formative period it must be remembered where those who had most use for guns were obtaining their ships – often from merchants. Certainly these traders, as powerful entrepreneurs, were often little different from the princes they were selling to. The distinction between military leaders or bishops, kings and queens or pretenders, admirals or merchants, was one of degree rather than of vocational criteria. The merchants of Lübeck from whom both Henry VIII and Gustav Vasa purchased ships were themselves rich and powerful, employing armed militia and owning land, castles and armed ships. So although state-forming and power-broking by 'new men' such as Henry VIII, Christian II and Gustav Vasa spurred the subsequent development of the northern European carvel-built warship, they were able to buy, 'second hand' or off the stocks, its ready-made precursor. However, these vessels were not bristling with ordnance like *Mary Rose* or *Mars*. These were second generation developments of earlier forms such as Gustav Vasa's kravel, privately built and merchant-owned. The adoption and subsequent development of a new technology can be seen, as Layton (1973) has observed, to be heavily dependent on individuals, but the initial furnace of change, in which so many of the precursive characteristics were forged, was mercantile: the north-south trade and exchange of the preceding centuries.

Caution is therefore needed when identifying various constructional features of early carvel ships as developments or adaptations stemming from the requirement to carry heavy guns. While the specific origin of gunports is uncertain (being traditionally ascribed to a Frenchman, Descharges in 1501) at least it is evident their systematic incorporation into hull construction to allow the mounting of large guns occurs in this period, i.e. after the eager adoption of carvel itself. It has also been reasoned that the square tuck or 'transom' stern as seen in the *Mary Rose* was developed to accommodate large stern chasers and combat the threat from galleys (e.g. Carr Laughton 1960:251; McKee 1973:22; Howard 1979:45; Hutchinson 1994:10; Rodger 1996:301). But if the earliest carvel ships built in northern Europe, similar to the 'Kravel', were built as merchant vessels this is questionable. The sterns of both the *Mary Rose* and the 'Kravel' have very close similarities to ships of the Basque tradition such as the galleon believed to be *San Juan* (1564) (Grenier 1988; Grenier et al. 2007). That all three ships have such similar stern constructions, despite their very different sizes, original functions, and countries of origin, suggests that this structural system was well developed before concerted attempts were made to mount large numbers of heavy guns on ships, firing through lidded gunports. Is it not possible that the square stern with its characteristic diagonal planking originates for other reasons? One possibility is a need to maximize capacity in the hull of ships like Basque naos and galleons for as much of the body length as possible. As ocean voyaging became longer, particularly in industries like whaling that required relatively large crews, cabin arrangements needed to be rather more generous than on vessels where the voyage length was days rather than weeks or months. Reducing the narrowing of the hull in the afterbody and leading it to a square stern would not only increase stowage capacity but also increase living space above. Fortuitously this configuration predisposed these ships, as did carvel construction itself, for the carrying of guns and the increased complement necessary to handle them.

The evidence therefore suggests that it was the builders of the caravels and of the naos on the Iberian Atlantic coast who had a formative influence on subsequent carvel shipbuilding of northern Europe. This is logical if one considers that it was this area through which the north-south-north interplay of ship technology occurred through the 13th to the 15th centuries. The Atlantic coast provided an operating environment which demanded characteristics of sea-keeping and robust construction. Hence this was the environmental and cultural melting pot implicated in so much of Europe's subsequent history. For the powerful (or power-hungry), highly motivated, state-builders of the 15th and 16th centuries, there is no doubt that these ships provided an efficient means to an end, both as an imposing visual transmitter of status and prestige and as a means of wielding that power through the use of guns. Viewed within a wider social trajectory, acceptance and then adoption of carvel shipbuilding was therefore expedient rather than traumatic, revolutionary but not mysterious. They can therefore be seen as part of 'a diachronic trajectory of material culture' (Shennan, 1989b:331) rather than a dislocated series of inexplicable phenomena.

With this in mind one can now view subsequent developments in northern European shipbuilding. First however, an apparent omission – another mystery – must be addressed.

Plate 1 The Swedish warship *Riksäpplet*, lost in 1676 near Dalarö (Painting: J. Adams).

Plate 2 *Anna Maria* (the 'salt ship') lost in Dalarö harbour in 1709 (Painting: J. Adams. Kester Keighley collection).

Plate 3 The 'Ghost Ship' (Courtesy of MMT).

Plate 4 The Dalarö wreck (Photo: Jens Lindström).

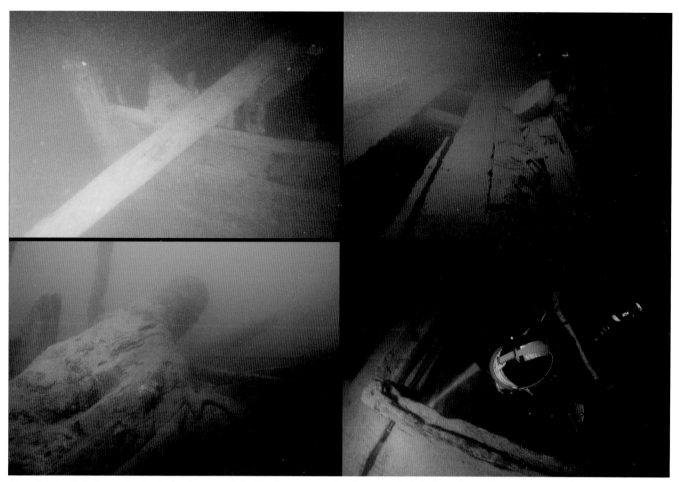

Plate 5 The Dalarö wreck, clockwise from top left: The bow, port side; the main deck looking forward; a gun mounted on its carriage; museum diver entering the main hatch (Photos: Jens Lindström).

Plate 6 The stern of the warship *Mars* (1564) (Photo: Tomasz Stacura, © Ocean Discovery).

Plate 7 The hull of *Mars* showing the heavy outer planks and wales (Photo: Tomasz Stacura, © Ocean Discovery).

Plate 8 The intact forward structure of the Swedish warship *Svärdet*, 'the Sword' (1676) (Photo: Jonas Dahm/MMT).

Plate 9 Painting of *Mary Rose* (1545), done prior to the raising and showing the site as it would have looked (if such visibility existed) towards the end of the excavation phase in 1981 (J. Adams).

Plate 10 The aft structure of the Swedish warship *Elefanten* (1564) (Painting: J. Adams).

Plate 11 Photomosaic of the warship *Mars* (© Ocean Discovery).

Plate 12 A representation of *Mary Rose* from an inventory of Henry VIII's ships drawn up in 1546 by Anthony Anthony (Pepys Library, Magdalene College, Cambridge).

Plate 13 The *Hynde* (80 tuns) depicted in the Anthony Anthony Roll (1546). (Pepys Library, Magdalene College, Cambridge).

Plate 14 The well-known image of a 16th-century ship by Mathew Baker, probably from the 1570s (Pepys Library, Magdalene College, Cambridge).

Plate 15 Lower hull structure of *Sea Venture* (1609) (J. Adams).

Plate 16 Starboard structure of *Warwick* (1619) (J. Adams).

5
The Mysterious Hulk:
Medieval tradition or modern myth?

Those already familiar with the principal stages of northern European ship development might be wondering why the narrative so far has barely mentioned a ship type that was surely central to the plot. Conventionally the seagoing ships of the medieval period in northern Europe have been treated as belonging to three principal traditions: the Nordic keel, the cog and the hulk (e.g. Heinsius 1956; Hutchinson 1994:5–20; McGrail 2001:223–243). Now, after more than a century of archaeological discoveries, we know well the sleek lines of the Viking long ship and the many variants built within the wider Nordic clinker tradition to which it belonged. We can also distinguish the very different approach to timber conversion and construction embodied by the straight-stemmed, high-sided vessels we call cogs but we look in vain for the hulk. This is odd, for the hulk is the type that apparently supplanted the cog for the carriage of bulk goods over long-distances around 1400 (e.g. Waskönig 1969:141, 165; McGrail 1987:118; Ellmers 1994:44; Greenhill 1995:250). On the eve of the coming of carvel this gives the hulk a pivotal place in the development of northern European shipping so it is strange that to date most scholars accept that we have yet to find any physical remains that can be unequivocally assigned to this third way of building ships. Yet this has been more a tacit acceptance of received opinion rooted in historical research more than half a century old. In reality, ideas of what the hulk was and what it looked like are confused and contradictory.

There is no doubt that hulks were an important ship type as they are mentioned consistently in historical sources over several hundred years. The earliest known reference to the 'hulc' is in *Laws of Aethelred* II from 1000 AD (McGrail 2001: 239). These and subsequent documents detail tolls for various craft including small boats, 'coels' and 'hulcs'. The tolls paid by hulks were the same or less than keels in the 12th century, but by the 14th century they paid more. The implications are that hulcs were medium to large ships that were in certain significant ways distinct from keels and that they had developed by the 10th century.

So why are they not represented in the archaeological record? They may be of course, for it is not long ago that cogs posed a similar puzzle. They too were well represented in documentary sources and in the 1950s and 60s various archaeological finds were tentatively identified as cogs. An example is Kalmar I, shown above in Figure 4.6, recorded and interpreted by Harald Åkerlund (1951) and used by Paul Heinsius in his discussion of cogs (Heinsius 1956). Then, following the discovery of a medieval wreck in the river Weser, Germany, Siegfried Fleidner (1964) realised that it was unmistakeably the sort of ship depicted on numerous town seals. Not only that but one of the more realistic images, the Stralsund seal of 1329, was referred to as a cog in near contemporary sources. The connection was made; the Bremen ship was a virtually complete cog (Fig. 5.1). Once that link had been made, several other finds that had defied identification were now realised to be cogs, such as the one found at Bossholmen in Sweden (Cederlund 1990). Of course this depends on what those medieval writers meant by 'cog' and there has been some debate as to whether the identification is sound (see Weski 1999 vs Crumlin-Pedersen 2000). Nevertheless, due to the various intersections of documentary and iconographic sources with archaeological finds the correlation is generally accepted. Are we now in a similar situation with respect to the hulk, awaiting the discovery of a Bremen equivalent that would enable us to correlate the historical and iconographic sources with reality? Basil Greenhill clearly thought so:

> *Somewhere in the mud of an estuary or buried in saltings, this most important of discoveries in the archaeology of boats and ships is still waiting to be made.* (Greenhill 1995:250).

His conviction was partly rooted in a correlation rather similar to that of the Stralsund seal with cogs, for Heinsius (1956:215) had pointed out that the Latin inscription on the seal of New Shoreham of 1295 read: *hoc hulci singno vocor os sic nomine dingno* (By this symbol of a hulk I am called mouth which is a worthy name) (Fig. 5.2). The old name of New Shoreham was indeed Hulkesmouth. This image therefore came to be seen as *prima facie* evidence for the physical characteristics of the hulk. It is certainly very different in appearance from any keel or cog and there are many others from the period (and later) rather like it on coins, manuscript illuminations and in carvings. Cumulatively they gave credence for the identity of a third way of building ships in the medieval period:

> *What is quite certain is that medieval craftsmen seeking to illustrate vessels in illuminated manuscripts, in stone carving, and in fine metalwork, were by the early twelfth century deliberately and carefully depicting a vessel quite different from the clinker-type with stem and sternpost, equally carefully depicted in other contemporary works of art.* (Greenhill, 1995: 251).

Examples in the various media he is referring to include the image carved on the font at Winchester Cathedral in England dated to *c.* 1180 (Fig. 5.3). The stone is Tournai marble from Belgium and a very similar one can be seen in Zedelghem near Bruges. Typical images are found on several denominations of gold coinage minted in England from the mid 14th century in the reign of Edward III (Fig. 5.4). Several examples were found on the *Mary Rose,* including 'angels', the earliest issued in the reign of Edward IV 1461–83 and the latest in the last coinage of Henry VIII between 1544–7. A type that looks similar in overall form although they are even less detailed, are seen on 9th-century coins from Dorestad (Ellmers 1995:36) and Quentovic (Vlek 1987: fig. 3.2.3). Of manuscript illustrations perhaps the best example depicts Henry I returning to England, in John of Worcester's Chronicle dated *c.* 1118–1140 (Fig. 5.5). Town seals range from the highly stylised New Shoreham seal to the more realistic second seal of Southampton, also 13th century (Fig. 5.6). Others noted by Greenhill included images on English medieval enamel plaques and carvings such as medieval misericords. These images, along with the documentary references and the support of ethnographic parallels, conveyed enough for him to affirm the existence of the hulk as

> *a distinct shipbuilding tradition, quite different from the traditions that produced the Scandinavian, Slav, or middle northern European clinker-built boats, and quite different from the traditions that produced the cog.* (Greenhill 1995:251).

Figure 5.1 (left) The Stralsund town seal of 1329, the explicit link to the appearance of medieval cogs (After Ellmers 1994).

Figure 5.2 (right) The town seal of New Shoreham (Hulksmouth) 1295.

Figure 5.3 (left)
The font at Winchester Cathedral, England. Believed to be the earliest representation of the stern rudder (J. Adams).

Figure 5.5. (right)
A manuscript illumination showing Henry I returning to England, in John of Worcester's Chronicle dated 1118–1140 (Corpus Christi College, Oxford Ms 157, f.383).

Proposed hulk characteristics

From the generic similarities of this family of images a series of characteristics has been proposed that together define the putative hulk. The hull is excessively curved, almost banana-shaped and many of the images show overlapping hull planking laid in the opposite way to conventional clinker, i.e. each strake overlaps the inboard side of the one below rather than the outboard. This is denoted 'reversed clinker' and is known to be used in boat building in other regions (Greenhill 1995:254; Blue et al. 1997; McGrail et al. 2003: 67–97). The other difference is that the strakes run parallel with the sheer line and end above the waterline rather than terminating in the posts as in normal clinker construction. Greenhill suggested that one reason for this was the difficulty in terminating a plank into a stem if the one below is already in place, as it would be if one was

building up from the keel in reverse clinker (Greenhill 1976:86). This and apparently similar plank arrangements have therefore been denoted 'hulk-style planking' (e.g. Greenhill 2000:12). What is also omitted from some of these images are stem posts and keels and so it was assumed that the vessels depicted had plank keels. The other feature often shown is some sort of collar at the termination of the planks, occasionally being at the base of small castle structures or in others seeming to be the lashed anchorage of the stays. Other characteristics such as the single mast and square sail, a side rudder in earlier images and later a stern rudder, are shared with images of other types.

Here then is the medieval hulk or rather it would be if we could find one, but to date they appear to be archaeologically invisible. Given the characteristics summarised above they should not be hard to recognise so have we

Figure 5.4 (left)
A gold Noble from the reign of Edward III. Coins like these were introduced in 1351.

Figure 5.6 (right)
The 13th-century town seal of Southampton (National Maritime Museum).

Figure 5.7 The Utrecht
ship now dated to the
11th century (After Vlek
1984).

simply been unlucky or might there be another
explanation?

In the course of his doctoral research, Joe
Flatman drew up a gazetteer of medieval and
early modern ship finds spanning the 6th to the
16th centuries. After subsequent revision for
publication it had reached 1,000 entries, of which
831 were northern European (Flatman 2007:87–
105). This database includes small craft such as
logboats but of the hundreds of ships the largest
group was of the wider Nordic clinker tradition.
Significantly, not a single one can be unambigu-
ously identified as a hulk, at least in terms of a
round-hulled, reversed clinker, 'hulk-planked',
keelless vessel with 'collars'.

Something is wrong, for if vessels of this type
existed in any numbers, especially over a period
of many centuries, then there must have been
losses, abandonments and re-use. It would be odd
then, even given the vagaries of the archaeological
record and all the other factors that influence
patterns of discovery, if none had been found.
Greenhill (2000:9) himself said as much: '...*it is
truly astonishing that no recognised remains of this
distinctive hull form have been found*'. Certainly
other ship types such as the Mediterranean
trireme elude us but there are reasons for that
which do not apply to the heavier, ballast-laden
constructions of northern Europe. Simple
statistics then raise what at first seems a rather
heretical possibility: that hulks in the form
deduced from iconography never existed. But as
we know that ships called hulks certainly did
exist, including their equivalents elsewhere such
as the Portuguese *urca*, in view of the number of
medieval ships and boats that have been found,
the implication is that among their number we
may have been looking at hulks all the time.

Proto-hulks?

In fact from a period not long after hulks are first
noted in historical documents there are some
boat finds that are clearly outside the cog and
keel building traditions, and which do resemble
the iconographic evidence in some ways. The best
known was found in Utrecht, Holland, in 1930
(Vlek 1987). Originally dated by C14 to the late
8th century, subsequent tree-ring dating has
demonstrated it to be early 11th century (Van de
Moortel 2003:184). The Utrecht boat is 17.45m
long with a beam of 3.85m (Fig. 5.7). It is an
extended logboat in that it has two additional
strakes and a half round wale built onto a logboat

base of 13.8m long by 1.9m wide. Recent analysis
by Aleydis Van de Moortel (2000, 2003) has also
shown it to have been expanded through heat
treatment. Nor it is unique. A very similar boat,
only slightly smaller was found at Waterstraat, also
in Utrecht, dated to the late 10th century (Van de
Moortel 2009:13) and a further small one at
Velsen not far distant in the province of North
Holland (Vlek 1987). Together with other more
fragmentary finds from the region (Zeewolde and
Antwerp) they are clearly from the same distinctive
boatbuilding tradition, but could they be the
banana-shaped craft that provided the subject for
so many representations and which brought goods
to London in the 11th century? In profile they do
bear a resemblance to some representations and
when it was believed that the Utrecht boat dated
to the late 8th century, it seemed as though it could
be an early or 'proto-hulk' such as those depicted
on the Carolingian coins (Crumlin-Pedersen
1965; Ellmers 1972, 1995). The most widely
accepted etymological root of the word, something
pod-like or hollowed out, also fits the process of
producing the hollowed out logboat base. In other
aspects its similarity is less convincing. For example
the strakes taper towards the bow and stern and
so do not seem consistent with the terminations
regarded as characteristic, although Van de
Moortel (2009:13) has questioned the veracity of
the original reconstruction. Otherwise, once the
true date was established, most scholars rejected
Utrecht as any sort of proto-hulk (Hutchinson
1994:12; McGrail 2001:242). The other problem
is that the Utrecht type was a river craft and, large
though Utrecht and Waterstraat are as boats (or
small ships), it is difficult to believe vessels like
these worked back and forth across the North Sea,
even with the very different attitudes towards risk
in the past. However, shipbuilding traditions often
produced variants for different environments and
Damian Goodburn has reported fragments of
what seems to be a vessel of the Utrecht type from

Bull Wharf in London. Perhaps seagoing variants did exist then which may not have been particularly large. If these are the vessels taxed under Aethelred's law codes in *c.* 1000 AD then they may have paid the same as larger keels because they were foreign. But whatever the true significance of the Utrecht finds, they seem unlikely precursors of the hulks that superseded the cogs in the late medieval period, so where are these?

Late medieval hulks

In 1980 Jerzy Litwin published a paper on the 'Copper Wreck', found in Gdansk, Poland, and suggested that it could be a hulk (Litwin 1980). As it seemed to be a conventional Nordic clinker-built ship this seemed odd for it had none of the characteristics described above. Since then, several other wreck finds have been tentatively identified as hulks: Adams and Rönnby (1996:96) speculated that the early 16th-century wreck known as *Ringaren*[1] in Sweden may be one (Fig. 5.8). A 15th-century wreck of a ship some 30m long, designated U 34, found in the polders in Flevoland has also been proposed (Reinders and Oosting 1989), as have a series of large heavily built clinker ships wrecked in Guernsey in the 13th/14th centuries (Adams and Black 2004:244). But like the copper wreck these are all conventional clinker construction so how can they be seen as hulks? Because ships of this large size, carrying bulk merchant goods were clearly called that in their day. As was noted in chapter 4, clench-built hulks are mentioned in English sources in the 1540s, and 'Ringaren' is contemporary with the

Swedish ship inventories that include 'holcs' along with other types of clinker-built ship.

It can be seen that the finds that have been proposed as hulks fall broadly into two groups. Firstly, they are distinct in date, the Utrecht type being earlier by several centuries than the later group. Secondly, they are the product of completely different building traditions. Perhaps the problems we have had in attempting to rationalise the hulk stems from the assumption that it was a single, distinct tradition that lasted throughout the medieval period. This is certainly what Greenhill concluded and in this he was closely aligned with Dagmar Waskönig, whose study of pictorial representations of hulks in the 15th and 16th centuries nevertheless also attributed great significance to the 13th-century New Shoreham seal (Waskönig 1969:142). Her conclusion that hulks were a distinct tradition that could be '*traced back through several centuries*' (Waskönig 1969:166). is what undermined her aim of removing '*...doubts and uncertainties in the appearance of the hulk*'.

If Goodburn is right about the Bull Wharf find, Vlek (1987:143–5) may have been premature in dismissing any connection between the Utrecht boat and what were called hulks at that time but he was surely right in concluding that it is not related to the large, seagoing hulks of the late medieval period (1987:89, 145). We are therefore dealing with different types of ship called hulk at different times and in different places. This is nothing unusual where ship names are concerned as expressed by Nicolaas Witsen: '*the breeds of ships are often mixed*' (Witsen 1690).

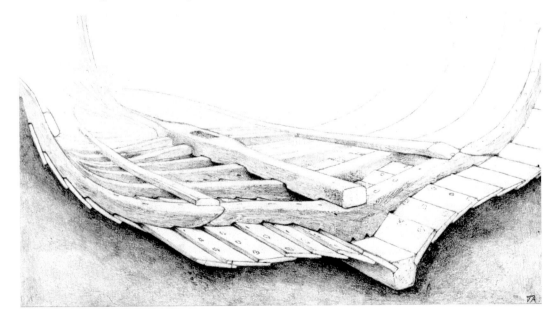

Figure 5.8 A late medieval clinker built ship known as *Ringaren* (the ringer) (J. Adams).

Table 5a

A representative sample of ship images from the 9th to the 16th centuries that have all been designated as hulks, tabulated against supposed hulk characteristics. Where planking is concerned 'indeterminate' refers to images where it is difficult or imposssible to distinguish between conventional or reversed clinker. 'Non-specific' is where the artist has depicted planking in a purely schematic way.

Perception and the medieval artist

As well as the unwarranted assumption of a continuous tradition, the other problem is the iconographic material from which the notion of the medieval hulk has been constructed. Perhaps more has been derived from these images than they had to give. The conveying of meaning through images is a complex process and the ways in which the subject is portrayed through a combination of text, figurative and abstract symbols and motifs are bound up with the conventions of representation and psychology of perception. This implicates the ideologies of those who commision the image, the knowledge, norms and conventions of the artists who produce them and the semiotic literacy of those who view them. These issues do not seem to have been taken into account in the rather overenthusiastic interpretations of what these images showed. In their time they were intended to convey aspects of community with economic, political and religious overtoncs, so attempting to define generic features of a ship type from them is problematic to say the least.

Table 5a summarises the features of some of the most widely known images that have commonly been designated as hulks. What is immediately striking is how few have all or even most of the characteristics believed to define the type. The ones that do are usually the most stylised, generally small and mostly made by artists who, due to the factors noted above, did not have representational realism in the modern sense as their priority. Where town seals were

Depiction	Date AD	No visible posts	Planks not ending at stem	Collars/ Stem ropes	Reversed clinker	Pronounced hull curvature
Coins from Quentovic and Dorestad in the reigns of Charlemagne and Louis the Pious	814–840	✓	✓	Indistinct	Non-specific	✓
Lewes capital (now BM)	c.1120	✓	✓	✓	Non-specific	✓
Henry I returning to England. Chronicle of John of Worcester Fig. 5.5	1118–40	✓	✓	✓	✓	✓
English enamel plaque: St Peter walking on water (Germanisches National Museum)	1170–80	✓	✓	No	Indeterminate	✓
Font at Winchester Cathedral Fig. 5.3	c.1180	✓	✓	✓	Indeterminate	✓
From 'Life of St Thomas of Canterbury'	1230–40	✓	✓	✓	✓	✓
Shoreham ('hulkesmouth') town seal. Fig. 5.2	1295	✓	✓	Small platforms	Non-specific	✓
Southampton 2nd town seal Fig. 5.6	13th C.	Stern	✓ Bow only	No	Non-specific	No
Holkam Bible Fig. 5.10	early 1300s	Both visible	✓	✓	✓	No
French Manuscript Fig. 5.11	14th C.	✓	✓	Castles	Non-specific	✓
Coin: Edward III Noble Fig. 5.4	1351	✓	✓	✓Bow only	Non-specific	✓
Rye town seal	c.1400	✓	Bow possibly	No	Non-specific	No
Danzig town seal Fig. 5.12	c.1400	Both visible	✓ Upper bow only	No	No	No
Paris Bolt maker's Guild Fig. 5.9	15th C.	✓	✓	Castles	✓?	✓
Admiralty seal of Thomas Beaufort	1418–26	✓	✓ Bow only	Castles	No	✓
Admiralty seal of John Holland	1435–42	✓	✓	Castles	No	✓
Seal of the Admiralty Court of Bristol	>1446	✓	At bow only	✓ Below castle	✓	No
Coin: Edward IV (Angel)	1473	✓	✓	Castles	Non-specific	✓
Coin: Henry VIII (Angel)	1546	✓	✓	Castles	Non-specific	✓
Misericord No 7, St. David's Cathedral, Pembrokeshire Fig. 5.13	Late 15th C.	Both visible	Upper planks only	No	No	No
Coin: Mary (Ryal)	1553–4	✓	✓	Castles	Non-specific	✓

concerned their primary function was to celebrate the identity and economic spirit of the town, not to provide us with structural information on medieval shipbuilding. The ship depicted on the seal of New Shoreham was not a realistic representation of anything that could possibly float, it was a symbol, a motif that had already acquired a readily understood meaning to those who saw it. As already indicated, the 'hulks' on English gold coinage of the mid 1500s are very similar to those on Nobles and half Nobles two centuries earlier. The ships on the seal of the 15th-century Paris Bolt Maker's Guild (Fig. 5.9) and the Admiralty seal of John Holland 1435–42, are similarly stylised. In the case of manuscript illuminations, Flatman (2007:64) notes that it is the ships that have hulk characteristics that are the most highly decorated, with heraldic shields, flags and pennants. This is consistent with a stylised motif that has more to do with the transmission of ideas than the technology of medieval ship construction. The reality of Henry VIII's *Mary Rose* is nothing like the ship motif on coins found in her wreck, in circulation both at her building in 1510 and her loss in 1545. Rather like the modern use of the obsolete copper helmet to portray a diver, this stylised image of a ship has endured right into our own time and

Figure 5.9 A ship on the Paris Bolt Maker's Guild. One of many stylized ship images from this period (After Ellmers 1994).

appears in innumerable company logos, municipal sculptures and town coats of arms thoughout Europe and beyond.

Reverse clinker

Of all the features that are held to be characteristic of the hulk, the most discussed is reverse clinker. Some images unequivocally show it but in most of the so-called hulks the planking is either conventional or completely indeterminate. In the

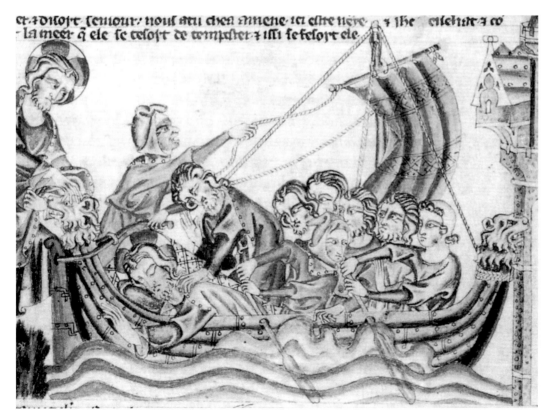

Figure 5.10. An illumination from the Holkam Bible, early 1300s (British Library MS Add. 47682, f. 24).

much discussed New Shoreham seal the planking looks more like courses of brickwork than strakes of planking, a style seen on many other seals of the period such as Melcombe Regis (1300) and Newtown, Isle of Wight (1330) (Ewe 1972:157, 165). In such cases the artists cannot have regarded an accurate depiction of planking as necessary, so, even where they chose to show overlapping planks, did they realise the significance of depicting them one way rather than another? Simply on the basis of other details shown in these images such as masts and rig, often shown in impossible relationships, it is probable that they did not. An example is the depiction of rope in either right-hand or left-hand lay. How rope and cables are laid (the direction of twist in which the fibres, yarns and strands are sequentially laid) is not a random matter but is related to the size of the cordage as well as its function. Yet in some of the representations of hulks, both right- and left-hand lay are depicted in the stays of the same vessel. An example is the 'hulk' shown in an illumination from the Holkam Bible (Fig. 5.10) of the early 1300s (reproduced in Friel 1995:89). Another is a 14th-century French manuscript (Fig. 5.11) where the lay changes in the same stay either side of a block. Clearly the artists did not realise the significance or afford it any importance so why should we assume they did when depicting planks? Another possible source of confusion in the case of coins and seals is the process of producing a positive image in relief from the negative intaglio of the matrix or die. However, the variability is seen across all media in which the images appear and the generic similarity of many suggests direct copying including the manner in which various features were depicted, accurately or otherwise.

None of this precludes the possibility that the reverse clinker technique might have been used in some medieval vessels but this cannot be demonstrated either way on the basis of these images. Only a detailed historical account of shipbuilding practice or an unequivocal archaeological discovery can do that. There are in fact two finds that caused some initial excitement when they were presented as being from reversed clinker vessels. One is a small section of hull planking re-used in a moat revetment in Southwark, London, dating from the late 16th century (Marsden 1996:136–44; Tyres 1996:198); the other is a joggled futtock from Kastrup in Denmark (McGrail 2001:242). Goodburn rejects the Southwark planking as

reverse clinker, pointing out that as conventional clinker (i.e. the other way up) it is perfectly consistent with various 'apple-cheeked' river craft of the period as well as surviving vernacular types both in England and on the continent (Goodburn 2002: 189). As for the futtock, its eroded state may have suggested reverse clinker but Crumlin-Pedersen was of the opinion that it came from a conventional Nordic vessel with an atypical upper plank (McGrail 2002:242). Indeed parts of the futtocks of some Swedish clinker vessels described in chapter 4, where the planking sequence changes, if seen in isolation would look similar.

The weight of evidence seen so far therefore suggests that reverse clinker, if used at all in the medieval period, was rare and not characteristic of the major building traditions. Similar cautions must surely apply to the so-called 'hulk-style planking' and 'collars'.

Hulk planking

In appearance the most obvious characteristic of the New Shoreham type is its exaggeratedly curved hull with planking running parallel to the sheer line. Greenhill's convictions about the existence of such ships were heavily influenced by apparent ethnographic parallels that he recorded in Bangladesh. Not only were some boats built using a reversed clinker technique but they had parallel bottom planking terminated, not at a stem or transom, but in a run of horizontal planks (Greenhill 1995: 254, fig. 325). As noted, he also offered an explanation for the parallel arrangement of plank ends by relating it to the construction sequence of building in reverse clinker. But not all the vessels he observed with 'hulk-style' planking were built in reverse clinker. So if the use of reverse clinker in medieval shipbuilding cannot be demonstrated, might there be another explanation for these planking systems?

In those images where the artists have chosen to represent the ship with more realism, for example the Southampton seal (Fig. 5.6), the Danzig seal of *c.* 1400 (Fig. 5.12) or the St Davids Cathedral misericord (Fig. 5.13), it becomes clearer what is being done. The lower planks of the bow are led into the stem in a conventional manner. It is only the higher strakes that sweep upwards into a platform or castling. The explanation is related to capacity. This is a clinker hull built to provide more capacity and better support for the more substantial upper works that were becoming common at this period. In fact many of the earlier images without such structures also show the same distinction between lower and upper planks such as the 'hulk' from a *Life of St Thomas of Canterbury, c.* 1230–40. (Hutchinson 1994:51), or the Holkam Bible image shown in figure 5.10. So it is only the most exaggerated forms typified by the New Shoreham seal that convey the impression that all the planks run parallel, perhaps for reasons discussed below.

So the Bangladeshi planking systems are not necessarily associated with reversed clinker construction. If this is doubted one only need look at remarkably similar plank arrangements in the lower hulls of postmedieval Dutch and English carvel vessels, also built for capacity. In the case of flutes, such as the *Anna Maria* (1709) sunk at Dalarö (Petersen 1987; Rönnby and Adams 1994:79–89), the Jutholmen wreck, *c.* 1700 (Cederlund 1982) and the English brig *Severn* (1834) lost near Herrhamra (Rönnby and Adams 1994:111–121), the bottom strakes run parallel to the keel and are terminated by the next run of planks. These, having run along the turn of the bilge, pass around the forebody, the lower ones running into the stem at an angle and the higher ones terminating at the horizontal wales (Fig. 5.14). In clinker construction it is not feasible to cut one line of strakes with another in this way. Nor in planking a bluff bow, can all the planks be brought to the stem unless they are drastically tapered. A remedy available to carvel builders was to reduce the number of planks with the use of stealers but this was not generally done in European clinker building. The answer was to limit the taper of the lower planks and continue

Figure 5.12 A town seal from Danzig, dated *c.* 1400 AD (After Waskönig 1969).

Figure 5.13 Misericord in St David's cathedral, Pembrokeshire. Late 15th–early 16th century (Rees 1995:7).

Figure 5.14 Like the English built *Severn* and the Dutch fluit *Anna Maria*, the Jutholmen wreck, a Dutch fluit built around 1650, shows a typical planking pattern to accommodate a bluff, full bow (J. Adams).

Figure 5.15 Comparison
of generic clinker
planking of the Viking
period (left) with a
system of late medieval
planking where the
upper strakes run into
the castling as in the
Danzig seal of 1400
(right) (J. Adams).

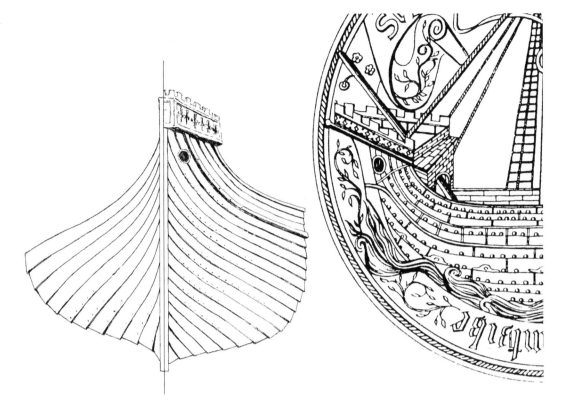

the upper ones with the sheer, up the platform
or castling as in the vessel shown in the Danzig
seal (Fig. 5.12, and 5.15). These planking patterns
are therefore a response to hull form, developed
in various regions by builders of both flush-laid
and lap-straked hulls

Collars

Perhaps the most enigmatic feature, the so-called
collar now makes more sense. Rather like the
banana-shaped hull, collars seem to be a feature
of the earlier more stylised images, rarely shown
if there is any superstructure or where there are
'stem-ropes' – in which the forestay lashed around
the stem in some way. Its representation as a collar
rather than a strop, etc., could simply be a stylistic
convention but as Greenhill (2000:7) suggested,
in the absence of a platform or castling as in the
earlier vessels, some sort of reinforcement at the
plank ends might have been necessary such as
the binding shown in the John of Worcester
Chronicle (1118–40).

Banana boats and stylistic convention

The last of the 'hulk' characteristics is also related
to issues of representation. The hull shape has
been seen partly as a product of the supposed
manner of construction as well as the known

mercantile function of hulks recorded in historical
sources. That it fitted the most commonly
believed etymology of the word only strengthened
the impression derived from the images. The
nature of imagery has been the focus of
considerable analysis. In the immediate context
of medieval ships, significant work includes Moll
(1929), Ewe (1972), Villain-Gandossi (1985,
1995) and more recently Flatman (2007). One
commonly acknowledged reason why ship images
on seals and coins are obviously distorted is said
to be because of the circular space within which
the ship has to be rendered (e.g. Vallain-Gandossi
1995:173). This does not apply to manuscript
illuminations or the vessel on the font at
Winchester, yet the shapes are remarkably similar.
Villain-Gandossi (1995:171) is nearer the mark
in observing that the ship's hull is never the most
important element in what is being portrayed or
rather of the meaning being conveyed. With the
number of times an image may be re-used or
copied, particularly long-lived motifs can become
accepted norms of representation. The use of a
compact, banana-shaped, archaic ship became
just such a norm and has remained in use for
centuries. Clues as to how the shape became
accepted as ship-like in the first place may be
related to the ways artists attempted to render

vessels seen foreshortened at sea or in harbour. Prior to the principles of geometrical perspective being understood in the 15th century, artists nevertheless tried to represent objects in ways that took account of what was visible and what hidden. The 14th-century image referred to above (Fig. 5.11) is a case in point. For although the artist's representation of the construction detail and rig is fantasy, the foreshortened hull as a three-dimensional form is shown quite successfully, even though it predates the earliest known geometrical perspective painting by Massaccio (around 1428). The resulting shape is very similar to the exaggerated banana-like hull of New Shoreham and the like. Small boats too were commonly represented so foreshortened that they seem almost folded in two. This can be the case even in relatively late depictions which are otherwise accurately detailed and realistic. Examples include two of the boats rescuing survivors from the sunken *Mary Rose* in 1545. The engraving is of a lost contemporary painting formerly at Cowdray House.

Similarly, the impression that the entire hull was composed of planks running parallel to the sheer line may be a result of drawing vessels as seen on the water. The upper planks would be visible sweeping down towards the waterline then up again to the other end. The lower planks running into the stems would not be so prominent. An artist unconcerned with reality and drawing only the upper planks might well create an image like New Shoreham or those on gold angels and, as already shown, once an image becomes culturally accepted, like the spurious Viking helmet with horns, it can be long-lived and resilient.

Conclusion

The hulk has posed a continuing problem in the understanding of medieval shipping because we have been looking for what did not exist. The tantalising but as yet unseen shipbuilding tradition is a myth. The early medieval hulks differentiated from keels for tax purposes might have included sea-going examples related to the Utrecht type trading between the low countries and London but we await further evidence of them doing so in any numbers. Even at that period the term might also have related to vessels of foreign origin with certain charateristics and functions rather than vessels from a building tradition which was of little concern to the authorities.

We can be more definitive about the late medieval hulk: the term was probably used more or less casually to refer to any generically large cargo vessel, rather than the product of a particular building tradition. Indeed, Glasgow suggested as much (Glasgow 1972:103–4). In northern Europe the obvious candidates were the large, capacious, clinker-built ships, i.e., a development of the Nordic tradition. It had already proven capable of generating hull forms of bewildering variation (Åkerlund 1951; Bill 1995, 1999). Clinker ships of 30m length or more were not uncommon and it is these that challenged the cogs, the largest known of which (Bremen) is only 24m long. Cogs also had a lower block coefficient than contemporary, full-hulled clinker ships. Figure 5.14 illustrates the planking systems of fine hulled Nordic construction compared to a bluff-bowed vessel with high block coefficient. It produces the characteristic lower hull where planks run to the stem in the normal way and the upper strakes continue up into the castling.

Clinker-built vessels, such as the Bergen 'great ship', the large clinker ship found in Sandwich, Kent, U 34, *Ringaren*, Guernsey 6, 7, and 8, and the 'Copper wreck', all may have been called hulcs in some places by some of the people who saw them, just as we know many large clinker vessels owned by Gustav Eriksson Vasa in the 1520s were. This concept of a hulk also makes sense of its equivalent terms used in France, the Atlantic coast and the Mediterranean, for example *hurque* or *hulcque* in France and *urca* in Portugal, Spain and Italy. These too were hulks and, as seen in the 16th-century English correspondence cited in chapter 4, by that time a hulk could be either clinker or carvel depending on the context and region of its production. This therefore is why nothing distinctive of a third great medieval building tradition enduring alongside keels and cogs has been seen in the archaeological record. It is a cautionary tale of how we synthesise data from different sources. Documentary records plus iconography do not necessarily equate to archaeological reality.

We now return to the carvel and the rapid developments that comprise its second flowering in northern Europe as the power of the ship begins to be fully exploited.

Note

1   *Ringaren* (the ringer) is the name given to a late medieval shipwreck that lies in 22m of water off Flatvarp in Sweden. This site was investigated during the 1970s and 80s by Nils Svenval, who then published his findings in a PhD thesis (Svenval 1994). In it he proposed that the ship could be termed a *Baltic carrack*, in view of various structural characteristics, including the framing arrangement and the method of joining the planks. Svenval was not a diver and relied on volunteer divers for detailed evidence of this kind. While the report provides an excellent overview of the ship and its cargo in particular, subsequent investigation of the site has demonstrated that many of its constructional features are not as Svenval believed (Rönnby and Adams 1994:35; Adams and Rönnby 1996:96). The hull is conventional clinker and as such falls squarely within the Nordic tradition.

6

Shipwrights, Status and Power

In the second half of the 16th century, a new type of ship appeared in England embodying fundamental changes that had occurred in almost every aspect of shipbuilding. The apparent suddenness with which this vessel burst upon the scene once caused a certain amount of puzzlement, though its antecedents can now be seen in the first generation of carvel ships such as the *Mary Rose* and other contemporary types. In other words, referring back to the closing emphasis of the previous chapter, there is a more diachronic quality to the interplay of events than was once realised. The apparent rapidity with which the new forms appeared was partly due to the way they were represented in iconography. Early 16th-century depictions of large merchant vessels and royal ships were highly stylised and emphasised the towering castle structures. As well as being the basis of the vessel's defence, in their use of architectural motifs they were also associated with power, status and importance. One of the very few broadly contemporary illustrations of the *Mary Rose* that survives is a good example, as indeed are all the illustrations in the manuscript from which it comes (Fig. 6.1). The 'Anthony Roll' is an illustrated manuscript presented to Henry VIII in 1546 by Anthony Anthony, an officer in the Royal Board of Ordnance, as part of *'A Declaration of the Royal Navy'* listing naval ships, their ordnance and other equipment. With the discovery of the real ship it could be seen how various elements had been depicted in the painting. Some were reasonably accurate but others had been either exaggerated or ignored. This is not surprising as the representations of each ship, though individual, are only a few centimetres across. Neither was accuracy a necessary adjunct to the function of the document. However, there are similar problems even in much larger works. A painting probably dating from the 1540s showing Henry VIII embarking at Dover in 1520 depicts similar characteristics. Fifty years later illustrations of ships are becoming less stylised as artists absorb the new conventions of perspective and proportion. The few finds we have of ships from this era show markedly less discrepancy with their representation in art. Now that we have a few archaeological finds from both eras these are very revealing when examined along with the iconographic sources. One can identify precursive features in the earlier vessels, see structural and stylistic relationships between them and later forms, and discern other connections as well as prominent features representing major change. For example, some of the ships depicted in the series of prints engraved in the 1560s by Frans Huys, after paintings by Peter Bruegel the Elder, show remarkable similarities to the *Mary Rose*, in particular one that has been designated 'an armed merchantman' (Fig. 6.2). Yet continuity does not mean 'sameness' for we are dealing with what is effectively a second generation of English carvel building. We see modifications in design procedures, associated changes in hull form, radically altered construction techniques, new configurations of rig, and as a result new capabilities. While all this happens within the established carvel building tradition, its comprehensive and wholesale nature arguably makes it as much of a revolution as the adoption of carvel building itself a century or so earlier. The breadth and depth of these changes also indicate that vessels of the first and second

generation of carvel building were being used in very different ways directly related to contemporary perceptions and needs. The causes and contextual circumstances in so far as we may unravel them are the focus of this chapter. What becomes apparent as one weighs the various factors that promoted change as well as those that resisted it, is that Elizabeth's ships were not simply bigger and/or better versions of those of Henry VIII. Their differences are altogether more complex.

Precedents

Despite her ignominious loss in 1545, as Admiral Howard had discovered in 1512, the *Mary Rose* in her original form had proved a highly successful vessel, possessed of both remarkable speed and manoeuvrability:

> *The Mary Rose, Sir, she is the noblest ship of sail and a great ship at this hour that I trow to be in Christendom. A ship of 100 tons will not be sooner about than she.*

By the middle of the 16th century, ships with carvel-built hulls and carrying ordnance in the manner of the *Mary Rose, Peter Pomegranate* and the *Henry Grace à Dieu* formed a large proportion of Henry VIII's fighting navy (as opposed to transports, barges and the like). Their appearance

demonstrated a decision to change the way warfare was conducted at sea. But radical though they were, to a great degree these ships represented a compromise. For the first time they carried integrated batteries of ordnance suitable for long range bombardment but were still capable of being used in the same fashion as the previous generation, i.e. resolving an engagement by boarding and hand to hand combat. Nor was commitment to the great sailing ships wholesale.

While the *Great Harry* represented one extreme in terms of size, propulsion and armament, at the other were vessels that attempted to combine the manoeuvrability of the oar-powered Mediterranean galley with the robustly constructed and heavier armed sailing ship of northern Europe. The smaller versions appear to have been called 'rowbarges' and the larger ones 'galleasses' or 'galliasses' (Fig. 6.3). Both figure in various manuscripts, paintings and inventories of the period. It has often been suggested that they were not a success (e.g. Anderson 1926:133) but they cannot have been complete failures either. In particular, four ships built in 1545/6 to similar specifications are illustrated in the Anthony Anthony Roll of 1546 and judging from their successive re-buildings must have been regarded as successful, at least in terms of their hull form and sailing characteristics. These were the *Bull, Greyhound* and *Tiger* of 180 tons and the *Hart* of

300 tons. They lasted a relatively long time for wooden ships. The *Hart* and the *Greyhound* were rebuilt in 1558, the latter being wrecked off Rye in 1562 (Oppenheim 1896a:123). The *Bull* was rebuilt in 1570 without oarports and finally broken up in 1594. The *Tiger*, also rebuilt in 1570 without oarports was being used on the Roanoake voyages in 1585 (Glasgow 1966:115–21; Quinn and Quinn 1973 *passim*; Durant 1981 *passim*). So rather than being failures as ships, it is more accurate to say that the direction in which naval development progressed removed the need for vessels of this type.

In any case, in the context of ship development, it is as components of the Tudor navy as a whole that they are of particular interest. For in effect this was a period of experimentation. Other ships depicted in the Anthony Anthony Roll, and in other iconography such as the Cowdray engraving (Fig. 6.4) suggest that between the two extremes represented by the carrack-like *Great Harry* and the oar-propelled rowbarges, there were already

Figure 6.4 Detail from an engraving of a topographical painting of the scene at Spithead on July 19th 1545. It was painted soon after the event and is surprisingly accurate. It was formerly in Cowdray House but destroyed in a fire. To the left of centre, the masts of the capsized *Mary Rose* show above the surface. Behind her the *Henry Grace à Dieu* (*Great Harry*) engages the French galleys, backed up by a large three-masted ship and various galleasses and rowbarges.

medium sized, relatively heavily armed, three-masted sailing ships with considerably lower castle structures than the great ships. Indeed, careful examination of the *Mary Rose* sterncastle structure indicates that it was never quite the towering edifice depicted in the Anthony Anthony Roll. Interestingly, the Cowdray engraving does not emphasise this aspect of the larger ships as much as Anthony's more stylised manuscript illuminations. This may reflect the purpose of the original painting (now destroyed) from which the engraving was copied. It was a pictorial document of the attempted French invasion of 1545 in which the *Mary Rose* was lost. It shows, in panoramic view, the whole of the eastern Solent, Portsmouth, Southsea, the Isle of Wight and the positions of the two fleets. Distinctly different ship types are shown and this, together with the general accuracy of topographic, architectural, military and costume details, suggests their representation could be more reliable than its relatively simplistic style suggests. The sunken *Mary Rose* is shown capsized on her starboard side at a severe angle of heel, lying roughly north-south. The masts still show above the waves indicating the approximate depth of water. All these things, together with the position of the catastrophe relative to Southsea Castle, where Henry VIII watched in horror, were born out by the excavation of the wreck following its discovery in 1967–1971.

It is impossible to judge the degree of intentionality or to what extent there was any co-ordination in the construction of the various ship types. Nor can we know the extent of any formal, central appraisal of their performance or how consciously the successful qualities of these mid 16th-century vessel types were integrated into later design and construction. But all of these things must have happened to a degree, for the net effect was that the ships built in the third quarter of the century undoubtedly combined the best characteristics of the various types afloat thirty years before. The new vessels were strongly constructed yet fast and sleek, heavily armed yet nimble and manoeuvrable. In effect qualities of the *Mary Rose* had been combined with those of the galleass. As more emphasis was now placed on long range gunnery, fewer soldiers were carried. This allowed a reduction in the fore and after castles which dramatically improved sailing qualities. The rig was also improved. The cut of the sails was changed from the more voluminous courses carried by the earlier carracks, becoming

flatter and as a result much more efficient (Anderson, 1928; Lees 1984; McGowan 1981:25). As with any ship type, they were a compromise but they seem to have been a fairly happy one, proving adaptable and successful in a number of roles. While much of the experience and knowledge that influenced the building of these vessels was undoubtedly home-grown, there must also have been a measure of influence drawn from foreign vessels, for in outward appearance there were undeniably similar characteristics between the three-masted English ships of the 1570s and those of France, the galleons of Spain and Portugal, the pinnas ships of Holland and the kravels of the Baltic. Phillips (1994:99) has pointed out that much writing about the characteristics and relative merits of these ships has been distorted by nationalistic preference. As we shall see however, as well as the general qualities referred to, there was a difference of substance that reflected English circumstances, needs and priorities.

The developmental path towards these new vessels was by no means straightforward nor was it obvious to much of the contemporary society. This applied both to those who actually built ships, those who co-ordinated and managed the practice and those with the power and resources to have them built in the first place. We know there was vigorous debate among those who had influence over shipbuilding, concerning the qualities that ought, as a matter of policy, to be incorporated in Her Majesty's ships. The person most associated with this debate was Sir John Hawkins, who was Treasurer to the Navy between 1578 and his death in 1595. Another was Sir William Wynter, Surveyor to the Navy between 1557 and 1589 and also an accomplished seaman. While they were hardly personal friends, quite the opposite, they certainly had a clear idea of the ships they wanted built. Ranged against them were those who disputed the necessity of change or the superiority of the characteristics Hawkins proposed (Oppenheim 1896a:127). He wanted low, sleek, vessels manoeuvrable enough to avoid being boarded and heavily armed enough to win an engagement by bombardment (even if the final victory involved boarding). Conservative opinion favoured the older 'high-charged' ships. Clerk of Ships, William Borough, irritated by the effect of Hawkins' strenuous rebuilding programme, charged him with turning them all into galleasses (Williamson 1941:355). In the event Hawkins' views held sway for several reasons. Quite apart from his position of influence, his case was immeasurably strengthened by being one of the most accomplished seamen of his day. As well as Wynter he also had the firm support of Mathew Baker, equally as eminent in his profession as Hawkins was in his. By implication, Hawkins' supporters must have included Peter Pett, also highly respected, the other of Elizabeth's Master shipwrights at this time, for he was building similar vessels to Baker (Glasgow 1964:186). Finally, Hawkins was able to call on personal experience and this must have weighed most heavily against his opponents' views. Hawkins was not advocating new untried qualities. He was pointing to examples already afloat.

Of the personal experience referred to, one of the events commonly held to have stiffened Hawkins' resolve in these matters occurred during his privateering exploits in the Caribbean for Queen Elizabeth. This was the violent engagement with the Spanish in the harbour at San Juan de Uloa in 1568. Anticipating trouble, he had moored his ships, the *Jesus* and the *Minion*, with stern lines. When trouble duly erupted he hauled his ships clear of the Spanish to prevent their getting close enough to board. Although heavily outnumbered, he proceeded to bombard them to such effect that he sank the *Capitana* and another vessel and caused a third, the *Almirante*, to explode (Waters 1949: 97; Unwin 1961; McGowan 1981:24). Although the *Jesus of Lübeck* was fairly heavily armed, she was a lumbering veteran of carrack-type, (having been in the Navy since purchased by Henry VIII in 1544). The lesson of experience was in two parts, firstly the devastating effect of stand-off gunnery, and secondly, the obsolescence of a ship like the *Jesus*. She had to be abandoned while Hawkins made his getaway in the more nimble *Minion*. This was not the only such incident he could call on. Only the year before, a close friend, George Fenner, in the *Castle of Comfort*, had fought off seven Portuguese ships in a two-day gun battle off Terceira (Waters 1949:98).

That Hawkins' views prevailed is often cited as one of the saving graces in the subsequent Armada campaign of 1588. By this time England's naval force included enough of these fast, manoeuvrable ships, if not to defeat the Spanish Armada, at least to enforce its continued defensive posture until its inherent logistic problems and the elements took effect (McGowan 1980; Martin and Parker 1988).

Cod's head and Mackerel's tail

As for their name, the terms 'galleon', 'Elizabethan galleon' or 'race-built galleon' have all been used to describe them, more for convenience than accuracy, as the word 'galleon' was very little used in England at the time (Glasgow (1964:177; Phillips 1994:98). Yet it may be significant that the term 'galleass' was clearly used to refer to a specific ship type in England, whereas the vessels they helped influence were usually simply called 'ships' both by those who built and those who sailed them. Whatever their nomenclature, nowhere are the processes of this revolution more beautifully illustrated than in the earliest known English manuscripts connected with ship design. These are a collection of notes, drawings and ship drafts by none other than Mathew Baker. He became Master Shipwright by letters patent in 1572; hence his influence as a supporter of Hawkins' energetic advocacy of the new form. Although Baker's drawings are the first known designs for English ships, recent work referred to in chapter 4 has strongly indicated that the principles involved had been used in the design of the *Mary Rose* (Barker and Loewen pers. comm.). Baker's drawings, together with those of John Wells, to whom he left them in his will, are collectively known as '*Fragments of Ancient English Shipwrightry*' now in the Pepysian Library, Magdalene College, Cambridge (MS 2820.). The folios of Baker's work fall broadly into two categories: The first are more highly finished, being watercoloured and were presumably intended to convey aspects of ships and their design to others. They include illustrated notes on shipbuilding in earlier times, midship sections demonstrating various methods of deriving hull form, and presentation drafts of complete ships or hulls. It is these watercolour drawings that have been so often reproduced. One of the most striking is the image in which the body of a fish is superimposed onto the lower hull to indicate the ideal hydrodynamic shape (Fig. 6.5). This was held to be a combination of the head of a cod and the tail of a mackerel. The second category consists of working drawings, many of which show alternative or experimental geometric constructions and added notes or arithmetical workings (Fig. 6.6).

As far as the designs are concerned, the drawings in '*Fragments*' show the outward appearance of these ships and various methods of drafting the lines from which the ship would

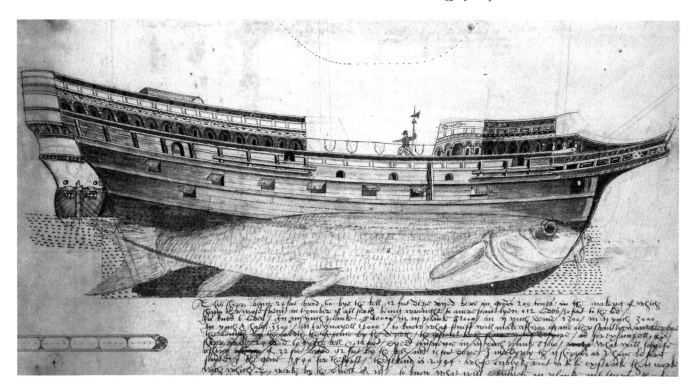

Figure 6.5 (above)
Illustration from
Mathew Baker's
*Fragments of Ancient
English Shipwrightry*,
MS 2820, Pepys Library,
Cambridge (Courtesy of
the Pepys Library,
Cambridge).

See also Plate 14

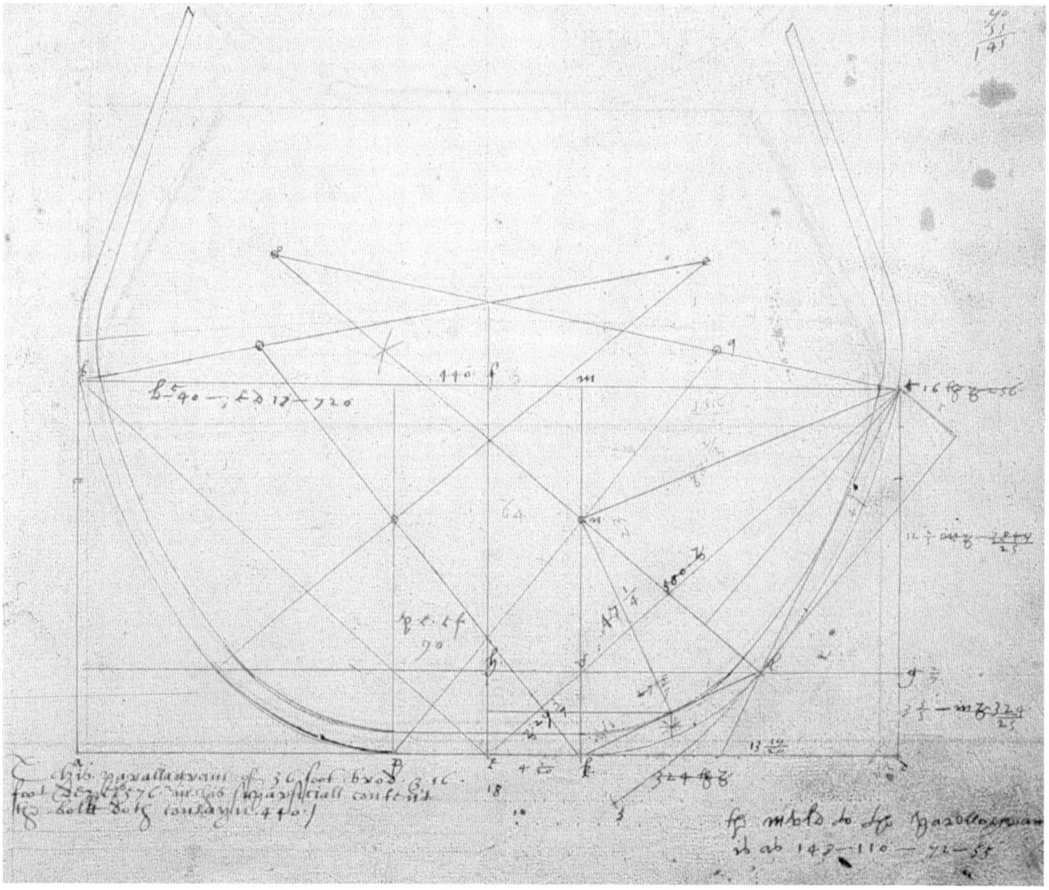

Figure 6.6 Illustration
from Mathew Baker's
*Fragments of Ancient
English Shipwrightry*,
MS 2820 (Courtesy of
the Pepys Library
Cambridge).

be built. As they are chiefly concerned with the philosophy and procedures involved in developing hull form, there is little information concerning the actual construction. So, while Baker lays bare many of his ideas about how ships should be, until recently we have not been able to see how they were translated into reality. For this we need parts of the ships themselves but no ship designed by Baker has been discovered. However, the design methods used by Baker's contemporaries were similar in principle, so the discovery of any vessel of this type would increase our understanding of the technology of early 17th-century shipbuilding. This would provide a basis from which the underlying influences and pressures that led to wholesale changes in shipbuilding could be discerned and understood in a wider social context, which after all is where they are rooted. Just such a discovery was made in Bermuda in 1958.

Sea Venture

Historical context

With the founding of Jamestown, Virginia, in 1607, England finally established a precarious foothold on the North American continent. Unlike previous unsuccessful attempts by individuals like Humphrey Gilbert and Walter Raleigh, this enterprise had been backed by the powerful syndicate of the Virginia Company of London. For while there was undoubtedly strong political backing and a heavily ideological component to colonial expansion, the more overt and pragmatic motives were commercial. The whole concept of the new 'plantation' was very much a commercial enterprise in which investors, or 'adventurers' were sought to fund the project – hence the term 'venture capital'. Energetic marketing of the opportunities is evident in the various pamphlets published, enthusing about the opportunities for profitable investment for those with the necessary capital, and of a rich new life for prospective colonists (Wingood et al. 1986:1).

Unfortunately, as those who bravely ventured themselves rather than their money found out, 'New World' reality was more harsh. The first colonists were not, as a group, ideal in terms of their backgrounds or their skills. This was undoubtedly one of the reasons the settlement did not quickly achieve self-sufficiency. The humidity of summer fostered disease. The numbing cold of winter demanded an adequate

diet, something that the first dismal attempts at agriculture could not provide. If that were not enough, the indigenous Indian population was, with good reason, decidedly hostile. The upshot was an appalling mortality, and only the annual supply fleets, bringing more colonists, stores and equipment kept the colony going.

In a determined attempt to put things on a stable footing, the Company assembled a fleet of nine vessels in the spring and early summer of 1609 to carry 600 colonists to Jamestown. This was to be the 'third supply' and after a rendezvous in London they made their way to Plymouth, the final port of embarkation. The flagship was the *Sea Venture*, which at 300 tons was '*the strongest and newest of our fleet*' (Jourdan 1610). The admiral of the fleet was to be Sir George Somers, a West Country seaman like Hawkins and Drake. He could also claim to have been one of Queen Elizabeth's élite sea captains and had commanded some of her most famous ships including the *Vanguard*, the *Swiftsure* and the *Warspite*. *Sea Venture*'s captain was Christopher Newport, also a veteran Elizabethan privateer. Acknowledged as one of the finest navigators of his day, he had also captained both previous fleets to Jamestown. Also to sail aboard the flagship was Sir Thomas Gates, Governor designate of the colony, who had with him a company of soldiery under Captain George Yeardley.

Sea Venture's history prior to being commissioned by the Virginia Company is at first sight obscure. Contradictory statements about the date and place of building have become ever more confused in transmission from one publication to another, now compounded by some utterly bizarre entries in web sites. Many authors refer to the ship being recently built (Kennedy 1971:26), newly built or indeed on its maiden voyage (e.g. Karwoski 2004:8), being built in East Anglia (Doherty 2007:18) or more specifically in Aldeburgh (e.g. Wright 1960; Raine 1987). Although one of the East Anglian yards is certainly possible at this period, the origins of this information are obscure. None of the authors cited here provide references.[1] The reference to *Sea Venture* being new may derive from Jordan's account cited above. 'New' of course is a relative term and some have interpreted this to mean that she was built in 1608, a 'factoid' that the archaeological evidence does not support.

As it happens, the historical record provides a strong contender in a '*Seaventure*' that had been built in 1603 and used in the cloth trade with the low countries. Intriguingly she disappears from the record when one of her owners, the prominent London merchant Lionel Cranfield, sold his share in the ship the very day before the Third Supply left for Virginia (Peterson 1988:45). What heightens this coincidence of dates is the relative rarity of the name *Sea Venture* (or variants thereof *Sea Adventure*, *Seaventure*, etc.) at this time. Other circumstantial evidence includes the fact that three of the other owners of Cranfield's ship became members of the Virginia Company prior to the departure of the Third Supply. It is also likely that Christopher Newport knew or at least knew of Peter Motham, the man who had been Master of *Sea Venture* and also a part owner. Indeed it was Peter Motham and an unnamed friend who purchased Cranfield's share of the ship on June 1st. Might that friend have been Newport?

This perfect circumstantial fit is only spoiled by puzzling references to the ship's tonnage as being variously 250 tons (PRO, SP 14/8/58) and 120 tons (PRO, E 190/12/3). For we are told that the *Sea Venture* of the 'Third Supply' carried 150 people and was around 300 tons, and this is borne out by the remains on the seabed. There are many reasons why tonnage figures can be recorded incorrectly accidentally or intentionally and one or other must be the case here. Firstly, we know that Cranfield's *Seaventure* carried eight minions and eight sakers. This would be too great a weight of ordnance for a ship of 120 tons (cf. Lavery 1988:12) but quite in keeping for a vessel of 300 tons. Another significant statistic concerns a letter sent to Cranfield by one of his factors which refers to two anchors, one broken and another lost, both of 12 cwt (Peterson 1988:44). According to Mainwaring's formula of 1cwt for every 25 of the vessel's tonnage, these would also be far too big for a ship of 120 and theoretically too big for a 250 ton vessel, especially two of them, presumably bower anchors. It is however, exactly consistent with the figure of 300 tons.

Given the above it would be strange if Cranfield's *Seaventure* and the *Sea Venture* of the Virginia Company were not one and the same ship. But if *Sea Venture's* history, strictly speaking, remains unproven, what happened after the fleet's departure from Plymouth on June 2nd 1609 constitutes one of the great stories of the sea. We are fortunate to have two highly detailed first hand accounts of the voyage written by William Strachey, Secretary to the Virginia Company, and

Silvanus Jourdan. Their vivid and evocative words best describe the ensuing events:

> *...upon Friday late in the evening we brake ground out of the Sound of Plymouth, our fleete then consisting of seven good ships and two pinnaces, all of which from the said second of June until the twenty-three of July, kept in friendly consort together, not a whole watch at any time losing the sight of each other... We were within seven or eight days at the most by Captain Newport's reckoning, of making Cape Henry upon the coast of Virginia: when on St. James his day, July the 24th,... the cloudes gathering thick upon us and windes singing and whistling most unusually,... a dreadful storm and hideous began to blow out the Northeast...*

> *Swelling and roaring as it were by fits, some houres with more violence than others, at length did beate all the light from heaven; which, like an hell of darknesse turned black upon us... Six and sometimes eight men were not enough to hold the whipstaffe... by which may be imagined the strength of the storme in which the sea swelled above the clouds and gave battel unto heaven. It could not be said to rain: the waters like whole rivers did flood in the air.*

Even allowing for a certain amount of poetic licence, this was no ordinary storm but a hurricane. The fleet was scattered, though amazingly, all except *Sea Venture* and the unfortunate '*Catch*' until then towed astern, eventually made safe haven in Virginia. *Catch* was never seen again, and for *Sea Venture's* company, this was the beginning of a four-day nightmare. As the ship rapidly began to take on water, they were divided into three shifts in order to maintain day and night bailing and pumping. Heavy equipment and guns were jettisoned in an attempt to lighten the ship but to no avail. The water in the hold, though held in check by superhuman effort, could not be reduced. As exhaustion set in they began to resign themselves to the inevitable. So it must have seemed like divine providence when after three and a half days of continuous struggle and with all hope lost, Admiral Sir George Somers sighted land. It was the Bermudas, or as they were known at the time: 'The Isle of Devils'.

Newport probably knew well enough where they must be, though that realisation was apparently little comfort to the ordinary crew. The fearsome reputation of the Bermudas had made them the place mariners most wanted to avoid, inhabited, it was believed, by demons and evil spirits and constantly racked by storms. With no choice in the matter, Newport tried to bring the ship to shore by picking his way through the reef, but three quarters of a mile out the ship lodged solidly in a 'v' shaped cut and stuck fast. In moderating weather, the whole company was safely ferried to shore in the boats. They found the Bermudas not a place of evil spirits but an island of benign climate and of plenty.

A revealing postscript to this particular aspect of the story occurred in 1989 when, after hurricane Dean had passed very near Bermuda, the wind directions that a ship in *Sea Venture's* circumstance would have experienced became clear. As a tropical storm moves in a generally northerly direction any ship to the west of its track could well be hit by north-easterly winds just as Strachey says. Once overtaken its direction would be dictated by the track of the storm, in this case to Bermuda. On the morning after hurricane Dean had moved north west of Bermuda the seas all around the island were still very rough, except the stretch of water over the reef where *Sea Venture* lay. That was almost flat, bringing to mind Governor Nathaniel Butler's words of 1620 describing the circumstances by which *Sea Venture's* company reached the shore:

> *...behold sodenly the wind gives waye to a calm.... and with extreame joye, almost to amazednesse, arrived all of them in safetye on the shore...* (Lefroy 1882).

Historical and archaeological evidence indicate that in the ensuing weeks repeated journeys were made back to the stranded vessel to salvage belongings, stores and equipment. They also removed timber, fittings and rigging for the building of two new vessels: *Deliverance* of 80 tons, under the supervision of Thomas Gates on St George's island, and *Patience* of 30 tons under the supervision of George Somers on the main island. In these two little ships they finally continued their journey to Jamestown after ten months on the Bermudas. In fact two men stayed behind, one who utterly refused to leave and another, under stay of execution for murder, absconded the night before embarkation. These two were later joined by a third when Sir George Somers returned for supplies (Wingood et al. 1986). Many more would probably have preferred to stay on Bermuda, for they knew only too well what rigours awaited them in Jamestown.

In due course news of the miraculous 'wreck and redemption' reached England, including the first hand accounts written by Strachey and Jourdan. They would have been shown to many, including those investors most closely involved in the enterprise. One of these was Henry Wriothesley, Earl of Southampton, who also happened to be the patron of William Shakespeare. It is presumably through Wriothesley that Shakespeare either got to see these 'repertories' or at least know details of their contents, for the very next year (1611) he wrote '*The Tempest*'. This is far more than a literary curiosity, for the play, while clearly basing its plot on the 'wreck and redemption' of a ship's company cast ashore on an enchanted island, is also rich in symbolism and allusion. Many of the audience would have recognised the parallels between the castaways of the play and European colonists and also the repression of indigenous peoples, for whom Caliban is a metaphor. It is a powerful indication of the significance of these early colonial ventures, not only in terms of their commercial potential but also their national and ideological importance. Hence *Sea Venture*, in marking the beginning of the island's permanent settlement and being the 'Tempest wreck', has a high symbolic profile, not just in the island's history but in its collective modern consciousness. Archaeological work on this site has therefore been an activity of sustained prominence in the media, as much to do with its iconic role in the genesis of the island community as with its acknowledged archaeological importance.

The island's qualities did not go unrecognised for long and it bacame a colony in its own right in 1612. As for the *Sea Venture*, the last recorded sortie to salvage from the site was by Governor Nathaniel Butler in 1620, who raised

> *a very fayre saker...a great shete anchor...divers barres of iron and steele, with some pigges of leade* (Lefroy 1882:290).

By this time the hull must have been substantially reduced and had presumably subsided to the gully floor. Eventually the remaining structure and contents were assimilated into the sandy deposits.

Discovery

In 1958, Edmund Downing, an American working on the US Airforce Base on Bermuda, set out to look for the wreck of the *Sea Venture*. He was descended from George Yeardley, Thomas

Gates' Captain of Soldiery. As a keen diver, Downing obviously saw finding the wreck of the ship on which his ancestor had reached Bermuda as a particularly attractive goal. After some historical research he reasoned that manoeuvring his boat over the reefs towards Bermuda in an attempt to follow the path of the stricken vessel might yield results. After many attempts, on the last dive of the season, he dropped anchor over a promising looking cut in the reef, donned his equipment and swam down. The gully floor was almost entirely covered in coral sand but gently fanning it away revealed flint pebbles. In a few places around the edge of the gully, dark eroded wood just showed above the sand. These were the oak timbers of a shipwreck and the flint pebbles were its shingle ballast. Ed Downing had found the *Sea Venture*.

At the time however, its identity was far from secure. After some further investigation by Downing, who could only pursue the work in his spare time, the Bermuda Government contracted Teddy Tucker to excavate the wreck. As the assemblage of recovered material grew and various structural features became apparent it seemed increasingly certain that this was indeed the *Sea Venture*. That was until photographs of a cast iron gun Teddy Tucker had raised were sent to the Royal Armouries at the Tower of London. In their opinion the gun seemed to be 18th-century, hence much too late to have been on the *Sea Venture*. Perhaps due to this, the project lost momentum and the site was subsequently closed down until the Bermuda Maritime Museum re-opened the files in 1978. A new phase of work was supervised by Allan Wingood and succeeded in putting the identity of the wreck beyond reasonable doubt (Wingood 1982). In 1982, with the importance of the site readily apparent, the 'Sea Venture Trust' was formed. The archaeological work of recording and reconstructing the hull now described was largely done under its auspices, in liaison with the Bermuda Maritime Museum (now the National Museum of Bermuda) where the archive and collection would reside.

Site formation

The ships considered in chapter 4: *Mary Rose*, *Elefanten*, and the 'Kravel', all comprise relatively well preserved sections of hull structure. Where less of the hull survives, as in the case of *Sea Venture*, some comment needs to be made about

the level of inference possible, especially as in this case a fairly comprehensive reconstruction is attempted from what are, by comparison, fragmentary remains. Of ships that wreck in tropical and sub-tropical environments, more often than not little survives of the hull structure. As discussed in chapter 2, it has often been assumed that a shipwreck is the chaotic result of natural forces. When faced with what appears to be a random scatter of more durable artefacts such as ceramics, ballast and lead shot, it is easy to understand how early workers failed to discern significant patterning in their distribution. However, a growing body of work has demonstrated that most wreck sites are anything but chaotic (Muckelroy 1975, 1976, 1978; Murphy and Johnson 1993; Ferrari and Adams 1990; Tomalin et al. 2000). On the *Sea Venture* site, as on the *Mary Rose*, analysis of the formation processes explained the presence/absence, distribution and condition of various classes of material that otherwise could not have been used to develop subsequent interpretations. In this sense it could be classed as middle range theory, integrated at one level with the raw data, being concerned with how the data came to be as observed, and at another with wider social considerations concerning the ship as 17th-century material culture (Merton 1968). In distinguishing between the component processes that form archaeological deposits various models have been developed. For terrestrial contexts Schiffer's concept of transformation (Schiffer 1987) draws a distinction between 'C Transforms' (those processes that were cultural in origin) and 'N Transforms' (transformation due to natural processes). In many of the events described above the human element is obvious. The process of wrecking too, though induced by natural forces, was clearly affected by human strategy. The subsequent salvage, also a cultural activity, was apparently extensive and long term. Both processes of wrecking and salvage are also implicated in the way natural environmental conditions on the wreck site acted upon the remaining material.

In the understanding of wreck sites, a seminal work that most closely paralleled Schiffer's was that of Keith Muckelroy. Rather than distinguishing between cultural and natural processes, he developed the concepts of 'extracting filters' – those mechanisms that removed material from the assemblage and 'scrambling devices' –

processes that reorganised materials in various ways. In *Sea Venture's* case, the equipment thrown overboard during the storm and subsequent salvage activities, particularly their selective nature, are examples of materials extracted from the assemblage. Various natural phenomena including wave action and the biogenic processes described below could be regarded as scrambling devices. However, the word 'scrambling' implies that the component processes are random, unpredictable and that their products are therefore unlikely to facilitate reconstruction. In fact much of Muckelroy's work, as well as more recent research (in particular Tomalin et al. 2000) has demonstrated that both his 'scrambling devices 'A': *The process of wrecking* and 'B': *Seabed movement*, include component natural processes that obey physical laws and which can therefore be modelled and reconstructed. In particular, understanding sediment transport mechanics in and around wrecks (Richardson 1968; Caston 1979; Quinn et al. 1997, 1998), has demonstrably improved understanding of the resulting assemblage and surviving associated structure (Rule 1982:44, Adams 1985:276–287; Ferrari 1993). At the time Muckelroy was able to report that there was no evidence suggesting that marine worms might have similar consequences to earthworms, as highlighted by Atkinson (1957) and of burrowing creatures analogous to moles and rabbits (Muckelroy 1978:181). Since then Ferrari and Adams (1990) have drawn attention to various species that are now known to be responsible for marked biogenic modifications of seabed deposits in and around wreck sites and which could have major implications for the survival, visibility and location of archaeological material. However, the organisms observed on the *Sea Venture* site do not appear to have transferred archaeological material from one layer to another or obscured interfaces between layers. They have almost certainly increased oxygenation of the deposits and this may have accelerated erosion and organic breakdown. Shipworm (*Teredo Navalis*) has in some cases destroyed timber elements entirely, particularly outer hull planks. This was a component process of site formation that also affected distribution of some classes of material (Adams 1985:280; Ferrari and Adams 1990).

Although there will always be lacunae in the evidence, if attention is paid to all the component processes of site formation, and to the fact that the principles of archaeological stratigraphy (Harris 1979, 1989) apply equally under water, a high degree of reconstruction may be possible, working from the fragmentary archaeological remains back to the original entity. Here lies the basis for the application of middle range theory in which analysis of the cultural and natural formation processes facilitates a greater level of inference to be drawn from the activities that led to the deposition, in this case the voyage, the stranding and the subsequent salvage. In turn this facilitates a greater understanding of the use of this vessel in the context of English colonial expansion.

Preservation and distribution

As Muckelroy observed, the wrecking process actually begins some time before a vessel actually sinks. This was certainly so in *Sea Venture's* case, a struggle to stay afloat lasting four days during which both the social and physical organisation of the ship had largely broken down before the ship struck the reef. Indeed an entirely different organisation had been imposed that at least partly removed the distinction between crew and passenger, and between those of different social and professional status. Some of the component events in this process can be identified from the archaeological record and in the historical sources: Damage during the storm to structure and rigging; probable springing of hull timbers with associated caulking loss allowing water to enter the seams; sediment in the limber passages preventing efficient use of the pump; emergency repairs carried out in order to reduce leakage with contents of the hold rearranged to gain access to leaks; splitting and spoilage of various containers in the flooded hold; jettisoning of heavy equipment including guns. These events, compounded by salvage activities, clearly affected what classes of material were subsequently represented on the site, what condition they were in and where on the site they were found.

Identification

Although details of the artefact assemblage is not of direct concern here, it was instrumental in putting the identity of the wreck beyond reasonable doubt. After examining the whole assemblage available up to 1981 Ivor Noël Hume said:

I have neither seen nor heard anything that precludes your ship from being the 'Sea Venture'. On the contrary, all the artefacts that I have examined are consistent with stores, possessions or cargo likely to be found aboard an English ship lost c. 1610. Collectively, however, they are quite definitely not what one would expect to find aboard a Spanish, Dutch or French vessel of the same period (Wingood 1982:346).

Together with the structural evidence and other materials such as the ballast, the case is closed. It is to the hull we now turn, as it embodies the substantial design changes that occurred in the time between the loss of the *Mary Rose* and the end of the century.

Hull Structure

As a result of the circumstances of wrecking, the majority of *Sea Venture*'s surviving hull structure comprises one integral unit, with various other elements such as fittings and fastenings lying on and around it (Figs 6.7 and 6.8; Plate 15). This may also have been partly promoted by subsequent salvage activity, for had the would-be colonists not removed much of the upper works and rigging for the construction of their new ships, subsequent storms might have fractured the hull and distributed it over a wider area. As it is, 15.5m of keel survive overlain by 14 floor timbers, and some internal planking. Although this is a relatively small proportion of the total hull, its survival as an articulated assemblage has preserved a great deal of information concerning hull form, construction and use. Its coherence has also been critical for the subsequent attempts at reconstruction described below.

The hull slopes some 18 degrees to the port, and due to the relatively shallow deposit, less of the higher starboard side survives. There are only a few fragments of outer hull planking, no ceiling, and some floors have been eroded almost in as far as the keel. A few first futtocks remain, again foreshortened by erosion, although in one slightly deeper pocket of sediment, two first futtocks in better condition flanked a relatively well preserved second futtock. On the port side the situation is better as the structure has been preserved by a greater depth of deposit including a substantial quantity of ballast. The floors amidships survive to their original length and support three runs of ceiling planks within two adjacent sleepers (stringers).

The keel is of oak (quercus) and is between 335–345mm (*c.* 13½ inches) wide amidships and tapers towards the bow and stern either side of the midship frames. Its original depth is uncertain

due to erosion but where it was possible to gain access it was still around 330mm deep. Originally it was probably at least as deep as it was wide. Sutherland (1711) gives 14 inches square as the midship keel dimensions of a ship of *500 tuns*. The keel was probably constructed from three timbers, the two forward sections of which comprise the surviving length. The aftmost section survives only as short dislocated fragments. Forward, the keel survives as far as the beginning of its scarf with the stem. Aft, the keel ends at what also appears to be an eroded scarf joint, but the joint between the two integral pieces is well preserved. This joint is tabled vertically (as are the other two), sealed with a luting compound of animal hair and tar except at the edge of the keel where oakum appears to have been used. A shallow rebate was cut into the top of the keel along the line of the joint. Capping pieces were let into this, also sealed with tar and hair. One end of the joint is hidden by a floor timber but it appears that one length was used to cover the main diagonal seam, while small pieces were placed over the butt ends. The visible end of the main capping piece was fastened with a small dowel and a spike.

To accommodate the rising line of the floors, a sloping ramp of timber was built onto the ends of the keel on which the floor timbers were erected. There are two such pieces above the forward end of *Sea Venture*'s keel. They are trapezoidal in section and are simply butted together. The aft section is rebated (although only by some 50mm) into the forward face of a floor timber. A sloping channel has been cut into it that would have allowed water to pass down to the limber channel proper and hence to the pump. The forward section either continued and tapered into the stem or into a run of timbers forming a kind of inner stem. In later periods this was the 'apron'. However, it is not certain that *Sea Venture* would have had one, or that if such timbers existed they would have had this name. As this particular timber is unlikely to have run very far before tapering off against the stem or being scarfed into another, it is therefore 'dead' in the sense that its function is more to provide a platform for the rising floors than to function as a primary strength member.

The surviving floors are all oak, and are cut from one piece of timber. They cross the keel and are bolted and/or treenailed to it. In the midship area they are around 305–330mm (12–13 inches) moulded. They diminish in size forward and aft.

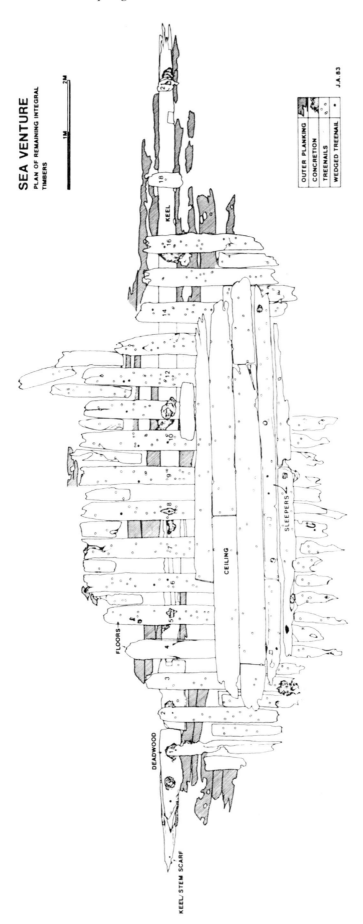

Figure 6.7 Plan of the hull remains of the *Sea Venture* (J. Adams, Sea Venture Trust).

Figure 6.8 *Sea Venture*, briefly uncovered for filming during the excavation season of 1986 (Photo: J. Adams. Courtesy of Sea Venture Trust).

Their quality also seems to diminish, for while they seem fairly well squared amidships, some, particularly those astern, are rather rounded and retain sapwood. On the underside of floors 4 to 16 a channel around 70–80mm square, has been cut to form a central limber passage, except in one case where the floor has been rebated over two wide slabs of timber with a gap between them forming the limber.

Unfortunately, the extent of erosion on the underside of the hull has robbed the joints between the floors and futtocks of some detail. However, taken collectively their primary characteristics can be outlined. The first futtocks overlap the ends of the floor timbers by a metre or more (3–4 feet) their squared butt ends lying about 1m from the keel. There were no direct fastenings between floors and adjacent futtocks. The latter seem to have been relatively short; perhaps around 1.5m, though erosion makes it difficult to be sure. It is probable that their upper ends were also plain butts. This might depend on whether the heel of the third futtock rested

on the end of the first or whether there was a gap or 'spurkett' (see below). The second futtocks lie at the ends of the floor timbers, overlapping in their turn the upper ends of the first futtocks. They appear to have butted against the floors in simple 'splayed' or angled butt joints rather than having a gap left between them as has been suggested on the basis of Navy Board models (See the lively debate in *Mariner's Mirror* between R. C. Anderson (1953:139), William Avery Baker (1954b:80–81), R. C. Anderson (1954:155–156), and William Salisbury (1954:156–159)). Unfortunately, none of *Sea Venture*'s second futtocks survive for anything like their original lengths. Nor do any timbers higher in the hull than the second futtock level survive in a condition that can provide detailed structural information. There are several timbers from these parts of the hull but they have collapsed out of position and lost their outer surface through degradation and erosion. Hence original dimensions and joint details, etc. are impossible to determine with any precision. Their positions can only give an approximate indication of where the timber might have been in the complete hull.

Due to the processes involved in the breaking up of the ship the underside of the hull is all very eroded. Therefore no outer hull planks have been seen that survive to their original thickness. In contrast, the inner surface is generally very sound, protected by sediment that had either already collected between the frames by the time the ship sank, or which found its way in soon after. Another reason for its preservation seems to be because it was scorched or charred. There are obvious signs of burning in many places, in some cases to the extent of causing the crazed, square pattern characteristic of partially burnt wood. However, this is only in the uppermost 1–2mm, and over the majority of the plank surfaces the charring has simply caused a black discolouration, indicating the process was carefully controlled. The charring extends over the majority of the inboard surface of the outer hull planks and had certainly been done before they were fastened in place. Charring is known to have been the technique used to soften the wood to facilitate planking the curved areas of the hull:

> *The ends of those planks that are bolted into the rabbet of the stem are called hoodings, which are more dangerous to spring than the rest because of the rounding of the bow, to which circle they grow not but are forced by burning to hollow somewhat near the matter.* (Admiralty Library MSS 9).

An archaeological example of this is provided by the Jutholmen wreck, a Dutch merchant vessel that sunk around 1700 near Dalarö, Sweden, and which was probably built around 1650 (Cederlund 1992). Scorching was noted on the curved planking (Cederlund pers. comm.).

An alternative was to heat the timber in wet sand. Both methods were superseded by steaming where the planks were heated in long steam boxes. However, most of the preserved areas of hull planking visible on the *Sea Venture* curves very little and would hardly have required this treatment in order to fit. This poses the question as to whether it might have been scorched for other reasons. One possibility is that, just as we have found the charred surface of these planks so well preserved after nearly four hundred years, so presumably would shipwrights have noticed during repair or breaking up old hulls, that charred wood does not rot. Knowing this was the case, charring as a general pre-treatment might well have become favoured by some shipwrights, if not common practice. A recent find on the Isle of Wight of a small carvel-built vessel also has scorched hull planks under the floors, i.e. in a flat part of the hull. The date of the vessel is uncertain at present. A dendrochronological sample has been dated to the 17th century but the lack of sapwood renders this a rough *terminus post quem*. The vessel may date from the 18th century. The fact that it exhibits several structural features that are seen in 17th-century construction is not surprising, as evidence from several building traditions attests to the longevity of some techniques and to their survival in the construction of smaller, local craft.

Unfortunately, nothing of *Sea Venture*'s keelson survives. The only remaining evidence of its existence is the cast impression of its underside in two of the keel bolt concretions. It was presumably a substantial strength member and, like the keel, would have been made of more than one section. The extent of concretion on the top of some floors indicates that, as one would expect, the keelson was through-bolted to the keel at intervals.

Three runs of ceiling plank survive, each becoming wider away from the keel (from around 420mm to over 500mm. These are large heavy planks, in places up to 80mm thick. They are solidly treenailed to the floors, and as such play an important part in hull strength. A gap between the innermost fastened ceiling strake and the keelson was filled with a series of short boards about 1.1m in length. These were limber boards and were not fastened so as to provide access to the space between floors. Their short length would have meant that any of them could be raised after shovelling aside a fairly small area of ballast.

Outside the ceiling planks, two heavy stringers, known at this period as 'sleepers' provided additional longitudinal strength, as well as binding the overlapping floors and first futtocks. They are substantial timbers, measuring up to 320mm wide and 160mm thick, which probably represents 12 × 6 inches. They were scarfed together to form a continuous belt of timber throughout the hull. However, the scarfs are fairly short and it is doubtful if they would have been a factor in their overall strength. Their longitudinal strength lay in the fact that they were overlapped and bolted as well as treenailed through to the frames. Their position served to provide a secure binding for the overlapping floors and first futtocks. Sir Henry Mainwaring in 'A Seaman's Dictionary' (1623) described them thus:

> *Sleepers are those timbers that lie fore and aft the bottom of the ship on either side of the keelson just as the rungheads do go. The lowermost is... bolted to the rungheads* [the ends of the 'rungs' or floors] *and the uppermost to the futtocks, and so these between them do strengthen and bind fast the futtocks and the rungs, which are let down by one another and have no bindings but these sleepers.* (Manwaring 1922:227).

For a ship of *Sea Venture's* size, there are likely to have been a series of three and this is suggested by the length of a bolt concretion in one of the floor timbers, which indicates that the adjacent timber would have been the same thickness.

The majority of hull fastenings are treenails cut from straight grained oak and finished to an approximate octagonal section with a draw-knife. This was the method used before the development of the moot, but it remained common practice to the end of the wooden shipbuilding era as will be seen in chapter 7. The average diameter (around 32–33mm) indicates that they were 1¼ inch treenails. At their inboard ends, some were tightened with wedges but most were not. Some were tightened with caulked cuts, though these were found where the surface of the timber was virtually pristine. More may have been tightened this way but are almost invisible in an eroded surface. However, even in the areas of generally uneroded timber, many do not appear to have been tightened in any way. This is not surprising if the treenail has been satisfactorily driven so its full width has emerged proud of the plank surface, especially where the planks are 70mm thick or more, as in the case of *Sea Venture's* ceiling. The treenails do not appear to have been driven in a strict pattern, although this is difficult to judge as most of the treenail holes will have been augered from outboard. However, a similar irregularity was noted in the outer hull planks of the *Dartmouth* (1690). It was probably intentional in order to avoid setting up lines of weakness, hence reduce the chance of the plank splitting (Martin 1978:48). This has certainly been the effect in *Sea Venture*. Another intentional variability that can be introduced when positioning treenails is to vary their angle slightly. This lessens the tendency for the plank to work away from the frame under stress. Many of *Sea Venture's* treenails show the characteristic elliptical section

that results from driving them this way. The impression that the variability in the position and angle of treenails was intentional is further reinforced by several cases where treenails have obviously been positioned very precisely when required.

A case in point may be a series of treenails that are placed exactly in a seam between two adjacent ceiling planks. A similar occurrence was noted on the *Dartmouth* (1690) (Martin, *ibid.*). In that case it was discussed whether this was pure chance or whether there might be some reason for intentionally driving treenails in this position. In Figure 6.7 it can be seen that although there are only three planks *in situ*, there are seven treenails that precisely cut a seam. That this should happen by chance seems unlikely, yet if it were intentional they would have had to have been driven from inboard. It also raises the question as to why it should have been done, as they can have no role in fastening the ceiling planks to the frames. Carvel hull structure depends for its integrity on the secure fastening of outer and inner planks to the frames. By definition there is no fastening between adjacent planks, and in many cases, as in *Sea Venture*, neither was there any direct fastening between the frame elements. For structural integrity there is a need to ensure that the two layers of parallel elements, i.e. the frame elements running one way and the planking running the other, cannot flex significantly in a diagonal plane. In many cases, due to the curvature and sheer of the hull, the timbers cross at a continually changing angle, something that automatically introduces a certain amount of longitudinal and diagonal bracing. The need for such bracing has been recognised at several stages in the building or rebuilding of large carvel hulls, the example of the *Mary Rose* (built 1510, rebuilt 1536, sunk 1545) being noted above in chapter 4. In her case the diagonal bracing is thought to be associated with the comprehensive strengthening necessary for the ship to carry the heavier battery of ordnance which it carried after 1536. In other cases, riders were fitted to older ships to reduce the working of an ageing hull. It is commonly asserted that merchant ships did not have riders as they reduce capacity. This is generally true but it was not unknown. Where there are no such heavy internal timbers incorporated in a hull structure (and there is no evidence for riders of any sort in *Sea Venture*) the lack of diagonal bracing is most acute in the more regular middle body of the hull where the frames and plank alignments are virtually at rightangles. By placing treenails along the seams in the manner seen in *Sea Venture*, the planks are effectively locked edge to edge. The so-called 'stopwaters' in keel joints, etc., provide a similar function. If this is so, such treenails might prove to be blind, i.e. only driven into the timber a few inches, rather than all the way through the hull. Unfortunately, it would be impossible to ascertain this without cutting out a section of the plank and floor timber, as the treenail wood is too degraded to attempt extraction.

A case where there is no doubt about the precision in which the treenails were placed is in the fastening of the garboard strake. As the hull lines become progressively finer either side of the midship section, there is a point where treenails start to be driven into the keel as well as the floor timbers (being impossible where the garboard is horizontal with the top of the keel). Obviously in this situation, treenails cannot avoid being placed along the same line, as the point of entry into the garboard is restricted by the height of the rabbet. However, this is alleviated by the garboard's extra thickness. Also, to achieve maximum cohesion, the angle at which the treenails are driven through to the keel is varied as much as possible in the vertical plane and quite considerably in the horizontal.

It is possible that not all the treenails in the ceiling plank were observed and marked on the plan, as even in Bermuda's waters they are often difficult to see. Even so, there is a distinct difference between the numbers visible in the ceiling planks and the number visible in the upper surface of the floors and most futtocks. This either suggests that the floors have been reused, or alternatively that the ceiling planks had been replaced. This is relevant in discussions of the age and origins of the vessel. We have one reference that refers to *Sea Venture* as the 'newest' in the fleet (Jourdan 1610). If Jourdan is right, then reused floors are a distinct possibility. Even if this is Lionel Cranfield's *Seaventure* built in 1603, would five years in the cloth trade have necessitated replacing ceiling planking of this thickness? If the floors are reused, this implies the ship from which they were taken had a compatible hull form and, as will become apparent, must itself therefore have been different from vessels like the *Mary Rose*. An obvious solution would be to date these timbers, though at the time of excavation removal of large enough samples for dendrochronological assay from such an iconic wreck caused concern.

Three decades on however, a new programme of work is planned that will include such sampling. As well as clarifying the date and status of individual timbers and perhaps the date of construction, it might also establish the region where the ship was built.

As well as treenails, some iron spikes were also used, probably for smaller internal timbers and repairs, etc. The major elements of construction were fastened with iron bolts. Amidships every third floor is bolted to the keel. Forward of the point where the deadwood begins every floor was bolted, though this may have included bolts that passed through the keelson as well. Astern the situation is less clear. The intervals are generally similar (every two or three stations) as far as the end of the central keel element. Beyond that some keel bolts were observed in a line, several still standing vertically, marking the line of the now degraded aft keel section. Their lengths and spacing would have provided invaluable information on the construction sequence and keel length, as well as what elements they might have been connecting. Unfortunately they were removed at some time in the late 1970s (Wingood pers. comm.). What is clear from the aft end of the middle keel section and the surviving fragments of the aft section, is that many of the timbers were not directly fastened to the keel at all. Amidships the intermediate floors are treenailed to the keel. Aft of frame 16 this is not the case. Therefore as the hull curvature became more pronounced towards the run, other arrangements were used. The forward rise of floor is assisted by two pieces of deadwood-like timber and it is possible that a similar arrangement was used in the stern. However, neither of the two fragments of the stern section of keel show signs of this. There was certainly no solid ramp of deadwood as extensive as that found in some later vessels. Arrangements seen in the *Elefanten* (chapter 4) and the *Sparrowhawk* (below) provide more likely parallels.

Iron bolts were also used to fasten the sleepers to the floors and first futtocks. Judging from the number of concreted bolts lying outboard of the main structure, as one would expect, they also provided the primary fastening for the stringers and knees above. The keel bolts all appear to have been clenched over washers but bolts from elsewhere in the hull were of the 'pin and forelock' type.

The rest of the structural inventory and associated fittings include various waterproofing materials associated with caulking and luting (a waterproof mastic applied to timbers before they are assembled), fittings such as rudder pintles, rigging elements: chains and deadeyes, repairs such as lead patches ('tingles') and 'Dutchmen' (wood pieces let into other elements such as planks to replace a defective area). In addition to the artefact assemblage, other significant materials include the shingle ballast, carried by English ships for centuries. As these classes of material are not directly relevant here, see Wingood 1982; Adams 1985; Wingood 1986; Wingood, Wingood and Adams 1986 for details.

Comparative material

One of the reasons the discovery of *Sea Venture* was so significant is because there are so few ship remains surviving from this period that fall within the same 'galleon-type' carvel building tradition. However, the following are among the most significant.

Sparrowhawk

In 1863 the timbers of a small ship were discovered in beach deposits in Orleans Marsh, Cape Cod. Historical research suggests this is the *Sparrowhawk*, lost in 1626 (Holly 1953). The timbers have been reassembled and are now on display in the Pilgrim Hall, Plymouth, Massachusetts. Although a much smaller vessel than *Sea Venture*, her timbers and general structural layout are similar. William Avery Baker

(1955:277) notes the keel is *c.* 28 feet (8.53 m) in length with a depth of around 9.5 inches (240 mm). However, there has inevitably been some radial shrinkage since these measurements were taken and this probably relates to the maximum depth amidships. The surviving framing consists of overlapping floors and first futtocks. As in *Sea Venture* they are not fastened to each other. Of particular interest is the arrangement of stern timbers as this part of *Sea Venture* does not survive. The lower part of *Sparrowhawk*'s sternpost survives and is rebated into the keel which, despite shrinkage, shows a distinct skeg. The joint is braced with a stern knee. A series of naturally grown, Y-shaped crooks continue the lower rising line of floor to the sternpost. The foremost of these stand on the keel, one side of the foot alternately let into the upper edge of the keel. The three aftmost crooks are variously rebated into the stern knee (Fig. 6.9). The lower limbs of these timbers stand in the space which in some later, larger constructions would be filled with deadwood. A method adopted in larger vessels, where finding timbers of this shape would have been both difficult and costly, was noted in chapter 4 (*Elefanten*). These *Sparrowhawk* timbers provide a possible analogy to *Sea Venture*, where between the bolted floors in the aft section of the keel (Fig. 6.7) the intermediate timbers, however they were arranged, were also not directly fastened to it.

Warwick

Lying in Castle Harbour, Bermuda, are the remains of another of the island's most significant shipwrecks, the *Warwick*. Like *Sea Venture*, she was on company business, though by this time it was the Somers Isles Company, an offshoot of the Virginia Company, formed in 1615 to administer the new colony. The *Warwick* was so named because she was owned by Robert Rich who had inherited the title Earl of Warwick in 1619 and who was a member of the new Somers Isles Company. That year the *Warwick* brought the new Governor Nathaniel Butler to Bermuda and was due to depart for Jamestown but while lying at anchor she was driven against the cliffs in a hurricane and lost. Due to the protected location and more heavily silted conditions, a large section of the hull has survived. Whereas in *Sea Venture* we have the flat of floor and part of the turn of the bilge, the remains of the *Warwick* comprise a large section of the starboard side (Plate 16). In this sense it is conveniently

Figure 6.9 Drawing to show construction details at the stern of the wreck believed to be the *Sparrowhawk* (1626) (J. Adams).

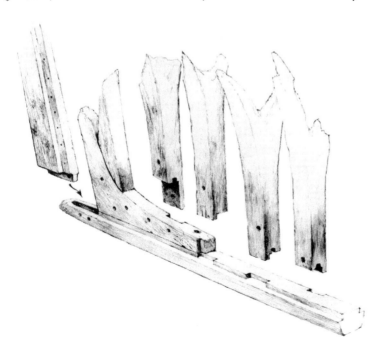

complementary to *Sea Venture* as the two ships were designed according to the same geometric principles. There are however, some intriguing differences in construction.

The wreck of the *Warwick* was extensively investigated by Teddy Tucker and a collection of artefacts are on display at the Bermuda National Museum. Drawings were also made which are on file at the Smithsonian Institute in Washington. With Tucker's kind cooperation two midship profiles were recorded by the *Sea Venture Trust* in 1988 (Adams and Rule 1991). On the basis of evidence he had seen in the hull Tucker believed the *Warwick* to be an old ship. In 1988 this seemed plausible because in some ways its structural layout resembled the *Mary Rose* of 1545 more than *Sea Venture* of 1609. For example the internal planking below decks, with its alternating arrangement of thick ceiling planks and even thicker stringers is similar to *Mary Rose* but very different from *Sea Venture*. The lodging knee arrangement is also similar to *Mary Rose*, as are some aspects of the framing. Of course we do not have *Sea Venture*'s structure at this height in the hull and it is certainly possible that it also had a similar deck structure arrangement.

In 2009, work was restarted on the *Warwick* and three seasons of work provided the opportunity not only to record the surviving structure comprehensively in three dimensions but also to carry out a comprehensive programme of dendrochronological analysis (Bojakowski and Custer 2010; Nayling 2012). This has shown that in fact the *Warwick* was a new ship, perhaps marking Rich's inheritance of his title. Although the ship was newly built, its resemblance to *Mary Rose* is not necessarily surprising. While the principles underlying its design were the same as those of *Sea Venture* (and *Mary Rose*) as will become apparent, *Sea Venture* was built according to a design method that represented the state-of-the-art in the early 17th century. The majority of shipwrights, perhaps including the one who oversaw the building of the *Warwick*, were using more traditional methods. In general the ship certainly seems to have been well built and the details of its design will become apparent when the current analysis is complete.

An intriguing aspect of the framing not seen in either of the other vessels (or indeed any other known to this author) came to light when the furthermost timbers that survive towards the bow were uncovered for the first time. This is the loof – the point at which the hull begins its curve through the bow to the stem. Here alternate futtocks were set at an angle to each other presumably in an attempt to integrate the diagonal bracing of a truss (Fig. 6.10). We do

Figure 6.10 Forward framing of *Warwick* near the bow (left) showing the alternate setting of the timbers. Fr 71 and alternate timbers running aft are set conventionally, perpendicular to the centreline. Timber Fr72 (far left) and the next four alternate timbers running aft are set at an angle (J. Adams).

not know how far forward this system went or in what way it related to the frames of the bow proper, particularly as they are canted in the opposite way to conventional cant frames. The system was not used in the main body of the hull or the part of the stern that survives and seems to be an ingenious way of stiffening an important part of the hull without the addition of riders.

Alderney

Discovered by divers off Alderney around 1990, this wreck was provisionally identified as the *Makeshift*, an Elizabethan vessel transporting arms that was lost off the Caskets in 1592. However, this now seems unlikely (Loades pers. comm.). Its finds assemblage consists of an impressive array of arms and armour but to date, little of the structure has been found. What has been seen so far is severely degraded and further work is projected to ascertain whether further, better preserved sections of structure survive elsewhere on the site. The rudder was raised in 1996 and its dimensions were used by Owain Roberts as a basis for reconstructing the hull (Roberts 1998). This is entirely possible theoretically (but see the comments below on reconstruction in general with regard to the *Sea Venture*). The finds and historical context of the ship are discussed in Bound and Monaghan (2001).

The Gresham Ship

In 2003, dredging operations in the Princes Channel of the Thames Estuary, by the Port of London Authority recovered parts of the structure of a timber wreck. Although it was severely damaged, underwater investigation by Wessex Archaeology resulted in the recovery of an anchor, four guns, some artefacts and five coherent sections of hull. Since being recorded, the anchor and timbers have been placed in an artifical lake to preserve them for further investigation if required.

Initially known as the Princes Channel wreck, one of the guns suggests a connection with the merchant Richard Gresham; hence the wreck's subsequent appellation (Auer and Firth 2007: 233). Dendrochronological dating puts the construction of the ship around 1570 (Nayling 2004). It was probably an armed merchantman and its size, estimated on the basis of its timbers, was between 150 and 250 tons (Auer and Firth 2007:234). Carvel-built in oak, it has some similarities to near contemporary vessels, for example the rebated joints between the ends of

the floors and the first futtocks are similar to those of the *Mary Rose*. A significant feature of the structure that has not been seen archaeologically before is that the ship had been furred, a remedial process carried out when a new ship was found to be too 'tender'. In other words the hull's righting moment was too weak and this necessitated increasing the breadth of the hull to stiffen it. One way this could be done was by simply adding a second layer of outer planking at and somewhat below the waterline. This was known as 'girdling'. Furring was a more drastic remedy where the outer planks were removed and large slivers of wood were added to increase the moulded dimension of the frames after which the planking was replaced. In this instance the breadth of the ship was increased by 300mm (approximately a foot) each side. Before shipwrights were able to mathematically predict performance these processes were not uncommon judging by the references to them in documents of the time (Mainwaring 1623 in Manwaring and Perrin 1922).

Principles of construction sequence

There is not enough of *Sea Venture*'s hull to determine every detail of the construction sequence but there is enough to indicate some of the fundamental principles involved in the lower hull, and these provide a solid testimony to the nature of 17th-century carvel building and its developments.

The keel was laid and the stem and stern assemblies were raised. Then some of the floors were laid across the keel and bolted in place. This would have included the midship floor and others at intervals along the hull. It was these that essentially controlled hull form. At this point ribbands were probably fastened along the ends of the rungs (floor timbers) at the sirmark of the floors and the first futtocks. The sirmark was the point at which the arc of the floor timbers met that of the futtocks. There was another at the junction of the second and third futtock sweeps. The ribbands were strips of timber that effectively acted as splines or battens, defining the longitudinal curvature of the hull. It was to these ribbands that the intermediate timbers were faired. The first futtock of each control frame may have been added at this stage for in one case in the accessible timbers a treenail was found that passed through a floor timber horizontally, and hence may have originally joined the first futtock to it. Such attachment can only have been to assist positioning during construction as it would have contributed little to hull strength.

At this point the garboard strake (the line of planking adjacent to the keel) was applied. Quite possibly more of the bottom planking was put in place as well, after which the intermediate floor timbers were fastened in place, though these were only treenailed at this stage. We know that at least the garboard was in place prior to the intermediate frames because treenails that fastened it to the keel were cut off flush with the top of the keel and some can be seen partially under the floors.

The keelson could now be bolted in place above the floors, the bolts passing through the intermediate floor timbers (hence the necessity of only treenailing them in the first instance).

The first futtocks that overlapped with the floors could now be put in place. They were not actually fastened to the floors in any substantial manner but simply overlapped. They may have been temporarily spiked to them to assist in positioning and then wedged in place by knocking in small blocks of wood between the floor and futtock. They were also supported by a line of props or 'shores'. This would have been a good reason to advance the planking out as far as the foot of the first futtock as this would have controlled the position and provided support.

The rest of the frame elements probably advanced in a similar alternating fashion. The second futtocks were probably set upon the ends of the floors but were not attached to them in any way. They were also shored and temporarily connected across the ship to each other with 'cross-palls' (temporary tie-bars). It is possible the third futtocks did not even rest on the heads of the first futtocks, leaving a gap called a 'spurket' (Manwaring 1922:233). Whether they did or not might have depended on how heavy the hull construction was required to be. A warship perhaps would have been more solidly timbered. The positions in which timbers have collapsed on the *Sea Venture* site make it difficult to say definitively but if the third futtock did rest on the first, here too there was no connection other than simple contact.

After this stage there are many possible sequences in which the rest of the principle elements could be assembled and above this point in *Sea Venture* we have no direct evidence.

Planking probably continued to be applied as the framing advanced. Once the framing was completed up to the level of the orlop deck beams, the internal planks could be fitted. The most important were the three runs of thick stringers or 'sleepers' that bound the overlap between the floors and first futtocks. Between these and the limber strake there was continuous ceiling and this was probably the case throughout the hold. This would have led up to a thick stringer or 'clamp' which effectively provided a shelf for the heads of the beams. Once this was in place, the beams could be fitted. Knees would have fastened them to the hull and they gained additional support from the stanchions mortised into the sleepers. As these beams appear to have been about six feet apart, the deck would have needed the fore and aft support of carlings rebated into them. Ledges or half beams would have completed the assembly onto which the planks were laid. As a merchant ship it is quite possible that *Sea Venture* had a run of undecked beams in the hold.

Beyond this point conjecture, albeit based on contemporary accounts such as Mainwaring, take over. However, the first stages of the sequence as deduced from the surviving hull tell us a great deal about the character of this phase of carvel construction. Perhaps the fundamental point that emerges is that the construction did not involve the erection of a complete 'skeleton' of frames prior to the planking being applied. As the vast majority of frame elements were not even fastened to each other, let alone scarfed, assembly must have been largely timber by timber. As so much of the subtle curvature of the fore and after bodies must have relied on the judgement of the shipwrights fairing the timbers to the form indicated by the ribbands (which could be adjusted if necessary), it is more appropriate to judge these ships as 'frame-led' rather than 'skeleton-built'. The latter term implies just the sort of free-standing framing system that is more typical of later 18th- and 19th-century practice in the larger dockyards. Although hull form and framing systems changed dramatically, the more organic, stepwise procedure of advancing the framing system and the planking, as in *Sea Venture*, had changed little in principle from the *Mary Rose* period. As will be seen, it not only continued in the smaller yards until the end of the wooden ship era in the 19th century but is still used in some parts of the world today.

Reconstructing Sea Venture

Although only a relatively small percentage of *Sea Venture's* hull survives, there is enough to produce a rather more extensive reconstruction than might be the case if one were dealing with other vessel types. This is because the principles of hull design demonstrated in the manuscripts of Mathew Baker and others are based on rules of proportion, geometric construction and arithmetic calculation. In principle, all the important dimensions of a ship can be determined on the basis of just one known value, such as the length of the keel or the main breadth. All other dimensions can be expressed as fractions or proportions of it. Hence from the relatively small proportion of *Sea Venture's* surviving hull, these rules can theoretically be used to reconstruct the missing parts. The problem is which rules. For each of the manuscripts and treatises that have survived vary from each other to a greater or lesser degree and would generate a concomitantly different result.

There have been several reconstructions of early 17th-century vessels attempted by various people for different purposes. Perhaps the first notable example in terms of scholarship and expertise was naval architect William Avery Baker's reconstruction of the *Mayflower* (1620). The *New Mayflower* was built at Upham's Yard in Devon in 1957 and was sailed across to America the following year. It is still afloat and on display at Plymouth, Massachusetts. Of the more recent projects, the most relevant for the *Sea Venture* is Brian Lavery's reconstruction of the *Susan Constant* (Lavery 1988). This vessel was directly comparable to the *Sea Venture* and although considerably smaller at 120 tons, the principles of her design, rig and general fitting out would all have been broadly similar. Another was Owain Roberts' reconstruction of the Alderney wreck (see above). In this case the reconstruction was based entirely on the height of the rudder.

These projects, together with various other reconstructions of English ships of this period, either on paper or in the form of models, have been based almost entirely on historical information. This exists basically in four forms: as descriptions of ship characteristics by contemporary authors such as Raleigh or Harriot; contemporary manuscripts relating to ship designs by working shipwrights or those directly concerned with their building; lists of dimensions,

armament or equipment resulting from surveys or other official procedures such as litigation; a few models, e.g. the so called 'Oxford Model' and the votive ship model of a galleon now in the Swedish National Maritime Museum in Stockholm (Kirsch 1990). It has been relatively recently that archaeology, through the excavation of surviving ship structure underwater has been able to furnish additional information. In this respect Brian Lavery's reconstruction of the *Susan Constant* was the first such project to be able to capitalise on this by incorporating information from the *Sea Venture*. Reconstructing the *Sea Venture* itself (at least on paper and with a computer) offered the prospect of taking the process one stage further, in that the historical manuscripts could be combined with the material reality of a known vessel.

The secret art

The procedure of hull design in the 17th century started with determining the principal dimensions of keel length, breadth and depth in hold. Governed by rules of proportion this might give ratios of 5 : 2 : 1, e.g. a ship with a keel of 60 feet would be 24 feet in breadth and 12 feet deep in hold. From these the other defining values such as the overall length, the height and rake of the stern post, sweep of the stem, etc., were determined. The actual shape of the hull could be generated by geometric construction. This essentially involved combining tangent arcs of circles of different radii (and later on more complex curves). The centre for each arc was either constructed geometrically or was a given proportion of one of the principal values such as the main breadth. Using these techniques the cross-sectional shape or 'body plan' of the hull was drawn, and the narrowing and rising of the hull fore and aft. Baker's Folio 19 is used to illustrate the principal dimensions and constructions that controlled hull form (Fig. 6.11). Figure 6.12 shows the midship section and the three tangent arcs which comprise the lower hull in Mathew Baker's Folio 35. The details of how this was done have been discussed at length by various authors, e.g. Baker (1954a), Lavery (1980, 1988) and more recently Barker (1994). Appendix 2 provides detailed examples.

In all methods it is the flat of floor and the radius of the turn of the bilge, the floor sweep, that are constructed or plotted first and which

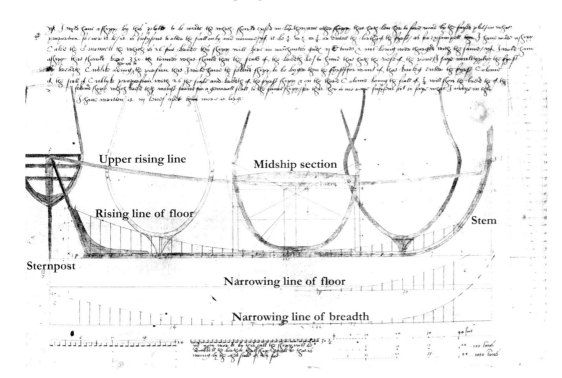

Figure 6.11 Mathew Baker's Folio 19, showing the principal elements of hull form.

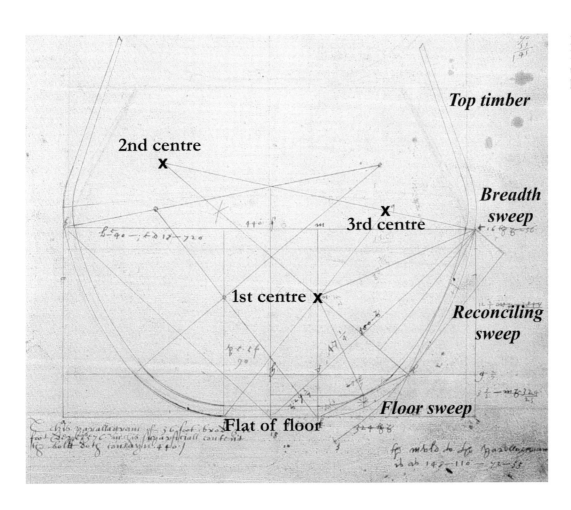

Figure 6.12 Mathew Baker's Folio 35 with the principal sweeps labelled.

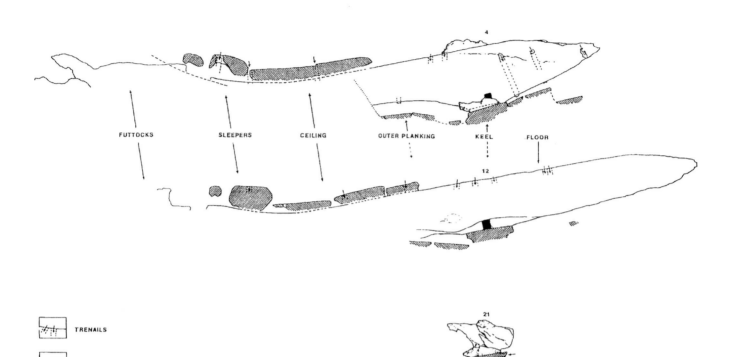

SEA VENTURE   sections 4, 12, & 21

FUTTOCKS   SLEEPERS   CEILING   OUTER PLANKING   KEEL   FLOOR

TRENAILS

CONCRETION

1 M

J A 84

Figure 6.13a (above) Three of the *Sea Venture* profiles drawn through the centre of each floor timber (J. Adams).

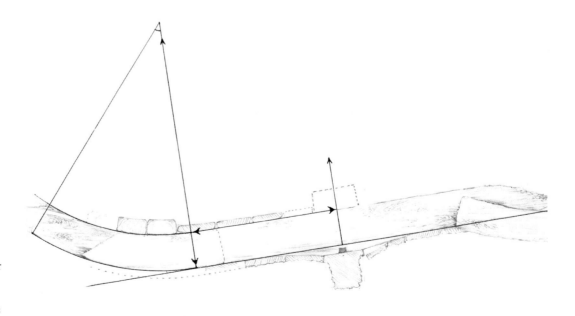

Figure 6.13b Diagram showing the flat of floor and the radius of the floor sweep in relation to the surviving timbers (J. Adams).

have most influence on the hull form. As it was exactly this part of *Sea Venture*'s hull that had survived, might both these values be determined from her timbers? In addition to plans and photomosaics, etc., the survey was directed to that end, in particular recording a profile along each surviving floor and any adjacent futtocks as accurately as possible (Fig. 6.13a). Each profile was drawn to a scale of 1:5. On those few floors whose upper surface was entirely exposed, the end of the flat of floor was identified as closely as possible underwater by placing a 1 m bar over the curve of the timber and sliding it back to the point where light could no longer be seen under it. Even given the hand-finished surface, the outer end of the bar would then be fairly close to beginning of the turn of the bilge. Even where the ceiling was still in place the seams were open enough to take measurements to the floors beneath, and while the edges of the ceiling itself were fairly eroded the surface of the floors were well preserved. However, the individual characteristics of hand-worked timber would make this variably accurate so other means were used on the drawing board once the profiles had been plotted. The radii were determined in two ways. Firstly a scaled series of concentric circles were used (similar to the procedure for determining pot circumference from rim sherds). Secondly, a geometric method was used. As the curve of the bilge is the arc of a circle, striking a series of chords through it enables the construction of a series of perpendiculars that will coincide at the centre of the circle. In practice a cluster of points is obtained from which the mean centre was calculated. The centre should in theory be vertically above the end of the flat and in general the results were reasonably close (Fig. 6.13b). This procedure was carried out on twelve timbers and the results are shown below.

Table 6a shows the values determined for the flat of floor and the radius of each floor timber. These procedures were repeated several times hence the value given for each radius and each flat are averages. The individual values for the radii were themselves averaged to give a working figure for the reconstruction. This was 7 feet 7 inches, including an estimated 10 inches for the depth of the floor at the 'rung head' (end or head of the floor) and taking into account very slight taper from the end of the flat to the rung head. The values for the flat of floor, as one would expect, show a reduction fore and aft of the midship point. Not surprisingly the pattern is not quite regular. The figure for floor 8 may be

too large. Similarly that for floor 11 too short. With those provisos, the flat amidship seems to be between 8 feet 2 inches and 8 feet 6 inches. From the table it seems as though *Sea Venture* had at least two frames either side of midship frame identical to it. This was a common expedient in merchant ships to produce a slightly fuller body and hence increase capacity. The number of identical frames could vary from one either side upwards.

With these two values identified with reasonable confidence, theoretically a set of lines could now be produced using a 17th-century method. How close this reconstruction would be to the original vessel and thus, how useful, depended on being able to identify which, if any, of the methods that survive is at all close to *Sea Venture*. As a fairly large merchant vessel she was capable of functioning as a warship if required. Hence one might expect that her hull would incorporate appropriate proportions. If she had also been fairly new and therefore Jacobean rather than Elizabethan, would her hull form have reflected the most up to date ideas on design or the practice of ten or twenty years before? William Avery Baker clearly felt that in the case of the colonial vessel *Mayflower*, at 180 tons, a somewhat smaller vessel than *Sea Venture*, the latter was more likely. That is why he based his reconstruction on Mathew Baker's folios in particular Folio 35 (Fig. 6.6).

In the attempt to reconstruct a viable set of lines from the remains of the *Sea Venture*, it was therefore necessary to compare the various methods of hull design that were current at the time, i.e. around 1603. The problem is that of the various manuscripts that survive, some are anonymous copies. Their dates, and thence the originals have been judged on the basis of the form of the writing, the style of the language, similarity to other sources, and other clues in the content and way the subject matter has been presented. The survey therefore included sources that spanned just over half a century either side of 1600, which could be taken as an approximate date for the method by which the *Sea Venture* was designed (Table 6b).

As well as identifying which method most closely matched the hull remains of *Sea Venture*, this range might also indicate the nature of any change in design that occurred over the period represented. All the methods are broadly similar in principle, varying only in detail. Hence they can be easily compared. They specify certain key proportions or ratios as described above but

Table 6a *Sea Venture*:
flat of floor and radii
taken from drawings of
each floor timber.

Floors (as numbered underwater)	Flat. Mean value in m/ft averaged from max/min measurements	Floor sweep (m/ft) estimated using concentric radii + 10" added for floor*	Rise of floor (mm)
3	1.1 = 3' 7"	7' 10" (2.39)	256
4	1.15 = 3' 9"	7' 10" (2.39)	186
5	1.2 = 3' 11"	7' 10" (2.39)	146
6	1.25 = 4' 1"	7' 9"? (2.36)	96
7	1.28 = 4' 2"	7' 6" (2.29)	96
8	1.3 = 4' 3"	7' 4" (2.23)	76
9	1.25 = 4' 1"	7' 3" (2.2)	76
10	1.25 = 4' 1"	8' 3" (2.51)	76
11	1.23 ?? = 4'	7' (2.13)	96
12	1.25 = 4' 1"	6' 10" (2.08)	106
13	Not surveyed		
14	1.15 = 3' 9"	8' 1" (2.46)	166
15	1.15? = 3' 9"	8' 1" (2.46)	156
16			196
	Flat amidships c. **8' 2"-8' 6"**	**Average 7' 7"***	

*Ten inches may be too much for the moulded depth of the end of the floor timbers, so 7' 6" is also possible.

usually in terms of minimum and maximum values that the prudent shipwright should stay within. When looking at several such works collectively the effect is to widen these parameters. For example if we are told in one document that a particular dimension can be between five ninths and three quarters of another, and in a second work that it can be between one half and seven tenths, the possible parameters now range from one half to three quarters. So unless one has evidence that points to specific methods the possible parameters for each of the design criteria are too wide for producing a useful reconstruction.

Hence in attempting to select the most appropriate values for a reconstruction of *Sea Venture*, the process has entailed trying to identify the methods closest in date, then determining a suitable mean value from as narrow a range as possible. The following tables (6b–6f) have been compiled from various manuscripts related to ship design dating from the mid 16th century to Anthony Deane's '*Doctrine*' of 1670 at which time some of the important variables stabilise. The earliest folios in Mathew Baker's *Fragments of Ancient English Shipwrightry* probably date from the 1570s. However, one of the drawings (Folio 13) is of the galleasses *Greyhound* built in 1545 and *Bull*, *Hart*, and *Tiger* built in 1546. The method of producing the hull shape in this drawing is a two-arc method and is different from

anything else in the collection. In view of its date it is interesting that it produces a rounded lower hull shape very similar to the *Mary Rose*. While it now appears as though she was designed using a three-arc method, this two-arc method is paralleled elsewhere, for example Fournier's 'old method' (1643) and Bushnell (1664). Also, in some of the moulds drawn by Baker, e.g. Folio 6 of the *Judith Borough*, a two-arc alternative is indicated. Does this represent an earlier and simpler form that became progressively less common as the 16th century proceeded? Not all the tables below are complete, either because the information is not available or not relevant to that particular manuscript.

As is apparent, even from a cursory reading of the data, there is a considerable range in the parameters of the various criteria. Of these, those that can be closely determined from the archaeological remains of *Sea Venture* are the flat of floor and the radius of the floor sweep. Draughting midship sections at a common scale using these various methods illustrates how they vary. Figure 6.14a shows four midship moulds superimposed. In order of age they are: Baker Folio 14 (an early four-arc method), Folio 35 (three-arc method), Wells (*c.* 1620), and Deane (*c.* 1670) both three-arc methods. The top timbers and second centres are numbered 1–4 in the same order.

Table 6b Manuscript and documentary sources.

Manuscript/folio	Possible date
Fragments of Ancient English Shipwrightry (Mathew Baker, John Wells) Pepys Library, MS 2820, Magdalene College, Cambridge: – Folio 13. (Midship mould of four galleasses: *Hart, Greyhound, Bull* and *Tiger* believed to have been built by Mathew Baker's father James).	As the vessels in question were built in 1545–6 and in view of the family connection, it is reasonable to suppose that this method was used around that date.
Fragments – Folio 11. A Venetian method on which several subsequent folios in the collection seem to be based.	Baker voyaged to the Mediterranean on a 'study visit' in the 1550s. The text says this method was used by the Venetians 'till within this 20 years'. If it was drawn around the 1570s this would imply the method was current at the time of his journey.
Fragments – Folio 10. The *Emanuel* (virtually identical to Folio 11)	1570s?
Fragments – Folio 15. Almost exactly reproduces the four-arc shape of Folio 11 but uses three arcs.	1580s?
Fragments – Folio 35. Possibly Baker's developed three-arc shape. A working drawing.	1590s? on the basis that it is significantly different from the moulds showing vessels of known date such as the *Emanuel* and *Foresite*.
Fragments – Folio 91. Almost certainly by John Wells the second author of 'Fragments', who inherited the collection on Baker's death in 1613.	1600–1620?
Thomas Harriot. Notes on shipbuilding. British Library. Not comprehensive but containing reliable core information. See Pepper 1981.	1608–1610
Admiralty Library MSS 9. Anon., though Salisbury (1958:2) suspected John Wells.	Salisbury estimated the date to be around 1620–25. It is very similar to Wells Folio 91.
Cambridge University Library **MSS Add 4005 Part 12** Anon. Recently discovered and dubbed the **Newton Manuscript** (Barker 1994) as it is filed with various documents in Sir Isaac Newton's hand.	c.1600.
Royal Institute of Naval Architects (**MS 798 The Scott Collection**). A copy of an anonymous work, though George Waymouth has been suggested.	Tentatively dated around 1600. John Coates (1981:285-6) thought 1595-1605, partly on the evidence of the watermarks. Lavery (1988:9) doubts the Waymouth attribution and thinks it is rather later. Certainly, dated watermarks would only provide a *terminus post quem*. Other characteristics might support Lavery, including designs for ships of a hull form that is more typical of the mid to late 17th century than c. 1600.
Dimensions of the *Royal Sovereign* built in 1637 by **Phineas Pett** (Perrin 1918; Anderson 1919; Abell 1948). Exact dimensions have been the subject of discussion (Anderson 1913, 1919)	First draft submitted 1634, adjusted thereafter.
'Doctrine' (Pepys Library, Cambridge, **MS 2910**) Midship section of a 70 gun ship by Sir Anthony Deane. See also Lavery 1981.	1670

Other comparative data are drawn from William Borough (c. 1600) and William Chapman Crane.

Table 6c Principal proportions of 16th- and 17th-century treaties and manuscripts.

MS	Keel Length:Breadth	Breadth:Depth	Flat of floor as % of main breadth
Fragments MS 2820/13	-	209:101 (48.3% of breadth) measured off draft	14.3%
MS 2820/15	-	207:112 (54% of breadth) measured off draft*	18.1%
MS 2820/35	-	8/9 of half breadth (16' depth to 18' half breadth). (44.4% of breadth)	By construction* which gives ½ floor of 4 1/20'. (22.5% of breadth)
Harriot	10:4 this work concerns small ships.	2:1	half the difference between breadth and depth, so 25% where depth is half the breadth but greater the less the depth.
MS 2820/91 (Wells)	-	For a ship of 36' breadth, depth = 15'6" (43%).	¼ of breadth (25%)
Admiralty Library MSS 9	Keel can be between 2 & 3 times breadth but recommends 25:9 e.g. 100:36	Can be the mean of ½ & ⅓ of breadth but recommends 7:3 so 36' gives 15'5" – though uses 15'6") (15.5% of L, 43% of B)	Can be between ¼ & ⅓ of breadth: for 36'; 9–12' Recommends ½ the difference (29.2%) but uses 9' (25%)
CUL MSS 4005/12	Breadth between ½ and ⅓ of keel	Depth between ½ and ½ of breadth	Between ½ and ¼ of the breadth (50–25%)
RINAS MS 798 (Scott)	-	40% of breadth	6' for a breadth of 20'. (30%)
Pett (*Sovereign*)	100:36.9 (Keel 126, breadth 46'6")	43% of breadth (20')	14' (30% breadth)
Deane MS 2910	10:3	36:13'8" (38% of breadth)	⅓ of breadth (33.3%)

*method of drafting produces a main breadth slightly wider than the grid

William Borough gives the proportions for general ships (presumably merchant vessels) as:
Length = 2.25 x Breadth. Depth 11/24 of the breadth, and for warships and galleons:
Length = 3 x Breadth. Depth = 2/5 of the breadth.

Table 6d Sweeps as proportion of main breadth (or given value).

MS	Floor sweep	Breadth sweep	Reconciling or futtock sweep
2820/35	Found by construction: approx. 64% of depth	By construction: approx. 70% of floor sweep	By construction from floor and breadth sweeps: approx. 77.5% of breadth
Harriot	From ½ to 7/12 of the half breadth	2/5 of the half breadth	17/10 of the half breadth (85% of main breadth
2820/91 (Wells)	¼ of breadth	24.3% of breadth	60.4% of breadth
MSS 9	Must be less than ½B & less than difference btwn. ½B & ½floor (18' - 4'6" = 13'6") Best is 1/3 of depth (15'6") + difference (13'6") div. by 3 = 9'8")	Can be equal (though not more) than floor sweep. Commonly ¼ breadth. Best proportion is as 15:19 of floor sweep = 7'8" (approx.). 21.3% breadth	No more than the breadth or less than half breadth. (Can be longer or shorter depending on desired fullness). Best is as 6:10 of breadth = 21'8"
Scott	30% of breadth	21.6% of breadth	65.1% of breadth
CUL 4005/12	¾ – ⅓* of the depth	¾ – ½ of depth	½ – ¾ of the breadth (50–75%)
Pett?	30% of breadth	23.5% of breadth	2/3 of breadth (66.6%)
Deane	¼ of breadth (9')	7/9 of the floor sweep (7') below the height of breadth and 17/18 of the half breadth above.	5/9 of the breadth (20') = 55%

* probably meant to be 2/3

Table 6e Proportions and sweep of top timbers.

MS	Height of top timbers	Breadth of top timbers	Reverse sweep
2820/35	Twice depth++	¾ of breadth (white lines suggest it could be between 2/3 and ¾).	¾ of the breadth
Harriot	Twice height of max. breadth	2/3 of the breadth	2/3 of the breadth
2820/91 (Wells)	Twice depth*	2/3 of the breadth	equal to the breadth
MSS 9	Twice depth*	Between 2/3 and ¾ of the breadth	equal to the breadth
Scott	Twice depth*	c. 70% of breadth	102.5% of breadth (20'6")
CUL 4005/12			c. 91% of breadth
Deane	Twice depth *	77.8% of breadth (*)	17/18 of the half breadth

++ refers to the height of the grid on which the mould is drawn, as the maximum breadth is in fact marginally higher.

* Height of maximum breadth in the mould, which in these methods equals the height of the grid.

(*) 4/6 of half breadth of floor = tumblehome, i.e. 4' for 36' breadth.

Figure 6.14a The midship moulds of Baker (F11 [1] and 35 [2]), Wells (F91 [3]), and Deane [4] superimposed. Showing the progressive drift in the principal design criteria (J. Adams).

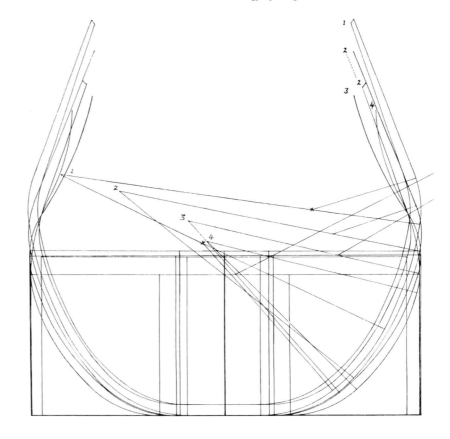

Figure 6.14b The same moulds as above but superimposed over the end of the flat. This shows that despite considerable increase in the breadth relative to the height, the curvature of the lower hull retains a similar character (J. Adams).

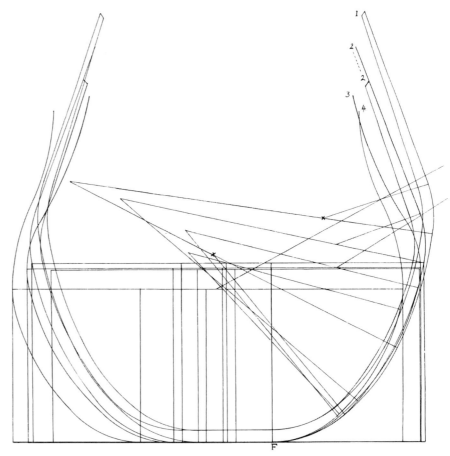

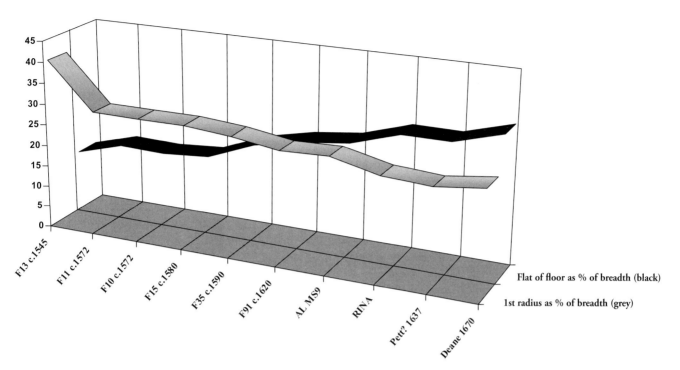

Figure 6.14b, shows the same moulds but aligned at the end of the flat of floor ('F'). This shows that despite considerable differences in the positions and lengths of the various radii, the curvature they produce is not dramatically different. The principal differences seem to be an increase in the breadth relative to the depth in hold and to the height of the upper works, together with a slightly more rounded lower hull form produced by a wider flat and a shorter second or 'reconciling' radius.

It also seems that the change is progressive throughout the period concerned, something that is shown even more clearly in graph form. Figure 6.15 shows the progressive change in the two criteria directly measurable in *Sea Venture*: the flat of floor and the radius of the floor timbers – the first radius or 'floor sweep'.

Early 16th-century vessels show a fairly deep, wedge-shaped hull and a narrow flat (around 14% of main breadth). By 1600 this had increased to around 20%. It appears to carry on increasing up to Anthony Deane's time. Thereafter it remains around 33.3% or a third of the breadth for some time. There are caveats to be born in mind of course, mainly concerning the size of the sample of surviving manuscripts. The examples used are those that appear to be generally of large merchant ships or warships. Other vessel types had wider and flatter hull shapes and are not directly comparable. The other problem is dating. There is no certainty that the chronological order in

which they have been arranged is correct. However, even if the most unreliably dated manuscripts are swapped around, it does not materially change the indication of fairly progressive change over the course of a century.

This steady change is also true for many of the other criteria governing hull form particularly the breadth sweep which also progressively decreases. Figure 6.16 shows the relationship of the flat of floor to the three other radii that constructed the hull: the floor sweep, the breadth sweep and the reconciling sweep. Likewise they are plotted as percentages of the main breadth. The peak in the reconciling sweep in the early moulds results from the use of four arcs instead of three. When Baker began drawing almost identical hull forms with three arcs his futtock radius (the second) was the average of the old second and third sweeps. Figure 6.17 therefore shows the same data but using a mean value of the second and third radii. If this is taken into account all the radii can be seen to reduce in contrast to the progressive increase of the flat of floor.

Now where would the values derived from the remains of *Sea Venture* lie on the graph? They appear to match the proportions in use around 1600–1620 quite closely. Similarly, using methods at either end of the time spectrum to reconstruct a hull on the basis of these dimensions produces hull forms unquestionably too large or small. The next step was to examine those methods either side of 1600 and see if any of

Figure 6.15 Graph to show the relationship between the flat of floor and the floor sweep over time. Against the vertical axis the two values are plotted as a percentage of the main breadth of the vessel. The horizontal axis shows the series of manuscript folios from *c.* 1545 to 1670 from which the criteria were taken (J. Adams).

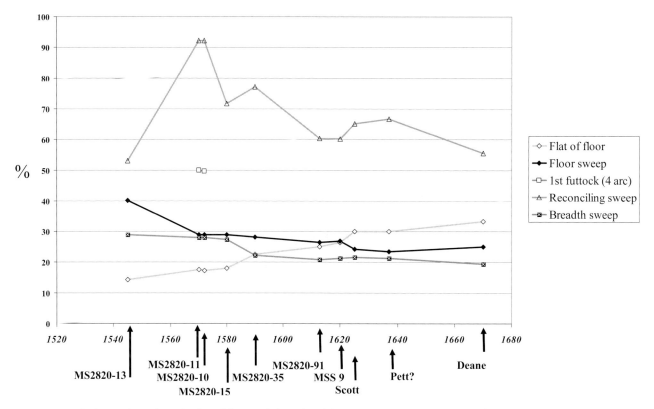

Figure 6.16 Graph to show the flat of floor and the radii of the tangent arcs as percentages of the main breadth (J. Adams).

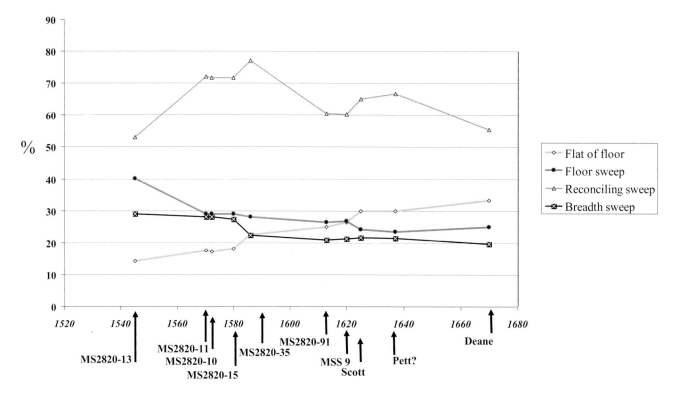

Figure 6.17 Graph to show the flat of floor and the radii of the three lower hull arcs as percentages of the main breadth. Second and third arcs of the early moulds have been averaged (J. Adams).

MS	Date	Flat of floor as % of main breadth	8'2"	8'4"	8'6"
2820/13	1545?	14.3%			
2820/15	1580s?	18.1%	45' 1"		
2820/35	1590?	22.5%	36' 3"	37'	
MSS 4005 (CUL)	c.1600	25%	*32' 8"*	*33' 4"*	*34'*
Harriot	1608	Half difference btwn B&D so 25%	*32' 8"*	*33' 4"*	*34'*
2820/91 (Wells)	1620?	25%	*32' 8"*	*33' 4"*	*34'*
MSS 9	1600 - 20?	Says between 25–33.3% Uses 25%	*32' 8"*	*33' 4"*	*34'*
"		Recommends ½ difference between ¼ and a ⅓ = 29.16%	*28'*	***28' 7"***	***29' 2"***
MS 798 (Scott)	1625 1600-1640?	30%	*27' 2"*	*27' 9"*	*28' 4"*
Pett (Sov. of Seas)	1637	30%	*27' 2"*	*27' 9"*	*28' 4"*
Deane's Doctrine.	1670	33.33%	24' 6"	25'	25' 6"

Table 6f The range of possible breadths using the maximum and minimum estimates of *Sea Venture*'s flat of floor (8'2" to 8'6").

them would fit the *Sea Venture* more closely than others. Firstly, the values for the flat of floor and the floor radius derived from the wreck were used to determine a range of main breadths using the proportions given in the various manuscripts (Table 6f).

Given that the weight of archaeological and historical evidence point to *Sea Venture* being around three hundred tons, the table shows that many of the calculated breadths fall outside the conceivable range for a ship of that size. Those in italics are possible. Those in bold italic seem the most probable.

Just as the proportions of the individual design criteria to the ship's principal dimensions can be used for comparative purposes so can the relationships between the criteria themselves. Hence the proportional relationship between *Sea Venture*'s flat of floor and the radius of the floor timbers was compared to that of the various manuscripts. Table 6g shows the proportional

relationship of the flat to the floor sweep. Table 6h shows the same relationship in the various manuscripts.

As with the calculated breadths, the closest correlation is with the Admiralty Library MSS 9. Therefore the conclusion is that *Sea Venture* had a main breadth of about 29 feet. The flat of floor and floor sweep would indicate a main breadth of around 29 feet 2 inches. Using MSS 9's length:breadth ratio would give too long a keel. However, using an average for merchant ships of this size, at this date: where the breadth was around 38–40% of the length, would give a keel between 72 feet 11 inches and 76 feet 9 inches. This also accords reasonably well with the archaeological evidence. MSS 9 says that the depth can be between a third and a half of the breadth and recommends the mean (15% of length) but this is less than most ships we know of for the period. What is more, MSS 9 actually uses 15.5% which accords with many large

Estimated flat of floor	Estimated floor sweep of 7' 7" as % of flat	Estimated floor sweep of 7' 6" as % of flat
8' 2"	93%	92%
8' 4"	**91%**	**90%**
8' 6"	89%	*88%*

Table 6g The relationship of *Sea Venture*'s flat of floor and floor sweep.

warships built over a long period: *Merhonour* (1590) *Prince Royal* (1610) *Sovereign of the Seas* (1637). *Sea Venture* as a medium sized merchant vessel could well have had a slightly deeper hold than this though probably not as much as half the depth. Depths in general seem to have reduced from around 20% of keel length (the old half of depth proportion) in the 16th century, to around 17–18% in the early 17th century. This would give *Sea Venture* dimensions in the region of 75' on the keel, 29'2" breadth and 13'6" depth in hold (see Table 6j). These figures would give 295 tons by the rule of the time (Length × Breadth × Depth, divided by 100).

The stronger relation between the physical remains of *Sea Venture* and the Admiralty Library MSS 9 suggests that the ship was designed according to a method that used similar proportions. There is a potential problem however in that the author of MSS 9 used logarithms to generate many of the curves such as the rising and narrowing lines. Logarithms were invented in 1615, so although men like John Wells were involved in their development it cannot be until around this date at the earliest that they are incorporated in the work of shipwrights. This obviously puts it some time after *Sea Venture* was lost. However, MSS 9 accords so closely in principle with other rules it must be a modernised treatment of a system originally generated by more primitive means. It is the same John Wells, author of the later additions to the Pepysian '*Fragments*' who was proposed as the possible author for MSS 9 by Salisbury (1958). Apart from obvious similarities between the midship section on Folio 91 of '*Fragments*' with that of MSS 9 there are various places in '*Fragments*', where Wells has made notes alongside Baker's calculations and recalculated the long-hand arithmetic using logarithms. In other words, MSS 9 may be a systematic treatment of the whole process of ship design by Wells (and collaborators?). So although the method for drafting a ship given in MSS 9 employs more complex curves than may have been used by the builder of *Sea Venture*, the fundamental proportions were evidently similar. Also, the more complex cubic and quartic curves are used in the upper hull, for example the upper rising and upper narrowing lines. Their effect on the lower hull is not great, that being largely dictated by arcs of circles as in earlier methods. As the reason for producing the reconstruction of *Sea Venture* was to analyse hull performance, the method that most closely correlated with the actual remains was judged the best option. For that reason a draft of *Sea Venture*'s hull was made using MSS 9's method allied to the dimensions of the preserved timbers.

The hull was surveyed using the metric system but obviously a conversion to the units in which the vessel was undoubtedly built is necessary. All dimensions are therefore given in feet and inches as well as metric. At the first attempt, problems were found in correlating the frame stations as recorded in the wreck with the numbers of frames fore and aft of the midship section in the reconstruction. Using the longer keel length resolved this problem giving an even number.

Table 6h The relationship between the flat of floor and the floor sweep in MSS.

	Flat as % of breadth	Floor sweep as % of breadth	Floor sweep as % of flat of floor
2820/13	14.3	40.2	284%
2820/15	18.3	28.9	158%
2820/35	22.5	28.2	125.3%
Harriot	25	25	100%
2820/91(Wells)	25	25	100%
MS 9	25	26.9	107.4%
'	29.16	26.2	**89.7%**
MS798 (Scott)	30	25	83%
Pett (Sov. of Seas)	30	23.7	78.8%
Deane's Doctrine.	33.33	25	75%

This slightly alters those dimensions that are given in MSS 9 as recommended proportions of the breadth, e.g. the radius of the stem, rather than those where a freer hand is indicated, such as the ratio of keel length to breadth. Both sets of figures are given below.

Figure 6.18 shows the midship bend of *Sea Venture* constructed using the proportions derived from MSS 9 (shown in Table 6k), based on the flat of floor derived from the actual timbers. Were a bend drawn to the same scale as Mathew Baker's Folio 35 (used by W. A. Baker for the reconstruction of the *New Mayflower*) it would give a vessel 37 feet 8 inches broad, far too big, while the values in Deane's '*Doctrine*' would give a vessel only 25 feet 6 inches broad. These two midship sections would, based on the average proportions of their respective periods, represent vessels of around 590 and 210 tons respectively. The values and proportions of MSS 9 however, give a tonnage figure very close to the 300 recorded for *Sea Venture*.

Hull lines

Having reconstructed the midship bend, the narrowing and rising lines were developed and drawn. These hand drawn lines were then input into an industrial lines-fairing package '*Wolfson Shipshape*' at the Department of Ship Science at the University of Southampton. This is one of a suite of programmes developed by the Wolfson Unit at Southampton for the performance analysis of ship hulls (Fig. 6.19). Once faired, the computer model is exported to a hydrostatics package '*Wolfson Hydrostatics*' for more advanced analysis, the provisional results of which are given below. The lines will also be used to cut a model for tank testing.

Performance analysis: provisional results

Initial results show that the *Sea Venture* model is very stable. Assuming even moderate fidelity with the original this is hardly a surprise. Tested with a variety of heights for the centre of gravity, the righting moment (the force acting on the hull to bring it upright) steadily increases with the angle of heel. With ports clamped shut and deck hatches well battened down, this hull form would recover from an angle of heel well past 45 degrees. This indicates a considerable sea-keeping ability for *Sea Venture* and ships of her general form. These results also suggest that this hull form is inherently more stable than the *Mary Rose* although this is currently being quantified with more comparative tests.

In one sense it is no surprise that the *Sea Venture* form proves stable. What nearly sunk her was leakage through overstressed hull planking, not instability. However, the concordance between the archaeological analysis and an otherwise cryptic historical record demonstrates that seabed data can be used to reconstruct form and performance in the manner shown above. That being the case, we can not only place *Sea Venture* more clearly in the trajectory of northern European shipping but address the social, technological and environmental factors that were responsible for the changes observed. We can also consider to what degree shipwrights were able to control those same factors in the design and construction process.

Element	Dimension (ft)	metres	*Alternative*	*Metres*
Keel	75'	22.86	*76' 9"*	*23.39*
Breadth	29' 2"	8.89	*29' 2"*	*8.89*
Depth	13' 6"	4.12	*13' 6"*	*4.12*
Sweep of the stem	23' 1"	7.04	*23' 10"*	*7.28*
Height of post	19' 5"	5.93	*18' 9"*	*5.72*
Height of tuck	9'	2.74	*9'*	*2.74*
Height of gripe*	7' 8"	2.34	*7' 8"*	*2.34*

Table 6j Showing possible principal dimensions of *Sea Venture* based on MSS 9.

* Salisbury says from base of keel but this does not work when constructing the rising lines, as all the offsets calculated cubically are read off the upper edge of the keel.

Table 6k Values for *Sea Venture* midship section using MSS 9 (with MS2820/35 and Deane's 'Doctrine' as comparisons).

Sea Venture	Feet & inches	metres	2820/35	Deane
Breadth	29' 2"	8.89	11.51	7.77
Depth	13' 6"	4.12	5.12	3.34
Flat of floor	8' 6"	2.59	2.59	2.59
Floor sweep	7' 7"	2.31	3.27	1.94
Breadth sweep	6'	1.83	2.29	1.51
Reconciling sweep	17' 6"	5.33	8.92	4.32
Top timbers (3/4 breadth)	21' 10½"	6.67	8.63	
" (2/3 Breadth)	19' 5"	5.94		6.91
Hollowing toptimber sweep	29' 2"	8.89	straight	8.40

Figure 6.18 Reconstruction of the midship bend of *Sea Venture* drawn using the proportions derived from MSS 9 (J. Adams).

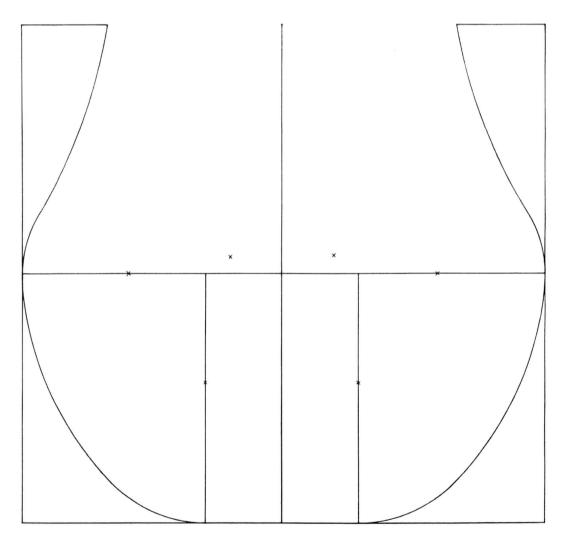

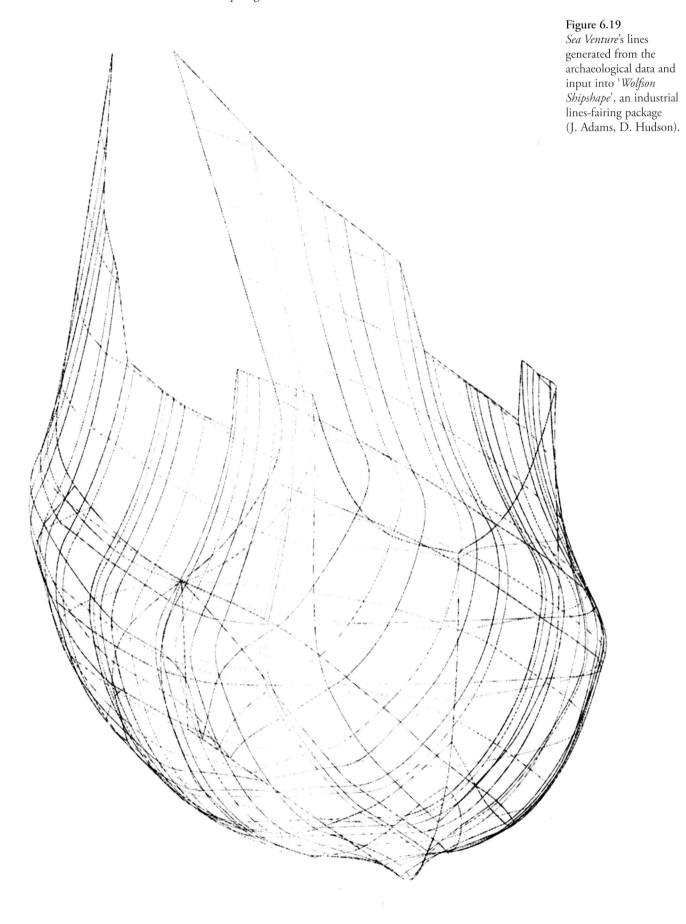

Figure 6.19
Sea Venture's lines generated from the archaeological data and input into '*Wolfson Shipshape*', an industrial lines-fairing package (J. Adams, D. Hudson).

Shipwrights and status

It has been suggested that Baker's more finished illustrative folios were probably produced to convey ideas on new ship construction to those in positions of influence. Richard Barker (1986) suggested this would logically have included Queen Elizabeth herself. McGowan (1981:28) had thought so too and included the Lord High Treasurer and Chief Minister, Lord Burghley. Both are highly likely and in looking at the original manuscripts, it is inconceivable that they were done simply as an exercise or as part of the normal design procedure. One is looking at drawings in all probability seen by Elizabeth I. However, other folios are clearly explanations of a specific mathematical procedure involved in hull design. It is highly unlikely that Elizabeth or her ministers would have required to know how to design a ship of 240 tuns burthen on the basis of a draft of a ship of 120 tuns or to calculate the volume 'contayned in the mould', etc. Those who would need such knowledge were Baker's apprentices. Baker, like any expert craftsmen, had students. The apprentice system was both the means of training the next generation and the source of part of his remuneration. These folios, with their tracts of geometry, arithmetic calculation and scaling devices are, among other things, components of an educational treatise. In earlier times it was possible to transmit the knowledge necessary for designing ships entirely orally. The practical skills of shipbuilding were passed on by what Hasslöf (1972:23) has described as the 'visual-motor tradition', where observation and imitation is the primary means of learning. But as ship designers attempted through mathematics to increase the control they had over the hull form and its eventual performance, this inexorably led the craft of shipwrightry towards the science of naval architecture. Though this transition was still some way off, it is in Baker's work and in the writings of his southern contemporaries like the Basque Diego García de Palacio, the Portuguese priest Fernando Oliveira, and the Venetian Theodoro de Nicolo that we see the beginnings of this process.

A corollary of this trend was that it pre-selected those who had or could acquire the necessary linguistic and arithmetic skills. Hence, as shipwrightry became more mathematical, so those who would become shipwrights in large yards and royal dockyards needed an increasingly high level of education. Many shipwrights and those directly associated with the administration of shipbuilding, like John Wells of Deptford, whose notes follow Baker's in the '*Fragments*' collection, were very capable mathematicians, and as noted above, quickly incorporated logarithms in the process of hull design. These were not only used in order to generate mathematically the required curves at the design stage rather than using more primitive rules of proportion and offsets, or drawing arcs with compasses, these also allowed more accurate transfer of body plans to the mould loft – the large wooden floor on which the frame shapes were drawn out at full size. As the procedures of designing and building ships began to become more complex and more indispensable to the business of running a nation state, skilled and educated shipwrights were increasingly integrated into that process. The importance of the new 'profession' was allowing shipwrights, some of them at least, to negotiate their way up the class ladder. Hence we see Mathew Baker, far from being simply the craftsman who was directed by great men, becoming an authority to whom they deferred for corroboration of their views and to bolster their policy recommendations. After Baker came Phineas Pett who, if the more snide comments of his contemporaries are to be believed, was something of a social climber (Abell 1948:43). With Sir Anthony Deane, as his title suggests, new precedents were set in terms of the status a shipwright held. He moved freely in society, being a long time friend of Samuel Pepys, then Secretary of the Navy. Not surprisingly, Deane's treatise or '*Doctrine*' is also in the Pepysian Library. It is significant that that particular word should have been chosen as a title for a treatise on the naval architecture of England, of such central importance to the state. It is possibly due to his exalted position (though he faired less well during the period of the commonwealth) that he is credited with developing the method for calculating displacement and hence predicting draught. As Lavery (1980:25) has pointed out, there is no evidence that he had done so. Mathew Baker, in calculating the volumes of the hulls he was designing a hundred years earlier, was probably moving towards the same goal. What is clear from this first century of shipbuilding from the preparation of Mathew Baker's manuscripts to the '*Doctrine*' of Sir Anthony Deane, is that the state now viewed shipbuilding as an industry in which it had a strong vested interest. Something that as Loewen has pointed out (Loewen 1994:18) was also happening in other developing nation states.

Ships of war and trade: divergence and convergence

What seems to have developed within a central enclave of carvel shipbuilding in the south of England was an ideologically robust formula for the production of an ideal known as the 'defensible ship'. With this formula, ships could be built across a wide range of tonnage that had essentially common features: robustly constructed and capable of carrying a heavy weight of ordnance relative to their size, a relatively fast hull form and an efficient rig. Conceptually ships of this type embodied ideas of offence and defence – a product of their time. They were warships, long distance, defensible merchant ships reaching out to the Levant, the Far East, and across the Atlantic, and, very much interconnected with all these functions, the vehicles of an increasingly determined colonial policy. If one is looking for a shipbuilding tradition in which an ideological framework strongly characterised and channelled the component concepts, skills and procedures, then this would rank highly among the examples one might find in a world-wide survey. So solidly embedded were these ideas of how a proper ship should be, both in terms of form and construction, that this may partly explain the developments in shipbuilding at the end of the 17th century, which were as much conceptual and social as they were technological.

Davis (1978:12–13) has pointed to the enormous number of Dutch merchant vessels that were captured during the three Dutch Wars. These vessels were transferred directly to the English merchant fleet and were primarily used for the carriage of bulk cargoes. Principally 'fluitships', their flatter bottoms and wall sides gave them a far greater block coefficient than the equivalent sized English ship. As Nicolaas Witsen put it in 1690: Dutch fluits 'measure little and stow much'. Davis's thesis is that it was the huge numbers of captured fluits that satisfied the English merchant fleet's needs for such vessels until the final cessation of hostilities in 1674 (Davis 1978 *ibid.*). Once the supply had dried up merchants began seeking vessels of similar capacity from elsewhere. Apparently English yards in the south were slow to respond.

Contemporary sources refer to the fact the English shipwrights could (or would) only build 'defensible ships', which were perfect for the trader of valuable commodities in waters where there was the very real threat of piracy, and where speed was at a greater premium than capacity. But for the trader in timber, grain, or coal, plying across the North Sea or into the Baltic, piracy in time of peace was not a major issue. Fluits were slower but neither was speed in these trades an issue, especially when capacity was so much greater and crew lists indicate that far smaller crews were required to sail them. In short the owners could make more money with a fluit than with a 'defensible ship'. What then appears to have happened is that yards in the north east began building the kind of vessels needed for these trades. These were collier-barks, timber 'cat-ships' and brigs that were ubiquitous in the English North Sea and coastal trades for the next hundred and fifty years.

Davis's thesis certainly fits the circumstances and it is undeniable that the centre of gravity for these forms of merchant shipbuilding had shifted irrevocably. It is also consistent with the discussion here concerning building traditions and the overall trajectory of carvel shipbuilding in England. However, there is another discernible trend during this period that must have contributed to the shift in momentum from south to north, and that is concerned with a long term oscillation between convergence and divergence of warships and merchant vessels.

In chapter 4 the medieval practice of procuring large merchant ships for naval use was noted, and its converse, that state-owned ships were routinely leased to merchants when not required for military purposes. In other words large carrack types, whether of Mediterranean origin or clinker-built in England, could function in either capacity. With the adoption of carvel building throughout Europe and Scandinavia, ships like the *Mary Rose* incorporated such a degree of specialisation that, as purpose-built warships, they differed in various material ways from equivalent sized merchant vessels. However, in the particular circumstances of the early 16th century, this distinction did not last. As a result of the developments in the second and third quarters of the 16th century, English warships and large merchant ships were once again, to all intents and purposes, indistinguishable. While ships built for the Crown might be of higher quality and perhaps more robustly constructed than an equivalent sized privately owned vessel (though we have no direct evidence for this), the principles of design and construction were the same. This was also the case with the galleon-types of other nations. The galleons of Spain for example were quite likely to function as warships on one voyage and merchant ships on the next. This compatibility is implicit in the longstanding English policy of 'bounty', in effect state sponsorship for private building of ships large enough to serve as warships if needed. As a practice this goes back at least to the reign of Henry VII (Davis 1978:305). By the second half of the reign of Elizabeth I a bounty of five shillings per ton was paid on any ship over 100 tons. *Sea Venture*'s owners would certainly have benefitted in this way (Petersen 1988:43). The threshold at which bounty became payable gradually increased as time went on and reflected the progressive increase in the mean size of warships. Hence for as long as the crown could not afford to build a fleet of vessels to be permanently available for naval duties, it was in its interests to maintain this similarity. This must therefore be a primary factor in the strength and durability among English shipbuilders of the concept of how ships should be. The ideology of the shipbuilders in the practice of their art was bolstered and materially sponsored by the ideology of the state. That this was most clearly defined in yards in the south of England, the region in which the crown built its own ships or contracted them from private yards is also not surprising. Hence when the opportunity arose to provide ships involving very different concepts of form and construction, private yards up and down the east coast were better placed to seize it. That there was a strong conceptual element in the process is also suggested by geography, as they were not as strategically placed for trade with France as the southern ports and not significantly better placed for trade with Holland and Germany than those in the south east. Only for the Baltic were they at a geographic advantage and the requirements for carrying the associated commodities, timber in particular, certainly influenced the subsequent designs. The ownership or repair of fluits and other related Dutch types common in the North Sea provided a basis of practical and conceptual experience.

However, throughout the century, the basis of a final divergence between ships of war and trade was being laid. In 1606, the same year that the Virginia Company of London received its royal charter, the 1000 ton *Trades Increase* sailed to the East Indies. She was lost, and with her an enormous investment, but the momentum was unchecked. This was the genesis of the *Honourable English East India Company*. As the East India Trade began to coalesce into a separate field of maritime enterprise, with it went the hybrid ship of war and trade. This precipitated the end of the long tradition of bounty as the size at which bounty was payable steadily increased. After a brief cessation due to financial difficulties in 1619 bounty was restored in 1626 but now only for ships of over 200 tons. As Davis points out, ideas of what was a 'large' ship were changing (Davis 1978:305). Revived again in 1662 after the Civil War, bounty was no longer determined by tonnage but amounted to a third of the customs duties incurred on the first two voyages. To be eligible ships needed significant offensive capability: '… *Three Decks and a Half with a Forecastle and five foot between each Deck mounted with Thirty Pieces of Ordnance…*'. This was revised in 1672. Eligible ships were divided into three-decked and two-decked ships, though the latter had to be over 300 tons and both still had to carry (or be capable of carrying) at least thirty guns. The final Act 'For building Good and Defensible Ships' was passed in 1694 stipulating ships of 450 tons or more, with three decks six feet apart and capable of carrying 32 guns (Davis *ibid.* 312). This only applied to East Indiamen and remained in force only ten years. After that the Crown no longer felt the need to subsidize auxiliary fighting vessels. Warships were becoming steadily larger and more heavily armed. This together with developments in naval tactics eventually outpaced the provisions for incorporating merchant vessels into fleets in time of war. Once large merchant ships began to be built dedicated to specific trades, divergence was irreversible. It is no coincidence that the majority of East India ships continued to be built in the south, whereas 'cat ships', collier barks and West Indiamen were subsequently built all round the coast and at this time particularly in the north east.

The swing northwards in the take-up of certain construction opportunities is therefore a part of this divergence in the purposes for which ships were built. Hulls were still robustly constructed to resist the stresses of North Sea voyaging and from sitting aground at low tide in the smaller harbours and on beaches where so much local trade was conducted. The hull forms however, were very different: Flatter bottomed, more wall-sided and with fuller fore and after bodies, much like their Dutch antecedents. The next chapter is concerned with a ship that, while of a relatively late, mid 19th century date, is nevertheless a product of this important north eastern development.

Note

1. Most of the references to *Sea Venture* being built in East Anglia seem to originate in P. M. Wright's '*The Sea Venture Story*' (1960) and an undated pamphlet 'Bermuda Epic' that he wrote for the Bermuda Government around that time. Kennedy (1971:26) drew her comments from Wright, while Glover and Blake Smith (2008:78) used Kennedy, and so on. The late David Raine could not remember the source for his statement that *Sea Venture* had been built in Aldeburgh (Raine pers. comm.) although it may have been Wright. Subsequent authors who state *Sea Venture* was brand new may have misread Kennedy's suggestions that the vessel had been 'newly acquired' by the Virginia Company and that this might have been her 'first long voyage' (Kennedy 1971:258). She was right on both counts if by 'long' we mean transatlantic.

7

A New Technology

Background

In 1986 several wrecks were discovered during a major Dutch dredging project off Rotterdam. The work involved the construction of an enormous basin or 'slufter' in which to pump polluted sediments dredged from the estuaries of the rivers Rhine and Maas. To create such a basin involved dredging over two square kilometres of seabed to a depth of 28 metres and constructing a ring-dike around it with the spoil. As the location of the slufter was in an area where there had been intensive maritime traffic for centuries, if not millennia, it was inevitable that this operation, involving the movement of 37 million cubic metres of sediment, would uncover wreck material. The first two 'hits' were made in the first days of dredging and, although that rapidity of discovery was not sustained, a new wreck was discovered every month (Adams, van Holk and Maarleveld 1990).

SL 4

The fourth, designated SL 4 (Slufter wrecksite 4) appeared to be of 19th-century date. Because of its relative youth it was initially believed to be of lesser importance than the others already discovered or were anticipated. As working on the site would also be extremely difficult and hazardous it was, with obvious reluctance, archaeologically abandoned at this stage. It was with a mixture of horror and awe that the archaeologists present watched a large section of the remains unceremoniously wrenched from the water by a large grab and dumped on a barge. This project set a precedent however, in that its

budgeting and organisation provided for an archaeological component. The remains were therefore transported to a land site for recording and analysis (Adams et al. 1990:72).

SL 4 turned out to be the wreck of an English collier from around the mid 19th century. But in spite of its relatively recent date and humble role, its recording and analysis proved a far more rewarding exercise than anyone anticipated. Structurally it was a physical synopsis of the entire northern European carvel building tradition, but it also illustrated the influences of dwindling natural resources and the use of new materials, principally iron. It was therefore an eloquent statement of technological change in a period when the effects of the industrial revolution were irrevocably changing traditional industries, generating new ones and dramatically affecting the demography and lifestyles of society on a global scale.

Hull Structure

The hull is wood-fastened in that the inner and outer planks are mainly held to the frames with wooden treenails. The main structural elements are also fastened with iron bolts. Figure 7.1 shows a schematic representation of the forward section of the hull which was salvaged as an integral unit.

Keel, posts and deadwood
The keel was probably made from four sections. The foremost section was recovered as part of the integral assemblage shown in Figure 7.1 and fragments of the others were recovered separately. It was assumed the keel was elm until closer

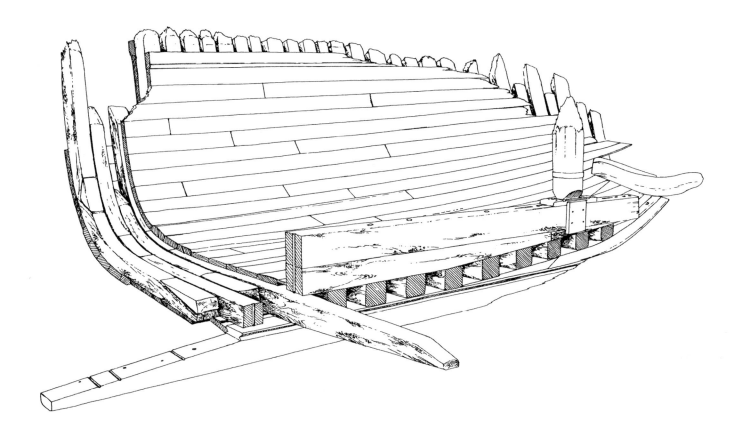

Figure 7.1 Schematic representation of the section of SL 4 recovered as a coherent unit. A similar proportion of structure was recovered in smaller sections or as single timbers (J. Adams).

inspection indicated otherwise. Species analysis identified all the pieces as birch. The keel tapered slightly either side of the midship section where it was 280mm in width by 370–80mm (11 × 15 inches) in depth. The scarf joints were around 1.8m in length, tabled horizontally and cut so the lower limb, as one would expect, angled down towards the stern. Judging from the deep rounded section of the keel and the lack of evidence for fastenings, there was no false keel or shoe. There are no keys or hooks in any of the scarfs and this is reflected in the number of stopwaters (now missing). These acted as keys and improved the longitudinal strength of the joint. In the central scarf there are four in the surviving 1.06m of tabling. The joints were fastened by clenched iron bolts 19–20mm (¾ inch) in diameter (in one case 25mm (1 inch)). These and the stopwaters are irregularly placed.

No sections of the stem or sternpost have survived. The only element of the stem assembly left *in situ* is the lower section of the apron. This lies above the keel, joined to a tapering piece that provides a ramp for the rising floors. At its forward end it terminates in an angled butt (Fig. 7.1). Although it continues the line of the apron it is

in effect deadwood as little if any of the stress taken by the apron was transmitted to it. The stern deadwood was similar but more substantial. The foremost 2.68 m of this survives; one broken fragment and two pieces in the dismembered assemblages of structure.

Framing

Of the frame timbers, all the floors and futtocks that were recovered are of oak. Heavy floors, between 290 and 305mm (11–12 inches) square, are set across the keel on approximately .58m centres (1 foot 11 inches). Amidships they are horizontal on their upper surface but their lower surface shows slight deadrise. They run out to the turn of the bilge where they butt against the second futtock. They are made from one piece except at the bow where one is formed from two pieces scarfed together. The intermediate first futtocks begin clear of the keel and continue through the turn of the bilge and butt against the third futtock. The first futtock overlaps the joint between the floors and the second futtock, just as the second futtock overlaps that between the first and the third. The result is a regular system (Fig. 7.2). At the joints the heads and

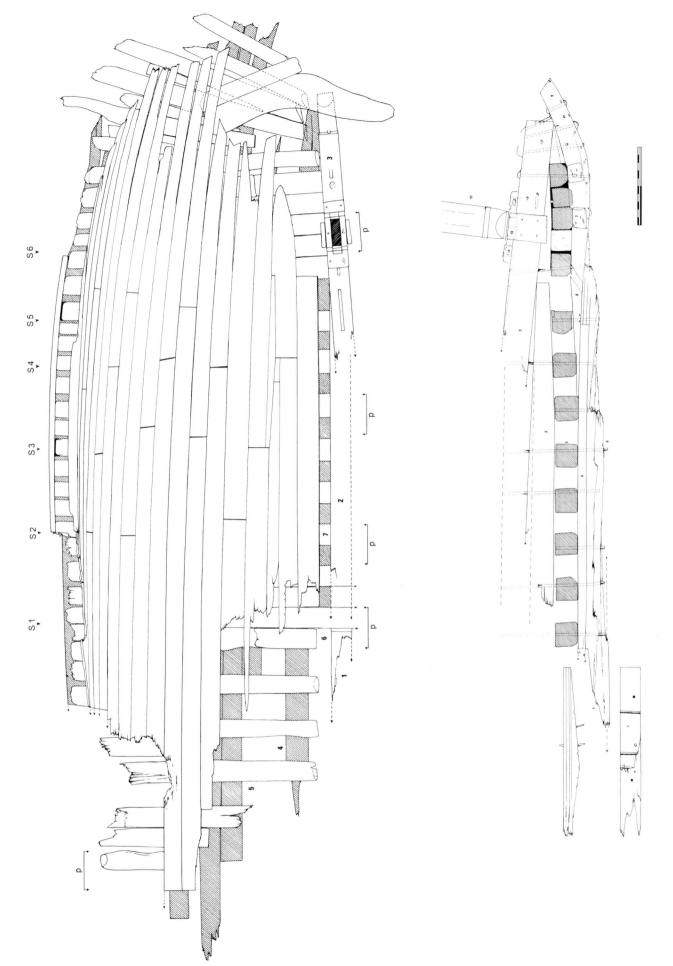

Figure 7.2 SL 4 plan and longitudinal section. Timbers paired ('in frame') indicated 'p' along keelson. Position of sections marked S1–S6. For explanation of other numerals, see Figure 7.4 (J. Adams).

heels of the timbers are cut at an angle and accommodate 'chocks' which are discussed below. In some cases the timbers were bolted horizontally to each other forming a paired frame. Where this was done, two 20mm (¾ inch) iron bolts fastened the adjacent timbers; the first to the second, second to third and third to fourth futtock. There were no bolts between the floor and the first futtock.

Representative timbers of each type are shown in Figure 7.3. Other frame elements include ten cant timbers on the starboard side. Although they have slumped out of position they are still correctly orientated as shown in the plan (Fig. 7.2). The main cant timbers are long curved pieces sided between 175 and 270mm and moulded 160–220mm. They were footed against the apron with shorter tapered pieces filling the space between them. The first cant frame was spiked to the last floor timber and bolted to the short tapered frame forward. None of the others are bolted but a cant timber that was recovered loose has two horizontal bolts, indicating that at least one pair of cant timbers a side (possibly from the stern) were joined.

Planking
Outer hull planking was predominantly elm below the waterline and oak above it. Amidships, the garboard strake was let into a rabbet cut 35–40mm below the top of the keel. It did not therefore lie flush against the bottom of the floors. A thin feather-edged pine board filled part of the resulting space and the channel left between that and the keel formed the limber passage. Either side of the midship area where the hull became more 'V'-shaped, the floors were supplemented by chocks or fillers. The garboard lay flush against these so a notch was cut in them to form the limber passage. On the port side there are 24 strakes remaining versus 8 to starboard. In the main body of the hull the bottom planks were approximately 300mm in width so these were probably cut to be one foot in width (305mm = one English foot). Above the turn of the bilge they are approximately 250mm wide (10 inches). Along the turn of the bilge there was a series of five thicker strakes to provide additional strength and wear resistance when the ship 'took the ground' (Fig. 7.4).

All the elm planks are rather roughly finished with an adze, not only on their outer surface but also along their edges. No attempt was made to produce the theoretically vital caulking bevel. In fact the scalloped surface produced by this treatment would appear to grip the caulking medium very securely. The outer planks of oak higher up also have no bevel although they are finished to a smoother edge. There is only one place where there is a bevel that must have been cut intentionally and that is at the butt joint on one of the oak planks.

The wales, also of oak, were 90–95mm thick (3½–3¾ inches) but were possibly a maximum of 100 mm (4 inches) thick amidships. Apart from an eroded fragment of the second, only the lower wale is still in place. Along its lower edge, where it is proud of the ordinary plank below, it was finished with a simple moulding. There were probably a series of four or five wales. The lowest is 190mm in width, probably 200mm at midships and the others are likely to have been the same.

The main fastenings of the planking were treenails. In addition the butt ends were secured by a bolt set in opposite sides of the plank. The majority of these bolts are 16mm in diameter (⅝ inch). Most are copper alloy although some appear to be nearer pure copper and are larger in diameter: 20mm (¾ inch) while a few in the bottom strakes are iron, also 20mm in diameter. These bolts are blind, i.e. they do not pass right through the hull, relying on friction for security. Those of copper appear to have been cut from cast rod, rolled and then beaten to roughly point the end. The faceted and split heads suggest they were driven with an iron hammer. The copper alloy bolts were individually cast and the mould marks filed off prior to use. The heads, in contrast to those of the copper bolts, show no signs of being driven with a hammer. As they were not as ductile as those of copper they were probably driven with a wooden mallet to lessen the chance of cracking. There is one case where this seems to have happened. Judging by the condition of the broken surface the break is old, certainly when compared to those broken during salvage. A second bolt had been placed only a few centimetres away. The metal of the broken bolt seemed to be a very porous cast which was presumably the reason it cracked.

Eighteen ceiling planks remain in place on the port side and six on the starboard, not including the limber boards. The ceiling planking is oak. There is great variation in width but most average 260–280mm amidships (approximating to 10 and 11 inches). Either side of the keelson there is a run of limber boards 150mm (6 inches) in

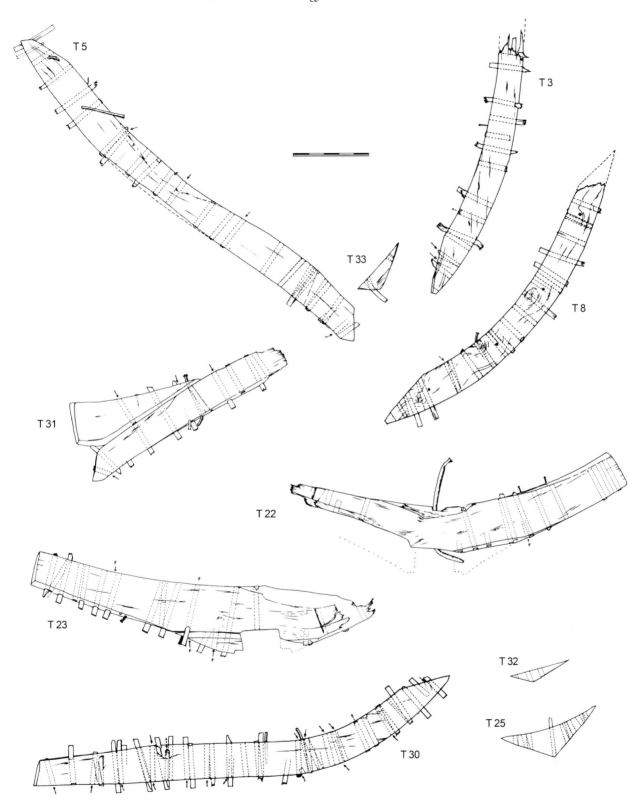

Figure 7.3 SL 4 Representative timbers recovered and recorded individually. From bottom: midship floor T14; first futtock T30; chocks between floor and second futtock T25 and T32; aft floor timber, made up with chocks or 'filling' (star-board chock missing) T23; asymmetric aft floor, chocks missing T 22; aft first futtock with filling chock T31; second futtock T8; chock between first and third futtock T33; cant timber T5; third futtock T3. Scale: 50 cm (J. Adams).

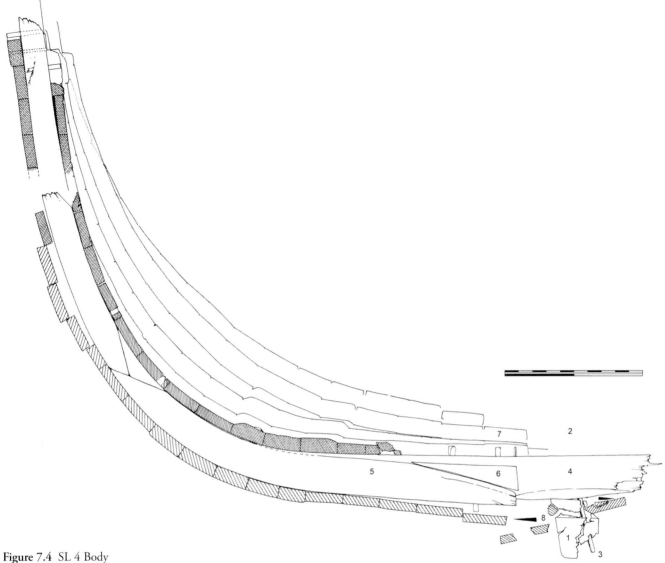

Figure 7.4 SL 4 Body
sections and profiles.
1   keel
2   position of keelson
3   keel bolt
4   floor
5   first futtock
6   first futtock chock
7   limber board
8   limber passage

Section 1 (S1) is labelled
at the upper limit of
preservation. S2 likewise
but shown as a profile
below the extent of S1.
Nos 3–6 are shown as
profiles. (Section
locations are marked on
the plan (Fig. 7.2))
(J. Adams).

width and 40 mm (1.⅗ inches) in depth. These
are supported on small blocks so as to lie at the
same level as the heavy limber strakes which are
70mm (3 inches) thick and 305mm wide (1 foot).
From these the ceiling runs out to the turn of the
bilge averaging 63 mm (2.5 inches) thick. At the
turn of the bilge there are three stringers or
'footwaling' 100mm (4 inches) thick.

From there up to the clamp the planks are
again 63mm thick (Fig. 7.4). These dimensions
are those near the midship section. All planks
and stringers reduce markedly in thickness
towards the bow and all except the limber strake
and limber board reduce in width. The fastenings

for the ceiling are treenails, the majority of which
are wedged with simple flat wedges. They were
supplemented by iron spikes. It is to the
footwaling stringers that the thick outer bilge
planking described above would correspond,
giving extra rigidity along the line of the joints
between the floors and the first futtocks. They
are additionally fastened with iron bolts
approximately 20mm in diameter that were
driven from outboard and clenched over rings
inboard. The planks from the bilge stringers
upwards seem to have been painted with tar and
it is possible that the whole ceiling had originally
been so treated.

Internal timbers

The keelson is formed of two timbers 280mm (11 inches) in width that are bolted through the floors to the keel with iron bolts 32mm in diameter. The maximum combined depth amidships was 71cm (28 inches). The lower element runs horizontally, reducing in depth as it runs forward over the rising floors. It ends in a butt just aft of the foremast which was stepped into the upper element. The resulting space is filled with deadwood. The upper element also runs horizontally and terminates in a simple butt above the apron (Fig. 7.2). Aft of the fore-mast the keelson was badly damaged by the dredger. One separate piece recovered shows the beginning of a horizontally tabled scarf joint. Both elements would have run to a point aft of the main mast. After that one or other element must have terminated or reduced with the rising of the floors towards the stern in a similar fashion to the bow.

One breasthook 3.04m long remains in place although it has slumped out of position with the rest of the bow section. Although it was not very regular in shape it was fashioned from good quality timber, 390 × 320mm in section tapering to the ends. It was positioned above the end of the remaining piece of the apron and bolted to the cant frames. The area between the breasthooks was planked by short pieces running parallel to them, one of which remains in place. The spacing between the two positions suggests that there were probably a series of five or six breasthooks up to and including the deckhook. Two halves of what are presumably breasthooks were salvaged as loose timbers.

The only beams surviving are fragmentary and none of them remains in place. Many were from the hold and were not decked over. They were spaced 1.83m apart (six feet) and rested on a beamshelf which is no longer present. This in turn rested on a stringer or clamp 90mm (3½ inches) thick. This was moulded along its lower edge in the same manner as the outer wale. There were no knees used to retain these hold beams. Instead, an iron strap 90mm in width and 20mm thick (3½ × ¾ inches) passed around the futtock against which the beam butted (Fig. 7.5). The futtock was trimmed to accommodate the thickness of the iron strap which was then bolted through the end of the beam with 20mm (¾ inch) iron bolts. The beam was also bolted vertically through its end to the shelf, the shelf in turn being bolted through the frames to the wale every other timber.

Both wooden and iron knees were recovered during salvage as separate elements and appear to be from the deck-beams (as distinct from the hold beams). The shape of the iron knees indicate a horizontally laid shelf above a clamp in the same configuration as those of the hold beams. The wood knees 'lodged' horizontally and some of their features were puzzling initially: the channel or rebate cut into one face, the varying distance between it and the side of the knee, as well as the curved back face of the long arm. This became clearer when looking at the deck-beams.

Two eroded beam ends were recovered during the inspection dives, having slightly flared ends. These had also been bolted horizontally and vertically. The horizontal bolt-holes correspond in principle to the pattern in the wooden knees, though no actual matches can be made. Some distance from the end of the beams on the upper side is a shallow rebate or channel into which a longitudinal beam appears to have been bolted. The channel corresponds to that in the wooden lodging knees. The knees are of various sizes and appear to have been paired, explaining the varying depth between the channel and the curved edge of some of the knees. The longitudinal timber rebated into the top of the beam would appear to a 'side binding strake' described by Andrew Murray in 1863, although he described it as a feature of naval ships (see glossary). Some of these deck elements were reassembled and reconstruction of both hold and deck-beam structure is shown in Figure 7.5.

Two mortises in the top of the keelson either side of the foremast step correspond to the position of the hold beams. Presumably they are for the pillars that supported them. One broken stanchion was recovered. This had a tenon of a size that corresponds to the mortises in the top of the keelson. On two of the mortises one side is sloped, enabling the tenon on the top of the stanchion to be located in the mortise in the underside of the hold beam. It could then be slid sideways into the mortise in the keelson and secured by a strip of wood nailed into the groove.

Keel Fastenings

The keel, floors and keelson were fastened with iron bolts 32mm (1 ¼ inches) in diameter. These were driven downwards, some only through a floor and the keel, others through both keelson timbers, floor and keel. This was a result of the construction sequence and is discussed below.

Figure 7.5 SL 4 deck reconstruction with wooden and iron knees (J. Adams).

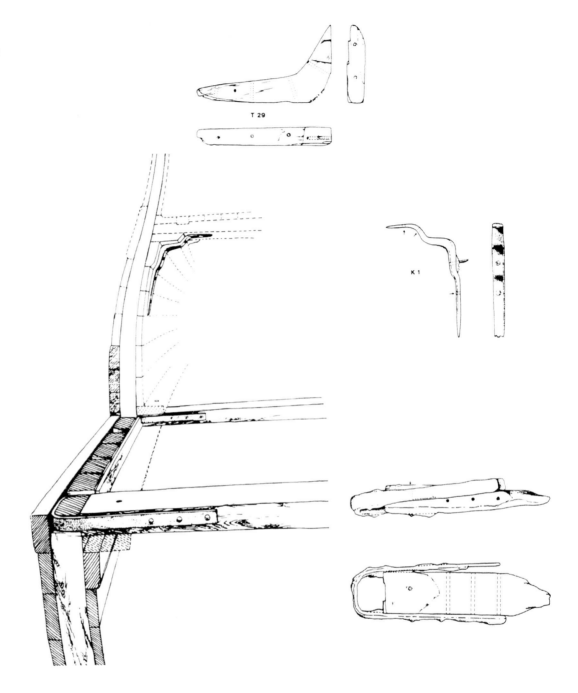

They did not have a washer under the head. The flared shape resulting from driving the bolt home was presumably adequate. The lower ends do not appear to have been clenched over a washer although it is possible that, without the protection of a false keel, these have been worn away. However, some appear to have ended well above the bottom of the keel and to have simply been left blind.

Main mast and mast-step

The stump of the pine foremast survives to a height of 1.4m where it shows severe shipworm attack. It is octagonally faceted and is 400mm in diameter at the highest preserved section. It is bound by an iron hoop 250mm above the mast step, presumably to prevent splitting. The mast-step is formed by a block of elm 910 × 280mm (36 × 11 inches) which is fastened to the top of the upper or false keelson by six spikes. The rectangular foot of the mast is stepped into it and also into the false keelson though only about 25mm (1 inch). The whole assembly was reinforced by two slabs of wood bolted to each other through the false keelson. Fore and aft of the foot of the mast two blocks of wood were set into the step filling the excess space. Transverse channels were cut across the top into which battens were nailed to retain the blocks (Fig. 7.2).

Of the remaining inventory of SL 4 the materials included ships fittings, such as the windlass, rigging elements, a substantial amount of the cargo of coal, remains of ballast presumably of earlier voyages, and artefacts. They are not directly relevant here but together with the material analyses (caulking, metallurgy, and palynological analysis of coal) are comprehensively described in Adams et al. (1990).

Analysis that is directly relevant to the development of building and of building traditions concerns the species of timber used, especially in the light of the discussion of its conversion below. SL 4, in line with contemporary surveys of other ships, used a variety of wood species in its construction. Table 7a shows the results of the analysis of 29 samples from various structural elements.

In general the wood species identified appear to be northern European and mid-European species. No obvious non European species were found although oak, elm, beech and birch all have closely related species in North America which are difficult to distinguish. This might be the reason some of the oak samples taken for dendrochronological analysis could not be dated, only European reference curves being then available.

The ship and its materials

The initial idea that the cargo of coal and various structural features indicated SL 4 was an English vessel from the first half of the 19th century was confirmed by subsequent research. For example the fastening of the butt-ends of planks with one treenail and a 'yellow metal' bolt had become fairly standard in English shipbuilding in the 18th century.

No.	Element	Position	Species
TS1	False keelson	midship	Quercus sp. (oak)
TS2	Keel	midship	Betula sp. (birch)
TS3	Garboard	midship stbd.	Betula sp.
TS5	Outer hull plank	lower midship port	Ulmus sp. (elm)
TS6	Outer hull bottom	lower midship port	Ulmus sp.
TS7	Outer hull bottom	midship	Quercus
TS8	Treenail	midship plank port	Quercus sp.
TS3/2	Treenail	midship stbd.	Fagus sp. (beech)
TS9	Deutel	from sample 8	Quercus sp.
TS10	Treenail	midship port plank	Quercus sp.
TS11	Wedge (punch) from TS10		Quercus sp.
TS12	Wedge (punch) from TS10		Ulmus sp.
TS13	Filling (under plank)	midship stbd.	Quercus sp.
TS15	Filling (under bilge stringer)	stbd. fwd.	Pinus sylvestris (pine)
TS14	Repair ('Dutchman')	port outer plank fwd.	Ulmus sp.
TS16	Mast step	keelson fwd.	Ulmus sp.
TS17	Foremast		Pinus sylvestris
TS19	Ceiling plank	port midship	Quercus sp.
TS20	Ceiling plank	port midship	Quercus sp.
TS21	Ceiling plank	port midship	Quercus sp.
TS23	Keelson	midship	Quercus sp.
TS22	False Keelson	midship	Quercus sp.
TS24	Floor timber	midship	Quercus sp.
TS25	Futtock	forward	Quercus sp.
TS26	Chock	midship	Quercus sp.
TS27-34	Keel		Betula sp.
TS36	Garboard	port side	Ulmus sp.
TS37	Garboard,	starboard side	Betula sp.
TS35	Garboard,	loose plank	Ulmus sp.

Table 7a Timber species of the various elements of SL 4. Analysis by Peter Stussen (Adams et al. 1990:99).

The variety of wood species used can certainly be attributed to cost and availability. Birch, for example, was not an ideal wood to use for the keel or a garboard plank. The only reason it was used was because it was cheaper and/or more readily available than oak or elm. The latter was by then long established as the species favoured for keels in English shipbuilding. The wide variety of wood species used in the ships of this period is well attested by Lloyds surveys of the period and show SL 4 was fairly typical in this respect. In a comparable Dutch vessel the hull timber would have been all of oak and mostly from European forests, while timber in an equivalent American vessel might include a similar number of species to SL 4's but they would have been locally obtained. The demands of both the Royal and merchant navies for wood of sufficient quality for shipbuilding had, if not exhausted the supply, long since overtaxed the infrastructure of management and supply from English forests. The severity of scarcity is debated (Albion 1926; Rackham 1976:94–96) but availability as well as increased costs prompted the industry to turn to overseas sources as the only alternative. The variety of species, although largely enforced by scarcity, were nevertheless used in situations that suited their natural characteristics. For example elm was used for the bottom planking in SL 4. Elm was available in reasonable lengths and has a very high resistance to rot as long as it remains wet, so its use was confined to the strakes below the 'light water mark'.

The dendrochronological results show all the frames of SL 4 to be of English provenance whereas the hull planks and keelson are from German or other European forests (Adams et al. 1990:102). This agrees with historical references that for particular structural elements, definite preference was given as to their area of origin. David Steel (1805) referred to the use of 'east country' oak (i.e. the Baltic, particularly Poland) for hull planking, except at the bow and the stern where English oak should be used. This may have been because English oak was thought to have greater strength. Fincham (1851) also wrote that oak planks from Danzig (modern Gdansk) were used especially for the bottom but were generally thought to be inferior to English oak. Perhaps by the mid 19th century this was an ideological preference as much as a reality for, as SL 4 shows, the quality of English oak available to shipyards on a tight budget was not the best. The preference was however based in fact, for the strength of oak

depends on how fast it has grown rather than where. Contrary to popular assumption, fast-grown oak is denser and stronger than slow-grown oak as it has a greater thickness of tissue between each annular ring. For climatic reasons therefore oak from the south of England is generally stronger than oak from the Baltic where the growing season is shorter. English oak was preferred for the frames for the same reason. Another functional explanation for Steel's recommendation was that Polish oak from large forest stands could be obtained in much greater lengths. The use of the shorter English planks in the curved fore and after body allowed the longer imported planks to be used to best advantage, reducing the number of butt joints in the hull.

Besides inducing the use of a variety of wood species the scarcity of appropriate timber also induced maximum economy. This had a considerable effect on the methods of converting and using the timber. As a result an accepted principle of framing large hulls, whether they were warships or merchant ships, had probably become established in England by the early 18th century. In merchant ships this general method of framing was followed almost until the end of the sailing ship era. This system and the related sequence of construction were dealt with in many treatises on naval architecture of the 18th and 19th centuries. However, many of the authors were writing about their own work and naturally tended to use the more impressive vessels they had built as examples. As a result these treatises were biased towards large warship construction rather than the far more numerous smaller merchant ships. Another aspect of these works was that in seeking to demonstrate the high degree of skill and knowledge that the work of the shipwright demanded, authors described procedures and techniques as they ought to be carried out in ideal circumstances. While they sometimes alluded to alternative methods it was often implied that the technique or procedure being described was the only way of doing something. The possibility of integrating the apparently comprehensive historical documentation with archaeological material such as SL 4 casts a new light on the industry.

A reconstruction

Just as various construction techniques used in SL 4 comprise a methodological summary of carvel building, so does the construction sequence. For, although some of the procedures were specific to the 19th century, the fundamental principles had changed little in four hundred years. As with shipbuilding traditions in general, which tend not to die but persist through smaller, regional craft, so core procedures may be modified but are often not radically changed. In describing the construction sequence of SL 4, one is also in large part describing that of the *Mary Rose, Sea Venture,* and the other vessels discussed above. One of the reasons is that SL 4 was a small to medium-sized vessel probably constructed by a small labour force in a local yard in the north east of England. Techniques that by then were established procedure in navy yards were either too costly or required labour and equipment not possessed in the average small family business that commonly turned out this kind of vessel. Methods were therefore used that had stood the test of time and were simpler, in short, those that had been around for centuries.

In SL 4 we have an example of how construction was actually carried out compared to the 'prestige' text book descriptions in the written record. It is this sort of opportunity to integrate archaeological data with historical documentation that was discussed in chapter 3 and which always reveals both insights and new questions that would not have arisen from using the sources in isolation. The sequence of construction of the SL 4 hull is therefore described alongside historical information from contemporary handbooks on shipbuilding.

The most useful treatise in this context proved to be *A Treatise on Marine Architecture* by Peter Hedderwick, a shipwright who ran a shipyard at Leith in Scotland and who had wide practical experience. His treatise was published in 1830 and deals exclusively with merchant vessels. It is therefore qualitatively different in its approach from most other works. It also makes constant reference to alternative practices found in other districts and thus gives a more accurate impression of the variety with which the basic principles of construction could be carried out than is usually the case. Slightly earlier is '*The Elements and Practice of Naval Architecture*' by David Steel, first published in 1805. More widely known than Hedderwick, it became a standard work, its third edition (1822) incorporating the views of such authorities as Hutchinson, Snodgrass and Seppings. Steel's work records 'high-end' practice in the yards that built warships and East

Indiamen. The two agree on the general principles of construction but Hedderwick's work is more relevant to vessels of the size of SL 4.

The description of the sequence of construction of SL 4 will therefore include references to Hedderwick and Steel, in particular plate X of Hedderwick's treatise (Fig. 7.6) which exhibits many of the features found in SL 4. The construction of SL 4 can also be used as a basis for commenting on that of the vessels discussed in earlier chapters, for while we do not yet have as much detailed information, some interesting aspects of the construction process come to light, especially with respect to shipbuilding traditions, associated ideas, and the temporal and geographic contexts of shipbuilding at those times.

SL 4 building sequence

Keel: Firstly the keel pieces were cut and scarfed. The evidence suggests there were four. Steel specifies four pieces for a merchant vessel of 330 tons but SL 4 was smaller than this. A higher quality or earlier vessel of this size would have had three. The scarf joints were tabled horizontally. On size Hedderwick says:

> ...the keel should be sided one half inch for every foot of the ship's extreme breadth and the hanging (depth) under the rabbet (should be) equal to the siding;... (Hedderwick 1830).

According to Hedderwick the dimensions of SL 4's keel which are approximately 280 × 380mm (11 × 15 inches) should have been more like 330 × 430mm (13 × 17 inches). For a West Indiaman of 330 tons, however, Steel specifies 12 inches breadth × 13 inches depth at the centre of the keel, tapering to 10 inches at the keel/stem scarf and 10 inches at the stern post. Steel's description assumes a vertically tabled scarf. Hedderwick's specifications are also for a vertical scarf but he outlines the arguments for both 'side scarfs' and 'flat scarfs':

> The seam of the scarph is sometimes laid horizontally, but oftener in an up and down way, as it is much stronger in the latter position. But there are various opinions respecting the scarphing of keels. In many parts of the west of England, the flat scarph is preferred, because it is easier to come at should it require caulking, and answers very well when covered with a false keel... (Hedderwick 1830 plate X: 4 and 5 (Fig. 7.6).

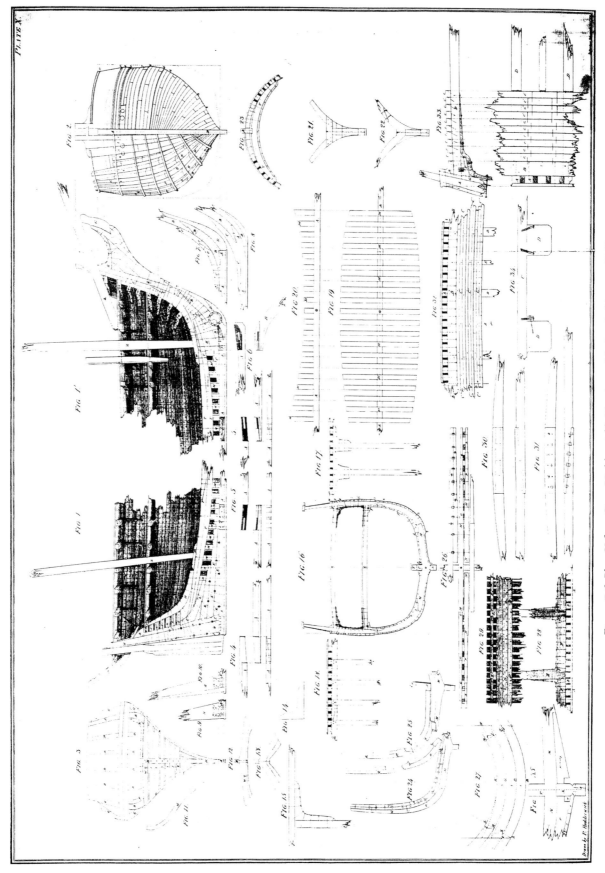

Figure 7.6 Plate X from Peter Hedderwick's *Treatise on Marine Architecture*. 1830.

However, as noted above, the flat scarfs of SL 4 do not seem to have been protected by a false keel.

The keel sections were then set up on a series of solidly bedded blocks, themselves carefully aligned at the correct angle of declination down the centre of the slipway. The pieces were then bolted together after the faces of the joints had been prepared with a luting compound. Both Hedderwick and Steel prescribed tarred felt or flannel. The bolts were to be large headed and 'clenched on rings'. The seam on the top surface was then sealed as follows:

> ...cut a groove in the upper side of the seam, one inch deep and 1/2" wide, caulk the seam with a strip of flannel, then a thread of oakum on top of it; then fit a piece of dry oak into the groove; tar the groove well, and drive the piece tight down with a piece of tarred flannel under and round it, and fasten it down with a few copper nails or oak pins. (Hedderwick 1830).

A similar technique had been in use for centuries and has been found in several archaeologically investigated ships: the *Dartmouth* (new keel 1678), *Sea Venture* (1609 built in 1603?) and the *Mary Rose* (built 1510, re-built 1536, lost 1545). These were all vertically tabled scarfs as described above. In SL 4 there was apparently no tarred felt or flannel in the scarfs but there are traces of what may have been an oakum-based luting compound. Preventing the entry of water also relied on stopwaters, a technique often used for horizontal seams and when used in a keel scarf also improving longitudinal strength by acting as a key in the same way as is suggested for the ceiling planks of *Sea Venture* (see chapter 5, hull structure).

In a keel with vertically tabled scarfs, as the pieces were assembled their alignment on the blocks was carefully checked and treenails were driven into them on either side to hold it absolutely straight. A flat-scarfed keel could be assembled on its side, the even surface of the blocks ensuring alignment. It could then be turned over when assembled and secured. Once the scarfs had been bolted together the 'rabbet' (rebate) for the garboard strake could be completed.

Stem, stern posts and transoms: The exact distance between the stem and stern posts was now marked off on the keel, then the positions of the floors. At this point both Steel and Hedderwick state that the deadwood is laid, although Hedderwick says it can be left until after the stem and stern assemblages are up. In describing these procedures Hedderwick is the more detailed. The stem and the apron also had to be made from several sections. The pieces were shaped and rabbeted (except for the scarfs as in the keel) then assembled and bolted. The apron was cut so its scarfs alternated with those of the stem and with those that would eventually fasten the breasthooks. The scarf was cut for the stem and the keel. Sheers were set up and the stem was hoisted and slung in its approximate position. The scarf was then tarred and flannelled after which the stem was joined to the keel. It was carefully adjusted into alignment with the keel, bolted and shored. The procedure for the stern post was similar. In small ships the transom, fashion pieces and filling transoms were assembled on the ground and raised as one unit. In larger ships, the filling transoms were then removed to lighten the load, being refitted later. For vessels of earlier periods this procedure would have been broadly similar, for the way the rest of the hull was assembled depended on the stem and sternpost as well as the control frames discussed below.

Deadwood: The small piece of forward deadwood in SL 4 could be viewed as the tail end of the apron. However, it is not properly scarfed to the rest of it and simply forms a ramp for the rising floor timbers. It was treenailed in place prior to the floors being laid and was through-bolted between the keel and the keelson. Due to the shape of the hull the stern deadwood was more substantial, though only recovered in fragments. The nature of deadwood, or whether there was any, depended on the hull design and on the period of construction. In earlier carvel hulls, the possibility of forming 'V'-shaped floor timbers out of grown timber made it unnecessary. The stern floors of *Elefanten* (chapter 4) are a good example. In the smaller 'kravel' (chapter 4) V-shaped floors are used all the way to the stern and in the even smaller *Sparrowhawk* (chapter 5), even more acute Y-shaped crooks were used. Later, as ships became larger and/or grown timber scarcer, solid timber had to be used aft of the point where the increasing deadrise made it impossible to use single or linked pieces. The alternative was to form the 'V'-shape required out of separate timbers or 'half floors'.

Frames: With the deadwoods in place the framing was begun.

The operation of joining together the different timbers in constructing the frames, or the methods taken for that purpose, may vary a little according to the custom of the place (Hedderwick 1830).

Both authors emphasise the necessity of avoiding 'grain cut' timber (floors or futtocks cut out of insufficiently curved wood). SL 4 shows several examples of 'grain cut' or 'cross-grained' pieces (Fig. 7.3: T3, T30). This is discussed in more detail below.

First the floor timbers were set on the keel. Steel implies all of them were bolted into position but often this was not the case even in warships or East Indiamen. Hedderwick says this should be done when building a 'fine' vessel but in his general text he refers to every other floor being bolted first. In humbler ships it was sometimes every third or every fourth. With these in place the futtocks for these floors were raised. The procedure for raising the futtocks of these main frames varied. Steel describes the system that was used in the naval and East India Company yards for large ships. The futtocks were cut and assembled on the ground. They were bolted together and the chocks were treenailed in place. The whole frame assembly was then hoisted into place with sheers but not without considerable reinforcement to prevent it losing its correct form. First the chocked joints had quartering (short lengths of plank) nailed over them. Then a brace was fixed in the inside of the frame, fastened at either end with cleats. Then a length of chain was passed round the back of the frame. This was a considerable rigging operation, although in smaller ships these frames would have been reasonably easy to handle. Hedderwick mentions a method for larger vessels (over 300 tons) that must have been much easier in small merchant yards with a small labour force.

For larger vessels, only the first and second, and third and fourth futtocks are bolted together on the ground; but the bolt-holes are all bored, and the bolts driven when the frames are set up... (Hedderwick 1830).

As they were set up they were supported by shores and connected athwartships by 'cross-pawls': temporary planks of wood nailed between opposite frames, tying them together until the beams were fitted.

In the main body of SL 4 generally every third floor was bolted in place. i.e. every third pair of timbers was 'framed'. Over the deadwood the system was less regular. The framed pairs are indicated on the plan (Fig. 7.2). The sequence was interrupted at the midship point where aft of that the frames were bolted in mirror image. This was because the floors forward of the midship section were moulded on the aft side, while those astern were moulded on their forward. The chocks or 'filling' under the floor timbers that increased in size as the floors became progressively more angled above the deadwood are illustrated by Hedderwick (Fig. 7.6) (see also Fig. 7.3: T22, T23).

Harpins and ribbands: When the main frames were up, strong strips of wood were nailed along their outer sides. The first was set at or just below the level of the floor heads. (Alternatively, Hedderwick says two of the bilge planks could be fitted instead.) The others were set at the first and second futtock heads and the level of the wales. Although temporary they were made out of good quality timber and carefully worked so that they formed an even curve. They provided precisely the same means of fairing and adjusting the intermediate frame timbers as was used in the *Mary Rose* and *Sea Venture*. By this period 'ribbands' were those used in the main frames and were usually made of pine. Where they curved round to the stem and stern post – the 'cant bodies' – they were called 'harpins' and were made of oak.

As chapters 4 and 6 have shown, this technique of controlling the shape of frame elements as they are assembled goes back to the earliest phase of carvel building. Whereas Steel at least implies the possibility of raising all the timbers as pre-fabricated frames, Hedderwick says it can be alternate frames (as in East Indiamen), every third as in SL 4 or even every fourth frame.

Staging: (the working platform erected around the ship) was then put up so as to be able to fix the upper ribbands (to the heads of the third futtocks and at the height of the wales and top timbers).

When the main frames were up, shored, cross-pawled, and the ribbands had been run, the intermediate floors were placed.

Keelson: After all the floors were in place the keelson was fitted. Also of necessity made of several lengths, the scarfs were arranged so as to alternate with those of the keel. There was often an upper and a lower keelson. Where this was the case Hedderwick says both pieces were individually scarfed and bolted as though they were single keelsons. They are usually termed a 'double keelson' or the lower timber the keelson and the upper a 'rider keelson' depending on whether the upper element ran all the way aft or not. Using straight timbers for the keelson assemblage as in SL 4 would be cheaper in both cost and labour than the large curved pieces shown in Hedderwick's plate (Fig. 7.6: 1 T). Lloyds surveys of vessels built at this period in the first half of the 19th century refer to the upper element as a 'false keelson' or 'riding keelson'.

When in place bolts were driven through both keelsons and the floors to the keel. In SL 4 the keelson bolts were driven through the intermediate floors. Through the floors of the built up frames there was already a bolt.

With all the floors bound by the keelson the futtocks of the 'filling' frames could be erected. Timbers were individually set up upon the head of the one below, temporarily nailed to the ribbands and chocked. The first futtocks in SL 4 begin about 20 cm from the keel. This was the practice in merchant ships whereas in warships the first futtocks were united across the keel by a 'cross chock'. The merchant ship practice allows water to collect and run to the pumps without coming above the ceiling and damaging the cargo.

> *...the heels of the lower futtocks run no lower than to take a treenail in the outer edge of the Garboard Strake in each timber. To have a bolt driven from the outside, and clenched upon the Limber Strake through the heel of every lower Futtock from the After Hatchway to the Formast* (Steel 1805).

Some of SL 4's limber strake fastenings are exactly as described but others are blind bolts driven from inboard.

All the timbers of SL 4, framed or otherwise, are similarly sided and set close together. In larger and finer ships small pieces of wood were usually set between the timbers through which the bolts passed. This is another aspect of framing well illustrated in the contemporary drawings and models (also Fig. 7.6:26). The chocked joints of SL 4 are also slightly different from those commonly illustrated in the manner the timbers are cut. The lower futtock is cut off at an angle while the foot of the futtock above is cut in a shallow angled butt. Perhaps this made a better platform for the upper futtock to rest on during building than if they were both left with one third of their depth as a butt. This would only apply if the futtocks were still being erected individually.

There would be no advantage in frames that were pre-assembled, yet the bolted frames of SL 4 also have this type of joint. A possible explanation is that the futtocks of the bolted frames were being erected in pairs as described by Hedderwick and in this case angled cuts would also ease handling. Another factor might be the way in which the futtocks were trimmed a little at a time until the shape of the futtock was fair with the ribbands. It would be easier to do this with an adze when the foot had been cut at an angle as the job could then be done more quickly and easily.

Cant frames: At the bow the first cant timbers forward of the frames proper were bolted and probably one or two other pairs of timbers were 'framed' each side both at the bow and the stern. The intermediate cant timbers were not fastened to each other but erected in a similar manner to the filling frames. Set in place supported by shores, they were then nailed to the harpins and possibly reinforced with temporary cleats.

Planking: Prior to planking Hedderwick recommended that the whole outer faces of the timbers be dressed to a smooth even surface so that the planks lay solidly against them. In some places in SL 4 hull there is a slight lip in the surface of the futtock at the seam between planks. This is a common effect of dressing the timber for each plank individually, as the planking proceeded. Although it was a less satisfactory alternative to the method prescribed by Hedderwick we must conclude that SL 4's planking was done that way.

> *There are various opinions respecting the methods of planking the bottom (the hull in general below the wales) some preferring to work from the bilge upwards, others to begin at the wales and work downwards;...* (Hedderwick 1830).

Hedderwick recommended working upwards as the weight of the plank made it easier to fit closely to the one below. Even when working upwards it was common to leave out the strake next to the bilge planking so the chips of wood resulting from work inside the hull could fall through. This too was probably done in SL 4 as very little in the way of shavings and offcuts was found between the frames.

First the outer bilge planks were fitted then a few more strakes were fitted working upwards so as to bind the feet of the second futtocks. If the framing had advanced far enough, the wales were begun at the same time starting with the second from top and working down as far as possible on the staging. Staging was then raised so the planking could proceed upwards. If the timber used was green the bottom planking was left off as long as possible while work proceeded with fitting deck beams. Hedderwick says this planking was worked from the garboard outward to the bilge planks, hence the last strake to be fitted would have been the one next to the lowest bilge plank. This was almost certainly the case in SL 4. A stealer (the tapered end of a plank necessitated by the converging strake alignments due to the curvature of the hull) had clearly been fitted in this position between existing planks. The upper one had to be cut back to accommodate the stealer, shown by two treenails that were cut in the process. The normal method of fastening a stealer is with a spike at the end and a treenail on the next frame back. Had the stealer been left any thinner it would have been too narrow to fasten in this manner without splitting.

'*Making good*': (shortcuts and work-arounds): In a number of places in SL 4 small pieces of wood were used in order to fair the run of the plank. Most common was the placing of a piece of oak board against the outer face of a futtock, filling it out to provide a continuous surface against which the outer plank could rest. A slightly different technique was used inboard. Thin pine board was laid under the central stringer on the starboard side, and several of the ceiling planks on the port side, to bring them up to the level of the planks adjacent to them. In many cases the pine was only a few millimetres thick but in others it seemed as though it was used to pack out two inch planks where two and a half inch planks were obviously required. In other words the filling was required under the outer planking due to a deficiency of the frame timbers, whereas inboard the deficiency was with the planks. This may partly be due to the progressive reduction in thickness of the planks towards the bow noted above or it might result from repair. While either feature might occur in a high quality hull occasionally, perhaps due to error, in SL 4 their frequency indicates they can only be due to economies either adopted expediently to save money or enforced by the highly competitive situation in which the builders and operators of ships in the 19th-century mercantile marine found themselves.

Beams:

> *There are many ways of fastening the deck beams to the ship's side, as by wooden for-and-aft knees and iron hanging knees. Others have no for-and-aft knees, but have their beams fastened by dovetailing them into the shelf and clamps, letting them down one third of their thickness; and then on the upper part are fastened the two legs of a strong plate of iron, which passes round the timber opposite the end of the beam* (Hedderwick 1830).

The first method is almost certainly the way that the decked upper beams of SL 4 were fastened. The alternative method described is similar to the hold beam fastenings in SL 4 except the ends of the beams were not dovetailed (Fig. 7.5). Although the iron knees illustrated by Hedderwick are 'staple knees' in that they are a compound hanging and rising knee in one piece, their shape, because of the horizontal shelf, is very similar to those of SL 4. A variation is that the shelf (Fig. 7.6: f) is placed against the clamp (Fig. 7.6: g) whereas in SL 4 it was placed above it, which would seem more logical and stronger.

Stanchions: Once the beams were in place, pillars or 'stanchions' were placed under them for support. In SL 4 there was probably one pillar to each hold beam stepped onto the false keelson. They could be located in a small mortise or in a small step nailed onto the top of the keelson.

Breasthooks and crutches: With the cant frames in position a series of large wooden knees were placed across the bow, binding the stem assembly and the forward cant frames. The equivalent timbers at the stern were called crutches. Both hooks and crutches were bolted at right angles to the fore and aft line. Consequently the arms of those low in the hull ran diagonally across the frames. The alternative arrangement in the stern consisted of timbers that ran diagonally up to the wing transom. They were called sleepers or pointers. Sometimes both crutches and pointers were used. Like deck knees these elements were later commonly made of iron.

Ceiling: Neither Steel or Hedderwick is explicit on the subject of internal planking. The limber strake (binding the feet of the first futtocks), bilge stringers (over the joint between the floors and second futtocks) and the beam clamps were fitted first (as with the wales and outer bilge planks).

Treenails: As the stringers and intermediate ceiling planks were fitted the rest of the treenails would now be driven right through from the outer hull planks. The outer planks were fastened initially with the butt end bolts and a small number of treenails.

...as to the treenailing of the bottom and the top sides, it is the general custom to double-bore each timber on the breadth of each strake if it exceed 10 inches and to double and single bore all the narrow strakes: that is, to double-bore one timber, and single-bore the next alternately. The size of auger for the bottom plank, for vessels of 100–300 tons measurement, is inch and quarter, and for the top-sides inch and eight. [32mm, 29mm] Hedderwick (1830).

The fastenings in SL 4 exhibit several different features. Fastenings in general can indicate many aspects of shipbuilding. They can be used to deduce the construction sequence, indicate areas of repair, and can also be diagnostic of building traditions. They can therefore also indicate different geographic regions in which a vessel has needed repair.

In SL 4 the outer hull planks wider than ten inches (254mm) were mostly double bored as Hedderwick specifies, while those less were 'double and single bored'. Those less than 7 inches wide (178mm) were single bored. The diameters of the treenails ranged from 25mm to 38mm but the majority were 32 and 35mm (1¼ inch, 1⅜ inch), the sizes recommended by Hedderwick. However, they were often irregular due to the force with which they were driven as well as their manufacture. Treenails were not initially turned on a lathe but split out of straight grained oak. In later periods they were sometimes finished with a circular plane or 'moot' in which case they were more evenly cylindrical. Alternatively they were hand finished with a drawknife hence the octagonal section and irregular shape. They continued to be made this way even in the 19th century as SL 4 shows. Hedderwick appears to prefer mooted treenails:

...treenails should be well rounded, and of equal thickness from the point to within 1-4th of their length from the head, where they should begin to swell a little. By properly driving such a treenail, it will draw the plank close up to the timbers... (Hedderwick 1830).

A selection of SL 4 treenails is illustrated in Fig. 7.7.

Tightening: Depending on certain factors such as wood variety, position in the vessel and its age, treenails were often wedged or otherwise tightened to increase their tightness. Its necessity in so many boat and shipbuilding traditions has resulted in the wide variation in methods used.

Those used in SL 4, included the flat wedges found in Scandinavian shipbuilding and throughout northern European shipbuilding both in clinker and carvel hulls (Fig. 7.7: 109b, 113). Another common form was the square wedge driven centrally into the treenail (Fig. 7.7: 110, 115). This is common in Dutch shipbuilding where it is known as a deutel. A third method seen in SL 4 was the use of several small wedges in one treenail (Fig. 7.7: 116); usually three but occasionally four and in at least two cases five.

Hedderwick's description of the latter is particularly interesting in the context of SL 4:

...in the north of England, where an immense number of vessels are employed in the coal and coasting trade, their vessels are much exposed to striking the ground in going over bars in entering and leaving harbours, and in lying on the ground at times with heavy cargoes. The ship builder and masters of such vessels ought to know well what methods answer best to keep their treenails tight, and prevent the planks from drawing or starting over them. Accordingly at these places, and several others, they tighten the treenails by driving three small tapering wedges or plugs into the head of each treenail. These plugs are made of well seasoned oak, and are about 1½ inches long, and 3-8ths of an inch square at the head, and drawn to a sharp point; they are called punches (Hedderwick 1830).

He goes on to say that punches were not favoured in vessels that were going to hot climates, being found to shrink and fall out. In these ships cutting then caulking the treenails in the manner of yards in the south of England was more effective. This latter method was not found in the hull of SL 4 but was prominent in the treenails of the *Dartmouth* (Martin 1978). Hedderwick implies the method he used himself was the single square wedge:

...the most general method used in Scotland is to drive one large plug or punch into the centre of each treenail, these being made of dry oak, about 2½ inches long and 5–8ths or 3–4ths of an inch square at the head (Hedderwick 1830).

In SL 4 the various types were generally applied according to function. Both plugs and punches were used almost exclusively on the outer hull planks and flat wedges almost exclusively in the ceiling. One reason is that square wedges, plugs and punches, tighten the treenail around its whole circumference without splitting it and are thus

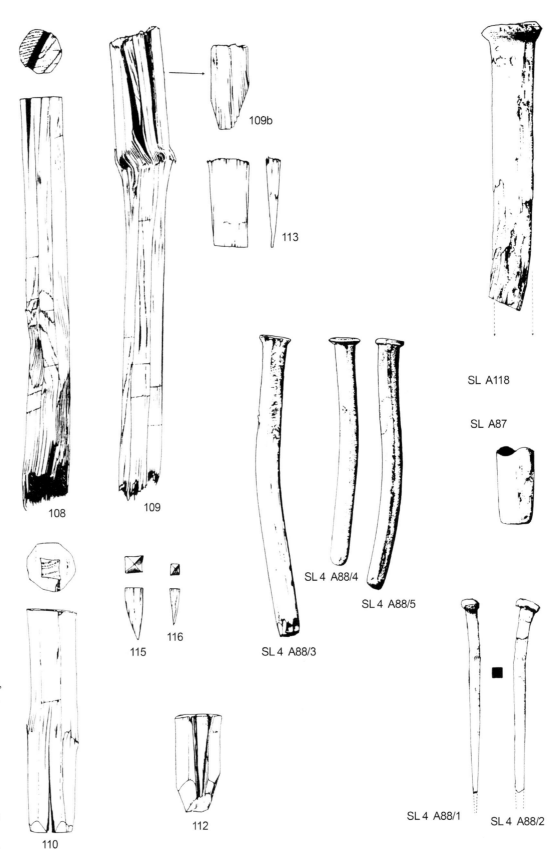

Figure 7.7
SL 4 fastenings: 32mm (1¼ inch) treenails (108, 109); flat wedges (109b, 113); 'rawl' treenail, wedged at the nose (110); plug (115); punch (116); false treenail (112); plank butt-end bolts (copper A88/3, A88/4 and 5 copper alloy); Keel bolts (A118, A87) and spikes A88/1, 88/2 (J. Adams).

more suitable for use outboard. A flat wedge on the other hand splits the treenail across its diameter which could result in leakage as the wedge is often nearly as long as the thickness of the plank. In the ceiling planking this is of no consequence. Of the three techniques flat wedges are probably the strongest. This may have been the reason for the main exception to the above, in that the treenails fastening the garboard and first three or four strakes of SL 4 were mostly flat wedged. On the bottom strakes and bilge planks single plugs predominated, then punches from there upwards.

Hedderwick says that the treenails on the bilge and other round parts of the ship should be wedged to prevent the plank from 'starting' (pulling off) over them with strain of caulking. This implies that the others need not be. Indeed they were commonly left plain for it was supposedly not necessary to wedge oak treenails outboard when new, especially if the ends were slightly flared as recommended by Hedderwick. The wood would swell when wet and become even tighter. Inboard this would not apply as long as the ship remained relatively leak free. In SL 4 it was obviously the standard to finish a treenail inboard with a flat wedge. In many other ships investigated archaeologically and spanning the medieval and modern periods, such as the Bossholmen cog (chapter 4), dating from the 13th century, the *Mary Rose* of 1545, and *Sea Venture* lost in 1609 (chapter 6), wedged or plugged treenails are in the minority.

In theory an oak treenail only needed to be wedged if driving it was found to be relatively easy. If so it was obviously not as tight as it could have been and so was wedged to make it as secure as possible. The ideal case was a treenail that could only just be driven through the timbers that were being fastened. Normally the faceted 'nose' of the treenail was driven 4–5 cm clear of the timber before being cut off. However, in some cases in SL 4 the treenail obviously proved so tight it could not be driven quite far enough, the nose of the treenail being visible below the surface of the plank. When this happened it was usually left unwedged and another treenail was driven nearby. In at least two cases a treenail in SL 4 could not be driven any farther than the inboard surface of the futtock. The hole in the ceiling was filled by a dummy treenail (probably an off-cut) that was duly wedged and so indistinguishable from the genuine fastenings (Fig 7.7: 112)! Another example was observed in an outboard

plank where a treenail hole was augered right at the edge of a futtock. The auger was deflected off the timber so another hole was drilled on the other side of the plank and the redundant hole plugged and wedged.

Repairs and miscellaneous features

In the same way as SL 4 constitutes a useful example of carvel construction in general, it was no exception to the rule that a vessel in use for any length of time needs repair and SL 4 was no exception. These repairs and constructional 'work-arounds', or shortcuts taken by the builders were rarely recorded in the contemporary documents but as techniques they have also been long-lived. On examining the outer surface of SL 4's loose frame timbers there are many treenails that have been cut off flush with the surface. This varies considerably from one timber to another but preliminary examination suggests this is most common in floor timbers. Some of them may be a result of the ceiling being laid before the garboard and lower strakes were fitted. Alternatively it indicates repair.

If outer hull planking was replaced this would necessitate cutting the treenails that had fastened the old planks flush to the frame before fitting the new ones. Prior to this they would have been drilled out to ease removal of the plank. In SL 4 there are several cases where this was done. This is indicated where the auger had penetrated a few millimetres too deep and slightly off line, leaving a shallow hole in the surface of the timber and the old treenail. In some cases the pattern of flush treenails is consistent with the number one would expect to fasten the old planks, i.e. one or two per strake on each frame, but there is great variation and, if this is associated with repair, not all planks were replaced. The other indication that some planks are replacements is that many of their treenails are blind. There could be several reasons for this. Some of the original treenails were blind but the majority were through-fastened. If the ceiling was already *in situ* (as it might have been in a minor repair) there would have been no need to fasten all the new treenails right through. To provide an effective connection a treenail only needs to be a little longer than twice the thickness of the plank.

According to Murray (1863) the grip of even a 6 inch (152mm) treenail is substantial (most of those seen in broken frames are between 20–30cm long). Table 7b lists the results of some experiments testing the resistance of treenails to a shearing force. It can be seen that there was not a great deal of difference in the force resisted. The treenails were observed to move about ½ inch (12mm) before shearing. These figures are an average of several experiments. The maximum force resisted by a 1 inch (25mm) treenail in a 3 inch plank in any experiment was 4.1 tons (Murray 1863).

Evidently effective, the use of blind treenails would avoid piercing any existing ceiling in double the number of places and weakening it. As the ceiling was also important to hull strength this was obviously desirable. One blind treenail (Fig. 7.7: 110), was wedged in its nose. The wedge tightened the treenail as it was driven against the end of the hole rather like a modern rawlbolt. This method of treenailing was described by Tideman (1861:367) although it was not stated whether it was specifically a Dutch technique. No other examples were found among the several blind treenails found loose or seen in fractured timbers of SL 4. It would seem a good technique for ensuring tightness without augering more than half way through the frame.

Around several treenails or treenail holes there are traces of tar or pitch indicating that it had been poured into or applied around the mouth of the hole. Several treenails recovered loose or from damaged timbers are black, suggesting that they had been dipped in pitch prior to being driven. This technique is very old and known to have been widely used in Scandinavian shipbuilding (Cederlund pers. comm.). As there are a relatively small proportion of these treenails they could have been additional fastenings or part of a repair.

If the present skin is the second, it was in place long enough itself to need repairs. Alternatively they are the original planks left in place when others were renewed. In many cases a crack has developed from the end of the plank either stemming from the bolt, which was only a few centimetres from the butt end, or the treenail in line with it. The cracks run from the butt past the bolt and usually to the nearest treenail in the line of the crack, so some could have occurred as the treenail was driven. In some cases these cracks have been caulked like a normal seam, one of them for a length of a metre.

There are other repairs to the outer planks in the form of 'Dutchmen' (small repair patches). These are small rectangular fillets of wood let into the plank and nailed in place. In one case the repair was to the corner of an oak plank and is fastened with 4 small iron nails. Another on the edge of an oak plank is fastened with one large iron spike. Both these patches are only some 20mm thick. Underneath the latter was a treenail which was very close to the edge of the plank and it is possible that a crack between the treenail and the edge necessitated the repair. Two other repair patches of elm, let into elm planks, are both fastened with two copper alloy spikes. One is a repair the full thickness of the plank, the other is a 'Dutchman' let into the plank like the other two. Being close together and so similar, they were probably fitted at the same time. Other spikes of the same type have been noted on loose timbers and possibly originate from the same repair or were carried out in the same place. The other two being differently fastened and both sitting proud of the surface of the plank are presumably repair(s) carried out at different times and/or elsewhere.

There are two other repair patches in the edges of planks that are similar but larger. One of them was fastened with two square pegs. This was a loose find but can only have been done either before the plank was fitted or after the adjacent plank had been removed. The latter is more likely and if so is additional evidence of a repair programme that entailed replacement of some planks and repair of others. Square pegs of the type noted here occur in other instances as well as dowels of 12–17mm diameter but these appear to be for filling nail holes, etc., and are not fastenings. A good example is a case where a hole for the butt-end bolt of a plank was being drilled into the futtock of a paired frame. The auger encountered one of the horizontal bolts, so the hole was plugged and another hole drilled for the bolt on the other side of the plank. In a similar case a hole for a butt-end bolt was drilled too near the edge of a timber and was then plugged with a small square peg of elm. Similar instances included two cases where a treenail hole had been started and then abandoned after 30–40 mm, perhaps because it was off line. The hole was filled with mortar.

There is a little suggestion of repair to the main structural timbers. In the bow the regularity of the framing system breaks down but this may be more a result of the change in the shape of the hull. There is one chock in this area that is so large as almost to be a short futtock. It might be the result of economy but alternatively it could be a repair. Rot often started around these chocks which might have necessitated cutting away the ends of the adjacent futtocks as well, thus requiring a

Treenail diameter inches (mm)	Average stress in tons before treenails fastening planks fracture in 6" and 3" planks respectively.	
	6" planks	3" planks
1 (25)	1.65	1.55
1.25 (32)	2.3	2.3
1.5 (38)	3.1	2.8

Table 7b The strength of treenails (Data from Murray 1863).

much larger replacement. Another chock nearby could be a replacement as it looks much newer than the surrounding timber. It is well shaped and does not include sapwood. Both chocks look as though they were covered in lime which was sometimes used as a preservative. If they are part of a repair it can only have been effected after the removal of the ceiling planks, in which case some of those (perhaps the strakes with pine filling under them) may be replacements. If this is the case one might expect more of the chocks to have been replaced at the same time, especially as many of them included rot-prone sapwood.

Implications

The hull of SL 4 as reconstructed above illustrates several very important factors in the long-term development of large ship carvel building. Although it provides an eloquent summary of northern European carvel construction, it also illustrates adaptations made for the design and construction of vessels to fulfil a specific role, in this case the carriage of bulk cargo. In comparison to Hedderwick's examples, SL 4 was evidently also a vessel very much built to a tight budget, with short-cuts, some of them perhaps deliberately intended to deceive the buyer and/or inspectors. It is highly likely that this was associated with the cost and difficulty of obtaining optimum materials, circumstances reflected in the use of iron by its builders. As a structure SL 4 is also a good example of how English framing systems changed in response to these and other constraints discussed in chapter 2. The system seen in SL 4 was widely used for two centuries or more in English building but is poorly represented in the remaining wooden hulls either afloat or preserved in museums. An overview of this technological trajectory now follows prior to considering aspects of innovation, change and links to wider society.

8

Carvel Building in Retrospect

Structures and materials

At present many aspects of the earliest carvel shipbuilding in northern Europe must be inferred until new documentary or archaeological material is discovered. However, through the ship finds discussed in chapters 4 to 7 we have a far more detailed appreciation of the first major phases of carvel shipbuilding where larger vessels are concerned, particularly those built for long distance mercantile and naval purposes. Clinker vessels by this time had exhibited the effects of dwindling resources and the pressures of cost on the size and quality of the timbers used in their planking. Carvel ships used the material in an entirely different way and in this first flush of activity, exhibit hulls in which choice of timber was largely unproblematic, even in the construction of very large vessels. These hulls are characterised by relatively round body sections, in which as a consequence the majority of the component frame timbers are curved, and by complex but flexible framing systems where some of the constituent frame elements were connected or scarfed to each other in a variety of ways. Although the basic systems were regular, as can be seen in the *Elefanten*, *Mars* and *Mary Rose*, variation due to the necessity of repair or simply through the use of different lengths and sided thickness of the timber to hand appear not to have compromised the overall strength of the hull (Fig. 8.1a).

Such systems, even when rigidly applied, distributed the futtock joints evenly over the whole hull but it seems that if a timber selected for its curvature happened to be long enough to run on another two or three feet then it was not cut short simply to conform to a formula. In other words the builders were not governed by a slavish adherence to formulaic arrangement. Up to a point *ad hoc* repairs would only enhance this effect. There was a certain amount of strength in the joints themselves. This was increased by heavy ceiling planks and stringers through-fastened to the outer hull planking. The result was a strong hull.

Then during the second half of the 16th century, relatively soon after the building of large carvel ships had become established in England, marked changes occurred in the hull form and construction of large ships. This is evident in the various contemporary manuscripts discussed in chapter 6 and supported by the archaeological evidence of the *Sea Venture*. The body section became much more angular, and this had major implications for the techniques of construction. Any sharp curve in the hull section tends to concentrate the futtock joints. The sharper the curve, the harder it is to find a timber that follows the radius of the curve and continues for any significant distance beyond. The shipwright therefore has to place the futtock joints either in the curve itself or not far either side of it purely because the timber will not allow otherwise (Fig. 8.2). Hence an angular hull, for example with a sharp chine and abrupt tumblehome, will have joints concentrated at those locations in the body section. Where this is the case, however well scarfed the component timbers are, there will be an inherent weakness unless other steps are taken.

The answer was to abandon end to end joints as contributors to hull strength in favour of overlapping the timbers. When this is done sufficient hull strength can be achieved with little

Figure 8.1 Framing
systems through time:
a) 15th/16th century,
b) 17th century,
c) late 17th/18th
century, d) 19th century
(J. Adams).

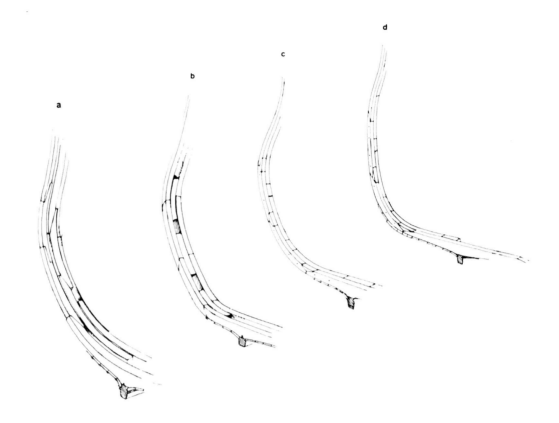

Figure 8.1 Framing systems through time: a) 15th/16th century, b) 17th century, c) late 17th/18th century, d) 19th century (J. Adams).

or no strength in the futtock joints and without any horizontal connection between adjacent timbers (Fig. 8.1b). In fact in this system many of the timbers did not even butt against each other (Mainwaring 1623). It is this system of framing which is exemplified by *Sea Venture* (chapter 6, Hull structure) and is radically different from those used in *Mary Rose* (1511–1545), or *Elefanten* (1559–1564)

Characteristic of late 16th- and early 17th-century shipbuilding in England, this system was also more economical in the use of timber. With all the joints concentrated in the most acutely curved section of the hull, a high proportion of the futtocks in the main body could be formed out of virtually straight timber. This was a continuing trend through to the 19th century (Fig. 8.1c & d). What the relationships are between these changes and the concepts of design is a fascinating question. Was it an increasing shortage of timber and associated expense that promoted the development of hull forms that were cheaper to build? Alternatively, was it developments in hull form in search of better performance to which new procedures of timber conversion and principles of construction had to be matched? Perhaps there is a case to be made for both. Even though by the end of the 17th

century the difference in the price of straight timber and curved timber does not seem to have been that great (see comparative tables for the cost of straight and compass timber in Sutherland 1711), it was enough to enable considerable savings to be made on the number of loads required to build even a moderately sized vessel. This would also depend on where the timber was, for the most significant factor was the cost of transporting it to the yard. In shipbuilding, curved timber was required for a far higher proportion of structural elements than in building houses, barns, etc., and as transporting a load of compass timber was physically harder and thus more expensive than moving the same volume of straight timber, the cost was greater. Thus cost was related to availability as well as location and procuring timbers of the right curvature remained one of the primary activities of shipwrights, apparently requiring them to travel long distances in search of the pieces they required.

It this light it is interesting that when these ships made their appearance the so-called timber crisis was still a century and a half away, yet in response to scarcity, there had already been legislation passed in Henry VIII's reign concerning the sale of timber (Albion 1926). A telling

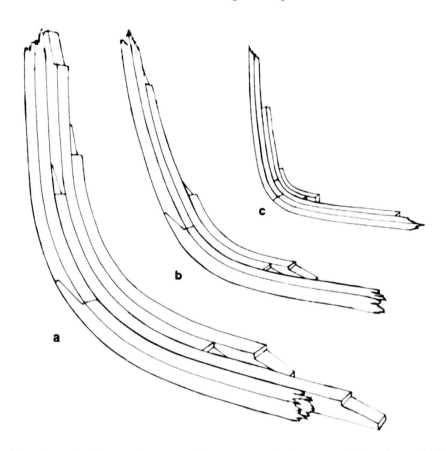

Figure 8.2 Diagram to show the effect of increasingly sharp hull curvature on the location of framing joints. In larger vessels, the sharper the hull, the more closely the joints will be confined to the region of hull curvature due to the way wood grows (J. Adams).

reference from the period in question appears in William Harrison's introduction to Holinshed's Chronicles in 1577:

> *...of cole mines,... we have such plentie in the north and westerne partes of our Islande as may suffice for all the Realme of Englande. And so must they doe hereafter indeede, if woode be not better cherished than it is at this present.*

A century later the scholar John Evelyn in his treatise on forest trees was writing in similarly doom-laden terms (Evelyn 1664). One of his motives for this work was to encourage land-owners to plant more timber for shipbuilding. So was the timber crisis a more deep-seated and gradually compounding problem than has been thought?

Whether there was one at all, in the sense of a shortage for shipbuilding induced by competing industries, has been challenged. Rackham (1976:85, 1986:23–24, 90–97), maintains that it is largely predicated on what he refers to as 'psuedo-history'. The received truths on which the perceived timber famine rests are that between 1550 and 1700 English woodlands were depleted by the charcoal and iron industries. This adversely impacted on shipbuilding, itself progressively over-exploiting the available timber supply for the ever-enlarging fleet. However, this supposed competition for the same resource is probably apocryphal for there is a difference between 'wood' used for fuel or fencing, and 'timber' used for construction of buildings and ships. Efficient charcoal is best made from the smaller branches, hence these industries used 'wood' which was a rapidly renewable resource. This, as Rackham points out, is precisely why extensive woodland survives in areas where these industries were most intensive such as the weald (Rackham 1986:91). As for timber availability, Rackham points to the rapid expansion of the British navy between 1724 and 1774 when it almost doubled in size and for which '*There was not the slightest real difficulty in producing the oak*' (Rackham 1986:24).

While this may be statistically correct in terms of the increase in tonnage, the fact remains that the archaeological record unequivocally indicates progressive change in the way timber was converted and assembled. The parallel (and related) trends towards lower quality, smaller pieces and the use of other wood species must, at least in part, reflect cost and availability. Figure 8.3 shows the increase in timber price per ton

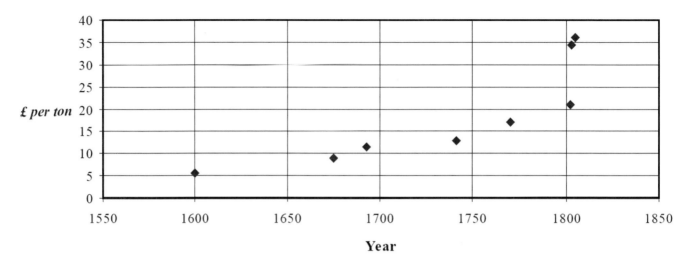

Figure 8.3 Graph to show the rise in price per ton of shipbuilding timber for the building of a third rate between the years 1600 and 1805 (Data from Albion 1952:14).

for the construction of a third rate between the years 1600 and 1805 (data taken from Albion 1952:14). While the increase up to the mid 17th century may not have been excessive against the general inflation over that time, the increase between the seven years war (1756–1763) and 1805 was acute.

Evidence for shortage also comes in other forms. In 1670, well before the period Rackham cites, we have the earliest evidence to date for the use of iron knees (or at least iron brackets of a sort) in the building of English warships. This comes from intriguing correspondence between Samuel Pepys and Sir Anthony Deane and suggests there were problems with obtaining the large grown timbers required for knees. Pepys admonishes Deane for using 'iron dogs' in the construction of the *Royal James*, without consulting the Navy Board. Deane replies:

> *...between you and myself, the King must build no more ships, if nothing can be invented but knees...,, we having not one knee in the yard.* (Goodwin 1998:26).

Even if such problems were intermittent, the acceleration in the shipbuilding of the 18th century was largely possible due to radically changed procedures in the use of timber. Many of these had been adopted well before 1724 and are described in detail below. Production of such enormous fleets without these changes would simply not have been possible. Even had the timber been available, it would have been terminally profligate and economically suicidal to produce the fleets of the 18th century using the technology of the 16th. Rackam (1976:94) is thus mistaken in stating that the *Mary Rose* is essentially the same structure as the *Victory*

(1765). In the sense of being planks on frames yes, but in terms of how the timber had been converted and used they were very different.

Economics related to timber supply must therefore be acknowledged as powerful constraints on shipbuilding but were these factors primary in the development of new hull designs? The power of socio-political circumstances and ideologies has already been highlighted, and associated with these must be the agency of those involved in shipbuilding. We have to credit shipwrights, not only with proprietary motives concerning the protection (and secrecy) of the precepts of their shipbuilding tradition but, in some cases at least, intentional innovation. Mathew Baker's work is a good example. Loewen (1994:18) points out that it was also in the interests of shipwrights like Baker to emphasise the sophistication of shipbuilding as part and parcel of their increasing social status. It has often been observed that innovation in shipbuilding is not something that is wisely done in radical leaps. However, there were clearly pressures on shipbuilders to construct hulls with specific characteristics and capabilities, both for those who were investing in mercantile enterprise and for those who sought or held naval power in these formative stages of state-building. In this context, we must assume that efforts to build hulls with certain qualities, such as speed, manoeuvrability, robust construction and the capability of carrying a heavy armament took careful account of the performance of previous examples. It is difficult to believe that the catastrophic capsize of the *Mary Rose* did not leave a profound impression on those who were charged with building subsequent vessels for the crown. Nor was her loss in this way by any means unique, or indeed the last. The elegant timber arrangement of the *Mary Rose* lower hull was clearly arranged to bear the weight of more heavy guns than ever before, as well as absorb their recoil on firing. The shipwrights who carried out the necessary modifications, perhaps during the rebuild around 1536 and thereafter, obviously understood wooden structures well. The shipwright James Baker, Mathew Baker's father, is credited with being the first to adapt ships to carry heavy guns (Oppenheim 1896a:73). This cannot be true if the *Mary Rose* carried guns firing through lidded ports in her original configuration of 1511, at least at either end of the gun deck (the arrangement shown for many of the ships depicted in the painting of Henry VIII departing for the Field of the Cloth of Gold in 1520). However, as Oppenheim (*ibid.*) points out, James Baker was the only shipwright of his generation who was remembered in the next century. He was made King's Shipwright in 1538 and so may have been centrally involved in the modifications to the *Mary Rose* around that time, giving her what amounted to two decks of heavy guns, the lower firing through lidded ports on the main deck. While highly skilled in wood engineering, what these shipwrights could not do was predict with any precision the effect of their work on stability. But the drive for increased weight of ordnance on ships continued unabated. Are we therefore seeing this as a factor in the designs of the later 16th century, with their deeper, more wedge-shaped hulls and their increased tumblehome? The fallacy of tumblehome improving stability by bringing the weight of guns inboard is well known. As to whether this was recognised prior to the 18th century is difficult to say. It did have an indirect benefit, as by lightening the deck structures above the waterline it lowered the centre of gravity and this may have been part of the thinking behind reducing castling. The author of Admiralty Library MS 9 implies as much when discussing the relative merits of a hollowing post as opposed to straight:

> *I rather commend the hollowing post, which is more comely to the eye and more ease to the ship's side; seeing by tumbling thereof the weight of ordnance and of the upper work is brought so far into the body of the ship that it is supported without stress, whereas in a straight post they both overhang the side, which is a great burden to it.* (MS 9: *sweeps*).

For other benefits of tumblehome see Bartlett (1997:478) and Barker (1998:95).

Irrespective of whether or not Mathew Baker believed a ship with tumblehome was intrinsically less likely to capsize, many of the ships he built were warships. It is therefore inconceivable that this was not a major consideration as he experimented with different ways of generating improved designs. Hence it is difficult to accept Gillmer's assertion that as 'frame-first' building was refined, hulls were designed by methods of some geometrical elegance which had little to do with performance (Gillmer 1985:261). From an opposing perspective one might maintain that the geometric procedures developed to generate the complex underwater body was elegantly simple. The initial analysis of the *Sea Venture* model, as reported in chapter 6, has indicated a highly stable hull form. More tests are planned that will give further insights into performance, but suffice to say, the sea-keeping ability of any vessel that could stay afloat in a hurricane for nearly four days must be judged fairly successful. As archaeological remains show, these vessels are materially different from those of the previous phase. Without falling victim to the sort of partisan representation of them referred to by Phillips (1994:99), as indicated above, there are many contemporary accounts that indicate their performance was significantly different too. As material culture, none of the changed aspects of hull form, construction, rig and use was random or unrelated to society. Interrelated causes underpin them all. While aspects of their timbering could be judged inferior, as compromises (which all ships are) their capabilities clearly exceeded those built a generation earlier.

Although the nature of the relationship between design, timber availability and framing systems in the 16th and early 17th centuries is difficult to quantify, other changes began to appear that were undoubtedly due to economy in timber conversion. The next significant development occurred, probably gradually, during the 17th century. This time it did not primarily concern the hull form, or at least it was independent of it, as it came to be used in English vessels of all shapes and sizes. Apart from the radically sharp hulls of the early frigates exemplified by the *Dartmouth* (1655), hull form changed fairly slowly. As the graphs in chapter 6 show there was a trend towards greater breadth relative to height and a more rounded lower section but the fundamental principles of designing hull form based on arcs of circles, though refined, essentially remained unchanged. In the framing system there was probably an increasing tendency to reduce the gaps or spurkets between the frames. This, coupled with the ever increasing cost as well as the difficulty in obtaining compass timber, directly influenced the next developments. That one can be specific with regard to cause in this case is because, as will be shown, there is hardly any other possible motive for the procedures that were adopted throughout the shipbuilding industry. That they were necessary of course implies adherence to designs, themselves born of accepted concepts, ideas and ultimately needs. It is these changes that can be seen in many of the vessels considered above. SL 4, representing the extremity of the process, best illustrates the principles involved.

On examining the frame elements of SL 4 it is clear that in most cases they have been cut out of timber that curves much less than it would in ideal circumstances. In general, true 'cross grain', i.e. where the wood grain passes from one side of the timber to the other, has been avoided but in many cases curved futtocks have been cut out of virtually straight timber and split as a result. The characteristic shape of these timbers is the angled end cut to accommodate the chock. The reason for the chock is illustrated by the diagrams in Figure 8.4a–c. Futtock *a* is cut from a timber closely matching the desired curvature. It is the maximum length and thickness that could be cut from this piece of timber without including rot-prone sapwood. The ends can be butted or scarfed to the next futtock by any method required (although if scarfed, the length of the overlap will be lost). Futtock *b* is of the same curvature and size but cut from a less curved timber, so there is no alternative to sacrificing the ends. Even where the discrepancy in the radius of the futtock and the timber is not so great, conscientious removal of sapwood will still result in an angular end. So too would this be the case if futtock *a*, was extended (*a2*). Although not ideal, the timber of futtock *b*, is sufficiently curved for the central grain to run continuously from end to end. Futtock *c*, on the other hand, is cut from virtually straight timber. If all the sapwood is removed, the outer surface of the futtock will have a rounded section, exactly what is seen in many SL 4 timbers. In extreme cases the futtocks cannot even conform to the required shape. Many of them are a compromise, being less rounded but only because a considerable quantity of sapwood has been left. In the terminology of the Lloyds

surveyors of the time, they are not 'well squared' or 'well sapped'.

Butting futtocks of type *b*, or *c*, to each other leaves an angular gap which if not filled reduces the area of hull available for solid bedding of the inner planking and for solid through-fastening of treenails. The triangular gap is therefore filled with a chock. The chocks vary in size depending on how much had to be trimmed off the futtock. 'T 30' (Fig. 7.3), is a better than average first futtock from SL 4. Yet it is still cut from almost straight timber. At its heel a large chock has been used to fill the gap. On others this chock is well over half the thickness of the futtock (Fig. 8.5). Of the chocks in the other futtock joints, some are diminutive (in a few cases there is no chock at all) while others are quite large. The latter make a reasonably coherent end to end joint between the futtocks but this is a secondary function. A joint made this way does not have the strength of a properly scarfed joint, demonstrated by the considerable reinforcement necessary when the frames were raised as a pre-assembled unit in the manner illustrated by Steel (1805).

Joints of this type are well illustrated in the various treatises on naval architecture in the 18th and 19th centuries. However, they are always shown as being butted and of a regular size (e.g. Fig. 8.6). As the majority of these works are by eminent shipwrights working in naval dockyards or large merchant yards, their treatises have a strong bias to warships or the finer, large merchant ships such as East Indiamen. On the proper jointing of timber in this fashion, Steel says:

...each [timber] should stand upon its proper head... The heads and the heels of all the timbers to have one third of the substance left in the moulding (Steel 1805).

In other words at least one third of the moulded depth of the futtock should meet in a true butt. The implication is that they were not necessarily to be the same size as long as they did not exceed the specified depth. If this was exceeded to the point where the chock became the same thickness as the frame this was a 'through chock':

...if one timber happens to be short, provide the next long enough to make good the deficient length, as through chocks should always be rejected... (Steel 1805).

He goes on to specify that: *'the seats of the chocks should not exceed once and a half the siding of the timber'* (Fig. 8.6). By limiting the amount that is

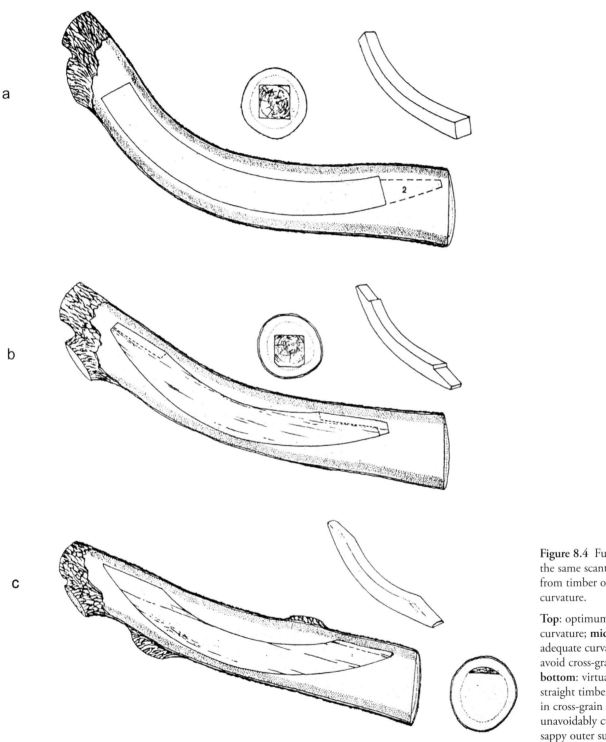

Figure 8.4 Futtocks of the same scantling cut from timber of different curvature.

Top: optimum curvature; **middle**: adequate curvature to avoid cross-grain; **bottom**: virtually straight timber resulting in cross-grain and an unavoidably curved, sappy outer surface (J. Adams).

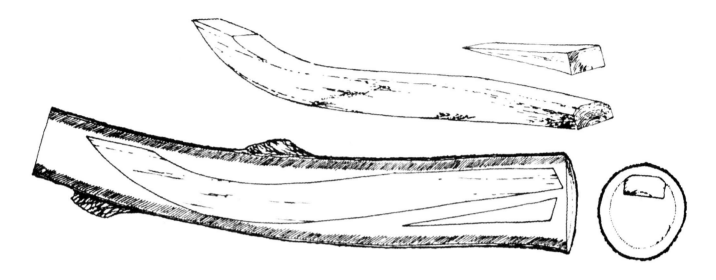

Figure 8.5 Drawing of a typical first futtock of SL 4. Cut from virtually straight timber, a large chock is needed to build up the heel. The photograph shows a typical heel chock. The run of the grain and the wainy corners of the floor it is fastened to can be clearly seen. The chock has come off the floor in the foreground, revealing even poorer quality, hardly any sapwood having been removed (Drawing and photo: J. Adams).

trimmed off the timber and the overall length of the chock, one is effectively limiting the extent to which the available timber can be utilised. It is interesting that rather than flout these rules he advocates compromising the regularity of the framing system as the lesser of two evils.

The chocks in the hull of SL 4 do not answer to a set proportion at all. As noted, one of the chocks is not a wedge but more like a very short futtock. Similarly a wreck on the beach between Zandvoort and Bloemendaal, investigated by the

Dutch Ministerie voor W.V.C. in April 1986, showed extremely long chocks. With its general characteristics and its yellow-metal bolts in the plank butts, it too looks like a 19th-century English vessel.

A further, much earlier example serves to show how the technique probably originated. In the Swedish National Maritime Museum, Stockholm there is a section of hull cut from the warship *Carolus XI*, also known as the *Konung Karl* (*King Charles*) built in 1679 and scuttled in 1733. It

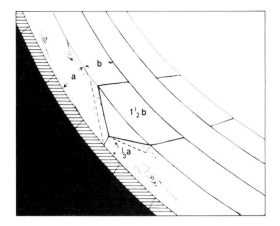

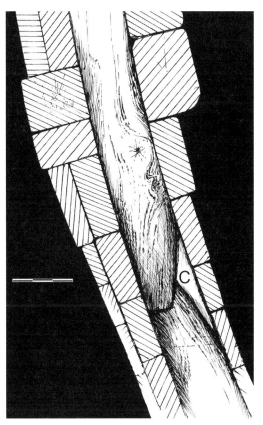

Figure 8.6 (left) Diagram of a futtock chock as specified by Steel. Maximum length not to exceed 1.5 x the sided dimension of the timer (b). Dotted line left indicates a through-chock, dotted line right indicates preferred dockyard 'butted' chocks (1805) (J. Adams).

Figure 8.7 (right) Reality as opposed to theory: Measured sketch of a chock in the 17th-century Swedish warship *Carolus XI*, a large warship that nevertheless reveals the real role of such fillers. Scale 30cm (J. Adams).

was excavated in the Naval shipyard at Karlskrona in 1941 (Cederlund 1983:55). The section is cut from the main gun deck and is massively timbered. The ends of two futtocks can be seen where, rather than cut them so they could be butted across their full depth, there is a slight gap left because both have been cut slightly beyond their optimum thickness. This has left the characteristic gap, which although relatively small has been duly filled with a small chock (Fig. 8.7). The grain of the wood and the slightly rounded profile of the timber as they curve towards the butt, show that this was not a formulaic way of finishing a futtock joint. It resulted from the way the timber was used. What is interesting is that modern scholars have drawn these very timbers as though they were really joined with a large, butted chock of the type specified by Steel and seen so commonly in diagrams of ship structure (e.g. Fincham 1851, Abell 1948, Dodds and Moore 1984; Longridge 1955). In other words, the way it is assumed futtock joints 'were' at this period seems to have subjugated observation of reality. It is probably significant that the *Carolus XI* was built by Robert Turner who, along with two other English shipwrights, Thomas Day and Francis Sheldon, arrived in Sweden in 1659 (Nilson 1985:42). It was Sheldon who had built *Riksäpplet* (1663) and then with Turner had built *Kronan* in 1665 (Haldin 1963:146). This appears to be the result of a decision by the Swedish monarchy to have ships built in the English manner rather than in the Dutch tradition that had been favoured for many years. The Sheldons prospered as a shipbuilding dynasty in Sweden and were still active until the early 19th century. Turner, building in the English manner, presumably made free use of the ubiquitous chock, something the Dutchmen who preceded him did not do.

The other development in the framing of ships was the use of bolts fastening adjacent futtocks horizontally. This may have begun as a constructional aid but it led to a change in the constructional sequence. It may have been connected with the new way of utilizing timber necessitating chocks and would have become economically more viable with the reducing cost of iron. As seen in the construction of the earlier ships, the majority of timbers were raised individually. They were supported on shores, nailed to the ribbands and, until planked, could be further secured by having wedges knocked between them or having additional temporary battens nailed across them. The details of the procedure certainly varied widely but it would not be so easy with chocks. Not only were there double the number of pieces involved but there was less surface for the heel of one futtock to rest upon the head of the one below. A logical step was to bolt the component futtocks of a frame together on the ground and then raise them in one unit. As a result the term 'frame' came to refer to a paired set of connected or 'framed' timbers as opposed to the 'filling frames' or 'filling timbers' installed separately. As has been emphasized, even when fully developed as a construction sequence not every frame was so formed, the filling frames being assembled timber by timber in the earlier manner.

In what order these changes occurred is difficult to say. Various authors have stated that the use of chocks was introduced in 1714. The source for this 'fact' can be traced back through various secondary sources to authorities like John Fincham (1851:205) who was writing when the method was still in use. He gives that date for the introduction of chocks when describing the system that Sir Robert Seppings developed and proposed as superior. Seppings presented his method to the Royal Society in a paper entitled: 'On a new Principle of Constructing Ships in the Mercantile Navy' being published in its *Philosophical Transactions for the year 1820*. In it he discussed the origin of chocks and cited '...*an old work in my possession, dedicated to GEORGE the First.*' On this basis he supposed the practice was introduced '*around 1714*', being the year in which George I came to the throne. William Sutherland's treatise: 'Britain's Glory or Ship-Building Unvail'd' was first published in 1717 and is dedicated to George I. The dedication is prominent, even more so in the 1729 edition where the date 1714 is emphasized, so this could well be the 'old work' to which Seppings refers.

In fact Sutherland (1717:120) describes chocks in some detail and, like Steel a century later, recommends correct proportions in relation to the futtock (Fig. 8.8). Although he does not mention them in his earlier, shorter work 'The Shipwright's Assistant' published in 1711, it is obvious that he is describing an established practice. The example of the *Carolus XI* has already been cited and as it was built by an English shipwright we can assume that the use of chocks was part of its original construction in 1679 and not a technique he learnt or invented in Sweden. They were also found during the excavation of the *Dartmouth*, built in 1655, rebuilt 1678 and lost 1690 (Martin 1978). Interestingly, in the *Dartmouth* there were no horizontal fastenings between the futtocks in the section of hull that was excavated and subsequently salvaged. This suggests a transitional stage although some bolts may have been used higher up.

Sutherland describes bolting the futtocks together, although he says that in large ships they were only bolted up to a certain height (a similar compromise to that recommended by Hedderwick over a century later). As with most new practices change probably occurred at different times in different areas. It is also possible that the use of chocks was a long established remedy, the occasional one being used where inadequacy of specific timbers made it necessary as in the *Carolus XI*. With rising timber prices its use presumably became increasingly widespread until it became standard practice. Becoming so, especially in the

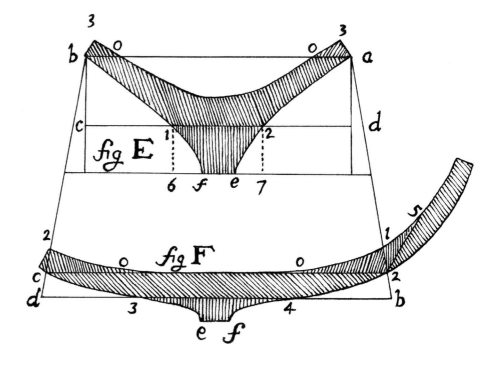

Figure 8.8 Chocks as illustrated in 'Britain's Glory' or Ship-Building Unvail'd (1717). In the lower diagram (Fig. F), the numerals 0-2-5 define the chock between the floor and second futtock. Note that rising floors in large ships needed a chock or filling piece (for example 1-2-f-e in Fig. E – resting on the keel at f-e (after Sutherland).

building of warships and East Indiamen subject to stricter quality control, not to mention insurance assessment, would necessitate establishing standards like those described by Steel.

Developed in the 17th century, the method was the norm throughout the 18th and well into the second half of the 19th century. The new method proposed by Sir Robert Seppings in 1818 involved butting the futtocks and joining them with circular 'coaks' (large dowels). The system made use of shorter futtocks which reduced the curvature required in each piece and enabled them to be butted across their full thickness (Fig. 8.9). In his Royal Society paper (Seppings 1820), he criticised the practice of only bolting alternate pairs of frame timbers:

In forming the frames or ribs, half the timbers only are united so as to constitute any part of an arch; every alternate couple only being connected together: the intermediate two timbers (termed fillings) being unconnected with each other, and merely resting on the outer planking, instead of giving support to it... This loose practice is, I believe, peculiar to the English merchant ship-builder; and indeed was persued till very lately even in His Majesty's Navy, while the preferable system of connecting the ribs was common to other maritime powers (Seppings 1820:134).

While ships with all their timbers horizontally bolted were undeniably stronger, his assertion that the filling frames were only 'resting' on the planking ignores the strong binding effect of the latter. More than two centuries earlier ships with virtually all their timbers 'resting' on the planks had circumnavigated the world.

But Seppings was even less complimentary about the use of chocks:

...the present mode of joining together the several pieces of the same rib, is also highly objectionable. It is done by the introduction of a third piece, technically termed a 'chock' or 'wedge piece'... Of these chocks not one in a hundred is ever replaced [i.e. reused] in the general repair of a ship; for they are not only found defective, but very generally to have communicated their own decay to the timbers to which they are attached. Besides this, the grain of the rib-pieces being much cut, to give them the curvature required, has a

Figure 8.9 Sir Robert Seppings' butt and coak system contrasted with the 'old' chock system (left) (from Fincham 1851).

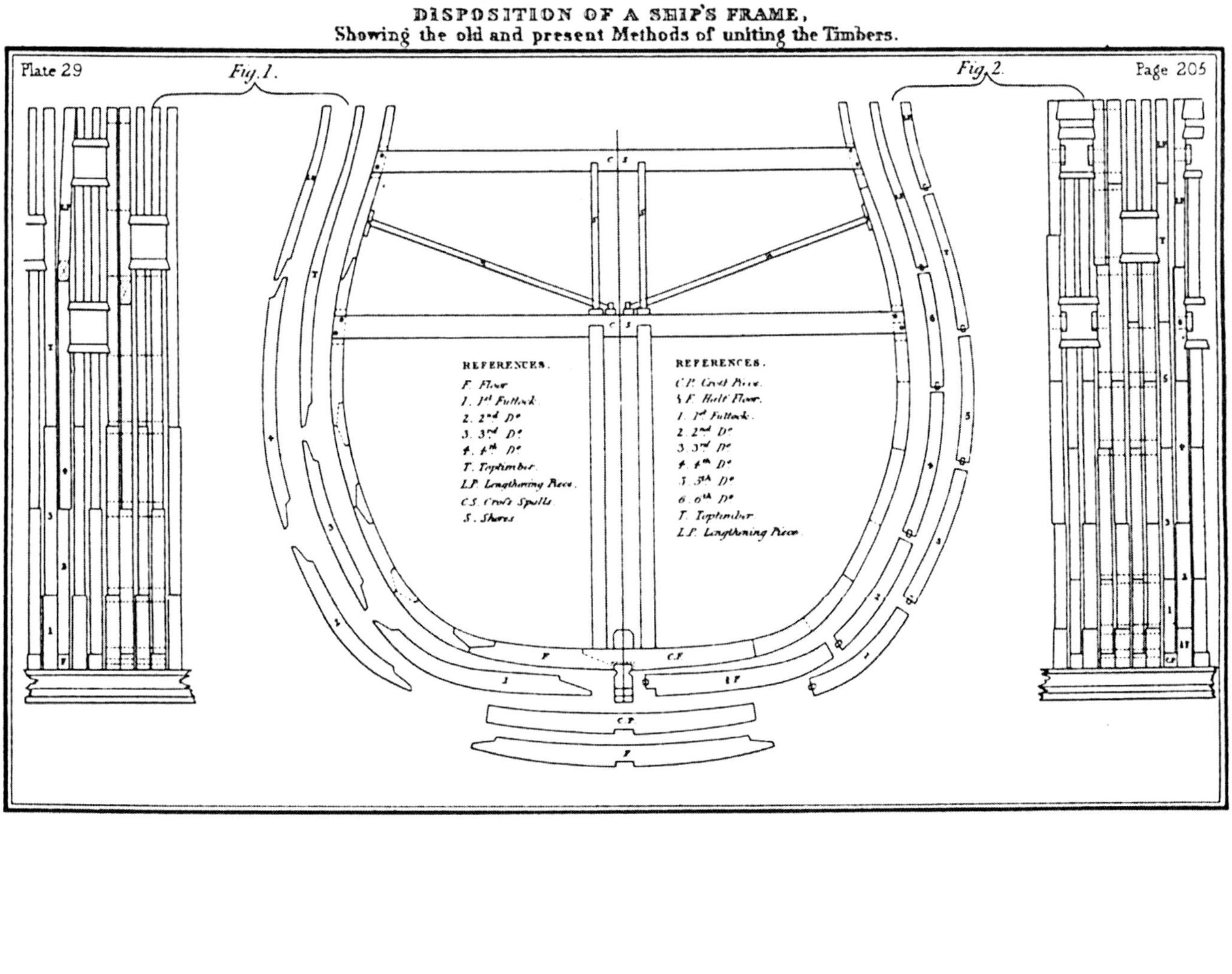

DISPOSITION OF A SHIP'S FRAME,
Showing the old and present Methods of uniting the Timbers.

considerable share in weakening the general fabric. That they occasion a great consumption of materials, is obvious, as the ends of the two rib pieces must first be cut away, and then be replaced by the chock (Seppings 1820:134–5).

This last statement is interesting, for as shown in Figures 8.4c and 8.5, in timbers where the grain was '*much cut, to obtain the curvature required*', the space occupied by the chock was not cut from solid timber at all. This apparent contradiction continues in the next paragraph:

The introduction of chocks was no doubt to procure that curvature which is so necessary in the formation of a ship, when crooked or compass timber became scarce (Seppings 1820:135).

This may stem from the fact that the chock system had become so formalized in the Royal dockyards, the timbers were cut and joined in this manner whether it was necessary or not. When a curved piece was cut from straight timber there was undeniably waste along its length, even though this could be used for chocks and other small pieces.

Seppings' alternative method was certainly a great improvement and survives in one of the ships he built; the *Unicorn* (1824) which is still afloat in Dundee. In his '*Philosophical Transactions*' paper Seppings also advocated the use of his system to merchant ship builders, particularly for East Indiamen. Apparently some merchant vessels were subsequently built using this principle and Hedderwick (1830) illustrated it in his treatise but, despite general consent that there were better ways, merchant yards continued to use chocks for many years. In 1842 William Hutchins proposed a 'new' method of framing and jointing for merchant ship construction very similar to and presumably derived from that advocated by Seppings, which by then had become the norm in the navy. John Fincham in 1851 referred to the use of chocks as the 'old method' but plans of merchant ships built well after this date, as well as Lloyds surveys, show that it had remained the standard method for wooden framed English ships.

SL4 and the ship from Zandvoort/Bloemendaal both indicate that unbutted 'sliver' chocks as they were called were normal in vessels up to about 350–400 tons. The great similarity with those illustrated by Sutherland (1729) and of the *Carolus XI* indicate this rougher application of the technique had probably remained constant since the 17th century. It had certainly stood the

test of time. Hedderwick's opinion was that although there were better methods, such as dove-tailing the chock, or the Seppings system of butt and coak used by '*some of the Navy People*', chocks if well fitted would '*answer every purpose*'. Whether it was chocks or the 'butt and coak' method, both were the result of the constraints imposed by the price and availability of timber. This is best summed up by Hedderwick's final remark on the subject of joining futtocks: '*I consider a method of scarphing them, where it can be obtained, as preferable to either.*'

Ribs and skins

All of this raises interesting questions about the prominence of various ideas and concepts embedded in the carvel tradition as practised in the English manner, which for a long period included Sweden and were presumably closely paralleled elsewhere. In an examination of what he has called 'Dutch-flush' building, Maarleveld (1992, 1994) draws ideological and socio-political distinctions between the Dutch method in its social context on the one hand, and those of other European regions on the other. In so doing he is one of the few maritime archaeologists who have ventured much beyond comparison of shipyard practices and operating environments. The Dutch bottom-based method of building a flush-planked hull was in a way a shell-first procedure (as seen in Fig. 4.5) which, as pointed out in chapter 4, was essentially the same as had been used to fabricate the lower hulls of cogs for centuries (far longer if continuity with Romano-Celtic vessels is accepted). Maarleveld's thesis argues that it is '*virtually impossible*' to separate the Dutch building procedure into a design phase and a construction phase. While the degree to which this is true could be debated, the Dutch shipbuilding process was certainly more transparent and thus potentially egalitarian in that the majority of the participating labour force not only had access to the requisite knowledge, they had to share, in part at least, the master shipwright's skills in order to achieve the construction successfully. In this way it has strong similarity to the building of Nordic clinker ships in the medieval period. Maarleveld is therefore correct in pointing out that the Dutch master builder would have found it far more difficult to keep his skills and knowledge secret in the manner claimed for shipwrights in England, or in most other regions for that matter. How effectively the master shipwrights could keep their secrets is questionable given the remarkable uniformity of the methods of design that we know about. But once the design procedure was committed to paper and resolved by increasingly sophisticated mathematics, it could be carried out behind closed doors. The differentiation of knowledge between master shipwright and ship carpenter was reinforced.

As technical procedure and social practice the Dutch approach was undoubtedly different from others. However, in demonstrating the distinctiveness of the Dutch manner, Maarleveld goes a little too far in generalising the practice of other regions, assuming they uniformly consisted of frame systems of interlocking timbers which were pre-erected and to which the planking was applied. This inference rests on the assumption that the fundamental importance of the midship section in Iberian and related traditions is necessarily transmitted throughout construction, where the frame is '...*the outstandingly essential element in the ship's strength*'. Drawing on the undeniably long-lived parallel between the 'ribs' of a ship and the skeleton of an animal, Maarleveld reasons: '...*in order to fulfil this conceptual function the constituent parts of the frames should be well connected indeed.*' (Maarleveld 1992:163). Hence the predesigned, built-up frame and the overall strength of '*this internal skeleton is deemed essential in the overall strength of the ship.*' (Maarleveld 1994:159). This is contrasted with the Dutch situation where the emphasis is unequivocally on the shell of planking. '*The zoological parallel and the concept of a skeletal framework do not apply.*' (Maarleveld 1992:163). This zoological analogy in Portuguese shipbuilding is certainly emphasized in the writings of Fernando Oliveira (Oliveira 1570 (1991:63). However, primary importance of the midship section in the design process did not necessarily translate into framing systems that had independent structural integrity or a segregated frames-then-planks construction sequence. Even in the Basque ships such as the Red Bay vessel, it is only the lower frames in the main body that were connected by dove-tailed mortises. The rest of these frame elements, and all of those fore and aft, were assembled piecemeal controlled by the ribbands, with the planking advancing in tandem, (Grenier, Loewen and Proulx 1994:139). A similar approach appears to have been used in the *Mary Rose* while in the *Sea Venture* a generation later, even fewer of the frame

elements were interconnected. In some cases they did not even meet (see chapter 6 *Hull construction*).

In the *Mary Rose* some of the frame elements are joined end to end but few securely enough to regard them as coherent strength members in the manner of later built-up frames. Admittedly, recent inspection (by this writer and Christopher Dobbs of the *Mary Rose Trust*) showed that there are simple, shallow hooks or keys between some floors and adjacent timbers but they are not the regular dovetailed mortises as seen in the Cattewater wreck (Redknap 1984:24), Red Bay and the many other archaeological finds of this tradition. Just as in the Iberian cases, these hooks presumably assisted the construction sequence based around control frames. Of the other *Mary Rose* futtock joints, some are crude scarfs where the ends are stepped and tapered but others are simply butted or overlapped side by side. Not only that but there are very few treenail fastenings between adjacent timbers. Those that there are also seem likely to be associated with the construction sequence. Even in the *Elefanten* built in 1559, where the frame timbers are scarfed together in a regular manner, what at first sight look like strength joints are fastened with only two iron spikes. Thus they too would appear to be associated as much with the procedures of controlling assembly than with the strength of individual frames or the system as a whole. While there is certainly end to end integrity in the framing elements of *Elefanten* and a certain amount in some of those in the *Mary Rose*, whether scarfed or not, the strength of their framing systems mostly derives from strong through-fastening of treenails and bolts between the thick inner and outer planking, from high quality timber, and the fact that the joints are positioned evenly throughout the hull. In other words, apart from the demonstrable bottom plank-first approach, many of the things proposed as characteristic of Dutch-flush framing are found elsewhere.

The point is, as the cases described in the previous chapters show, that much, if not most carvel building in the 16th and 17th centuries was not 'skeleton' construction in the sense of a complete framing system of 'ribs' erected prior to the application of a plank 'skin'. In reality, the two advanced side by side which, *de facto*, precluded any possibility of the majority of the timbers constituting 'frames' in the sense of a coherent unit. Apart from the control frames, of which there might only be three, there would be precious little access to fasten adjacent timbers anyway. Recent ethnographic work shows that this flexible approach to carvel building is still practised world wide (Sarsfield 1992; Blue et al. 1998; McGrail et al. 2003).

In a wider sense this doesn't detract from Maarleveld's case where the conceptual influences on shipbuilding are concerned, in that we can postulate that there are always connections between the social practice of ship construction (or that of any other craft tradition) and the society at large. In the Dutch case, this open, efficient method of construction suited Dutch entrepreneurial maritime mercantile enterprise. In the late 17th century change in society at large and mercantile practice in particular, created tensions and contradictions that forced the issue. A case in point would have been the highly organised Dutch East India Company, *Veerinigde Oostindishe Compagnie* (VOC). This forerunner of modern multi-national corporations was highly autonomous in many respects, more so than the larger *Honourable English East India Company*. The various chambers of the VOC built their own ships according to specifications drawn up by committees similar to the British Admiralty Board. As Maarleveld suggests, the existing methods, executed without elaborate design drawings, probably did not mesh well with bureaucratic infrastructures like the VOC which increasingly required control, consultation and second opinions. It is perhaps no coincidence that change occurred in the VOC yards partly through the head-hunting of English expertise, primarily administered and controlled within the Amsterdam Chamber. In the 1740s a wholesale revision of the company's ships was undertaken and provides a fascinating insight into the mechanisms whereby a new form of vessel is eventually realised. Charles Bentam, one of three English shipwrights brought to Holland in the 1720s, was commissioned to design the new 150 foot class of East Indiaman. He duly made or supervised the building of a dockyard model to his design in 1742. The *Amsterdam* was to be one of eight ships constructed according to these specifications. Launched in 1748, on her maiden voyage in 1749 the ill-fated *Amsterdam* sailed into one of the worst recorded gales in history (Marsden 1975, 1985; Gawronski 1986, 1987). Seeking shelter in Pevensey Bay on the south coast of England, she grounded in the heavy seas and lost her rudder. Though still two miles

offshore the captain had no choice but to anchor in the hope of riding out the storm. After ten days the gale showed no signs of abating and with an appalling number of fatalities exacerbated by the freezing cold of January, the anchor cables were cut and the ship run ashore at Bulverhythe near Hastings. The spot where the ship was driven ashore (perhaps intentionally) is the silted up mouth of a former river. The hull did not therefore break up but rapidly subsided into the deep sediments to be preserved in remarkably complete condition, a high-resolution view of the VOC. When parts of the ship were comprehensively recorded during three seasons of excavation between 1984 and 1986 (Marsden 1985; Gawronski 1986, 1987), the construction was found to be very different from what had been expected on the basis of Bentam's detailed model. As documentary sources were already being routinely interrogated and used to generate questions that archaeology might answer, this discrepancy put the ball back in the archival court. It was not long before some of the reasons began to emerge, not least the long interval between the completion of Bentam's design and the start of actual construction. One significant but entirely fortuitous event occurred in 1744 when three French ships were captured by the British and sold to the VOC at Cape Town. French construction and sailing qualities were much admired even by their arch rivals and all the ships were examined thoroughly. Elements of their construction were noted and recommended for use in subsequent VOC ships (Kist 1986:43). By the time the *Amsterdam* was finally on the ways in the VOC's Amsterdam yard, it appears that some of this rethinking had worked its way through. Also at this time Dutch construction methods in the VOC yards involved a considerable amount of prefabrication of major elements such as beams and knees. When comparing the actual disposition of the *Amsterdam's* internal timbers, they have far more similarity to earlier specifications for 145 foot ships (the largest class prior to the new 150 footers), particularly those built in the VOC yard at Middleburg (Adams 1986b:25; Kist 1986:43). Perhaps a compromise was arrived at to avoid the waste of large numbers of preformed timbers that could not be used in the locations required by the new design. Perhaps less functional and all too human influences might also have been at work, in the form of conservative resistance to new-fangled ideas of the English designer.

In referring to the integration of historical and archaeological material discussed in chapter 3, this is a case where both sources generated questions that would never have been raised, let alone answered in discrete enquiries. The actual vessel, though recent in archaeological terms, proved very different from anything that could have been predicted from the historical sources alone. Similarly, without them many of the answers to questions arising from inspection of the actual ship would have remained conjectural. Perhaps the holistic nature of such enquiry can be partly attributed to fresh connections: the information was there all the time but without the stimulus of archaeological enquiry, it would have remained as a series of disparate records, the relationships unsuspected. Intergrated into a broader enquiry they provide a new insight into why the changes and differences are as observed.

'Dutch-flush' building had essentially developed as the particular response to the requirements of shipbuilding as they were in the late 16th century. Rather than adopting a new method of design and construction they adapted a long established local technique. It was only when there were changes in the way shipping was organised and controlled that traditional procedures in the shipyards were put under stress. Maarleveld's analysis of Dutch flush construction and its building sequence is thorough (1994:160–161) but it is his comments relating it to wider society that point the way to really understanding it in the context of northern European shipping and the maritime development of northern Europe. Might we see similar approaches or even the use of the Dutch method itself in similar societies?

In fact Dutch shipbuilding expertise and methods had been drafted into the service of the Swedish state for the construction of its large warships. At first sight this example might appear to refute Maarleveld's case, for if Dutch practice reflected its social context, how could it have been used in Sweden in the service of a hierarchical state system headed by a competitive monarchy? Perhaps the answer is indicated by the fate of the *Vasa* in 1628 which clearly reveals problematic communication between the commissioning authority and the shipwrights (Soop 1992:14–15). Recent research (Cederlund and Hocker 2006:44–46) has debunked the myth that the loss of the ship was due to the King's insistence on the addition of a second gun

deck at too late a stage in the building process. But if, as it now seems, *Vasa* was very close to what was originally intended, master shipwright Henrik Hybertsson clearly had enough autonomy to exasperate the king (Hocker 2006:45). The Swedish Crown finally abandoned Dutch expertise some 20 years later. Apparently King Karl X Gustav was much taken with an English ship he saw in Denmark. While this may have precipitated the decision, taking such a step on a whim seems unlikely. The reasons were probably deeper and more complex. The English shipwrights who were brought to Sweden evidently prospered and this may indicate that the whole process of designs on paper, consultation on the basis of models, and hierarchical management in the English manner was much more compatible with the Swedish Nation State than the less quantifiable (and less controllable) Dutch approach. As Hocker put it: '*in a system where the builder also had administrative responsibility, there was little to complain about until it was too late*' (Hocker 2006:46).

While pots, as the most ubiquitous form of archaeological material, are often employed in discussions on the meaning of material culture (e.g. Hodder 1986; Shanks 1995), there is an interesting parallel here between Maarleveld's egalitarian model of the Dutch manner and the more hierarchical systems in place elsewhere. Sander van der Leeuw has studied the production of pots in Mexican communities where the design process and their actual manufacture are almost completely segregated. In other words those who design the pots are not the ones who make them. This may have arisen because pots in these communities are made in moulds rather than being built up or formed under the potter's hands on the wheel. This promoted a difference of status between those who are the guardians of the 'tradition' and custodians of its designs (the 'molderos'), and the artisans – a system that would scarcely be possible where other fabrication techniques were used. The status quo is also maintained by the community at large who accept that moulded pots are the way pots should be, so demand for established forms is maintained (van der Leeuw et al. 1991; van der Leeuw and Papousek 1992). There is an analogous situation between van der Leeuw's 'molderos' and carvel shipbuilding, in that the primary design elements were also 'moulds', literally so in 16th-century English terminology. The master shipwright, in being privy to the 'secrets of the arte' was both the producer of the design and custodian of the central precepts underpinning the tradition. Ordinary shipwrights, apprentices, carpenters, caulkers, etc., and general labourers actually built the ship to his design. In this way carvel shipbuilding was a manifestation of the social system in which master shipwrights had successfully negotiated their path upwards. In the process they had hardened the distinction between them and their subordinates. Dutch shipbuilders on the other hand were more like a cooperative of potters at their wheels, generating the hull form under their hands and adjusting it as they proceeded.

New materials and new ideas

If SL 4 constitutes a metaphor for the whole trajectory of carvel building it also provides insight into how shipbuilders began to respond to the challenges of material availability and the social and demographic upheavals of 18th-century society associated with the industrial revolution. Ironically, the result was the end of carvel building as the dominant paradigm in the construction of large ships.

Although iron, and other metals, chiefly copper and various copper alloys had by then been used for fastening ship elements for millennia, in the 18th century we see iron in particular begin to be used for other purposes. Initially, cost and related limitations in the technology of its production restricted its use but by the end of the 18th century technological breakthroughs had markedly improved quality and reduced cost. One of the motive forces driving the industrial revolution had been the development of steam power. The development of practical steam engines had a dramatic effect on the coal mining industry. Rich seams below the water table, previously inaccessible, could now be exploited. Steam pumps could keep down water levels and raise the coal mined from far greater depths with ease. Vitally, with the development of the steam railway, coal could now be transported to railheads at ports like Sunderland, Newcastle, Shields and Hull. From there ships transported it to ports all round the coasts and overseas. Cheaper and more readily abundant fuel was linked to the improvements noted in the smelting of iron and as a result production was dramatically increased.

In an industry struggling to obtain key structural elements in traditional materials, namely certain species of wood, the alternatives included compromising standards and using other timber species, both of which were done in ships like SL 4. The other option was to use another material entirely, and this is what had been tried in various ships sporadically for some years. The elements most difficult to obtain by the end of the 18th century were the long curved 'compass' timbers and the grown crooked timbers used to make knees and 'V'-shaped floors, etc. To a great extent the requirement for compass timber had first been lessened by the development of hull forms in which a large proportion of the component timbers could be virtually straight – a process that had started in English shipping in the 16th century. Subsequently systems like Seppings' allowed shorter timbers to be used where curvature was unavoidable. The requirement for knees on the other hand was less dependent on hull form and even more dependent on size, hence other solutions had to be found. As shown in recent work on the *Invincible*, a 74 gun ship captured from the French and lost in 1758, French ships had long made use of iron knees (Lavery 1988b: *passim*). In English ships a more usual compromise was to form the knee out of more than one piece of wood and then bracket the whole assembly with a heavy iron strap (Longridge 1955: *passim*). Where they were available, wooden knees continued to be used.

A small English brig *Severn*, built in Chepstow in 1817 and sunk in Sweden in 1836 is entirely constructed of wood, including transom knees and the paired knees lodged between the deck beams (Rönnby and Adams 1994:111–121). *Severn* was only built a generation or so before SL 4 but is a good deal smaller, hence wooden knees were feasible. The threshold at which iron became the more realistic alternative to wood occurred somewhere between the size and construction date of the two ships.

When iron was finally adopted for knees on a wider scale it was first used to fabricate what is in effect an iron equivalent of a wooden knee. This is an imitative trait that is characteristic of many new technologies, in that they are first used to mimic the familiar. In other words the concept of what a knee is governed how the new material was used. Once the qualities and potential of iron began to be understood, the ways in which it was used resulted from lateral thinking rather than linear or imitative thinking. SL 4 illustrates both stages. The iron hanging knees are a similar shape and support the deck beams in the same way as wooden knees (Fig. 7.5). However, the hold beams were fastened to the hull in a novel way. The use of an iron strap passed around the futtock and through-bolted to the beam is both simple and elegant, but more to the point, it owes nothing to the older way of doing things. It is conceived and executed by people conversant with iron as a construction material as well as (though not necessarily) wood. Interestingly it is a technique that seems, on the basis of Lloyds surveys, to be characteristic of ships built in Sunderland from the 1830s (Adams et al. 1990:124). It is no coincidence that this was one of the principal railheads for the coal industry, itself linked through steam power and railways to iron technology.

Just as iron began to be used in ways that better exploited its inherent properties, so its use for single elements like knees and straps provided the basis for re-thinking the whole process of shipbuilding from an iron worker's point of view. The end of the carvel dominated era was in sight.

9

Maritime Material Culture

The foregoing analyses, although not sequential in a narrative sense, nevertheless comprise an overview of the adoption and development of the carvel shipbuilding tradition in northern Europe. Across a trajectory of several centuries the focus has been on major episodes of technological change. Their re-analysis in the contexts of their contemporary societies has not only enabled them to be understood with more clarity but has shown that they relate to significant changes in society. In looking at these shifts in the conception of ships and in the processes of their design, construction, use and disposal, one is reading the history of Europe in a new light.

Throughout medieval northern Europe we see the long-lived and widespread Nordic tradition of clinker construction displaying radical adaptation in response to the plethora of social needs, as well as external competition from other forms, and the stresses imposed by material availability and cost. As the impetus of European economic development in the late medieval period brought carvel technology northward, its widespread adoption was promoted by associated social change. Most prominent are those socio-political developments in which the ship becomes a major factor in state-building and long distance trade, exploration, imperialism and associated colonial expansion. In the latter half of the 16th and early 17th centuries, in response to these new roles, there was a revolution in the whole process of hull design, construction and use. The factors involved span materials to mathematics, linked to the vested interest of the state in the procurement of ships and the concomitant increase in the status of those who built them.

Just as ships played a key role in state building, so they were subsequently vital to the security and prosperity of the nation states so formed. Not for nothing does the title of Sutherland's 1717 treatise on shipbuilding begin: '*Britain's Glory…*'.

The principles established for design and construction during these two first phases of carvel building provide a foundation for all subsequent adaptations in shipbuilding for the next two centuries. This is not to imply that there was no change between the 17th and 19th centuries in shipbuilding. It is rather that the period is characterized by iterative changes and refinement rather than dramatic jumps. The basic format had been determined and subsequent change within it was a steady development of capacity, efficiency of rig and sailing qualities, weight of ordnance, and the technology of control, particularly steerage. All this takes place within the shifts in economic and political cycles of war and peace and against the backdrop of a steady decline in the availability and quality of resources. By the end of this time, in the 19th century, sourcing timber for the construction of large wooden ships had become increasingly problematic. This was coupled with the social upheaval of the industrial revolution, which generated new needs and new technologies. The final solution for shipbuilding was a shift to a new material: iron. The use of iron as a supplementary material had begun relatively early but the ways it was used in response to the constraints and needs of the industrial age demonstrate how a new technology can incrementally infiltrate centuries of tradition.

The new versus the old: 'Innovators and laggards'

No matter how the interrelated circumstances that promote change arise, and no matter how a technological innovation is developed and executed, whether it is actually taken up or not is less dependent on the intrinsic characteristics of the 'new' than on the bias of the agents involved. Layton (1973) and Rogers (1962) both observed that the adoption of an innovation is heavily influenced by the relationship between the innovators and the potential 'acceptors' (Layton 1973:41). In seeking to understand the whole process of innovation, one must therefore examine the process of acceptance that must precede adoption. Rogers subdivided the process of acceptance into phases: awareness, interest, evaluation, trial, adoption. However, in cases involving major technological change in shipping, so much is at stake that it is less of a passive or leisurely process than these stages imply. Acceptance or rejection of innovation is often the result of protracted debate and complex socio-political relationships. In other words, adoption may finally occur under duress or resignation in the face of unalterable forces.

Heated debate certainly attended many of the developments considered in this book. The changes to design advocated by Hawkins discussed in chapter 6 were the subject of one of the earliest (partially) documented debates of this sort. The objections raised by his opponents bring to mind subsequent episodes of naval innovation which have apparently polarised radical, innovative, versus traditional, conservative thinking. Examples include the 19th-century 'wooden walls' debate in which the traditionalists resolutely favoured continuing the construction of wooden-hulled warships in spite of a growing body of evidence that demonstrated their ineffectiveness against exploding shells. By the end of 1860 the ironclads *La Gloire* and *Warrior* were afloat and armour plating was the inevitable future, yet Lord Palmerston still voiced his faith in wooden ships. Nor was he alone, for Parliament at this time was providing the means for the Admiralty to procure more timber than ever (Albion 1952:20).

Another famous instance was the introduction of the screw propeller over the paddle wheel, dramatically demonstrated in the famous 'contest' between the steam-powered stern wheeler *Alecto* and the screw-propelled *Rattler*. The showdown was staged on the Thames in front of the Houses of Parliament in 1845, where the *Rattler* proved capable of towing the *Alecto* astern on half power against the futile efforts of the latter's paddle wheel delivering full power. Other controversies erupted over warships with turret guns championed by Captain Cowper Phipps Coles in the 1860s and Admiral John Fisher's ardent promotion of the all-big-gun battleship, resulting in the launch of HMS *Dreadnought* in 1906.

In most cases the innovators prevailed, though by no means in a straightforward way. As we have seen, Layton argued that the perceived character and social status of the innovator is all-important. The case of Coles provides a good example. The inventor of a successful turret gun, his ambition throughout the 1860s was to build a ship so armed, the benefits of which he summarized in his catch phrase, 'turn the gun, not the ship'. An extrovert self-publicist with the backing of Parliament, royalty, the press and the general public, he was (not entirely unjustly) cast in the role of brilliant innovator while the Admiralty were cast as obstructively incompetent advocates of outmoded broadside battery. After years of politically-charged controversy, Coles was finally cleared to find a private builder to construct a turret ship to his design, despite his being unqualified as a naval architect. Tragically on her second voyage in September 1870 HMS *Captain* capsized in a moderate gale with the loss of 481 people including Coles himself (Sandler 1973).

An even more recent example that was presented to the public in a similar way, also seemed to show that established practice dies just as hard in the modern world. In 1982, in response to the Royal Navy's search for a possible alternative to its Type 23 anti submarine warfare frigate, a consortium of ship designers and marine engineers headed by Thornycroft, Giles and Associates, submitted a proposal for a revolutionary design. Their *Sirius 90* concept embodied the idea that warships with a low length to breadth ratio (L/B 5 or 6) would be superior to the traditional long, thin form (L/B 8 or more) historically favoured by the Navy (Lloyds 1988:3–1). They argued that the additional capacity would increase weapons carrying ability, increase security from air-to-ship and ship-to-ship missiles such as the *Exocet*, and improve sea-keeping abilities, all for no loss of speed. With the precedent of supply vessels used year-round in environments like the North Sea, the 'short/

fat' proponents for a time seemed to have a powerful case. Resistance from the Navy was held up as blinkered traditionalism of exactly the same type that had resisted armour-plating and dreadnoughts. What is striking about this affair was that such polarised disagreement could develop with both lobbies basing their case on the supposedly 'hard' data of ship science in which the performance of the two hull forms could (supposedly) be modelled objectively.

Of course in none of these examples were the issues as clear cut as they are usually portrayed. Political interests inevitably colour the arguments and our knowledge of them is subject to the usual provisos about the writing of history. That Hawkins and Winter carried the day where Elizabeth I's new ships were concerned was no doubt assisted by the fact that so many other practical seamen and shipbuilders were of a similar opinion. In the *Rattler*-versus-*Alecto* challenge, it is apparent that it was more for the benefit of the politicians (hence the location of the demonstration) than the Navy, who were clearly aware of the relative merits of the two methods of propulsion. They knew perfectly well which ship would 'win'. Where turret guns were concerned the Navy was not opposed to them at all. It had after all purchased many of the Coles design. It was just highly dubious, quite rightly as it turned out, as to how their advantages could be realized in a seagoing ship. Until marine engines became both powerful and reliable enough to enable ships to dispense with a sailing rig, the problem of mounting turrets presented insurmountable difficulties. In hindsight it can be seen that the whole episode, ending with the tragic loss of the *Captain* was driven by personalities rather than policy. Ironically, the Navy was already working on a design to circumvent the problem. HMS *Devastation*, driven only by twin engines and screws, was launched the year after in 1871. In recalling Layton's observation of the importance of the perceived status of the innovator, Coles had built a vessel for the Navy that was fundamentally flawed because of who he was as much as what he was.

In the 'short/fat vs long/thin' debate of the 1980s, despite the demonstrable advantages of broader hulls in some situations, the Navy opted for long, thin vessels, as it judged that few of those advantages would prove significant in the contexts of use it could foresee. The hidden factors that never emerged in the row reported with such relish by the media, related to cost of building,

through-life costs, noise levels and power requirements, etc., all of which threw up valid questions as to the ultimate viability of the S90 concept. As in so many of these areas, the precise figures were impossible to predict accurately enough to put the matter entirely beyond doubt. The consortium therefore still felt aggrieved even after Lloyds' evaluation had exonerated the Navy's decision (Lloyds 1988). If even the hard data of economics and ship science could not provide closure, could it be that embedded aesthetic and symbolic considerations had the casting vote? The sleek, rakish and powerfully aggressive grey hulls are certainly how we expect warships to look today, just as the *Henry Grace à Dieu* was what the Tudors expected.

In terms of the phenomenon of innovation and its component processes, all these episodes have a common characteristic, and that is the nature of the disagreement. In all cases what underlies the details of argument over specification is the fundamental concept of what a ship is. In all the archaeological examples examined above, one can see that the technical procedure of adapting a design or adopting a new one can be relatively easy. It is the ideological component that is often the most significant hurdle and which, until a sufficiently important social reason to overcome it occurs, remains the most powerful impediment to change. An interesting aspect of these ideological struggles is that they often involve an informed lobby who advocate change, seeking to convert those who cannot reconcile the proposals with their fixed ideas, in these cases of what ships were and how they should be used. In Rogers' terms: innovators were opposed by 'laggards' whose frame of reference lies in the past (Rogers 1962:171). In the case of the laggards opposing John Hawkins, they clung to the concept of their 'high-charged' carracks because that is how they 'knew' warships were. Compared to the 'race-built' galleons championed by Hawkins and his allies, the old 'great ships' were more imposing, more 'royal', conveyed power effectively and in their opinion, were clearly how her Majesty's ships should be. Hence, as in all the other cases of change examined here on the basis of archaeological material, while the process may be seen as a technical one, subsequent analysis inexorably begins to reveal the motives and relations that were interwoven with and ultimately responsible for it. One wonders if similar arguments raged as to whether King Henry VII's new ships *Regent* and *Sovereign* should be built carvel or in the traditional clencher construction of royal ships that had stood the test of time.

If change is the result of tensions between various social and environmental factors, do these episodes reveal anything of the relative balance between them? Much archaeological debate has centred around the degree to which the environment determines human action in a cultural sense (Binford 1972; Hodder and Preucel 1996:205–219). Historians have considered a similar conundrum, i.e., to what extent technology drives history, or *vice versa* (Smith and Marx 1994; Heilbroner 1967, 1997). While environmental determinism models society as a system, an organism-like whole, maintaining stasis or adapting in response to environmental pressures, technological determinism is almost the opposite. Here technology shapes opportunity, facilitates action and so patterns behaviour, very much akin to the notion of 'active material culture' where things, once made, act back on society. One only has to consider the way people's lives in the present are influenced, indeed patterned by such things as the internal combustion engine, digital technology and telecommunications. Yet these things do not spontaneously arise of their own volition but from the continual flux of social momentum.

Material culture and its entrained technology are products of people's intentions and behaviour but created and used within an existing context (McGuire 1992:95). Hence the relationship between technology and history is dialectic: contexts for change are created by human motivation, social tensions and contradictions. Technological developments are both a product of this social furnace and a flux for subsequent action and change. The archaeology of water transport demonstrates both processes and the role of agency. Once carvel ships existed in the north, initially driven by mercantile motives, new political, naval and colonial agendas were facilitated on an increasingly global scale, themselves fuelling further technological development. In this sense the material culture of ships assisted people in the shaping of their world and the making of their own history, always within the context of prior action and of course not always as they could have foreseen or would have intended:

Men make their own history but they do not make it just as they please (Karl Marx (1852) 1926:9).

Specific circumstances and general explanations

If this study reinforces the impression that explanation of social change through reference to general principles is problematic and that each case needs to be taken 'on its merits', then it sits quite happily alongside various others that have reached the same conclusion such as Barrett (1988:40) who rejects what he terms general and spurious models of social totalities. Whether there are in fact useful generalities that can be identified is discussed below, but at the level of identifiable causality, not only are the three main cases discussed in this book very different, it is also difficult in each case to allocate a single factor responsible. Monocausal explanations, e.g. dwindling natural resources, the gun, economics, etc., are, at least in the three cases dealt with here, individually inadequate to explain why change came about and how it was implemented. We may refer to the social phenomena with which these changes in ship technology were connected, such as state-building, nation state or industrial revolution, but while these characterise the context of change they cannot in themselves function as explanations. Focusing on any single factor suspected of being causal in a processual sense tends to reveal other relationships which are implicit in its operation. Certainly some factors will exert greater influence or leverage but in each case they form part of an interrelated set or network of causal relations specific to each case and historically unique. This does not mean that the same factors, such as material availability, economics or indeed any of the constraints discussed in chapter 2, are not implicated in different episodes of change, but that they operate at different levels of amplitude. For example, a strong case has been made for the influence of timber supply on the designs of 17th-century hull design, but it has been argued that it did not exert as much leverage as political and ideological factors connected to state power, social class, personal status and prestige. By comparison, the way various species of timber were used in SL 4, together with innovative ways of incorporating iron, shows that in this case material availability was a factor of much greater prominence in the changes observed. Even here it was a constraint exacerbated by many other factors.

It is through the identification and analysis of these sets of causal relationships that these episodes of change are better understood, and as a result, throw new light on the social context within which that change took place. In gaining new insight into the development of carvel shipbuilding as major technological enterprise and widespread craft tradition, we are achieving a better perspective on the role of maritime activities in the development of northern Europe. Major transformative processes of state-forming such as imperialism, colonial expansion and industrial revolution cannot be fully understood without considering the role of ships and the roles of those who conceived, designed, built and used them.

While the specific nature of each set of circumstances is obvious, are there any generalities, above the level of the banal, that can be identified and which might help explain other episodes of change? The similarity in the character of debates about change might be one possibility, although as Layton (1973) showed, the deciding factor is often the individual. We might postulate that debate always accompanies change, even though it is invisible in the archaeological record. Perhaps the first place to look is in the building traditions themselves. Van der Leeuw and Papousek's analysis of the nature of innovation specifically in relation to pottery traditions has already been mentioned (van der Leeuw et al. 1991; van der Leeuw and Papousek 1992). They cite examples that could be interpreted as 'rogue designs' or attempts by individual potters to break out of prescribed practice, who by creating their own moulds, attempted to appropriate the whole process of production. However, more often than not, these initiatives failed in a predominantly conservative system maintained by those in control of designs and by an acquiescent community who subscribed to the traditional norms. Recalling Layton's observations (see chapter 4) concerning the perceived status of the innovating individual, potters were of lesser status than the 'molderos', the traditional mould-makers, and so were unlikely to get away with going against convention (van der Leeuw et al. 1991). Recently however, the pace of modern development and more communication with distant, as well as adjacent communities has produced hitherto unknown stress on the stability of convention (van der Leeuw and Papousek 1992:154).

Stress response

If one views a craft tradition as a body of concepts and related methodologies within a coded ideological framework, such a social entity, through its very nature of being 'traditional' is likely to be put under stress if social and environmental conditions impinge on what it produces and how. Emphasis has to be transferred to the other tendency of 'traditions', that of absorbing new ideas and innovating. However, if van der Leeuw is right in believing that the conservative tendencies of craft traditions predominated, this implies that stimuli for change need to be powerful enough to overcome them. The identification (through changes in their output) of craft traditions under stress may prove a useful indicator of social change that otherwise might not be so apparent. This may be more so if sets of circumstances tend to promote change in one craft tradition more than another. Shipbuilding, being implicated in contact between people, movement of goods and hence ideas, might be a more sensitive indicator of social change than other forms of material culture. Unfortunately this is unlikely to be a 'universal' but could prove useful in elucidating the complexities of the Mediterranean situation discussed in chapter 4.

In the north one can read change in the maritime record a little more easily. Perhaps the most eloquent individual indicator of a tradition under stress is the *Grace Dieu* (1418). Its triple plank construction shows the Nordic tradition taken beyond the rational limitations of the materials and technology implicit in its fundamental principles. A similar situation arises at the end of the carvel ship period of dominance. Scarcity of resources coupled with increased volumes of trade and competing maritime powers that required ever more powerful navies, placed increased stress on the norms of the tradition. In the better funded English yards with larger labour forces, even if they could afford timber of optimum quality, it often was not available. Inordinate measures were taken to build increasingly large wooden hulls of sufficient rigidity. In these situations other solutions had to be found: trussed frames, diagonal bracing, butt and coak joints and increasing quantities of supplementary iron components. The conceptual framework of production thus gradually began to break down as conventional methods, no matter how cherished, failed to manufacture the products required. In the end, the use of new materials won through and carvel building was progressively reduced, first to the building of specialist types, then to smaller and smaller local craft.

History to prehistory: directions and potential

Throughout this archaeological analysis of ships, the opportunity has been taken of integrating historical data with the material record, where observed technology has been used as the basis for a better understanding of the social context in which it arose. As a result the relationships within that context explain why the technological expression of change manifested itself in the way it did. Any success in this approach leads to the obvious, fundamental question: can the investigation of maritime material culture, especially investigation which capitalises on high-resolution finds from aquatic environments, further our understanding of prehistory?

At first sight it might seem impossible, especially in view of the 'disjunctions' between the historical and prehistoric worlds discussed in chapter 2. But although we do not have written sources to integrate with material remains, we are dealing with classes of material culture produced by people for various purposes. They have symbolic and ideological aspects as well as functionality. In this sense the material culture of prehistory is no different from ours. Various levels of functionality and symbolism are always present. The balance between the two is not always the same but they are different facets of the way material culture is. Hence in prehistoric maritime settings we can infer that aspects of social action and meaning will have been present. We can therefore look for the same richness of contextual inference and a similarly strong relationship between material culture and its context. For although in prehistory we cannot relate a particular object to a named person, or a certain site with an historical event, we can explore the social circumstances in which they were developed and used. Unlike Dennis Potter's play '*Cold Lazarus*' (Potter 1996), in which the events of the subject's past life are viewed on a screen by tapping into his cryogenically preserved brain, we cannot tap into the frozen, suspended animation of past users of material culture and know 'their' thoughts, any more than we can know those of a historical figure like Gustav Vasa's. But just as we can move closer to understanding the context

of his actions, so through a similar approach we can engage with the context of prehistoric action and its production of material culture.

As Hodder has pointed out, simply by analysing an object (for Hodder a pot but here a boat) we are assuming that our and their concepts of 'boats' are at least compatible, that the watercraft we call 'boat' meant something similar to them. Of course the totality of their ideas of what 'boat' meant in various contexts must have been different. That is precisely the challenge. For if material culture is meaningfully constituted, evidence of how people viewed their world and the boats within it will be embedded, albeit partially and selectively, in the boats' material remains. We are not confined to describing a prehistoric boat in terms of its construction characteristics and its capacity – as the static result of decisions and practice. Instead, on the basis of those characteristics, we can work our way towards a better understanding of the context in which those actions were carried out – the 'chaîne opératoire', in which a vessel is conceived, designed, produced, used and discarded. So while the terms in which we express the results of such enquiry will be different for sites and materials of prehistoric as opposed to historical periods, the results themselves may not be.

A case that could be discussed arises from the previous discussion of boatbuilding traditions: One of the characteristics many of them seem to share is a tenacious longevity in the face of competing forms. Repeatedly the prominent traditions of earlier periods have survived in the form of small boats. It is because of this, as much as the similar technical traits, that a possible continuity between Romano-Celtic craft and medieval cogs has been proposed, for physical similarities in construction on their own are not proof of a common tradition. For example the technique, so characteristic of cogs, of turning nails back into the wood to effect a fastening, was also used centuries earlier in the Mediterranean as well as in Romano-Celtic vessels. There could conceivably be a connection between all three but a comparable technique in itself does not prove that. The case for the cog's ancestry gains far more weight from arguing that the Romano-Celtic tradition is unlikely to have simply evaporated after the 4th century AD. The time between the last known Romano-Celtic find and the earliest cog is not a problem considering that the two types were built and used in a similar geographic region, and that we see the survival over a similar time span into the modern age of Nordic craft (e.g. Osler 1983) and perhaps cogs (Litwin 1991) in the form of small boats.

Even if subsequent finds demonstrate a different or more complex trajectory for cogs, the nature of long-lived traditions may shed light on other apparent gaps in the evidence. One of the most intriguing discontinuities in the prehistoric archaeological record concerns the watercraft of the European Bronze and Iron Ages. English Bronze Age finds provide a rich enough database to show there was a widespread, plank boat building tradition of considerable complexity and that it existed alongside the use of simpler logboats and perhaps skin boats for more than a thousand years. As summarised in chapter 4, current dating runs from around 1900 BC for Ferriby 3 to *c*. 800 BC for Brigg, and possibly far longer, though dating and identification for the later Ferriby finds (4 and 5) are less certain. That this tradition exhibits continuity for this length of time is not in itself unique but it endured through the changes brought by the *Urnfield period* which Harding (1994:304) has referred to as '...*an age of revolutions: industrial, social, military, and religious.*'

It is in the next phase of cultural change that a major hiatus in boat technology appears to have occurred. Although the size of the sample is too small to postulate trends, it is odd that in the Iron Age there are so far no certain seagoing (or at least estuary-going) craft comparable to the Dover boat or Ferriby 1. If Ferriby 5 is a craft of this type this would extend the contenuity into the middle pre-Roman Iron Age. Even this extension leaves an apparent discontinuity of several centuries between these plank boats and those of the next identifiable building tradition grouped under the terms Gallo-Roman or Romano-Celtic. Arnold (1999) has tried to plot connections between these earlier and later plank boat traditions. However, the very different technologies employed in their construction suggest that major change had occurred but not how. We could of course wait for further discoveries to be made, and judging by recent finds at Goldcliff, Caldicot and Spurn Head (Kilnsea), they will be. In fact a recent find of a plank fragment that has a cleat typical of the form has been made at Testwood in Hampshire, though as yet it remains unpublished. New finds may narrow the time frame for when change occurred and could eventually indicate how sudden it was. But while they should provide the basis for a more satistactory interpretation there is no

guarantee that the reasons for change will be self-evident. Carrying on from the rationale outlined in chapter 3, can we do a little better than simply wait for new finds to fill the gaps?

In advance of anticipated finds, there are various statements we can make: If the three cases of technological change analysed in the previous chapters indicate a general correlation, the major technological differences between the watercraft of the Bronze Age and the Roman periods must have resulted from similarly profound changes in society. Unlike the eclipse of the Nordic ship and the carvel-built sailing ship in more recent times, there is no evidence to suggest that a lack of suitable materials was a contributory factor at the end of the Bronze Age. Nor is there yet evidence of a new, competing technology. Is the boat record therefore telling us that the social changes between the production of craft in the late Bronze Age and Romano-Celtic vessels like Blackfriars 1 and St Peter Port, involved fundamental and traumatic cultural disruption, more so than occurred, for example, in post-Roman northern Europe, in late medieval Europe during the Black Death, Renaissance and Reformation, or as a result of the industrial revolution?

Circumstances more cataclysmic than these might include such things as invasion and population displacement, catastrophic climate change impacting settlement patterns and agriculture, the collapse of social organization, and technological revolution. All of these have been offered to explain the transitions that moved Europe from the Bronze into the Iron Age (Champion et al. 1984; Harding 1994, 2000; Kristiansen 1998). Such changes might not have significantly changed the production and use of logboats (for these were used throughout the periods under discussion) but could have quite easily removed or made redundant those with the knowledge and skills to produce more complex craft such as Ferriby 1 and Dover. A people simply moving in and displacing another provides a scenario, but to do without boats or at least radically change the methods of their production implies new needs and strategies. One possibility may involve exactly these changes, and be connected to transformations in the power structures of late Bronze Age societies.

A widely accepted model of Bronze Age society involves a network of powerful elites who maintained their position through the control of those resources from which power, status and prestige were derived. These included vital substances like salt, crafted materials such as textiles and precious objects of gold, jet and amber, but pre-eminent was bronze itself. The need to control its procurement, accumulation and distribution through status-enhancing exchange practices necessitated an international network of communication and transport simply because its raw materials, copper and tin ores, were relatively rare and very widespread (Kristiansen 1998:211). From around 1300 BC, the onset of the Urnfield period, the scale of metal production increases dramatically. This further promoted the importance of long distance communication and exchange, and in view of the distances and routes involved, the need for boats in procurement and distribution can be assumed. Of two underwater Bronze Age finds in England one (Langdon Bay in Kent) is difficult to interpret any other way than as a wreck (Muckelroy 1981). The other (Salcombe in Devon) could certainly be a wreck too. Assuming the Langdon Bay site is a wreck, the boat was carrying a large hoard of continental bronze objects. It was mostly scrapped axes, presumably being transported to Britain for reuse and distribution. The Salcombe site has likewise released bronze artefacts, swords and a dagger (Muckelroy 1981). Though far fewer in number, further finds have been made by divers more recently and there are clearly more present.

Boats in the mind – boats in reality

There are no European or Scandinavian assemblages of Bronze Age plank boats as extensive as the British finds. However, many thousands of the rock carvings known in Scandinavia depict boats. This, together with their frequent appearance on bronze objects, demonstrates their degree of importance as material culture both symbolically and functionally. Few fields of archaeological research have generated such a disparate range of interpretations as rock art in general and of the Scandinavian material in particular. However, a relationship that would seem worthy of further study is the possible link between images of boats and the transport networks such boats were undoubtedly used in. As well as the frequency of the images themselves, many of their locations are on the former Bronze Age shore line (Coles 1994:9; 2008; Ling 2004). Not only that. Many of these places would have provided sheltered landing spots, i.e. the images of boats were made where real boats could have been.

Recent interpretations of these images, particularly on artefacts, has focused on the religious (e.g. Kaul 1998). Similarly, interpretations of the rock art have tended to downplay functional association with the use of boats themselves, promoting symbolic, cosmological and religious connections instead. Indeed Kristiansen has summarised the theoretical approaches to rock art over the last two centuries as a cyclical oscillation between romanticism and rationalism (Kristiansen 1998: fig. 14, 2010: fig 6:1). Yet religious, cultic or other ceremonial functions and meanings for these images are not at all incompatible with events, practice and functional associations. Indeed the Bronze Age mind could hardly have conceived a spiritual boat without having experienced a corporeal one. Similar observations have been made about bronze tools and weapons, often regarded as symbolic or ritual rather than functional, whereas they could easily have been both (e.g. Bridgford 1997; O'Flaherty 2007).

Modern western society has progressively divorced the religious from the secular, but this is a separation unrecognised in other cultures as it surely was in the past. The images proclaim the boat as a symbol of enormous power. The river crossings, sea shores or bays where boats were brought, and where images were carved, must also have been similarly significant. Boats carried people to and from far away places. They carried materials of importance to the way society worked, of importance to how people defined and negotiated their identities, of importance in maintaining contact between widely separated communities. These could, and surely would, have had cosmological significance. The places where this happened were after all interfaces between the land and water, between near and far, and between the familiar (here) and the exotic (there). There might have seemed to be parallels between the use of boats in this world for transporting people and things from one place to the other, and the spiritual in which one is transported from one state to another: Shamanistic passage to altered states of consciousness, crossing from life to afterlife, or deities passing from night to day. Images created as part of the practice of seafaring could thus be related both to the social relations of the people involved, and to their cosmos. This is perhaps reinforced by their juxtaposition with images of other forms.

Recently, rock art researchers have begun to focus not just on the experience of viewing the

images but on the act of carving them (e.g. Hauptman Wahlgren 2000:90). Maybe the act of creating images of boats was inextricably linked to their use in the minds of the actors, just as burning incense sticks to the Goddess Kali is linked to practical seafaring for the sailors of the Patia in Orissa (Blue et al. 1997). At Himmelstalund near Norrköping in southern Sweden (Fig. 9.1), there are many hundreds of boat images at several sites (see Fig. 9.2a). Several things about them may have significance. At Himmelstalung itself, while most of the hunting-related, animal, footprint and other motifs are carved on the top of the rock, facing the sky, the boat images are more commonly carved on the slopes of the rock facing the water (or where the water would have been). In a few cases there are also axes and swords carved alongside them (Fig. 9.2b). People in boats on the water could have seen the boat images, and people in the act of carving them could have seen the boats. Viewers could have seen both. Coles (2008: 29, 32) has discussed the position of the viewer relative to the carvings, as well as the effect of light conditions at certain times of the day or season. Distribution of motifs varies widely, whether at major sites such as at Kville hundred, Bohuslän, Sweden (Hedengran 1995), or the smaller sites such as many of those in Uppland (Coles 1994). But at Himmelstalund the segregation of motifs suggests a relationship

between the place the boats were used, carved and viewed, all of which could have been played out in ritual and ceremony. Nor is this more holistic view of social practice and the use of boats in the widest sense incompatible with recent varied approaches to interpretation, e.g. Tilley's semiotic anlysis of the images at Nämforsen, northern Sweden (Tilley 1991b).

How this relates to understanding the British Bronze Age where the boats survive as physical remains but not in the far smaller, non-figurative corpus of rock art is intriguing. But similar speculation on the ritualistic nature of the practice of using and disposing of boats has been prompted by some of the recent finds, as well as the reconsideration of earlier discoveries. Champion (2004) has constructed a plausible case for seeing the deposition of the Dover boat, not as discard in the modern sense but as intentional placement relating to its passage from one phase of existence to another. Van de Noort, while sceptical about the mode of deposition in this case (Van de Noort 2006), nevertheless argues for the particular social significance of travel and seafaring in the Bronze Age and the concomitant symbolic power of the boat (Van de Noort 2004a, 2004b). Irrespective of whether the Dover boat was ritually disposed of or not, the context of many other prehistoric boat finds, in addition to obvious examples like Hjortspring (Randsborg

9.2a (right) Rock art boats at Himmelstalund in southern Sweden.

9.2b (opposite) A Himmelstalund boat with adjacent sword (photos: J. Adams).

1995) and Nydam (Rieck 1995) certainly allows for their interpretation as intentional placement. This is made more plausible by the various objects often found in association with them. Many of these objects do not seem to have been worn beyond the possibility of repair or further use but instead to have been intentionally damaged. In other words these may have been objects of continued significance, not worn out utilities, especially in view of the investment of time, effort and skill required to produce them. We may therefore conclude that these boats were important in every sense of the word. But if the finds that so far comprise the archaeological record approximate even broadly to the actual temporal distribution, then something happened to change all this. For these boats seem to disappear.

If boats were implicit in maintaining the status of the elite, and thus the structure of Bronze Age society, maybe the change relates to what was carried. (Remember the adjacent images of weapon and boats.) With the introduction of iron the system of procurement of copper and tin ore over long distances, as well as exchange and distribution of its bronze products, was ultimately compromised. It took some time for this to happen. For although iron ore was widespread and thus readily available, the knowledge and skills necessary to smelt it were not. This is partly why the increase in the quantity of iron objects in circulation was so slow, but in fact they do not

seem to have been regarded as material equivalents to bronze objects at all. Iron was first used for an entirely different range of things. This may be because the yield of metal from inefficient iron smelting is small, so until the technology improved, fabricating swords and axes was a tall order. Gradually expertise was accumulated and those who acquired the knowledge and skills to smelt iron reliably must have acquired a power along with it. It was 'power to' as opposed to the 'power over' (Miller and Tilley 1984) enjoyed by the Bronze Age elite, but a power that nevertheless could insidiously undermine a bronze-articulated system, especially in those areas poor in bronze production. In this scenario the longstanding system of procurement and exchange over long distances became redundant. Thus the defining element of Bronze Age social structure collapsed (Huth 2000:191). The notion of cultural collapse caused by the introduction of iron *per se* is old and much criticized, rightly so if this is offered as a monocausal explanation. It is clear however, that in Britain a different metal technology might have assumed new roles in societies demonstrably affected by climatic change and soil condition, in turn precipitating changes in settlement patterns and agriculture.

Is the social upheaval associated with this period reflected in the boat record? With the collapse of long distance control networks, the needs for the craft involved in the associated water

transport would have radically changed and perhaps substantially reduced. If this prestige exchange utilised complex plank-built boats of the Dover and Ferriby I type, such a change might account for their apparent disappearance at this time (vagaries of preservation notwithstanding). Transcontinental exchange certainly continued but perhaps utilising radically changed networks and modes of water transport.

In Scandinavia, the situation was very different. Here, iron began to appear at similar dates to elsewhere in Europe (Levinson 1989:441), yet it was centuries before iron made a similarly profound impact. Sørensen (1989:195), makes the point that when the use of iron finally became common, it played a role different from that of both bronze and iron in the Bronze Age. In a society where bronze retained its prominent role for so long, and where society seems to have undergone generally less traumatic change, it may be significant that boat technology of considerable sophistication not only survived the transition to the Iron Age but developed into arguably the most widespread and long-lived boat building tradition of all: the Nordic.

These questions are discussed here by way of a parting shot. Beyond the tentative suggestions made above they must await new discoveries as well as re-analysis of earlier finds to produce answers. Other episodes of change or discontinuity in the maritime record might also be fruitfully investigated. Investigating the relations between technological development and social change can promote the study of ships from one of technology for its own sake to one of technology as a manifestation of, and means of social action. In an important sense any archaeological study must have this sort of holistic approach if its results are not to be circumscribed within the descriptive confines of a specific class of material. As a result, the study of boats and ships, both in historical and prehistoric periods, acquires the ability to advance dramatically our understanding about people's articulation with their maritime environments, with their material culture in general, and with each other. From this perspective, maritime archaeology, through explicating human maritime enterprise, can help to provide answers to some of archaeology's big questions.

Glossary

This glossary is essentially concerned with the terms used in this book. For a broader, illustrated glossary for both construction and rig of watercraft of all kinds, see Steffy 1994 and McGrail 2001.

Words or terms in *italics* are defined in their own entries.

Adze
Woodworking tool in which the blade is set at right-angles to the haft. Used extensively in *carvel* shipbuilding.

Apron
Part of the *stem* construction, running concentrically inboard the stem and fastened to it. Sometimes called a false stem.

Auger
A large wood-boring drill with a simple wooden T-bar as a handle. The design of the cutting head varied according to date.

Bark (*barque*)
Originally a specific hull form but later a vessel with three or more masts in which the aftmost mast is rigged fore and aft, the others being square rigged.

Beam
Heavy athwartship timber with its ends strongly fastened or otherwise lodged against the hull, effecting a strong connection between the sides of the vessel and contributing to hull stiffness. In most vessels they are set at appropriate heights in the hull to support the decks where they are *deckbeams*. Their position in the hull is the reason the term can also refer to the breadth of the vessel.

Beamshelf (shelf)
The large *stringer* on which the *beams* and *deckbeams* rest, also known as a *clamp* presumably as the beam is usually rebated into it.

Bevel
An angled face on the edge of a timber where it is cut to fit against another. In particular the term refers to the shape of the inner and outer faces of the *frames* which must be bevelled to follow the inward curve of the hull fore and aft of the midship section thus providing a fair surface for the outer planks and *ceiling*.

Bilge

The lowest part of the hold of a ship or the flattest part of the hull upon which the ship rests when aground.

Bitts

A pair of heavy vertical timbers acting as bollards to take the strain of the anchor cables.

Bitt beam

A heavy beam against which or into which the bitts are set.

Block

The wooden block or 'shell' enclosing one or more sheaves (or holes in the case of a *deadeye*) through which ropes are passed. A block can be positioned to lead a rope in a convenient direction for pulling. Two or more blocks can be rigged together to form a 'tackle' (pronounced taykle) giving mechanical advantage for various tasks on a ship, such as raising or lowering topmasts and yards, controlling sails and lifting or restraining heavy equipment. Blocks vary in size, number of sheaves and shape depending on their purpose and where in the vessel they are rigged.

Block coefficient (Cb)

The ratio between the volume of the submerged hull and the product of its waterline length, waterline breadth and draught. Streamlined V-shaped hulls have a low Cb while merchant vessels such as fluits or modern tankers have a high Cb.

Bolt

Large metal pin of iron, copper or copper alloy used for fastening structural elements such as *beams, floors, knees, keelson*, etc. Either driven into a blind augered hole with a slight drift, i.e., the bolt is of slightly greater diameter than the hole to ensure a tight fit, or driven right through the elements to be fastened and secured by various means. Modern bolts are threaded to take a nut but formerly it was done by deforming the end of the bolt over a washer or rove. Alternatively the end of the bolt was pierced with a slot to take a forelock, a curved wedge-shaped pin that when driven through the slot tightened against a washer so preventing the bolt from drawing out.

Bowsprit

The spar projecting forward from the bow, either above or to the side of the *stem*.

Breasthook

Large *grown timber* that is placed internally across the *stem* (or the *apron* in larger vessels) forming a strong connection between the two sides of the hull.

Brig

A vessel having two masts: a foremast and a mainmast, both of which are square rigged.

Butt

The end of a timber or plank when cut square. (**Butt joint:** The junction of two timbers finished in this manner.)

Cant frame

In the main body of the ship the *frame* timbers were laid at rightangles to the keel but where the hull curved in towards the bow, the frames were often set radiating outwards, approximately from where the *stem scarfed* to the *keel*. Timbers were often canted in a similar fashion at the stern in double–ended hull forms.

Carling

A deck support timber running between the *deckbeams* i.e. longitudinally.

Carvel

A term believed to derive from the Portuguese ship 'caravela' that has come to mean the method of ship construction where the hull planks are laid flush onto the frame timbers and are fastened to the frames, not to each other. See chapter 4.

Castle

In earlier warships, the defensible structures at the bow (bow or fore castle (fo'c's'l)) and stern (stern or aft castle).

Castle deck

Deck in the bow or stern castle.

Caulking

The method of making a seam between planks watertight, for instance in deck planks or the hull planking of *carvel*-built ships. Various materials such as sphagnum moss, animal hair, *oakum* (the teased out fibres of old rope) or wood fibres were twisted into lengths, often with a binding material such as tar or clay. In some regions caulkers favoured specific materials while others used mixtures of both fibres and the binding medium (Adams et al 1990:). Several strands of these were driven into the seam with a 'caulking iron' and a 'caulking mallet'. They were then usually sealed with a waterproofing compound such as tar.

The term is also used for the process of laying a mastic waterproofing medium, typically tar and hair, between the planks of a clinker vessel during construction or repair. However, as this is a different process some prefer to describe this as *luting*, though the historical distinction between the terms is unclear.

Ceiling

The internal structural planking of the hull, i.e. not lining or panelling.

Chain plate (chains)

Originally chains bolted to the side of the ship. Their upper ends were linked to the iron binding of the lower *deadeye*. Later, flat iron straps were used (hence the term 'plate').

Chamfer

The angled surface formed when the sharp edges of a timber are cut back for safety and/or aesthetic appearance, such as the lower edges of *deckbeams* or the edges of deck supports.

Chasers

Guns positioned to fire forward (bow chasers) or aft (stern chasers).

Chine

The point at which the hull section curves upwards towards the waterline. Also referred to as the turn of the bilge.

Chock

Generally any angled or wedge-shaped block of wood added as packing to constructional timbers to build them up to the required dimensions, or between them to effect a joint.

Clamp

1. The stringer upon which the ends of the beams are supported. They are often rebated into it in various ways. The term is used synonymously with *beamshelf* or *shelf*.
2. A general term for offcuts or small pieces of wood used for temporary fastenings. In the context of the Dutch shipbuilding tradition, particularly those pieces used to fasten hull planking during construction, prior to fitting the frames.

Cleat
1. A small piece of wood used in construction to hold timbers in place or prevent them from moving until permanently fastened (such as preventing a *shore* from slipping). See also clamp 2.
2. A small piece of wood attached to for example a spar in order that a rope can be belayed.

Clench (clinch)
To secure a metal fastening by deforming the end so it cannot work loose or pull out. In Nordic construction this involved hammering the end of a 'clinch-nail' over a washer or *rove*. Another method involved turning the end of the nail back into the plank in the manner seen in medieval cogs. This turned, or 'twice-bent-nail' technique was also used for fastening timbers in Roman ship construction (Pomey 1991; Rival 1991) and in the Romano-Celtic tradition (Rule & Monaghan 1993; Marsden 1994; Nayling & McGrail 2004).

Clinker, clinker-built (clencher-built)
A plank-orientated method of boat and shipbuilding in which the edges of the hull planks overlap and are fastened by clenching (see above). Although deriving from a specific procedure, the term is often imprecisely applied to any hull that is constructed or partly so from overlapping planks, even where the planks are sewn together and therefore where no clenching is involved. In such cases the term 'lapstrake' is more accurate.

Coak
A block of wood, squared or cylindrical, set into closely fitting rebates in the corresponding faces of adjacent timbers, locking them together and preventing lateral movement.

Compass timber
Naturally curved wood used for correspondingly curved elements in ship construction. The term is sometimes used synonymously with *grown* or *crooked* timber, although it is more suitable for describing the evenly curved pieces required for frame timbers. *Grown* timber is a general term while *crooked* timber often refers to the sharply curved use for knees, etc.

Crook (crooked timber)
Grown timber of acute curvature used for *knees* or the 'V' shaped *floors* used in the fore and after bodies of ships.

Cross grain
A curved timber cut from straight wood to the extent that the wood grain passes from one side of the piece to the other, a potentially serious weakness in constructional elements but one that for reasons of economy was often tolerated.

Cross-pall (crosspawls, cross-spall, cross-spales)
A temporary plank or beam used to tie the frames together during construction prior to fitting the deckbeams.

Crutch
Similar to a *breasthook* but positioned at the stern.

Deadrise
A term referring to the upward angle of the *floor timbers* as they run out from the *keel* towards the turn of the *bilge*.

Deadeye
A *block* with holes instead of sheaves, used in pairs to tighten the *shrouds*.

Deadwood
In large ships, as the hull becomes sharper forward and aft, the floors can no longer be made in one piece so the futtocks are fitted on or against solid pieces of filling timber built up over the keel. Increasingly common in northern Europe from the 17th century onwards.

Deckbeam
See *beam*.

Deckhook
A *breasthook* that is at the level of a *deck* and so forms part of its support in addition to binding the forward or *cant* frames.

Deck pillar
Deck support or *stanchion*.

Dutchman
A repair to a timber where the flawed or damaged section is cut out so as to form a *rebate*. After preparing with a luting compound a new piece of wood is let into it and fastened in place.

False keel
A protective layer of timber fastened along the bottom of the keel, being relatively easy to replace when worn.

Fashion piece
The curved timbers set across the *stern post* forming the base of the stern.

Floor (floor timber, rung)
The lowest component of a ship's frame running across the keel.

Frame (see also *rib*)
Structural elements that either stiffen a plank-orientated construction, e.g. a *clinker-built* vessel, or which form the framework to which a watertight skin is fastened in frame-orientated construction, e.g. planks in *carvel* building and hides in skin boat construction. 'Frame' is a general term that can refer to vessels of any size. In larger craft a frame is made from several pieces each of which has its specific name (see *floors, futtocks, top timbers*).

Framed timbers
A term associated with *carvel* building in which *floors, futtocks* and *top timbers* are fastened together forming an integral unit. In later periods the component timbers were sometimes pre-assembled on the ground and raised as a single unit.

Futtock (foothook)
The timbers that together with the *floors* and the top *timbers* form a *frame*. They are numbered 1st, 2nd, 3rd, 4th, the 1st being the lowest and the 4th the highest.

Garboard
The plank next to the keel (garboard strake: the lowest *strake* of planking).

Grown timber
General term for naturally curved wood suitable for shipbuilding but it often refers to the sharply angled pieces from the branches of trees used for *knees* (see also *crook*).

Half beam (ledge)
The small timbers supporting the deck planking that lie between and parallel to the *deckbeams*. They are rebated into the *carlings* and the *beamshelves*.

Handspike
A wooden lever used for turning a *windlass* (as distinct from the 'hand spike' used like a crow bar for manoeuvring guns).

Harpins (harpings)
Lengths of timber (usually oak) used to support and bind the *cant* frames at the bow and the stern during construction. They are *scarfed* to the *ribbands* so forming a band of timber running the whole length of the ship.

Hawse hole/ timbers/ pipes
The holes through which the cables from the anchors pass into the ship. In large wooden ships they are generally cut through the *cant* frame timbers next but one to, and either side of the *stem* (hence 'hawse pieces' or 'hawse timbers'). They were often lined with lead, or later, iron 'hawse pipes'.

Heartwood
As successive rings of new *sapwood* are formed, the cells of older growth rings become progressively too far from the growth region below the cambium to function. Various chemical changes occur including the deposition of cellulose and lignin within the cells. This is 'heartwood' and is mechanically much stronger than sapwood and less liable to rot.

Hold
The lowest space within the body of a ship, used for cargo, stores and ballast where required.

Keel
1. The lowermost fore and aft structural element, in larger wooden ships formed from more than one timber, running along the centre line and joined to the *stern post* and *stem*.
2. Old term for Nordic clinker-built ships, surviving in the names of regional craft.

Keelson
The internal backbone of a ship. A large timber (or timbers) running parallel to the *keel* above the *floors*. It clamps the floors by being through-fastened to the keel.

Knee
An angled piece of wood or iron used to connect various elements of the hull that lie in different planes, such as the *deckbeams* to the *frames*. When made of wood they were best cut from *grown* timber but were superseded by iron knees as grown timber became increasingly scarce. Those set with one arm running downwards from the side of a beam or from its underside are referred to as 'hanging knees'. Those set horizontally against the beam are 'lodging knees' and those rising vertically from the top of the beam are 'rising knees' or 'standards'. Knees set at an angle, e.g. to avoid a gunport were called 'dagger knees'. When iron knees became common, the forms they could take became more varied. A 'staple knee' is a double iron knee: either a hanging knee where the lower arm continues down and along the top of the deck beam below (becoming the standard) or where two lodging knees are combined in a similar way.

Lateen
Triangular sail set fore and aft.

Limber /-hole /-passage /-channel
Channels for the passage of water to the pumps. They were usually cut in the underside of the *floor timbers*. Alternatively they were formed by the gaps left between timbers for the purpose.

Limber boards
A series of short boards between the *keelson* and the *limber strake* that were removable to allow access to the space between the *floor timbers* and to the limber channels.

Limber strake
The first *ceiling* plank either side of the *keelson*.

Mast step
The slot into which the foot or 'heel' of the mast is stepped. It can be constructed from several timbers or cut as a mortise into a structural element such as a *floor* or *keelson*.

Moot
A rotary plane for finishing treenails, producing a smooth, consistent section as opposed to the faceted surface of a treenail made with a draw-knife.

Mortise
A square or rectangular recess cut into a timber into which the *tenon* of another timber fits, forming a mortise and tenon joint.

Moulded depth
The depth or thickness of a ship's timber when viewed in section i.e. looking forward or aft (from the old term 'mould' referring to the cross section of a ship).

Nordic
Culturally, of Scandinavia but in this context the name given to a boat and shipbuilding tradition that originated in Scandinavia, probably in the Bronze Age, and which subsequently spread to most of northern Europe. Nordic craft were *shell-built* in terms of the principle of their construction, and *clinker-built* in the way that principle was applied.

Oakum
Fibres of old rope teased apart and then twisted together in strands for *caulking* seams between the *planks*.

Orlop
The lowest deck in the ship.

Plank (planking)
Technically the slabs of timber sawn or split from a bole that are between 1.5 inches (38 mm) and 4 inches (101 mm) in thickness. Timber thicker than this is referred to as 'thick stuff' and thinner timber as 'board'.

Plug
A square hardwood wedge driven into the centre of the end of a *treenail* to tighten it.

Punch
Small square wedge three or four of which are used to tighten a *treenail* as opposed to a single square *plug* or flat wedge.

Rabbet (Rebate)
A recessed channel cut in a timber to accommodate another, such as the 'V' shaped rabbet cut into the side of the *keel* into which the *garboard* is fitted or *rabbeted*.

Ribs
An old term for the frames of a ship, still loosely applied in this context but now more specifically to the frames of small boats.

Ribband
Lengths of timber (usually softwood such as pine) nailed along the outside of the *frames* at specific heights both to bind and support them during construction. As the ribband was carefully worked it would take up an even curvature as it passed over the standing timbers, effectively acting as a spline. It thus defined hull curvature for the insertion of the intermediate timbers, especially in the trickier fore and after bodies, where in later periods they were known as *harpins* and were often of oak.

Rider
Heavy internal reinforcing member of wood and later of iron, laid across the *keelson*, *ceiling* and *stringers*, usually in line with the frames to which they were strongly fastened. Standard in warships, they were sometimes added to merchant ships during repairs or in old age.

Rig
1. Collective term referring to the entire propulsion system of sailing vessels, comprising the masts, sails and *rigging*.
2. A term referring to the configuration of masts and sails where this accords to more or less standard patterns (see *ship rig*, *bark*, *brig*).

Rigging
The collective term for the rope and later, wire and chain, that brace the masts and spars and control the sails. 'Standing rigging' is the static components such as *shrouds* and *stays* that support the masts and *spars*. 'Running rigging' is the moving components such as *sheets* and *halyards* used to control the sails.

Rise of floor
A term describing the progressive increase in the depth of the *floors* or the height that they are set above the keel fore and aft of the midship section.

Rove
A round washer or square metal plate over which a nail or bolt is turned or *clenched* to effect a secure fastening.

Running rigging see Rigging

Sapwood (xylem)
The outer rings of wood formed within the cambium of a tree through which sap is transported and in which nutrients are stored. Most of it is generally trimmed off timbers in the process of shipbuilding as it has much less strength and rots much faster than *heartwood*. Even in higher quality building however, some sapwood is always present which is useful for tree-ring dating.

Scantlings
The dimensions specified for a ship's timbers.

Scarf (scarf joint, scarph)
A method of joining two pieces of timber end to end with a tapering overlap, generally so that the width and thickness of the timber is not altered. There are many types of scarf joint varying in complexity. 'To scarf': to join two timbers in this fashion.

Scupper
A pipe, earlier of wood then later of lead, that passes through the ship's side at deck level to allow any water taken onboard due to waves or spray, etc., to run off.

Settee
A fore and aft sail similar to a *lateen* but having a short vertical leading edge.

Sheathing
The layer applied to a ship's hull to protect the planking from attack by marine borers such as 'gribble' (limnoria) and shipworm (teredo navalis). It was made of various materials at various times. In the 18th and 19th centuries there were various combinations dictated by price and the destination of the vessel concerned. Tarred paper or tarred felt covered by pine boards was a common and relatively cheap option. A final layer of copper sheeting was more expensive but the most effective.

Shell (shell-built)
A boat or ship built in such a manner that the hull forms an integral, watertight unit, and into which further stiffening or strengthening 'frame' elements may be added.

Sheers (sheerlegs)
Two or three long timbers or poles lashed together to form an 'A' frame or tripod from which a *block* could be hung, enabling heavy weights to be hoisted (such as *frame* timbers in ship construction).

Sheer strake
The uppermost *strake* of the outer planking.

Shelf
See *beamshelf.*

Ship rig
A vessel with a bowsprit and three or more masts (including topmasts and topgallants) all of which are square rigged.

Shore
A timber used as a temporary prop or support for frames, stem and stern post etc., during construction of the vessel.

Shrouds
The ropes that provide the masts lateral and aft support.

Side-binding strake
... is scored (rebated) down and into the beam-ends at some distance from the side, and bolted through the side between the beams. The scoring into the beams connects the in and out fastenings of this strake with the longitudinal tie of the beams... (Andrew Murray 1863).

Skeg
The triangular projection or toe formed by the sloping aft end of the *keel,* The bottom corner of the rudder was chamfered to match.

Sleeper (pointer)
1. Internal stern reinforcing members of wood or (later) iron, running diagonally upwards and inwards to the underside of the *transom* or just below it.
2. In the 17th century they referred to what were later called *footwaling* or *bilge stringers*.

Snow
A vessel with two masts: fore and main, which are both square-rigged but with an additional small mast (a 'trysail mast') stepped immediately behind the main mast. It is the trysail mast that distinguishes a snow from a *brig.*

Spar
Any of the timbers used to support the rigging and sails, e.g. masts, yards and booms, etc.

Spike
A large square-shanked metal nail used for general fastening purposes, particularly planking.

Spurket
When frame timbers are assembled so they do not contact each other end to end the spurket is the resulting gap. (Not to be confused with 'spirketting': the stringer set above the ends of the deckbeams or above the waterway if present.)

Stanchion (deck pillar)
In general a vertical support pillar, for example of a *deckbeam* usually *stepped* into the *keelson* or *riders*.

Standing rigging see Rigging

Staple knee (see *knee*).

Stays
The thick ropes or wires that support the masts and bowsprit of sailing vessels.

Stealer
An additional plank introduced to accommodate the progressive widening of the strakes as they run towards the stern or conversely, reduction of the number of strakes where the planks taper towards the stem.

Stem
The large timber *scarfed* onto the keel that largely determines the shape of the bow of a ship and into which the ends of the outer planking are *rabbeted*.

Step
The rectangular recess into which the 'heel' or foot of the mast is locked or 'stepped' so that it cannot move. It can be cut into the keelson or formed by blocks of timber above the keelson or a deck depending on the size of the vessel and the position of the mast.

Stern post
The large timber set on the upper face of the aft end of the keel to which it was joined. It can be variously formed depending on the type of vessel but commonly the ends of the outer hull planking are rabbeted into it in a similar fashion as with the stem and the rudder is hung on its aft side.

Stopwater
A dowel set in the seam of *scarfed* timbers in order to prevent movement and hence leakage. It is a technique used in seams that cannot be effectively caulked, such as scarf joints of a keel. As well as the dowel, moss, grease or other waterproof material can be rammed into the hole which is then plugged with short treenails.

Strake
A run of *planking*. In a small plank-built boat each strake may be made of one plank but in larger boats and ships each strake will comprise several planks.

Stringer
A thick internal plank running longitudinally along the hull. They can either alternate with the *ceiling* planks or are placed where extra strength is required such as over a line of joints or under *beams*. *Sleepers*, *beamshelves* and *clamps*, etc., are all types of stringer.

Siding

The thickness of a ship's timber e.g. a *futtock* or a *deckbeam* when viewed from the side or above.

Tabling

The face of timbers cut to be *scarfed* together, often including quite complex keys and notches.

Tenon

A square or rectangular projecting tongue of wood cut to fit into a *mortise* so forming a 'mortise and tenon' joint.

Thimble

A heart shaped eye of wood or metal around which the end of a rope is spliced to make a 'hard eye' (as opposed to a 'soft eye' without the thimble).

Third rate

Relats to the English system of classifying warships according to the number of heavy guns carried. A third rate carried between 64 and 80 guns.

Tiller

The lever by which the rudder is turned.

Timbers

In the context of shipbuilding the term can refer collectively to all the pieces used, of whatever species. Later it came to refer specifically to the *frames*.

Tingle

A temporary repair patch of lead nailed over seams of deck planking or hull planking to stop leaks.

Tonnage

The measurement of capacity, formerly in all ships, now in merchant-ships only (war-ships being classified by their 'displacement tonnage' i.e. their actual weight). In English ships the capacity had originally equated to the number of Bordeaux wine casks or 'tuns' that could be stowed. The early formulae by which this could be calculated was based on multiplying the length of keel by the breadth, by the depth in the hold and then dividing the product, commonly by 100. This remained the basic principle of the many methods of tonnage measurement until 1836. The differences were the exact points between which the measurements were taken and the divisor used. In some methods the depth in hold and keel length were not actually measured but were proportions of those distances that were. The rule in force between 1773 and 1836 is a good example: In common with the majority of methods the calculation entailed multiplying length x breadth x depth, where the breadth was measured between the outside of the plank at the widest part of the hull. The length was the distance along the *rabbet* of the *keel* from the aft side of the *stern post* to a perpendicular dropped from the foreside of the *stem* below the bowsprit. From this was subtracted the rake of the stem which for convenience was taken to be three fifths of the extreme breadth. This gave a theoretical keel length. This was multiplied by the breadth which in turn was multiplied by half the breadth (taken to be the depth). The sum was divided by 94, the answer being the tonnage.

This method was inaccurate in many cases as it took no account of hull form. The method introduced in 1836 attempted to remedy this. It involved measuring the internal breadth at various heights and the depth from the underside of the *deckbeams* to the ceiling beside the *keelson*. This was done at three specific stations along the length of the hull, thus the resulting figure more accurately reflected the true capacity.

In other countries, similar arithmetical formulae were used, though in north west Europe and the Low Countries a ship's carrying capacity was expressed in 'lasten' (Dutch) 'laster' (Swedish), a weight, commonly of grain, being roughly two tuns. However, the actual weight of a last varied slightly depending on the commodity concerned. Nevertheless a general conversion from tuns into lasts was frequently done.

Top timber
The uppermost timber of a *frame*.

Transom
Heavy horizontal stern frame timbers set across the sternpost. The uppermost is the 'wing transom', set just below the top of the *stern post*. Set at the height of the deck is the 'deck transom', the others being 'filling transoms'.

Treenail (trenail, trunnel)
Wooden dowel used for fastening timbers together.

Tumblehome
The inward slope of the sides of the upper hull.

Turn of the bilge
The upward curve of the ship's hull approximately at the end of the *floor* timbers.

Wale
A thick outer hull strake corresponding to internal *stringers* providing additional longitudinal strength such as at the height of decks, the water line or below gunports, etc.

Waney (wainy)
A converted timber that retains some sapwood is 'waney', usually along its edges (hence the term 'waney edge').

Waterway
The outermost deck plank, often made from hard wood and usually thickened towards its outer edge to prevent water lying over the seam and seeping down between the frames.

Weather deck
A deck or section of deck that was open to the weather.

Whelps
Timber (later iron) ribs bolted longitudinally around drum of a capstan or windlass to protect the drum from wear and increase the bite of the cable being hauled.

Windlass
A winch for raising anchors or yards that was set horizontally on the deck and in early forms turned manually by levers (*handspikes*) located in sockets in the 'barrel' or shaft. In the 1830s various 'patent' mechanical devices were introduced to reduce the workload, in which pump handles were used to lever two vertical bars acting in ratchet fashion on the barrel.

Wrain (wrainstave)
In shipbuilding, an aid for forcing a plank into its required curvature against the frames, consisting of a length of wood set across the plank and connected to two wrain bolts temporarily anchored in a frame.

Appendix 1

NARROW ESCAPE FROM SHIPWRECK

This letter was published in the Hastings and St. Leonards News on Friday, March 12th 1852. It graphically illustrates the problems of voyaging in the days of sail. Although this vessel escaped sinking by a hair's breadth, the account also illustrates how unrelated a wreck site may be to the ports of lading and destination, or of the intended sailing route. (With thanks to Peter Barrie (Amsterdam Project) for drawing this to my attention).

'Narrow Escape From Shipwreck'

The following letter has been received by Mr Daniel Sargent, of Hastings, from his brother Mr George Sargent, who sailed from Newcastle in the middle of last month, in the Charles Kerr, of which he had the command, bound with a cargo of coals for the depot at Aden. The spirited and unvarnished story of the perils which were encountered in the endeavour to make the voyage, though the letter was not intended to meet the public eye, will doubtless repay our readers for the trouble of a perusal. The letter is dated from Cuxhaven, February 25.

My dear Dan, – Have this time had a narrow escape, the ship was leaky in harbour, but not so much so as I thought 'twould be a risk to go the voyage, but the first night at sea it came on to blow heavy at S.W. with a heavy sea; the ship being deep, nearly 1000 tons of coal on board, she laboured very much, I double-reefed topsails and reefed courses, and stood to the S.S.E., as with such a ship, drawing 19ft. 6in., I wanted sea-room.

The second night, gale and sea increasing, being on the starboard tack washed away our fore and main guard boards, they being the old fashioned ones, two feet broad, our starboard rigging was then all adrift, immediately wore ship to secure our masts, but in rounding-too a heavy sea came on board

carrying away the gripes of the long boat and stove her broadside in, we got her secured to the ring bolts to leeward, the ship all this time making much water, kept the pumps constantly going, took in the slack of our starboard rigging and again wore bend to southward; close-reefed topsails and handed courses, water in hold having increased to four feet. The remainder of time at sea, heavy gales, hove-to four days, no rest, and after a week at sea five men laid up, so you see we had few enough at the pumps, the leak gradually increasing on us. At all events we fetched the Texel, more moderate, gave her canvass, wind lulled round to N.W., hoping to get to some port in the English Channel, or if I could have got into the Downs I would have taken her up to London, sold the coal, and again taken her to the north to be repaired, but the wind again came round to the S.W. and blew a heavy gale with rain and thick hazy weather, the crew fairly tired out, myself also; bore up for Shields and had got half way over when it again flew into the N.W., having at this time double-reefed topsails and reefed courses, rattling the old barque through the water to get hold of the land, but no go. I then made up my mind to run for the Elbe, but nothing but thick hazy weather and not getting a sight of Heligoland, but knowing by my soundings I was in the Channel on the fair way of the Elbe, I made up my mind to run while daylight continued; wind at N.W., very thick with rain, kept the lead going, shoaling our water gradually into seven fathoms, when it cleared up a little, and as Providence ordered it got a sight of the Light Vessel before it thickened in again, at this time six feet water in her hold, shoaled our water to four fathoms, when all at once bump she goes. I thought the masts would have gone by the board, laid all flat aback. The tide making, she came off after about fifteen minutes, water increased in that time to eight feet, it again cleared up, when we saw the Light Ship about a mile off, dark coming on fast; we rounded the Light Ship close to the Dark, asked them for a pilot and told them we were sinking, but they could not give me one. I then gave her all the sail I could pack on, up the Elbe for the second Light Ship, but coming on very thick, gale increasing, could not hail the second Light Vessel, so steered for the pilot galliot she having a small light, expecting the masts to go over the side with the quantity of sail on the vessel, but neck or nothing, a pilot or a bump; sure enough bump it was, eleven feet when we struck, after a time managed to get the sails stowed, then out boats, after which got the people's clothes on the poop in case we should have to leave her before daylight. Our long boat being stove we had only a gig and second cutter, having left our first cutter in Shields. While busy with getting the clothes on the poop, the wind having backed into the West, she came off the sand all at once into deep water, a pretty predicament for a sinking ship; let go both bowers slap, sorry I did not do so to keep her fast when I had her fast, nothing now but the pumps for it. Poor George asleep on the poop among the people's bags covered over with a sail, pumps going all night, leak still increasing, twice the people knocked off and wanted to take to the boats, but I refused, as I thought she would keep up till daylight and then we should be sure of assistance. At daylight they saw our signals of distress, when they came to our assistance from the pilot ship, ten pilots and five sailors with two boats, they all clapped on to the pumps, now having twelve feet in well. Eleven a.m.,

flood having made, hove the anchors up and made sail, thank god fair wind up, but just as we got off Cuxhaven the wind came right out, and, expecting her to go down under our feet, a steam-boat came to our assistance and in half an hour stuck her in the mud, 15ft. 6in. in the hold, a near touch Dan my boy; thank God, all right. Poor George saw no danger, he left the poop in the night without my knowledge, went into the cabin, took a book of maps and my dictionary that he has had at school, went back again, crawled under the sail, and went again to sleep; whe[re] I found him when the people came to our assistance fast asleep with the books in his arms. I awoke him and asked him what he had there, he told me, and said that if he was saved he should save those books.

The Charles Kerr was a bark of 463 tons built in Sunderland in 1826 and was registered in Shields (near Newcastle). She was therefore a fairly old vessel by the time of this voyage. Surveyed in January 1852, she was noted in Lloyds' register as having had 'some repair' and 'part' new deck. In the 1853 register she is noted as having had a 'large repair', presumably precipitated by the rigorous voyage described above. In 1853 George Sargent is no longer listed as her master and she no longer appears in Lloyds' Register after 1857.

Appendix 2

17TH-CENTURY SHIP DESIGN

The following are two 17th century examples of generating the midship mould (midship section). The first is from Mathew Baker's *Fragments of Ancient English Shipwrightry.* MS 2820, folio 35 (Fig. 5.11). The second is the anonymous (possibly John Wells) Admiralty Library MSS 9 used for the *Sea Venture* reconstruction (Fig. 5.17).

Baker's method is the earlier and is an entirely geometric construction on the basis of the given breadth and depth. No other values are needed. The rest of the ship draft was then developed in a similar fashion (see Lavery 1988a). The diagram overleaf is labelled in line with the following text.

Baker, Folio 35

Fyrst ther must be maed with the bredth and depth of the shipp a paralillogram whose half shall souffyes for this worke. The bredth I sopose .36. foot the depth 16. of this proportion I have maed the paralillogram in the pag foling whose haef let be efcd now for the atayning of the flat or flower of the shipp I most take the 1/5 of ed and subetrakt that frome dc the lyn ed is .18. the lyn d.c. is 16 the one 5 of 18 subtracted from 16 doth leve 12 2/5 so is the lyn g.d. is 3 3/5. a lyn drawen from e to c will cut or crose the lyne h.g. in the poynt J. a parpendicular must be erected from. e.d. to .f.c. cuting the poynt .J. which which will be a parell to e.f. whose poynt or prik apone the lyn .e.d. is .k. now saye I the space between .e.k. is the half flower. the knowleg of which is that I seke fore. whose calculation is as foloth.

(8 lines crossed out)

the same preportion that .e.d..dothe beare to d.c. doth .J.g. bear .g.c. the lyn .e.d. is 18. the lyn .d.c. is 16 the on 5 of 18 subtracted from 16 as is sayd before doth leve 12 2/5 which is the lyn

g.c.so by the ruell of proportion I fynd the lyn J.g. to be 13 and 19/20 which being substracted from 18 dothe leve 4 & 1/20 the lyn .e.k. which is the halff flower of the shipp / the lyn h.l. is allways the 2/3 of e.d. so the 2/3 of 18 is 12. ther moust be a sentur found ought apon the lyn k.m. that maye tuch in the point K&L the which will be in the poynt .n. ther most allso be a lyn drane from the pric L. To N a long to the poynt O. on which lyne will be the sekon centur. the thord centor is found by the croseng of .2. lynes that goeth from .P. to .n. and from .c. to .o. croseng in the poynt .q. the centur of the hed of the futteke. the same depth that the mould is from .q. downward the leke depth will it be upward & ther will it be brod 2/3 of the lyn .b.c.

The following is a little simpler:

First a parallelogram is made ABCD (clockwise, A being bottom left). BC is the breadth (36 foot) and the depth CD is 16 foot. Then raise the centreline E to F.

Take ⅕ of the half breadth ED (3 ⅗ths), then measure that distance up the line DC to a point G so that DG = 3 ⅗th and GC = 12 ⅖ths, and similarly to point H on the centre line EF. The line HG can now be drawn parallel to ED.

Draw a diagonal from E to C which will cut HG at J. Construct a perpendicular from HG at J to meet FC at M and ED at K. EK is the half floor.

Mark point L ⅔rds of the way along HG (so that HL is twice LG). Join K and L.

Bisect KL and raise a perpendicular cutting KM at N. N is the first centre. The floor sweep can now be struck from K to L.

To find the second centre project the line LN for a distance as yet unknown. The second arc must run from L to C. So draw a line from L to C.

Now bisect LC and raise a perpendicular. Where it cuts the line projected from LN is the second centre O. The second arc can now be drawn from L to C.

To find the third centre, draw a line from O to C. Draw a line from P to N and extend it to cut OC at Q which is the third centre. Draw the third arc for a distance as yet unknown.

The height of the mould is twice the height that Q is above AD. The breadth at the top timbers R and S is ⅔rds of the main breadth = 24 foot.

Now draw the line of the top timber from S so that it meets the 3rd arc at a tangent.

Now repeat the procedure to construct the other side of the mould.

To draw the moulded thickness of the timbers the scantlings need to be known. The timbers progressively taper as they rise upwards. To draw them requires shifting the centres of the arcs slightly. On the basis of Baker's work it seems that this was a matter of establishing the correct moulded depth of the timber at the junction of each arc and drawing them by trial and error. There are numerous compass pricks in some of the folios. Experiment produces exactly the same effect.

Admiralty library MSS 9

In this method the flat of floor and the various radii are given as proportions or combinations of other values such as the breadth and depth, etc. The only arc that needs to be constructed geometrically is that joining the floor sweep and the breadth sweep, hence the name by which it is sometimes known: the reconciling sweep. Transcription is taken from Salisbury (in Salisbury and Anderson 1958). Salisbury's

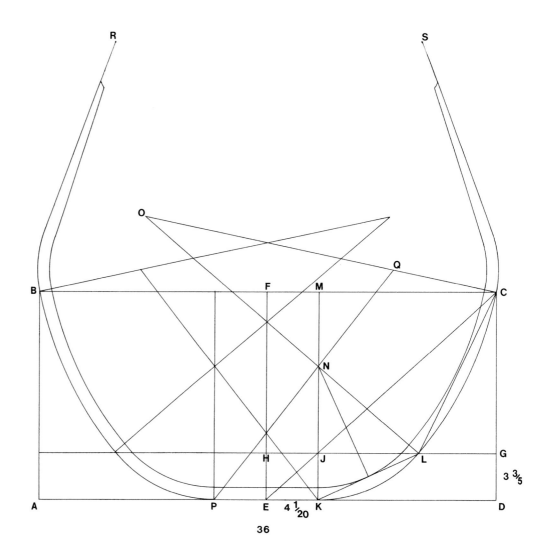

36

annotations are in [square brackets], my annotations [bold] and comments in normal text.

…to make a plot for a ship of 550 Tunns or thereabouts, which will be of most ordinary use and near a mean proportion between the greatest and the least…

…Suppose that the breadth were 36 foot: the ½ is 18 and the ⅓ is 12 which added together makes 30; the half thereof is 15, which is [a] mean between both and were a good proportion for the depth…But the best proportion of the breadth to the depth is as 7 to 3, and of the breadth to the length as 9 to 25, and 36 foot of breadth will have 15 ½ [foot] of depth and 100 foot of [**keel**] length.

For the flat of floor …In a good man of war the floor must never be more than ⅓ nor less than ¼ of the breadth… but more particularly ½ the difference between the breadth and the depth will be considered [**appropriate**] for all kinds of shipping. Which in this case would be 36'–15' 6" = 10' 6". However, ¼ breadth (9 foot) is used in the worked example.

Every bend [**body section**] consists of 3 sweeps, and if you use a hollowing post [**the reverse curve of the top timbers**], of 4.

First therefore make a parallelogram of the breadth and depth A.B.C.D. Divide A, B and C, D into halves at E and F; from each side thereof set the half floor to G and K

The lengths of the four sweeps are then given:

The first is called the sweep of the wrong head [**'rung head' the head of the floor or 'rung'**] … This must always be less than the depth and less the difference [between] half the breadth [**18**] and half the floor (**4' 6"**)… The best proportion will be one third of the depth and difference added together; so the depth is 15 foot 6 inches and the difference 13 foot 6 inches [18 foot less 4 foot 6 inches) both together is 29 foot … the ⅓ thereof is 9 foot 8 inches for the… first sweep.

The third sweep is the sweep of the breadth or naval timbers,…and the best proportion is as 15 to 19 of the lower [**floor**] sweep, and then the radius is near 7 foot 8 inches for the upper sweep.

The middle sweep, called the futtock sweep, doth only touch and include the other two and so makes one entire circular line of all three…. The best proportion will be as 6 to 10 of the breadth so the radius of this sweep will be 21 foot 8 inches.

The breadth of the ship is the best proportion for the sweep of the hollowing post…so…is 36 foot.

(See Figure 6.17)

References

Abbreviations
BAR   British Archaeological reports
CBA   Council for British Archaeology
IJNA   International Journal of Nautical Archaeology
JMA   Journal of Maritime Archaeology
MM   Mariner's Mirror
NMM   National Maritime Museum, Greenwich
PRO   Public Record Office
SNR   Society for Nautical Research
WARP   Wetlands Archaeological Project

Abell, Sir W. 1948. *The Shipwright's Trade*. London: Conway Maritime Press.

Adams, J. 1985. Sea Venture: A second interim report, part 1. *IJNA* 14.4: 275–299.

Adams, J. 1986a. Excavation strategies and recording. In J. Gawronski (ed.) VO*C Schip Amsterdam 1985*: 15–22. Amsterdam: Stichting VOC Schip Amsterdam.

Adams, J. 1986b. Hull structure. In J. Gawronski (ed.) *VOC Schip Amsterdam 1985*: 22–28. Amsterdam: Stichting VOC Schip Amsterdam.

Adams, J. 1995. The Oskarshamn Cog – Hull recording. In C. O. Cederlund (ed.) *Medieval Ship Archaeology*. Stockholm: Stockholm University/ Nautical Archaeology Society.

Adams, J. 1999. *The Kravel Project: The Survey and Recording of an Early Sixteenth Century Wreck in the Baltic*. Centre for Maritime Archaeology Interim Report. http://www.cma.soton.ac.uk/cma/ Research/kravel/ index.html (1.3.2000)

Adams, J. 2001. Ships and boats as archaeological source material. In D. Gibbins and J. Adams (eds) Shipwrecks. *World Archaeology* 32.3: 292–310.

Adams, J. 2002a. Maritime Archaeology. In C. Orser (ed.) *Encyclopedia of Historical Archaeology*: 328–330. London: Routledge.

Adams, J. 2002b. Excavation methods under water, in C. Orser (ed.). *Encyclopaedia of Historical Archaeology*: 192–196. London: Routledge.

Adams, J. 2006. From the water margins to the centre ground. Editorial article. *Journal of Maritime Archaeology*. 1.1: 1–8.

Adams, J. 2007. Alchemy or Science? Compromising Archaeology in the Deep Sea. *JMA* 2.1: 48–56

Adams, J., van Holk, A. F. L. and Maarleveld. Th. J. 1990. *Dredgers and Archaeology, Ship finds from the Slufter*. Alphen aan den Rijn: Ministerie WVC.

Adams, J., Norman, P. and Rönnby, J. 1991. *Rapport från marinarkeologisk vrakbesiktning, Franska Stenarna, Nämdöfjärden*. Marinarkeologisk tidskrift 2: 8–10. Stockholm.

Adams, J. and Rule, N. 1991. *'DSM' An Evaluation of a three dimensional method of survey on underwater sites*. In R. Reinders (ed.) *Scheepsarchaeologie: prioriteiten en lopend onderzoek*: 145–155. Proceedings of the Glavimans Symposia 1986 and 88. Flevobericht no. 322. Rijksdienst Ijsselmeerpolders.

Adams, J. and Rönnby, J. 1996. *Furstens Fartyg*. Stockholm: Swedish National Maritime Museum.

Adams, J. and Rönnby, J. 2002. Kuggmaren 1: the first cog find in the Stockholm archipelago, Sweden. *IJNA* 31.2: 172–181.

Adams, J. and Black, J. 2004. From Rescue to Research. Medieval Wrecks in St Peter Port, Guernsey. *IJNA* 35.2: 230–252.

Adams, J. and Rönnby, J. 2013a. One of His Majesty's '*Beste Kraffwells*': the wreck of an early carvel-built ship at Franska Sternarna, Sweden. *IJNA* 42.1: 103–117.

Adams, J. and Rönnby, J. 2013b. Interpreting Shipwrecks. Maritime Archaeological Possibilities. Oxford: University of Southampton/Södertörn University

Ahlström, C. 1978. Documentary research on the Baltic. Three case studies. *IJNA* 7.1: 59–70.

Ahlström, C. 1997. *Looking for Leads. Shipwrecks of the past revealed by contemporary documents and the archaeological record.* Helsinki: Finish Academy of Science and letters.

Albion, R. G. 1926. *Forests and Sea Power: The Timber Problem of the Royal Navy 1652–1862.* Cambridge: Harvard University Press.

Albion, R. G. 1952. The timber problem in the Royal Navy 1652–1868. *MM* 38.1: 4–20.

Alvik, R. and Tikanen, S. 2004. Introduction. In C. O. Cederlund (ed.) MoSS Project Final Report. Helsinki: National Board of Antiquities.

Andersen, S. H. 1986. Mesolithic Dug-outs and paddles from Tybrind Vig, Denmark. *Acta Archaeologica* 57: 87–106.

Andersen, S. H. 1987. Tybrind Vig: A Submerged Ertebølle Settlement in Denmark. In J. M. Coles and A. J. Lawson (eds) *European Wetlands in Prehistory.* Oxford: 253–280.

Andersen, S. H. 1994. New Finds of Mesolithic Logboats in Denmark. In C. Westerdahl (ed.) *Crossroads in Ancient Shipbuilding*: 1–10. IBSA 6. Oxbow Monograph 40. Oxford: Oxbow Books.

Anderson, A. 1946. Om svensk skeppsmätning I äldre tid. *Sjöhistorisk Årsbok.* Föreningen sveriges sjöfartsmuseum I Stockholm.

Anderson, R. C. 1913a. Big Ships in History. *MM* 3. 1: 43–45.

Anderson, R. C. 1913b. The Royal Sovereign of 1637. *MM* 3. 2: 208–211.

Anderson, R. C. 1919. The Midship Section of the "Sovereign". *MM* 5.4: 125–126.

Anderson, R. C. 1925. Italian naval architecture *c.* 1445. *MM* 11.2 : 135–163.

Anderson, R. C. 1926 (1980). *The Sailing Ship.* London: Harrap.

Anderson, R. C. 1927 (1982). *The Rigging of Ships in the Days of the Spritsail Topmast 1600–1720.* London: Conway Maritime Press.

Anderson, R. C. 1934. The Bursledon Ship. *MM.* 20: 154–170.

Anderson, R. C. 1953. The Framing of models. *MM.* 39. 2: 139.

Anderson, R. C. 1945. Jal's Mémoire no. 5 and manuscript Fabrica di galere, *MM* 31:160–167

Anderson, R. C. 1954. The Framing of models – and of Actual Ships. *MM.* 40.2: 155–156.

Anderson, R. C. 1962 (1976) *Oared Fighting Ships.* London: Argus.

Andersson, H. 1992. Makten och Borgarna. In Andersson, Hall and Öborn (eds) *Borgar från fortid och medeltid i Västsverige*: 87–91. Arkeologi i Västsverige 5. Gothenburg: Göteborgs arkeologiska Museum.

Andrén, A. 1993. Doors to other worlds: Scandinavian death rituals in Gotlandic perspectives. *Journal of European Archaeology* 1: 33–56.

Appadurai, A. (ed.) 1986. *The social life of things: commodities in cultural perspective.* Cambridge: Cambridge University Press.

Arens, I. 1987. (translated by C. Westerdahl). Nytt Vrakfyng I Estland. *Bottnisk Kontakt III.* Jacobstads Museum Publikationer No. 20: 46–50. Jacobstad: Jacobstads Museum.

Arnold, B. 1975. Gallo-Roman boat from the Bay of Bevaix, Lake Neuchâtel, Switzerland. *IJNA* 4.1:123–141.

Arnold, B. 1991. The Gallo-Roman Boat of Bevaix and the Bottom Based Construction. In R. Reinders and K. Paul (eds) *Carvel Construction Technique*: 19–23. Oxbow Monograph No. 12. Oxford: Oxbow Books.

Arnold, B. 1999. Some remarks on Romano-Celtic boat construction and Bronze Age wood technology. *IJNA* 28.1: 34–44.

Arnold, J. B. III and Weddle, R. 1978. *The Nautical Archaeology of Padre Island, the Spanish Shipwrecks of 1514.* New York.

Auer, J. and Firth, A. 2007. The 'Gresham Ship': an interim report on a 16th-century wreck from Princes Channel, Thames Estuary. *Post-Medieval Archaeology* 41.2: 222–241.

Bailey, G. and Sakellariou, D. 2012. SPLASHCOS: Submerged Prehistoric Archaeology and Landscapes of the Continental Shelf. *Antiquity* 86. 334: 20-1-2013.

Baker, W. A. 1954a. Early Seventeenth Century Ship Design. *American Neptune* 14. 4: 262–277.

Baker, W. A. 1954b. More on the Framing of Models. *MM.* 40.1: 80–81.

Baker, W. A. 1955. The arrangement and Construction of Early Seventeenth-Century Ships. *American Neptune* 15. 4: 259–286.

Baker, W. A. 1983. *The Mayflower and other colonial vessels.* London: Conway Maritime Press.

Barker, P. 1977. *Techniques of Archaeological Excavation.* London: Batsford.

Barker, R. 1986. Fragments from the Pepysian Library. IV International Reunion for Nautical Science and Hydrography, Sagres 1983. In *Revista da Universidade de Coimbra* 32: 161–178

Barker, R. 1988. Many may peruse us: ribbands, moulds & models in the dockyards. *Revista da Universidade de Coimbra,* 34: 539–559.

Barker, R. 1991. Design in the dockyard c.1600. In R. Reinders, and K. Paul (eds) *Carvel Construction Techniques*: 61–9. Oxbow Monograph 12. Oxford. Oxbow Books.

Barker, R. 1993. J. P. Sarsfield's Santa Clara: an addendum. *IJNA* 22.2: 161–5.

Barker, R. 1994. A manuscript on shipbuilding, circa 1600, Copied by Newton. *MM.* 88, 1: 16–29.

Barker. R. 1998. Why Tumblehome? *MM* 84.1: 95–97.

Barker, R. 1998. English shipbuilding in the sixteenth century: evidence for the processes of conception and construction. In E. Rieth (ed.) *Technologies,*

Idéologies, Pratiques Vol. XIII.1: 107–26. Concevoir et construire navires.

Barrett, J. C. 1987. Contextual Archaeology. *Antiquity* 61: 468–73.

Barrett, J. C. 1988. The Living, the Dead and the Ancestors: Neolithic and Early Bronze Age Mortuary Practices. In J. Barrett, and I. Kinnes (eds) *The Archaeology of Context in the Bronze Age and Neolithic. Recent Trends*: 30–41. Sheffield: Sheffield University press.

Bartlett, J. V. 1997. Why Tumblehome? *MM* 83.3: 478.

Basalla, G. 1988. *The evolution of Technology*. Cambridge: Cambridge University Press.

Basch, L. 1972. Ancient Wrecks and the Archaeology of Ships. *IJNA* 1.1: 1–58

Bass, G. F. 1966. *Archaeology Under Water*. London: Thames & Hudson.

Bass, G. F. 1967. Cape Gelidonya, a Bronze Age shipwreck. *Trans. American Philosoph. Soc.* 57. 8: 1–177

Bass, G. F. (ed.) 1972. *A history of seafaring based on underwater archaeology. London*: Thames & Hudson.

Bass, G. F. 1983. A Plea for historical Particularism in Nautical Archaeology. In R. Gould (ed.) *Shipwreck Anthropology*: 91–104. Albuquerque: University of New Mexico.

Bass, G. F. 1987. Oldest Known Shipwreck. *National Geographic* 172 (6): 693–734.

Bass, G. F. 1988. *Ships and Shipwrecks of the Americas*. A History Based on Underwater Archaeology. London.

Bass, G. F. 1991. Evidence of trade from Bronze Age shipwrecks. In N. Gale (ed.) *Bronze Age trade in the Mediterranean*. Studies in Mediterranean Archaeology XC. Jonsered: Åströms.

Bass, G. F. and Van Doorninck, F. H. Jr. 1978. An Eleventh-Century Shipwreck at Serçe Liman, Turkey. *International Journal of Nautical Archaeology* 7. 2: 119–132.

Bass, G. F. and Van Doorninck, F. H. 1982. *Yassi Ada, Volume 1: A seventh Century Byzantine Shipwreck*. College Station: Texas A&M University Press.

Bass, G. F., Matthews, S. D., Steffy, J. R. and Van Doorninck, F. H. Jr (eds) 2004. *Serçe Limani, an Eleventh-Century Shipwreck Volume 1: The Ship and its Anchorage, Crew and Passengers*. College Station: Texas A&M University Press.

Bates, C. R., Lawrence, M., Dean, M. and Robertson, P. 2011. Geophysical Methods for Wreck-Site Monitoring: the Rapid Archaeological Site Surveying and Evaluation (RASSE) programme. *IJNA* 40.2: 406–416

Bayliss, A., Groves, C., McCormac, F. G., Ramsey, C. B., Baillie, M. G. L., Brown, D., Cook, G. T. and Switsur, R. 2004. Dating, in P. Clark (ed.) *The Dover Bronze Age Boat*: 250–255. London: English Heritage.

Bellabarba, S. 1993. The Ancient Methods of Designing Hulls. *MM* 79. 3: 274–292.

Bellabarba, S. 1996. Origins of the ancient methods of designing hulls: a hypothesis. *MM* 82: 259–268.

van Beylen, J. 1970. *Schepen van de Nederlanden Van de late middeleeuwen tot het einde van de 17e eeuw*. Amsterdam. Van Kempen.

Bill, J. 1995. Getting into business. Reflections of a market economy in medieval Scandinavian shipbuilding. In O. Olsen, J. Skamby Madsen and F. Rieck (Eds), *Shipshape. Essays for Ole Crumlin-Pedersen*. Roskilde: The Viking Ship Museum.

Bill, J. 1999. Fra vikingeskib til bondeskude. *Nationalmuseets Arbejdsmark 1999*: 171–185. Copenhagen: National Museum of Denmark.

Bill, J., Gøthche, M. and Myrhøj, H. M. 1998. Nordeuropas største skibsfund. Ni vrag fra vikingetid og middelalder under museumsøen i Roskilde. *Nationalmuseets Arbejdsmark 1998*: 136–158. Copenhagen: National Museum of Denmark.

Binford, L. R. 1972. *An Archaeological Perspective*. New York. Seminar Press.

Binford, L. R. 1981. *Bones: ancient men and modern myths*. New York: Academic Press.

Binford, L. R. 1989. *Debating Archaeology*. New York: Academic Press.

Binford, L. R. and Sabloff, J. A. 1982. Paradigms, systematics, and archaeology. *Journal of Anthropological Research* 38: 137–153.

Bintliff, J. 1991. *The Annales School and Archaeology*. Leicester: Leicester University Press.

Bintliff, J. 1993. Why Indiana Jones is Smarter than the Post-Processualists. *Norwegian Archaeological Review*. 26. 2: 91–100.

Bird, M. I., Hope, G. and Taylor, D. 2004. Populating PEP II: the dispersal of humans and agriculture through Austral-Asia and Oceania. *Quaternary International* 118–119: 145–163.

Bloesch, P. 1983. Mediterranean Whole Moulding. *MM* 69: 305–6.

Blot, J-Y. 1996. *Underwater Archaeology. Exploring the World Beneath the Sea*. London: Thames and Hudson.

Blue, L., Kentley, E., McGrail, S. and Mishra, U. 1997. The Patia Fishing Boat of Orissa: A Case Study in Ethnoarchaeology. *South Asian Studies* 13: 198–207.

Blue, L., Kentley, E. and. McGrail, S. 1998. The Vattai Fishing Boat and Related Frame-first Vessels of Tamil Nadu. *South Asian Studies*. 14: 41–74.

Bojakowski, P. and Custer, K. 2011. The Warwick: results of the survey of an early 17th-century Virginia Company ship. Post-Medieval Archaeology 45.1: 41–53.

Bonney, R. 1991. *The European Dynastic States 1494–1660*. Oxford: Oxford University Press.

Bonino, M. 1978. Lateen-rigged medieval ships. New evidence from the Po Delta (Italy) and notes on pictorial and other documents. *IJNA* 7.1: 7–28.

Bound, M. and Monaghan, J. 2001. *A Ship Cast Away About Alderney: Investigations of an Elizabethan Shipwreck*. Alderney Maritime Trust.

Bradley, R. 1979. The interpretation of later Bronze Age metalwork from British rivers. *IJNA* 8.1: 3–6.

Braudel, F. 1972. *The Mediterranean and the Mediterranean World in the Age of Phillip II.* London: Collins.

Breen, C. 2007. *An Archaeology of Southwest Ireland, 1570–1670.* Dublin: Four Courts Press.

Bridgford, S. 1997. Mightier than the pen? An edgewise look at Irish Bronze Age swords. In J. Carman (ed.) *Material harm: archaeological studies of war and violence*: 95–115. Glasgow: Cruithne Press.

Broodbank, C. 1989. The Longboat and Society in the Cyclades in the Keros-Syros Culture. *American Journal of Archaeology* 93: 319–377.

Broodbank, C. 2006. The Origins and Early Development of Mediterranean Maritime Activity. *Journal of Mediterranean Archaeology* 19.2: 199–230.

Brown, A. 1988. *The Renaissance.* London: Longman.

Bruce-Mitford, R. 1975–1983. *The Sutton Hoo Ship-Burial.* Volumes 1–3. London: British Museum Press.

Brown, P., Sutikna, T., Morwood, M. J., Soejono, R. P., Jatmiko, Wayhu Saptomo, E. and Awe Due, R. 2004. A new small-bodied hominin from the Late Pleistocene of Flores, Indonesia. *Nature* 431, 1055–1061.

Brumm, A., Jense, G. M., van den Bergh, G. D., Morwood, M. J., Kurniawan, I., Aziz, F. and M. Storey. 2010. Hominins on Flores, Indonesia, by one million years ago. *Nature* 464: 748–752

Brück, J. 1999. Ritual and Rationality: some problems of interpretation in European Archaeology. *European Journal of Archaeology* 2. 3: 313–44.

Buchli and Lucas. 2001. *Archaeologies of the Contemporary Past.* London: Routledge.

Burström, M. 2004. In H. Bolin (ed.) *The Interplay of Past and Present.* Södertörn Archaeological Studies 1. Huddinge: Södertörn University College.

Burwash, D. 1969. *English Merchant Shipping: 1460–1540.* Newton Abbot.

Bushnell, E. 1664. *The Compleat Ship-Wright.* London.

Carr Laughton, L. G. 1960 (posthumously edited by Michael Lewis). Early Tudor Ship-Guns. *MM.* 46. 4: 241–285.

Casson, L. 1971. *Ships and Seamanship in the Ancient World.* New Jersey: Princeton University press.

Carver, M. 1995. Boat-burial in Britain: Ancient Custom or Political Signal?. In O. Crumlin-Pedersen and B. Thye (eds). *The Ship as Symbol in Prehistoric and Medieval Scandinavia*: 111–124. Copenhagen: National Museum of Denmark.

Carver, M. 1998. *Sutton Hoo. Burial Ground of Kings?* London: British Museum Press.

Caston, G. F. 1979. Wreck Marks: indicators of net sand transport. *Marine Geology.* 33: 193–204.

Cavers, M. G. and Henderson, J. C. 2005. Underwater Excavation at Ederline Crannog, Loch Awe, Argyll, Scotland. *IJNA* 34.2: 282–298.

Cederlund, C. O. 1978. *Ett fartyg byggt med syteknik. En studie I marinarkeologisk dokumentation.* Statens Sjöhistoriska Museum. Rapport 7. Stockholm: Swedish National Maritime Museum.

Cederlund, C. O. 1981. *Vraket vid Älvsnabben. Fartygets byggnad.* Statens Sjöhistoriska Museum. Rapport 14. Stockholm: Swedish National Maritime Museum.

Cederlund, C. O. 1982. *Vraket vid Jutholmen. Fartygets byggnad.* Statens Sjöhistoriska Museum. Rapport 16. Stockholm: Swedish National Maritime Museum.

Cederlund, C. O. 1983. *The Old Wrecks of the Baltic Sea.* BAR International series 186. Oxford: BAR.

Cederlund, C. O. 1984. A systematic approach to the study of the remains of old boats and ships. In S. McGrail (ed.) *Aspects of Maritime Archaeology and Ethnography in Northern Europe*: 173–209. Greenwich: NMM.

Cederlund, C. O. (ed.) 1985. *Postmedieval Boat and Ship Archaeology.* BAR S256. Oxford: BAR.

Cederlund, C. O. 1990. The Oskarshamn Cog. Part 1. *IJNA* 19.3: 193–206.

Cederlund, C. O. 1994. The Royal Ships and Divine Kingdom. *Current Swedish Archaeology.* 2: 47–85.

Cederlund, C. O. (ed.) 1995a. *Medieval Ship Archaeology. Documentation-Conservation-Theoretical Aspects-The management perspective.* Stockholm: Stockholm University/NAS.

Cederlund, C. O. 1995b. *Marine archaeology in society and science. IJNA* 24.1: 9–13.

Cederlund, C. O. 1995c. *Svanen Som Blev en Anka. Vrakidentifiering och marknadsföring av nationella myter.* Tvärsnitt, 1. Swedish Science Press. Uppsala.

Cederlund, C.O. 2004. What is Visualisation? MoSS Project *Newsletter 1/2004.* Helsinki: National Board of Antiquities.

Cederlund, C. O. and Hocker, F. (ed.) 2006. *Vasa 1. The Archaeology of a Swedish Royal Ship of 1628.* Stockholm: The Swedish National Maritime Museums.

Cervin de, Rubin, G. B. 1967. *The Catalan Ship.* In J. Jobé (ed.), *The Great Age of Sail*: 19–24. Cambridge: Patrick Stephens.

Champion, T., Gamble, C., Shennan, S. and Whittle, A. 1984. *Prehistoric Europe.* London: Academic Press.

Champion, T. 2004. The Dover Boat: its deposition. In P. Clark (ed.) *The Bronze Age Dover Boat.* London: English Heritage.

Chapman, F. H. 1768. *Architectura Navalis Mercatoria.* Stockholm. (Reprint 1971. London: Adlard Coles)

Chappelle, H. I. 1967. (reprinted 1983) *The Search for Speed Under Sail.* London: Conway Maritime Press.

Christensen, A. E. 1972. Boatbuilding Tools and the Process of Learning. In O. Hasslöf et al. (eds) *Ships and Shipyards*: 235–259. Copenhagen: Rosenkilde and Bagger.

Christensen, A. E. (ed.) 1996. *The Earliest Ships*. London: Conway Maritime Press.

Christensen, A. E. 1985. *Boat finds from Bryggen*. Bryggen Papers M.S.1, 47–280. Bergen: Universitetsforlaget.

Claassen, C. 1983. Answering our questions with experiments. In R. Gould (ed.) *Shipwreck Anthropology*. Albuquerque: University of New Mexico Press.

Clark, Sir G. 1966. *Early Modern Europe*. Oxford.

Clarke, D. Dean, M., Hutchinson, G., McGrail, S. and Squirrell, J. 1993. Recent work on the R. Hamble wreck near Bursledon, Hampshire. *IJNA* 22.1: 21–44

Coates, J. F. 1981. The Authorship of a Manuscript on Shipbuilding *c.* 1600–1620. *MM*. 67: 285–826.

Coates, J. F. and Morrison, J. 1987. Authenticity in the replica Athenian Trireme. *Antiquity* 61: 87–90.

Coates, J. F. 1977. Hypothetical reconstruction and the naval architect. In S. McGrail (ed.) *Sources and techniques in Boat Archaeology*: 215–226. BAR 29. Oxford.

Colebourn, P. 1983. *Hampshire's Countryside Heritage: 2 Ancient Woodland*. Winchester: Hampshire County Council.

Coles, J. M. 1994. *Rock Carvings of Uppland. A Guide*. Uppsala: Societas Archaeologica Upsaliensis and the Regional Museum of Uppland.

Coles, J. 2005. *Shadows of a Northern Past. Rock Carvings of Bohuslän and Østfold*. Oxford : Oxbow Books

Coles J. M. and Lawson A. J. (eds) 1987. *European Wetlands in Prehistory* 253–280. Oxford.

Coles, J. M. and Coles, B. J. (eds) 1989. *The archaeology of rural wetlands in England*. Wetland Archaeology Research Project occasional Paper 2. Exeter: WARP.

Coles, J., Fenwick, V. and Hutchinson, G. 1993. *A Spirit of Enquiry. Essays for Ted Wright*. Exeter: WARP, NAS & NMM.

Conway, T. M. 1989. When is a ship a he? *MM* 75.1:96–97.

Corbishley, M. 2011. *Pinning Down the Past: Archaeology, Heritage and Education Today*. Woodbridge: The Boydell Press.

Cordingly, D. 1996. *Under the Black Flag. The Romance and the Reality of Life Among the Pirates*. New York: Random House.

Creighton M. S. and Norling, L. (eds) 1996. *Iron Men, Wooden Women. Gender and Seafaring in the Atlantic World 1700–1920*. Baltimore, Maryland: Johns Hopkins University Press.

Crumlin-Pedersen, O. 1965. Cog-kogge-kaag. Handels-og søfartsmuseet på Kronborg Årbog: 81–144. Helsingör

Crumlin-Pedersen, O. 1972. Skin or Wood?. In O. Hasslöf et al. (eds) *Ships and Shipyards*: 208–234. Copenhagen: Rosenkilde and Bagger.

Crumlin-Pedersen, O. 1986. Aspects of Wood Technology in Medieval Shipbuilding. In O.

Crumlin-Pedersen and M. Vinner (eds) *Sailing Into the Past*: 138–148. Roskilde: Viking Ship Museum.

Crumlin-Pedersen, O. 1989. Wood Technology and the Forest Resources in the Light of Medieval Shipbuilding. In C. Villain Gandossi et al. (eds) *Medieval ships and the Birth of Technological Societies*: 25–42. Malta.

Crumlin-Pedersen, O. 1990. The Boats of the Angles and Jutes. In S. McGrail (ed.) *Maritime Celts, Frisians and Saxons*: 98–116. CBA Research Report No. 71. London: CBA..

Crumlin-Pedersen, O. 1994. Medieval Ships in Danish Waters. In C. Westerdahl (ed.) *Crossroads in Ancient Shipbuilding*: 65–72. IBSA 6. Oxbow Monograph 40. Oxford: Oxbow Books..

Crumlin-Pedersen, O. 1995. Experimental archaeology & ships – bridging the arts & the sciences. *IJNA* 24.4: 303–6.

Crumlin-Pedersen, O. 1996. Problems of reconstruction & the estimation of performance. In A. E. Christensen (ed.) *The Earliest Ships*: 110–119. London: Conway Maritime Press.

Crumlin-Pedersen, O. 1997. *Viking-Age Ships and Shipbuilding in Hedeby/Haithabu and Schleswig*. Ships and Boats of the North. Volume 2. Odense: Viking Ship Museum, Roskilde.

Crumlin-Pedersen, O. 2010. *Archaeology and the Sea in Scandinavia and Britain*. Maritime Culture of the North Vol. 3. Roskilde: The Viking Ship Museum.

Crumlin-Pedersen, O. and Vinner, M. (eds) 1986. *Sailing Into the Past*. Roskilde: Viking Ship Museum.

Crumlin-Pedersen, O. and Thye, B. M. (eds) 1995. *The Ship as Symbol in Prehistoric and Medieval Scandinavia*. Copenhagen: National Museum of Denmark.

Crumlin-Pedersen, O. 2000. To be or not to be a cog: the Bremen cog in perspective. *IJNA* 29.2: 230–246.

Crumlin-Pedersen, O. and Olsen, O. (eds) 2002. *The Skuldelev Ships 1*. Ships and Boats of the North 4.1. Copenhagen: National Museum of Denmark.

Cullen, B. R. S. 1993. The Darwinian Resurgence and the Cultural Virus critique. *Cambridge Archaeological Journal* 3. 179–202.

Cullen, B. R. S. 1996. Cultural Virus Theory and the Eusocial Pottery Assemblage. In H. Maschner (ed). *Darwinian Archaeologies*. New York: Plenum Press.

Cunliffe, B. (ed.) 1994. *The Oxford Illustrated Prehistory of Europe*. Oxford: Oxford University Press.

Cunliffe, B. 2001. *Facing the Ocean*. Oxford: Oxford University Press.

Daggfeldt, B. 1963. Lybska Svan. *Tidskrift I sjöväsendet* 1963: 3–27.

Davis, R. 1972. *The Rise of English Merchant Shipping in the 17th and 18th centuries*. Newton Abbot: David & Charles.

Davis, R. 1975. *English merchant shipping and Anglo-Dutch rivalry in the seventeenth century.* London: HMSO.

Davis, R. 1979. *The Industrial Revolution and British overseas trade.* Leicester: Leicester University Press.

Deetz, J. 1999. *In Small Things Forgotten.* An Archaeology of Early American Life. New York: Anchor Doubleday.

Delgado, J. P. 1997 (ed.) *Encyclopaedia of Underwater and Maritime Archaeology.* London: British Museum Press.

Derry, T. K. 1979. *A History of Scandinavia.* Minneapolis: University of Minnesota Press.

Diole, P. 1954. *4,000 Years Under the Sea. Excursions in undersea archaeology.* London: Sidgwick and Jackson.

Dixon, N. 1982. Excavation of Oakbank Crannog, Loch Tay – interim report. *IJNA* 11.2: 125–132.

Dixon, N. 1991. The history of crannog survey and excavation in Scotland. *IJNA* 20.1: 1–8.

Dixon, N. 2004. *The Crannogs of Scotland. An Underwater Archaeology.* Stroud: Tempus.

Dobb, M. 1963. (ed.) *The Transition from Feudalism to Capitalism.* London.

Dodds, J. and J. Moore. 1984. *Building the Wooden Fighting Ship.* London: Hutchinson.

Doe, H. 2009. *Enterprising Women and Shipping in the Nineteenth Century.* Woodbridge: The Boydell Press.

Dolwick, J. 2008. In Search of the Social: Steamboats, Square Wheels, Reindeer and Other Things. *Journal of Maritime Archaeology* 3. 1: 14–51.

Dolwick, J. 2009. The Social and beyond: Introducing Actor-Network Theory. *Journal of Maritime Archaeology* 4. 1: 21–49.

Dommasnes, L. H. 1992. Two Decades of Women in Prehistory and Archaeology in Norway: A Review. *Norwegian Archaeological Review* 25. 1: 1–14.

Dotson, J. E. 1994. Treatises on Shipbuilding before 1650. In R. Unger (ed.) *Cogs, Caravels and Galleons.* London: Conway Maritime Press.

Dugaw, D. 1996. Female Sailors Bold: Transvestite Heroines and the Markers of Gender and Class. In M. Creighton and L. Norling (eds) *Iron Men, Wooden Women. Gender and Seafaring in the Atlantic World*: 34–54. *1700–1920.* Baltimore, Maryland: Johns Hopkins University Press.

Duller, G. A. T. 2001. Dating methods: The role of geochronology in studies of human evolution and migration in southeast Asia and Australia. *Progress in Physical Geography* 25: 267–76.

Dunnell, R. C. 1989. Aspects of the application of evolutionary theory in archaeology. In C. Lamberg-Karlovsky (ed.) *Archaeological thought in America*: 35–49. Cambridge: Cambridge University Press.

Durant, D. 1981 *Raleigh's Lost Colony.* London: Weidenfeld and Nicolson.

Einarsson, L. 1990. Kronan - underwater archaeological investigations of a 17th-century man-of-war. The

nature, aims and development of a maritime cultural project. *IJNA* 19.4: 279–297.

Ekman, C. 1934. Sjöhistoriska undersökningar vid Björkcnäs. *Sancte Christophers gilles chroenica* 8: 21–35.

Ekman, C. 1942. Stora Kraveln Elefanten. In revised edition of A. Zettersten (1890). *Svenska Flottans Historia I, 1522–1634*: 89–98. Malmö: Allhems Förlag.

Ellmers, D. 1969. *Keltischer Schiffbau.* Jarbuch des Romish-Germanischen Zentralmuseums. Mainz.

Ellmers, D. 1972. *Frühmittelalterliche Handelsschiffahrt in Mittel- und Nordeuropa.* Neumünster: Karl Wachholtz Verlag.

Ellmers, D. 1984. The earliest evidence for skinboats in late-Palaeolithic Europe. In S. McGrail (ed.) *Aspects of Maritime Archaeology and Ethnography.* London: NMM.

Ellmers, D. 1985. Frisian and Hanseatic Merchants sailed the Cog. In A. Anderson, B. Greenhill, and E. Grude (eds) *The North Sea: A Highway of Economic and Cultural Exchange*: 79–96. Stavanger: Norwegian University Press.

Ellmers, D. 1994. The Cog as Cargo Carrier. In R. Unger (ed.) *Cogs, Caravels and Galleons*: 29–46. London: Conway Maritime Press.

Ellmers, D. 1995. Valhalla and the Gotland Stones. In O. Crumlin-Pedersen and B. M. Thye (eds). *The Ship as Symbol in Prehistoric and Medieval Scandinavia*: 165–171. Copenhagen: National Museum of Denmark.

Ellmers, D. 1996. The Beginnings of Boatbuilding in Central Europe. In A. E. Christensen (ed.) *The Earliest Ships*: 11–23. London: Conway Maritime Press.

English Heritage/RCHME, 1996. *England's Coastal Heritage. A statement on the management of coastal archaeology.* London: HMSO.

Eriksson, N. 2008. An early 'half-carvel' in the northern Baltic. Maritime Archaeology Newsletter 23: 4–9.

Eriksson, N. and Rönnby, J. 2012. The Ghost Ship. An Intact *Fluyt* from *c.* 1650 in the Middle of the Baltic Sea. *IJNA* 41.2: 350–361.

Eriksson, N. 2013. Sailing, sleeping and eating on board 17th century ships: Tapping into the Potential of Baltic Sea Shipwrecks with regard to the Archaeology of Space. In J. Adams and J. Rönnby (eds). *Interpreting Shipwrecks: Maritime Archaeological possibilities.* Oxford: University of Southampton/Södertörn University.

Eriksson, N., During, C., Holmlund, J., Rönnby, J., Sjöblom, I. and Ågren, M. 2012. *Resande mannen* (1660). Marinarkeologisk rapport 2012. Södertörn: Södertörn arkeologiska rapporter och studier.

Eskeröd, A. 1956. Early Nordic-Arctic Boats. A Survey and Some Problems. *Arctica.* Studia Ethnographica Upsaliensia. XI. Uppsala: 57–87.

Evans, A. C. and Bruce Mitford. R. 1975. The Ship. In R. Bruce Mitford (ed.) *The Sutton Hoo Ship-Burial* Volume 1: 345–435. London: British Museum Press.

Evans, A. M., Russell, M. A. and Leshikar-Denton, M. E. (eds) 2010. Navigating Contentious Waters: International Responses to the 2001 UNESCO Convention on the Protection of the Underwater Cultural Heritage. *JMA* 5.2

Evelyn, J. 1664. *Sylva, or A Discourse of Forest–Trees and the Propagation of Timber in His Majesty's Dominions.* London.

Ewe, H. 1972. *Schiffe auf Siegeln.* Rostock: Hinstorff Verlag.

Farr, H. 2006. Seafaring as Social Action. *JMA.* 1.1: 85–99

Fenwick, V. (ed.), 1978. *The Graveney Boat.* BAR British series No. 53. Oxford: BAR.

Ferrari, B. 1995. *Physical, biological and cultural factors influencing the formation, stabilisation and protection of archaeological deposits in U.K. coastal waters.* PhD Thesis. St Andrews.

Ferrari, B. and Adams, J. 1990. Biogenic Modification of Marine Sediments and their influence on archaeological material. *IJNA* 19.2: 139–151.

Fincham, J. 1851. *A History of Naval Architecture.* (reprinted, Scholar Press 1979)

Firth, A. 1995. *Three Facets of Maritime Archaeology: Society, Landscape and Critique.* (Unpublished based on paper given at TAG 93) see Univ. Soon WW1. home page (current research).

Fischer, A. 1995. *Man and Sea in the Mesolithic: coastal settlement above and below present sea level.* Oxford: Oxbow Books.

Fischer, A., Richards, M., Olsen, J. Robinson, D. E., Bennike, P., Kubiak-Martens, L. and Heinemeier, J. 2007. Coast–inland mobility and diet in the Danish Mesolithic and Neolithic: evidence from stable isotope values of humans and dogs, 2125–2150. *Journal of Archaeological Science* 34. 12: 163–178.

Fischer, A., Nilsson, B. and Sturt, F. (eds) In press. Flooded Stone Age: towards an overview of submerged settlements and landscapes on the Continental Shelf. *Journal of Maritime Archaeology*

Flatman J. 2003. Cultural biographies, cognitive landscapes and dirty old bits of boat: 'theory' in maritime archaeology. *IJNA* 32.2: 143–157

Flatman, J. 2007. *The Illuminated Ark. Interrogating Evidence from Manuscript Illuminations and Archaeological Remains for Medieval Vessels.* BAR International Series 1616. Oxford: BAR.

Flannery, K. 1967. Culture History v. Cultural Process: A Debate in American Archaeology. Reprinted in M. P. Leone (ed.) 1972, *Contemporary Archaeology: A guide to Theory and Contributions.* Carbondale: S. Illinois University Press.

Flannery, K. V. and Marcus, J. 1995. Cognitive Archaeology. In I. Hodder et al. (eds) *Interpreting Archaeology.* London: Routledge.

Fleidner, S. 1964. *Die Bremer Cogge.* Bremen: Focke Museums.

Foley, B. P., DellaPorta, K., Sakellariou, D., Bingham, B., Camilli, R., Eustice, R., Evagelistis, D., Ferrini, V., Hansson, M., Katsaros, K., Kourkoumelis, D., Mallios, A., Micha, P., Mindell, D., Roman, C., Singh, H., Switzer, D. and Theodoulou, T. 2009. The 2005 Chios Ancient Shipwreck Survey: New Methods for Underwater Archaeology. *Hesperia* 78: 269–305.

Foote, P. G. (ed.) 1996. *Olaus Magnus. A Description of the Northern Peoples 1555.* Volume 1.

Hakluyt Society. Second series No. 182. London: Hakluyt Society.

Flemming, N. C. 2005. *Submarine Archaeology of the North Sea: Priorities and Collaboration with Industry.* CBA research report. London: CBA.

Fredell, Å, C., Kristiansen, K. and Criado Boado, F. 2010. *Representations and communications: creating an archaeological matrix of late prehistoric rock art.* Oxford: Oxbow Books.

Franzén, A. 1967. *The Warship Vasa. Deep Diving and Marine Archaeology in Stockholm.* Stockholm: Norstedt and Bonnier.

Friel, I. 1983a. Documentary sources and the medieval ship: some aspects of the evidence. *IJNA* 12.1: 41–62.

Friel, I. 1983b. *England and the advent of the three masted ship.* International Congress of Maritime Museums. 4th conference proceedings. Paris: ICMM.

Friel, I. 1993c. Henry V's 'Grace Dieu' and the wreck in the Hamble River near Bursledon, Hampshire. *IJNA* 22.1: 3–19.

Friel, I. 1994. The Carrack: The Advent of the Full Rigged Ship. In R. Unger (ed.) *Cogs, Caravels and Galleons*: 77–90. London: Conway Maritime Press.

Friel, I. 1995. *The Good Ship: Ships, Shipbuilding and Technology in England 1200–1520.* London: British Museum Press.

Frost, H. 1963. *Under the Mediterranean.* London: Thames & Hudson.

Frost, H. 1972. Ancient harbours and anchorages in the eastern Mediterranean. In *Underwater Archaeology: A nascent discipline.* Paris: UNESCO. 95–114.

Fulford, M., Champion, T. and Long, A. (eds) 1997. *England's Coastal Heritage. A survey for English Heritage and the RCHME.* London: English Heritage and RCHME.

Gaimster, D. 1997. *German Stoneware 1200–1900: Archaeology and Cultural history.* London: British Museum Press.

Gale, A. 1993. *Hydroarchaeology: a subject framework.* *IJNA* 22.3: 209–217.

Gamble, C. 2001. *Archaeology: The Basics.* London: Routledge.

Gardiner, J. (ed.) 2005. *Before the Mast: Life and Death Aboard the Mary Rose.* The Archaeology of the Mary Rose Vol. 4. Oxford: Mary Rose Trust.

Garrow, D. and Sturt, F. 2011. Grey waters bright with Neolithic argonauts? Maritime connections and the Mesolithic–Neolithic transition within the 'western seaways' of Britain, *c.* 5000–3500 BC, *Antiquity*, 85, 327: 59–72

Gawronski, J. (ed.) 1986. *VOC Schip Amsterdam 1985.* Amsterdam: Stichting VOC Schip Amsterdam.

Gawronski, J. (ed.) 1987. *VOC Schip Amsterdam 1986.* Amsterdam: Stichting VOC Schip Amsterdam.

Gawronski, J. 1991. The Archaeological and Historical Research of the Dutch EastIndiaman *Amsterdam* (1749). In R. Reinders and K. Paul (eds) *Carvel Construction Technique.* Oxbow Monograph 12. Oxford: Oxbow Books: 81–84.

Gawronski, J. 1992. Aims and theory of the Archaeology of Dutch East Indiamen. In J. Gawronski, B. Kist, and O. Stokvis-van Boetzelaer. *Hollandia Compendium.* Amsterdam: Elsevier.

Gawronski, J. 1992. Research of Dutch East Indiamen and Underwater Archaeology. In J. Gawronski, B. Kist and O. Stokvis-van Boetzelaer. *Hollandia Compendium.* Amsterdam: Elsevier.

Gelder, K. 2007. *Subcultures: Cultural Histories and Social Practice.* Abingdon: Routledge.

Gellner, E. 1995. Interpretative anthropology. In I. Hodder et al. *Interpreting Archaeology.* London: Routledge.

Gerout, M., Reith, E. and J. M. Gassend. 1989. *Le Navire Genois de Villefranche.* Archaeonautica, 9. CNRS. Paris.

Gibbins, D. 1990. Analytical approaches in maritime archaeology: a Mediterranean perspective. *Antiquity* 64. 376–89.

Gibbins, D. and Adams, J. (eds) 2001. Shipwrecks. *World Archaeology* 32.3.

Gibbon, G. 1989. *Explanation in Archaeology.* Oxford: Blackwell.

Giddens, A. 1979. *Central Problems in Social theory: Action, Structure, and Contradiction in Social Analysis.* London: Palgrave Macmillan.

Giddens, A. 1984. *The Constitution of Society.* Cambridge: Polity Press.

Gillmer, T. 1985. Evolving ship design technology revealed in wrecks of postmedieval ships. In C. O. Cederlund (ed.) *Postmedieval Boat and Ship Archaeology*: 255–267. BAR S256. Oxford: BAR.

Glasgow, T. Jr. 1964. The Shape of the Ships that Defeated the Spanish Armada. *MM* 50. 3: 177–189.

Glasgow, T. Jr. 1966. H.M.S. Tiger. *North Carolina History Review* LIII: 115–121.

Glasgow, T. Jr. 1972. The Hulk. *MM* 58. 1: 103

Glete, J. 1977. Svenska örlogsfartyg 1521–1560. Flottans uppbyggnad under ett tekniskt brytningsskede. *Forum Navale. Skrifter utgivna av Sjöhistoriska Samfundet* 31: 23–119.

Glete, J. 1993. *Navies and Nations. Warships, Navies and State Building in Europe and America, 1500–1860.* Stockholm: Almqvist & Wiksell International.

Glete, J. 2000. *Warfare at Sea 1500–1650. Maritime Conflicts and the Transformation of Europe.* London: Routledge.

Glete, J. 2002. *War and the State in Early Modern Europe.* London: Routledge.

Good, G., Jones, R. H. and Ponsford, M. W. 1991. *Waterfront Archaeology.* Proceedings of the third international conference on waterfront archaeology held at Bristol 23–26 September 1988. Oxford: Alden Press.

Goodburn, D. 1988. Recent finds of Ancient Boats from the London area. *London Archaeologist* 5.16: 423–428.

Goodburn, D. 1991. New light on early ship and boatbuilding in the London area. In Good, et al. (eds) *Waterfront Archaeology*: 105–115. CBA Research report No. 74. York: CBA.

Goodburn, D. 1992. *An archaeology of medieval boat building practice.* Pre-prints: Medieval Europe 1992 Conference: Maritime session. York: York University.

Goodburn, D. 1993. Some further thoughts on reconstructions, replicas and simulations of ancient boats and ships. *IJNA* 22.3: 199–203.

Goodburn, D. 2002. *An Archaeology of Early English Boatbuilding c. 900–1600 AD: Based mainly on finds from SE England.* PhD thesis. Institute of Archaeology. London.

Goodwin, P. 1998. The Influence of Iron on Ship Construction 1660–1830. *MM* 84.1: 26–40.

Gosden, C. 1999. *Anthropology and archaeology: a changing relationship.* London: Routledge.

Gosden, C. and Marshall, Y. 1999. The Cultural Biography of Objects. *World Archaeology* 31: 169–178.

Gould, R. (ed.) 1983. *Shipwreck Anthropology.* Albuquerque: University of New Mexico.

Gould, R. 2000. *Archaeology and the Social History of Ships.* Cambridge: Cambridge University Press.

Green, J. N. 1975. The VOC ship *Batavia* wrecked in 1629 on the Houtman Abrolhos, Western Australia. *IJNA* 4.1: 43–63.

Greenhill, B. 1976. *Archaeology of the Boat.* London: Adam and Charles Black.

Greenhill, B. 1995. *The Archaeology of Boats and Ships, an Introduction.* London: Conway Maritime Press.

Greenhill. B. 2000. *The Mysterious Hulc. MM* 86.1: 3–18.

Greenhill, B. and Manning, S. 1988. *The Evolution of the Wooden Ship.* London: Conway Maritime Press.

Grenier, R. 1988. Basque Whalers in the New World. In G. Bass (ed.), *Ships and Shipwrecks of the Americas*: 69–84. London: Thames & Hudson.

Grenier, R., Loewen, B. and Prouix, J-P. 1994. Basque shipbuilding technology c. 1560–1580: The Red Bay Project. In C. Westerdahl, (ed.) *Crossroads in Ancient Shipbuilding*: 137–141. IBSA 6. Oxbow Monograph 40. Oxford: Oxbow Books.

Grenier, R., Bernier, M-A. and W. Stevens (eds) 2007. *The Underwater Archaeology of Red Bay. Basque Shipbuilding and Whaling in the 16ᵗʰ Century*. Ottawa: Parks Canada.

Groot, I. de and R. Vorstman. 1980. *Maritime Prints by Dutch Masters*. London: Gordon Fraser.

Grundvad, B. 2011. A clinker vessel converted. Maritime Archaeology Newsletter from Denmark 26: 24–27

Guilmartin, J. F. Jr. 1974. *Gunpowder and Galleys*. Cambridge. Cambridge University Press.

Gurevich, A. 1995. The French historical revolution: The Annales school. In I. Hodder et al. *Interpreting Archaeology*. London: Routledge.

Guy, J. 1988. *Tudor England*. Oxford: Oxford University Press.

Haldin, G. (ed.) 1963. *Svenskt Skeppsbyggeri: en översikt av utvecklingen genom tiderna*. Malmö: Allhems Förlag.

Hampshire & Wight Trust for Maritime Archaeology 2010. *Solent Marine heritage Assets: Defining, investigating, monitoring and reporting 2008–2011* five reports). Southampton: Hampshire & Wight Trust for Maritime Archaeology/English Heritage.

Harding, A. 1994. Reformation in Barbarian Europe 1300–600 BC. In B. Cunliffe (ed.) *The Oxford Illustrated Prehistory of Europe*: 304–335.Oxford: Oxford University Press,

Harding, A. 2000. *European Societies in the Bronze Age*. Cambridge: Cambridge University Press.

Harding D. W. 1997. Forts, Duns, Brochs and Crannochs: Iron Age Settlements in Argyll. In G. Ritchie (ed.) *The Archaeology of Argyll*: 116–140. Edinburgh.

Harriot, Thomas. 1608–10. (See Pepper, J. V.)

Harris, E. 1979. *Principles of Archaeological Stratigraphy*. London: Academic press. (second edition 1989).

Hasslöf, O. 1958. Carvel Construction Technique, Nature and Origin. *Folkliv* 1957–1958: 49–60. Stockholm.

Hasslöf, O. 1972a. Maritime Ethnology and its Associated Disciplines. In O. Hasslöf et al. (eds). *Ships & Shipyards – Sailors and Fishermen*: 9–19. Copenhagen: Rosenkilde and Bagger.

Hasslöf, O. 1972b. The Concept of Living Tradition. In O. Hasslöf et al. (eds). *Ships & Shipyards – Sailors and Fishermen*: 20–26. Copenhagen: Rosenkilde and Bagger.

Hasslöf, O. 1972c. Main principles in the Technology of Ship-Building. In O. Hasslöf et al. (eds). *Ships & Shipyards – Sailors and Fishermen*: 27–72. Copenhagen: Rosenkilde and Bagger.

Hasslöf, O. 1972d. Maritime Commerce as a Socio-Historical Phenomenon. In O. Hasslöf et al. (eds). *Ships & Shipyards – Sailors and Fishermen*: 73–122. Copenhagen: Rosenkilde and Bagger.

Hasslöf, O. 1977. Ethnography and the living tradition. In S. McGrail. (ed.) *Sources and techniques in Boat Archaeology*. BAR. 29. Oxford: BAR.

Hasslöf, O., Henningsen, H. and Christensen A. E. (eds). 1972. *Ships and Shipyards – Sailors and Fishermen*. Copenhagen: Rosenkilde and Bagger.

Hauptman Wahlgren, K. 2000. The Lonesome Sailing Ship. Reflections on the Rock Carvings of Sweden and their Interpreters. *Current Swedish Archaeology* 8: 67–96.

Hay, D. 1966. *Europe in the Fourteenth & Fifteenth Centuries*. London: Longman.

Hedderwick, P. 1830. *A Treatise on Marine Architecture*. Edinburgh.

Hedengran, I. 1995. The Shipwrecked and their Rescuer. In O. Crumlin-Pedersen and B. M. Thye (eds) *The Ship as Symbol*: 76–85. Copenhagen: National Museum of Denmark.

Heilbroner, R. L. 1967. Do Machines Make History. *Technology and Culture* 8. July: 335–345.

Heilbroner, R. L. 1994. Technological Determinism Revisited. In M. R. Smith and L. Marx (eds) *Does Technology Drive History?*: 67–78. Cambridge: MIT Press.

Heinsius, P. 1956. *Das Schiff der Hansischen Frühzeit*. Weimar: Herman Bolan.

Henderson, J. 2007. *The Atlantic Iron Age: Settlement and Identity in the First Millennium BC*. London: Routledge.

Herlihy, D. 1997. *The Black Death and the Transformation of the West*. Cambridge, Mass.: Harvard University Press.

Herrera, J. M. 2009. *The Reflexive Navigator: theory and directions in maritime archaeology*. PhD thesis, University of Southampton.

Herrera. J. M. (in preparation) *The Reflexive Navigator: theory and directions in maritime archaeology*.

Herrera. J. M., Buffa, V., Cordero, A., Francia, G. and Adams, J. 2010. Maritime Archaeology in Uruguay: Towards a Manifesto. *JMA* 5.1: 57–69

Hildred, A. and Rule, M. 1984. Armaments from the Mary Rose. *Antique Arms and Militaria*. May 1984: 17–24.

Hildred, A. 2011. *Weapons of Warre: The Armaments of the Mary Rose*. The Archaeology of the Mary Rose Vol 3. Exeter: Mary Rose Trust.

Hill, J. D. 1995. *Ritual and Rubbish in the Iron Age of Wessex*. BAR British series. 242. Oxford: Tempus Reparatum.

Hinton, D. A. 1990. *Archaeology, Economy & Society. England from the fifth to the fifteenth century*. London: Seaby.

Hocker, F. 1991. Development of a bottom-based shipbuilding tradition in Northwestern Europe and the New World. PhD thesis. College Station: Texas A&M University.

Hocker, F. and Vlierman, K. 1996. *A small cog wrecked on the Zuiderzee in the early fifteenth century*. Excavation Report 19. Flevobericht 408. Lelystad: NISA.

Hocker, F. and Dokkedal, L. 2001, News from the Kolding cog. *Maritime Archaeology Newsleter from Roskilde*. 16: 16–17.

Hocker, F. and Ward, C. (eds) 2004. *The Philosophy of Shipbuilding: Conceptual Approaches to the Study of Wooden Ships*. College Station: Texas A&M University Press.

Hodder, I. (ed.) 1982a. *Symbols in Action. Ethno-archaeological Studies of Material Culture*. Cambridge: Cambridge University Press.

Hodder, I. 1982b. Theoretical archaeology: a reactionary view. In I. Hodder (ed.) *Symbolic and Structural Archaeology*. Cambridge: Cambridge University Press.

Hodder, I. (ed.) 1982. *Symbolic and Structural Archaeology*. Cambridge: Cambridge University Press.

Hodder, I. 1986. *Reading the Past*. Cambridge: Cambridge University Press.

Hodder, I. (ed.) 1989. *The Meaning of Things*, One World Archaeology 6. London: Harper Collins.

Hodder, I. 1991a. Interpretative Archaeology and its Role. *American Antiquity*. 56.1: 7–18.

Hodder, I. 1991b. To Interpret is to Act: the need for an Interpretative Archaeology. *Scottish Archaeological Review* 8: 8–13.

Hodder, I. 1992. *Theory and Practice in Archaeology*. London: Routledge.

Hodder, I. 1999. *The Archaeological Process. An Introduction*. Oxford: Blackwell.

Hodder, I. (ed.) 2000. *Towards reflexive method in archaeology: The example at Çatalhöyük*. Cambridge: McDonald Institute for Archaeological Research/ British Institute of Archaeology at Ankara.

Hodder, I. and Shanks, M. 1995. Interpretative archaeologies: some themes and questions. In I. Hodder et al. (eds) *Interpreting Archaeology*. London: Routledge.

Hodder, I. and Shanks, M. 1995. Processual, postprocessual and interpretative archaeologies. In I. Hodder et al.. *Interpreting Archaeology*: 3–29. London: Routledge.

Hodder, I., Shanks, M., Alexandri, A., Buchli, V., Carman, J., Last, J. and Lucas L. (eds) 1995. *Interpreting Archaeology*. London: Routledge.

Hodges, R. 1989. *Dark Age Economics. The Origins of Towns and Trade AD 600–1000*. London: Dukworth.

Holinshed, R. 1577. *Holinshed's Chronicles of England, Scotland, and Ireland*. London.

Holk, A. F. L. van 1997. *Archeologie van de binnenvaart. Wonen en werken aan boord van binnenvaartschepen (1600–1900)*. Groningen: University of Groningen.

Holly, H. H. 1953. *Sparrow-Hawk*, A Seventeenth Century Vessel in Twentieth Century America. *American Neptune* XIII: 51–64.

Hornberg, G. 1963. Svenska Flottans Fartygstyper och Fartygsbggen. In G. Haldin (ed.) *Svenskt Skepps Byggeri*: 155–190. Malmö: Allhems Förlag.

Hornell, J. 1946/1970. *Water Transport. Origins and Early Evolution*. Cambridge: Cambridge University Press.

Hoving, A. 2012. *Nicolaes Witsen and Shipbuilding in the Dutch Golden Age*. College Station: Texas A & M University Press.

Howard, F. 1979. *Sailing Ships of war 1400–1860*. London: Conway Maritime Press.

Howard, F., 1986, Early Ship Guns, Part I: Built-up Breech-loaders. *Mariner's Mirror* 72.4: 440–48.

Humbla. P. 1934. Klink och Kravel. *Svenska kryssarklubbens årsskrift 1934*: 83–102. Stockholm.

Humbla, P. 1949. Om Björkebåten från Hille socken. In *Fran Gastrikland 1949*. Gavle.

Humbla, P. and von Post, L. 1937. *Galtabäcksbåten och Tidigt Båtbyggeri i Norden*. Gothenburg.

Hunter, J. R. 1994. 'Maritime Culture': notes from the land. *IJNA* 23.4: 261–264.

Hutchinson, G. 1991. The Early 16th century Wreck at Studland Bay, Dorset. In R. Reinders and K. Paul (eds) *Carvel Construction Techniques*: 171–175. Oxbow Monograph 12. Oxford: Oxbow Books.

Hutchinson, G. 1994. *Medieval Ships and Shipping*. London: Leicester University Press.

Huth, C. 2000. Metal circulation, communication and traditions of craftsmanship in Late Bronze Age and Early Iron Age Europe. In C. Pare (ed.) *Metals Make the World go Round. The Supply and Circulation of Metals in Bronze Age Europe*. Oxford: Oxbow Books.

Ingold, T. 2007. Materials against materiality. *Archaeological Dialogues* 14.1: 1–16.

Ingstad, A. S. 1995. The Interpretation of the Oseberg Find. In O. Crumlin-Pedersen and B. Thye (eds). *The Ship as Symbol in Prehistoric and Medieval Scandinavia*: 139–148. Copenhagen: Danish National Museum:

Irwin, G. 1992. *Prehistoric Exploration and Colonisation of the Pacific*. Cambridge: Cambridge University Press.

Jay, M. 1993. *Downcast eyes. The denigration of vision in twentieth century French thought*. Berkeley: University of California Press.

Jenks, C. 1995. (ed.) 1995. *Visual Culture*. London: Routledge.

Rieu, R., Jestin, O. and Carrazé, F., 1980. Mediterranean hull types compared: An unusual type of construction. The hull of wreck I at Bon Porte. *IJNA* 9.1: 70–72.

Johansson, B. A. (ed.) 1985. *Regalskeppet Kronan*. Höganäs: Bra Böcker.

Johnson, M. 1993. Housing culture: traditional architecture in an English landscape. Washington DC: Smithsonian Institution Press.

Johnson, M. 1996. *An Archaeology of Capitalism*. Oxford: Blackwell.

Johnson, M. 1999. *Archaeological Theory. An Introduction*. Oxford: Blackwell.

Johnson, M. 2006a. The tide reversed: projects and potentials for an historical archaeology of Europe. In M. Hall, and S. Silliman (eds) *Historical*

Archaeology: 313–331. Blackwell Studies in Global Archaeology. Oxford: Blackwell.

Johnson, M. 2006b. Houses, power and everyday life in early modern England. In, J. Maran, C. Juwig, H. Schwengel, and U. Thaler (eds) *Constructing Power – Architecture, Ideology and Social Practice. Konstruktion der Macht – Architektur, Ideologie und soziales Handeln*: 285–298. Hamburg: Verlag.

Johnston, S. 1996. *Ship design and the master shipwright*. Paper read at the Vasamuseet, Stockholm. 6.11.96.

Jones, A. 2002. *Archaeological Theory and Scientific Practice*. Cambridge: Cambridge University press.

Joncheray, J. P. 1976. Excavations on the Wreck of Bon Porte, Six century B.C. *IJNA* 5.1: 88–89.

Jones, A. 2004. Archaeometry and Materiality: Materials-Based Analysis in Theory and Practice. *Archaeometry* 46. 3: 327–338.

Jones, M. 2003. *For Future Generations: Conservation of a Tudor Maritime Collection*. The Archaeology of the Mary Rose Vol. 5. Oxford: Mary Rose Trust.

Jourdan, S. 1610. *Discovery of the Bermudas otherwise called the 'Isle of Devils'*. London. (See Wright, L. B. 1964)

Joint Nautical Archaeology Policy Committee. 2000. *Heritage Law at Sea. Proposals for Change*. Wolverhampton: University of Wolverhampton, School of Legal Studies.

Jørgensen, L. Storgaard, B. and Thomsen, L. G. (eds) 2003. *The Spoils of Victory: The North in the Shadow of the Roman Empire*. Copenhagen: National Museum of Denmark.

Kahanov, Y. 1996. Conflicting Evidence for Defining the Origin of the Ma'agan Mikhael Shipwreck. In Tzalas, H. (ed.) Tropis VI, Proceedings of the 4th International Conference on Ship Construction in Antiquity. Athens: Hellenic Institute.

Kaul, F. 1998. *Ships on Bronzes, A study in Bronze Age Religion and Iconography*. Copenhagen: National Museum of Denmark.

Keay S. and Paroli, L (eds) (2011). *Portus and its Hinterland: Recent Archaeological Research*. Archaeological Monographs of the British School at Rome 18. London: British School at Rome.

Keay, S. (ed.) 2012. *Rome, Portus and the Mediterranean*. Archaeological Monographs of the British School at Rome 21. London: British School at Rome.

Keith, D. H. and Simmons, J. J. 1985. Analysis of hull remains, ballast, and artefact distribution of a sixteenth century shipwreck, Molasses Reef, British West Indies. *Journal of Field Archaeology*, 12: 411–424.

Kirsch, P. 1990. *The Galleon*. London: Conway Maritime Press.

Kist, B. 1986. A design for the research of historical sources. In J. Gawronski (ed.) *VOC Schip Amsterdam 1985*: 42–44. Amsterdam.

Kist, B. 1992. Integrating Archaeological and Historical Records in Dutch East India Company Research. In D. Keith and T. Carrell, T (eds).

Underwater Archaeology Proceedings: 53–57. Tuscon: The Society of Historical Archaeology.

Knighton, C. S. and Loades, D. (eds) 2000. *The Anthony Roll of Henry VIII's Navy. Pepys Library 2991*. Navy Records Society Occasional Publications No. 2. London: Navy Records Society.

Kopytoff, I. 1986. The Cultural Biography of Things: Commoditization as Process. In A. Appadurai (ed.). *The Social Life of Things: Commodities in Cultural Perspective*: 64–91. Cambridge: Cambridge University Press.

Kobylinski, Z. 1995. Ships, Society, Symbols and Archaeologists. In O. Crumlin-Pedersen and B. Thye (eds). *The Ship as Symbol in Prehistoric and Medieval Scandinavia*: 9–19. Copenhagen: National Museum of Denmark.

Kristiansen, K. 1998. *Europe before history*. Cambridge: Cambridge University Press.

Kristiansen, K. 2004. Seafaring voyages and rock art ships. In P. Clark (ed.) *The Dover Bronze Age Boat in Context*: 111–21. Oxford: Oxbow Books.

Kristiansen, K. 2010. Rock Art and Religion: The sun journey in Indo-European mythology and Bronze Age rock art. In Å, C. Fredel et al. (eds) *Representations and communications: creating an archaeological matrix of late prehistoric rock art*. Oxford: Oxbow Books.

Kuhn, T. S. 1970. *The Structure of Scientific Revolutions*. Chicago: Chicago University Press.

Lamberg-Karlovsky, C. C. (ed.) 1989 *Archaeological thought in America*. Cambridge: Cambridge University Press.

Lane, F. C. 1934. (1979) *Venetian Ships and Shipbuilders of the Renaissance*. Baltimore (New York).

Lane, F. C. 1934. Venetian Naval Architecture about 1550. *MM*. 20.1: 24–49.

Last, J. 1995. The nature of history. In I. Hodder et al. *Interpreting Archaeology*: 141–157. London: Routledge.

Latour, B. 2005. *Reassembling the Social: An Introduction to Actor-Network-Theory*. Oxford: Oxford University Press.

Laughton, L. G. C. 1923. The Great Ship of 1419. *MM* IX. 3: 83–87.

Laughton, L. G. C. 1960. Early Tudor ship guns. *MM* 46. 242–285.

Laughton, L. G. C. 1961. The Square Stern and the Gun Deck. *MM* 47. 2: 100–105.

Lavery, B. 1981. *Deane's Doctrine of Naval Architecture, 1670*. London: Conway Maritime Press.

Lavery, B. 1983. *The Ship of the Line* (2 volumes), London: Conway Maritime Press.

Lavery, B. 1988. *The Colonial Merchantman Susan Constant 1605*. London: Conway Maritime Press.

Lavery, B. 1988. *The Royal Navy's first Invincible*. Portsmouth: Invincible Conservations.

Layton, R. 1989. Pellaport. In S van der Leeuw and R. Torrence (eds) *What's New? A Closer Look at the Process of Innovation*. 33–53. One World Archaeology 14. London.

Layard, J. 1942. *Stone Men of Malekula, Vao*. London: Chatto & Windus.

Lees, J. 1984. *The Masting and Rigging of English Ships of War* 1625–1860. London: Conway Maritime Press.

Leeuw, S. E. van der and Torrence, R. (eds) 1989. *What's New? A Closer Look at the Process of Innovation*. One World Archaeology 14. London: Unwin Hyman.

Leeuw S. E. van der, Papousek, D. A. and Coudart, A. 1991. Technical traditions and unquestioned assumptions: the case of pottery in Michoacan. *Techniques et Culture* 17–18: 145–173.

Leeuw S. E. van der and Papousek, D. A. 1992. Tradition and Innovation. *Ethnoarchéologie: Justification, Problèmes, Limites*. X11e Recontres Internationales d'Archéologie et d'Histoire d'Antibes. Éditions APDCA Juan-les-Pins: 135–158.

Lefroy, Gen. Sir J. H., R.A. 1882. The Historye of the Bermudaes or Summer Islands. Edited from a manuscript in the Sloane Collection, British Museum. London: Hakluyt Society.

Leino, M. and Klemelä, U. 2003. The Field Research of the Maritime Museum of Finland at the Wreck Site of Vrouw Maria in 2001–2002. In C. O. Cederlund (ed.) MoSS Project *Newsletter 1/2003*. Helsinki: Finnish National Board of Antiquities.

Leino, M., Jöns, H., Wessman, S. and Cederlund, C. O. 2004. Visualizing Underwater Cultural Heritage in the MoSS-project. In C. O. Cederlund (ed.) MoSS Project *Final Report*. Helsinki: National Board of Antiquities.

Lemonnier, P. 1993. Technological Choices. London: Routledge.

Lenihan, D. 1983. Rethinking Shipwreck Archaeology: A History of Ideas and Considerations for New Directions. In R. Gould (ed.) *Shipwreck Anthropology*: 37–64. Albuquerque: University of New Mexico.

Levey, M. 1967. *Early Renaissance*. Harmondsworth: Penguin.

L'Hour, M. and Veyrat, E. 1989. A mid-15th century clinker boat off the north coast of France, the Aber Wrac'h I wreck: A preliminary report. *IJNA* 18.4: 285–298.

L'Hour, M. and Veyrat, E. 1994. The French Medieval Clinker Wreck from Aber Wrac'h. In C. Westerdahl (ed.) *Crossroads in Ancient Shipbuilding*: 165–180. Oxbow Monograph 40. IBSA 6. Oxbow Monograph 40. Oxford: Oxbow Books.

Lindberg, A. 1985. *Riddarholmsskeppet: documentation av rekonstruktionen i Medeltidsmuseet*. Report on file. National Maritime Museum, Stockholm.

Lipke, P. 1984. *The Royal Ship of Cheops*. BAR International Series 225. Oxford: BAR.

Lipke, P. 1985. Retrospective on the Royal Ship of Cheops. In McGrail and Kentley (eds) *Sewn Plank Boats*: 19–34. BAR International Series 276. Oxford: BAR

Litwin, J. 1980. 'The Copper Wreck'. The wreck of a medieval ship raised by the Central Maritime Museum in Gdansk, Poland. *IJNA* 9.3: 217–225.

Litwin, J. 1991. Clinker and Carvel Working Boats on Polish Waters. Their Origin, Development and Transformations. In R. Reinders and K. Paul (eds) *Carvel Construction Technique*: 112–121. Oxbow Monograph 12. Oxford: Oxbow Books.

Litwin, J. 1995. Boats, cogs, holks and other medieval ship types in the south of the Baltic. In C. O. Cederlund (ed.) *Medieval Ship Archaeology*: 19–25. Stockholm: Stockholm University/NAS.

Litwin, J. (ed.) 2000. *Down the River to the Sea* (Proceedings of ISBSA 8, Gdańsk, 1997). Gdańsk: Polish Maritime Museum.

Lloyds Register of Shipping, 1988. *Warship Hull Design Inquiry*. Prepared for the Ministry of Defence. London: HMSO.

Loades, D. M. 1992. *The Tudor Navy: an administrative, political and military history*. Aldershot: Scholar Press.

Loewen, B. 1994. Codo, Carvel, Mould and Ribband: The Archaeology of Ships, 1450–1620. *Mémoires Vives*, 6–7: 6–21. Montréal.

Loewen, B. 1997. The Master-mould – shipbuilding tool of the Renaissance. *IJNA* 26. 2: 169–172.

Loewen, B. 1998. Recent Advances in Ship History and Archaeology, 1450–1650: Hull Design, Regional typologies and Wood Studies. *Material History Review* 48: 45–55.

Longfellow, H. W. 1850. *The Seaside and the Fireside*. Boston.

Longridge, C. N. 1955. *The Anatomy of Nelson's Ships*. London: Percival Marshall.

Lundström, P. 1962. Utgrävningen av Wasa. *Wasastudier* No. 2. Stockholm.

Maarleveld, T. J. 1992. Archaeology and Early Modern Ships. Building sequence and consequences. An introductory review. In A. Carmiggelt (ed.) *Rotterdam Papers VII*: 155–173. Alphen aan den Rijn.

Maarleveld, T. J. 1994. Double Dutch Solutions in Flush-Planked Shipbuilding: Continuity and Adaptations at the start of Modern History. In C. Westerdahl (ed.) *Crossroads in Ancient Shipbuilding*: IBSA 6. Oxbow Monograph 40. Oxford: Oxbow Books.

Maarleveld, T. J. 1995. Type or technique: some thoughts on boat and ship finds as indicative of cultural traditions. *IJNA* 24.1: 3–7.

Maarleveld, T. J. Goudswaard, B. and Oosting, R. 1994. New data on early modern Dutch-flush shipbuilding: Scheurrak T24 and Inschot/Zuidoostrak. *IJNA* 23.1: 13–25.

MacGregor, D. R. 1984. *Merchant Sailing Ships* (Three volumes: 1775–1815, 1815–50, 1850–75). London: Conway Maritime Press.

Machiavelli, N. see Skinner, Q, and Price, R. (eds) 1988.

MacKenzie, D. and Wajcman, J. (eds) 1999. *The Social Shaping of Technology*. Maidenhead: Open University Press.

Maginley, C. D. 1989. When is a ship a he? *MM* 75.1: 97–98.

Magnus, O. 1539. *Carta Marina. Karta och Beskrivning Över de Nordiska Länderna Samt de Underbara Ting som Där Finnas*. Facsimile edition 1964. Uppsala: Bokgillet.

Malmer, M. P. 1981. *A Chorological Study of North European Rock Art*. Antikvariska serien 32. Stockholm: Borgström.

Malmer, M. P. 1993. On Theoretical Realism in Archaeology. *Current Swedish Archaeology*. Vol 1: 145–148.

Malmer, M. P. 1997. On objectivity and Actualism in Archaeology. *Swedish Current Archaeology*. Vol. 5: 7–18.

Manwaring, G. E. (ed.) 1920. *The Life and Works of Sir Henry Mainwaring*. Vol. I. London: *Navy Records Society*.

Manwaring, G. E. and W. G. Perrin (eds) 1922. *The Life and Works of Sir Henry Mainwaring*. Vol. II. London: *Navy Records Society*.

Manwaring, G. E. 1922. A Ship of 1419. *MM* 8, 12:376.

Mainwaring, Sir H. 1623. A Seaman's Dictionary. In G. Manwaring and G. Perrin (eds). 1922. *The Life and Works of Sir Henry Mainwaring*. Vol. II. London: *Navy Records Society*.

Pujol i Hamelink, M. A 15th-Century clinker-built shipwreck in Barcelona. Conference paper, ISBSA 13, Amsterdam.

Marsden, P. 1967. *A ship of the Roman period, from Blackfriars in the City of London*. London: Guildhall Museum.

Marsden, P. 1976. A boat of the Roman period found at Bruges, Belgium in 1899 and related finds. *IJNA* 5.1: 23–55.

Marsden, P. 1975. *The Wreck of the Amsterdam*. London: Hutchinson.

Marsden, P. 1985. *The Wreck of the Amsterdam*. London: Hutchinson.

Marsden, P. 1994. *Ships of the Port of London. First to eleventh centuries AD*. English Heritage Archaeological Report 3. London: English Heritage.

Marsden, P. 1997. Ships and Shipwrecks. London: Batsford.

Marsden, P. 1996. *Ships of the Port of London. Twelfth to seventeenth centuries AD*. English Heritage Archaeological Report 5. London: English Heritage.

Marsden, P. 2003. *Sealed by Time. The loss and Recovery of the Mary Rose*. The Archaeology of the Mary Rose Vol 1. Trowbridge: Mary Rose Trust.

Marsden, P. 2009. *The Mary Rose: 'Your Noblest Shippe'. Anatomy of a Tudor Warship*. The Archaeology of the Mary Rose Vol 2. Exeter: Mary Rose Trust.

Martin, C. J. M. 1975. *Full Fathom Five. The Wrecks of the Spanish Armada*. London: Viking Press.

Martin, C. J. M. 1978. The Dartmouth an English Frigate Wrecked off Mull in 1690. *IJNA* 7.1: 29–58.

Martin, C. J. M. 1979. La Trinidad Valencera: an Armada invasion transport lost off Donegal. Interim site report, 1971–76. *IJNA* 8.1: 13–38.

Martin, C. J. M. 1995. The Cromwellian shipwreck off Duart Point, Mull: an interim report. *IJNA* 24.1: 15–32.

Martin, C. J. M. and Parker, G. 1988. The Spanish Armada. New York: Norton.

Marx, K. 1926. *The Eighteenth Brumaire of Louis Bonaparte*. Trans. Eden and Cedar Paul. London: Allen & Unwin.

Maschner, H. D. G. (ed.) 1996. *Darwinian Archaeologies*. New York: Plenum Press.

Mazel, C. and W. Reiss. 1979. An inexpensive method for real-time, accurate navigational control of marine surveys. *IJNA* 8.4: 333–338.

McElearn, T., McConkey, R. and Forsyth, W. 2002. *Strangford Lough: An Archaeological Survey of the Maritime Cultural Landscape*. Belfast: Blackstaff Press.

McGhee, F. L. 1997. Towards a Postcolonial Nautical Archaeology. *Assemblage* 3. University of Sheffield. http://www.shef.ac.uk/~assem/3/3mcghee.html (28.1.98)

McGowan, A. 1981. *Tiller and Whipstaff. The Development of the Sailing Ship 1400–1700*. The Ship Vol. 3. London: NMM/HMSO.

McGrail, S. 1975. *Models, replicas & experiments in nautical archaeology*. *MM* 61: 3–8.

McGrail, S. (ed.) 1977. *Sources and Techniques in Boat Archaeology*. BAR S29. Oxford.

McGrail, S. 1982. *Woodworking Techniques before 1500*. NMM Archaeological series No. 7. BAR S129. Oxford

McGrail, S. (ed.) 1984. *Aspects of Maritime Archaeology and Ethnology*. London: NMM.

McGrail, S. 1987 (1998). *Ancient Boats in North West Europe. The archaeology of water transport to AD 1500*. London: Longman.

McGrail, S. 1988. Assessing the performance of an ancient boat: the Hasholme Logoat. *Oxford Journal of Archaeology* 7: 35–46.

McGrail, S. 1990. *Maritime Celts, Frisians and Saxons*. CBA Research Report no 71. London: CBA.

McGrail, S. 1992. Replicas, reconstructions and floating hypotheses. *IJNA* 21.4: 353–5

McGrail, S. 1993. *Medieval Boat & Ship Timbers from Dublin*. Dublin: Royal Irish Academy.

McGrail, S. 1995. Romano-Celtic boats and ships: characteristic features. *IJNA* 24.2: 139–145.

McGrail, S. 1996a. The Bronze Age in Northwest Europe. In A. E. Christensen (ed.) *The Earliest Ships*: 24–38. London: Conway Maritime Press.

McGrail, S. 1996b. The Ship: Carrier of Goods, People and Ideas. In E. Rice (ed.) *The Sea and History*: 67–96. Stroud: Sutton.

McGrail, S. 1997. Early frame-first methods of building wooden boats and ships. *MM* 83: 76–80.

McGrail, S. 2001. *Boats of the World. From the Stone Age to Medieval Times*. Oxford: Oxford University Press.

McGrail. S. 2004. The Barlands Farm Boat Within the Romano-Celtic Tradition. In N. Nayling and S. McGrail. *Barland's Farm Romano-Celtic Boat*. London: CBA.

McGrail, S. and Kentley, E. (eds) 1985. *Sewn Plank Boats. Archaeological and Ethnographic papers based on those presented to a conference at Greenwich in November 1984*. NMM Archaeological series No. 10. BAR International series 276. Oxford: BAR.

McGrail, S. and E. McKee. 1974. *The Building and Trials of the Replica of an Ancient Boat: The Gokstad Faering*. NMM Monographs and Reports No. 11 (two parts). Greenwich.

McGrail, S. and Roberts, O. 1999. A Romano-British Boat from the Shores of the Severn Estuary. *MM* 85. 2: 133–146.

McGrail, S., Blue, L. K., Kentley, E. and Palmer, C. 2003. *Boats of South Asia*. London: Routledge Curzon.

McGuire, R. 1992. *A Marxist Archaeology*. London: Academic Press.

McKee, A. 1968. *History From the Sea*. London: Hutchinson.

McKee, A. 1973. *King Henry VIII's Mary Rose*. London: Souvenir Press.

McKee, A. 1972. The Hulk. *MM* 58. 4: 395.

McKee, E. 1976. Identification of timbers from old ships of north-western European origin. *IJNA* 5.1: 3–12.

McKee, E. 1983. *Working Boats of Britain*. London: Conway Maritime Press.

Menotti, F. (ed.) 2004. *Living on the Lake in Prehistoric Europe*. London: Routledge.

Merleau-Ponty, M. 1962. *Phenomenology of Perception* (trans. by Colin Smith), London: Routledge & Kegan Paul

Merton, R. K. 1968. *Social Theory and Social Structure* (3rd edition). New York: Free Press.

Miller, D. (ed.) 2005. *Materiality*. Durham: Duke University Press.

Miller, D. 2010. *Stuff*. Cambridge: Polity Press.

Miller, D. and Tilley. C. (eds) 1984. *Ideology, Power and Prehistory*. Cambridge: Cambridge University Press.

Milne, G. with J. Flatman and K. Brandon. 2004. The 14th-Century merchant ship from Sandwich: a study in medieval maritime archaeology. *Archaeologia cantiana* 124: 227–63.

Milne, G., McKewan, C. and Goodburn, D. 1998. *Nautical Archaeology on the foreshore. Hulk recording on the Medway*. Swindon: Royal Commission on the Historical Monuments of England.

Mindell, D. 1995. *War, Technology and Experience aboard the USS Monitor*. Baltimore: Johns Hopkins Press.

Mol, F. 1929. *Das Schiff in der Bildenden Kunst*. Bonn: Kurt Frelag.

Momber, G., Tomalin, D., Scaife, R., Satchell, J. and Gillespie, J. (eds) 2011. *Mesolthic occupation at Bouldnor Cliff and the submerged prehistoric landscapes of the Solent*. York: The CBA

Moser, S. 2003. Community archaeology in Quseir, Egypt. In L. Peers (ed.) *Museums and Source Communities*: 208–226. London: Routledge.

Morrison, I. 1985. *Landscape with Lake Dwellings: The Crannogs of Scotland*. Edinburgh: Edinburgh University Press.

Morrison J. S. 1984. Techniques of reconstruction. In J. Coates and S. McGrail (eds) *The Greek Trireme of the 5th century BC*. NMM Monograph. Greenwich. NMM.

Morwood, M. J., O'Sullivan, P., Aziz, F. and Raza, A. 1998. Fission track age of stone tools and fossils on the east Indonesian Island of Flores. *Nature* 392, 172–176.

Morwood, M. J. 2001. Early hominid occupation of Flores, East Indonesia, and its wider significance. In I. Metcalfe, J. M. B. Smith, M. Morwood, and I. Davidson (eds) *Faunal and Floral Migrations and Evolution in SE Asia–Australasia*: 387–398. Lisse: Balkema.

Morwood, M. J., Brown, P., Jatmiko., Sutikna, T., Wahyu Saptomo, E., Westaway, K. E., Awe Due, R., Roberts, R. G., Maeda, T., Wasisto, S. and Djubiantono, T. 2005. Further evidence for small-bodied hominins from the Late Pleistocene of Flores, Indonesia. *Nature* 437, 1012–1017

Mortenssøn, O. 1995. *Renæssancens Fartøjer – sejlads og søfart I Danmark 1550–1650*. Rudkøbing: Langelands Museum.

Muckelroy, K. 1975. A systematic approach to the investigation of scattered wreck sites. *IJNA* 4.2: 173–190.

Muckelroy, K. 1976. The integration of historical and archaeological data concerning an historic wreck site: the *Kennemerland*. *World Archaeology* 7.3: 280–90.

Muckelroy, K. 1975. Historic wreck sites in Britain and their environments. *IJNA* 6.1: 47–57.

Muckelroy, K. 1978. *Maritime Archaeology*. Cambridge: Cambridge University Press.

Muckelroy, K. 1981. Middle Bronze Age trade between Britain and Europe. *PPS* 47: 275–297.

Murphy, L. E. 1983. Shipwrecks as a database for human behavioural studies. In R. Gould (ed.) *Shipwreck Anthropology*: 65–90. Albuquerque: University of Mexico press.

Murphy, L. E. (ed.) 1993. *Dry Tortugas National Park*. Sante Fe: National Park Service.

Murphy, L. E. and Johnson, R. W. 1993. Environmental factors affecting vessel casualties and site preservation. In L. Murphy (ed.) 1993. *Dry Tortugas National Park*: 97–109. Sante Fe: National Park Service.

Murray, A. 1863. *Ship-Building in Iron and Wood.* Edinburgh.

Müller-Wille, M. 1995. Boat Graves, Old and New Views. In O. Crumlin-Pedersen and B. M. Thye (eds). *The Ship as Symbol in Prehistoric and Medieval Scandinavia*: 101–110. Copenhagen: National Museum of Denmark.

Myhre, B. 1985. Boathouses as Indicators of Political Organization. *Norwegian Archaeological Review* 18, 1–2: 36–60.

Mäss, V. 1994. A Unique 16th Century Estonian Ship Find. In C. Westerdahl (ed.) *Crossroads in Ancient Shipbuilding*: 189–194. IBSA 6. Oxbow Monograph 40. Oxford: Oxbow Books..

National Maritime Museum, Sweden. *http://www. sjohistoriska.se/en/Cultural-heritage/Marine-archaeology/Wrecks-in-the-Baltic-Sea/The-Dalaro-wreck-and-other-wrecks-at-Dalaro* (12/2/2013)

Nayling, N., Maynard, D. and McGrail. S. 1994. Barland's Fram, Magor, Gwent: a Romano-Celtic boat. *Antiquity* 68: 596–603.

Nayling, N. and McGrail, S. 2004. *Barland's Farm Romano-Celtic Boat.* London: CBA.

Nayling, N. 2004. *Tree-ring Analysis of Framing Timbers from the Princes Channel Wreck, Thames Estuary.* Unpublished report, University of Wales, Lampeter, Heritage & Archaeological Research Practice Dendrochronology Rep. 2004/02.

Nayling, N. and Jones, T. 2012. Three-Dimensional Recording and Hull Form modelling of the Newport (Wales) Medieval Ship. In N. Gunsenin (ed.), *Between Continents. Proceedings of the Twelfth Symposium on Boat and Ship Archaeology, Istanbul. IJNA*

Nilson, A. 1985. Det Engelska Maneret Införs. In Johansson (ed.) *Regalskeppet Kronan.* Höganäs: Bra Böcker.

Noble, G. 2006. Harnessing the waves: monuments and ceremonial complexes in Orkney and beyond. *JMA* 1.1: 100–117.

Noël Hume, I. 1969 (1991) *A Guide to the Artefacts of Colonial America.* New York: Vintage Books.

O'Flaherty, R. 2007. A weapon of choice – experiments with a replica Irish Early Bronze Age Halberd. *Antiquity* 81. 312: 423–434.

O'Sullivan, A. 2001. *Foragers, Farmers and Fishers in a Coastal Landscape.* Discovery Programme Monograph 5. Dublin: Royal Irish Academy.

O' Sullivan, A. and Breen, C. 2007. *Maritime Ireland – Coastal Archaeology of an Island People.* Stroud: Tempus.

Olechnowitz, K. 1960. *Der Schiffbau Der Hansischen Spätzeit. Eine Untersuchung zur Sozial- und Wirtschaftsgeschichte der Hanse.* Leipzig.

Olsen, B. 2003. Material Culture after Text: Re-Membering Things. *Norwegian Archaeological Review* 36. 2: 87–104.

Olsen, O. and Crumlin-Pedersen, O. 1967. The Skuldelev Ships. *Acta Archaeologica* 38: 73–174.

Olsen, O. and Crumlin-Pedersen, O. 1985. *Five Viking Ships from Roskilde Fjord.* Copenhagen.

Oppenheim, M. A. 1896a. *A history of the Administration of the Royal Navy and of Merchant Shipping 1509–1660.* Navy Records Society. London: The Bodley Head.

Oppenheim, M. A. (ed.) 1896b. *Naval Accounts and Inventories of the Reign of Henry VII 1485–8 and 1495–7.* Navy Records Society Vol. VIII. London. Navy Records Society..

Orser, C. E. 1996. *A Historical Archaeology of the Modern World.* New York: Plenum Press.

Osler, A. G. 1983. *The Shetland Boat.* Maritime Monographs and Reports No. 58. Greenwich: NMM.

Outhwaite, W. and Bottomore, T. (eds) 1993. *The Blackwell Dictionary of Social Thought.* Oxford: Blackwell.

Pacey, A. 1992. *The Maze of Ingenuity. Ideas and Idealism in the Development of Technology.* Cambridge, Mass.: MIT Press.

Parker, A. J. 1984. Shipwrecks and ancient trade in the Mediterranean. *Archaeological Review from Cambridge* 3: 99–113.

Parker, A. J. 1992. *Ancient Shipwrecks of the Mediterranean & the Roman Provinces.* BAR International series 580. Oxford: BAR.

Parthesius, R. 1987. Fusion of two disciplines: the historical-archaeological research of the Amsterdam. In J. Gawronski (ed.) *V.O.C. Schip Amsterdam 1986*: 31–36. Amsterdam: Stichting V.O.C. Schip Amsterdam.

Peacock, D. P. S. and Blue, L. K. 2000. *Myos Hormos – Quseir al-Qadim: Roman and Islamic Ports on the Red sea.* Oxford: Oxbow Books.

Peake, M. 1946. *The Craft of the Lead Pencil.* Wingate, reproduced in M. Gilmore, and S. Johnson. 1974. *Mervyn Peake. Writings and Drawings.* London: Academy Editions.

Pepper, J. V. 1981. Harriot's Ms. on Shipbuilding and Rigging (1608–1610). In D. Howse (ed.) *500 Years of Nautical Science, 1400–1900*: 24–28. Greenwich: NMM.

Perrin, W. G. (ed.) 1918. *The Autobiography of Phineas Pett.* Navy Records Society Vol. 51. London: Navy Records Society.

Peterson, M. L. 1988. The Sea Venture. *MM* 74.1: 37–48.

Phillips, C. R. 1994. The Caravel and the Galleon. In R. Unger (ed.) *Cogs, Caravels and Galleons*: 91–114. London: Conway Maritime Press.

Platt, C. 1996. King Death. *The Black Death and its aftermath in late-medieval England.* London: University College London Press.

Plets, R. M. K., Dix, J. K., Adams, J. R., Bull, J. M., Henstock, T., Gutowski, M. and Best, A. I. 2006. 3D reconstruction of a shallow archaeological site from high-resolution acoustic imagery – a case study. In, S. N. Jesus, and Rodriguez, O. C. (eds) *Proceedings of the 8th European Conference on*

Underwater Acoustics, 12–15 June 2006. Carvoeiro, Portugal: 757–762. Carvoeiro: ECUA Secretariat.

Plets, R. M. K., Dix, J. K., Adams, J. R. and Best, A. I. 2008. 3D reconstruction of a shallow archaeological site from high-resolution acoustic imagery: the Grace Dieu. *Applied Acoustics* 69. 5: 399–411.

Plets, R., Dix, J., Adams, J., Bull, J., Henstock, T., Gutowski, M and Best, A. 2009. The use of a high-resolution 3D Chirp sub-bottom profiler for the reconstruction of the shallow water archaeological site of the Grace Dieu (1439), River Hamble, UK. *Journal of Archaeological Science*, 36. 2: 408–418.

Tchernia, A., Pomey, P. and Hesnard, A. 1978. L'épave romaine de la Madrague de Giens, Var: campagnes 1972–1975 (XXXIV supplément à Gallia ed.). Paris: Centre National de la Recherche Scientifique.

Pomey, P. 1995. Les épaves grecques et romaines de la place Jules-Verne à Marseille. *Académy des inscriptions and belles lettres* Aviil–June: 470–79.

Pomey, 1997. Bon Porté Wreck. In J. Delgado (ed.) Encyclopaedia of Underwater and Maritime Archaeology. London: British Museum Press.

Pomey, P. and Rieth, E. 2005. *L'archeologie Navale*. Paris: Editions Errance.

Potter, D. 1996. *Karaoke and Cold Lazarus*. London: Faber & Faber.

Pounds, N. J. G. 1990. *The Medieval Castle in England and Wales. A social and political history.* Cambridge: Cambridge University Press.

Preucel, R. and Hodder. I. (eds) 1996. *Contemporary Archaeology in Theory.* Oxford: Blackwell.

Prins, A. 1986. A *Handbook of Sewn Boats*. NMM. Monograph No. 59. Greenwich: NMM.

Pryor, F. 1991. *English Heritage book of Flag Fen prehistoric Fenland Centre.* London: Batsford.

Pryor, F. and M. Taylor. 1993. Use, Re-use, or Pre-use? Aspects of the interpretation of ancient wood. In J. Coles et al. (eds) *A Spirit of Enquiry*: 81–84. Exeter: WARP, NAS & NMM.

Pulak, C. 1998. The Uluburun shipwreck: an overview. *IJNA* 27.3: 188–224.

Quinn, R., Bull, J. M., Dix, J. K. and Adams, J. 1997. The Mary Rose site – geophysical evidence for palaeo-scour marks. *IJNA* 26. 1: 3–16.

Quinn, R., Adams, J., Dix, J. K. and Bull, J. M. 1998. The Invincible (1758) site – an integrated geophysical assessment. *IJNA* 27. 2: 126–138.

Quinn, D. B and Quinn, A. M. (eds) 1973. *Virginia Voyages from Hakluyt.* London: Oxford University Press.

Rackham, O. 1976. *Trees and Woodland in the British Landscape.* London: Dent.

Rackham, O. 1986. *The History of the Countryside.* London: Dent.

Randsborg, K. 1995. *Hjortspring. Warfare & Sacrifice in Early Europe.* Aarhus University Press: Cambridge University Press.

Ransley, J. 2011. Maritime communities and traditions. In, Catsambis, Alexis, Ford, Ben and Hamilton, Donny L. (eds) *The Oxford Handbook of Maritime Archaeology*: 879–903. New York: Oxford University Press.

Ransley, J., Sturt, F., Dix, J., Adams, J. and Blue, L. (eds) 2013. *People and the Sea. The Maritime and Marine Historic Environment Research Framework for England.* York: CBA.

Rawson, K. J. and Tupper, E. C. 1994. (4th edition) *Basic Ship Theory* (two volumes). London: Longman.

Redknap, M. 1984. *The Cattewater Wreck. The investigation of an armed vessel of the early sixteenth century.* BAR British series 131. (NMM Archaeological series no. 8). Oxford: BAR.

Redknap, M. 1997. *Artefacts from Wrecks: Dated Assemblages from the Late Middle Ages to the Industrial Revolution.* Oxbow monograph 84. Oxford: Oxbow Books.

Rees, N. 1995. *The Misericords of St Davids Cathedral Pembrokeshire.* Much Wenlock: St Davids Cathedral.

Reinders, R. 1985. *cog finds from the ijsselmeerpolders.* Flevobericht. No. 248. Lelystad: Rijksdienst voor de Ijsselmeerpolders.

Reinders, H. R. and Oosting, R. 1989. Mittelalterliche Schiffsfunde in den ljsselmeerpoldern. In H. Zitnniertnann and L. Spath (eds). *Ländliche und städtische Küstensiedlungen im ersten und zweiten Jahrtausend* (Wilhemshavener Tage Nr.2: 106–122). Wilhelmshaven.

Reinders, R. and C. Paul. (eds) 1991. *Carvel Construction Technique.* Fifth International Symposium on Boat and Ship Archaeology, Amsterdam 1988. Oxbow monograph 12. Oxford: Oxbow Books.

Renfrew, A. C. 1986. Varna and the emergence of wealth in prehistoric Europe. In A. Appadurai (ed.) *The social life of things: commodities in cultural perspective.* Cambridge: Cambridge University Press.

Renfrew, C. and Aspinall, A. 1990. Aegean obsidian and Franchthi Cave. In C. Perlès, *Excavations at Franchthi Cave, Greece,* Fascicle 5: *Les industries lithiques taillées de Franchthi (Argolide, Grèce)* II. *Les industries du Mésolithique et du Néolithique initial,* 257–70. Bloomington and Indianapolis: Indiana University Press.

Renfrew, C. and Zubrow, E. 1994. *The Ancient Mind: Elements of Cognitive Archaeology.* Cambridge: Cambridge University Press.

Renfrew, C. and Bahn, P. 1991. *Archaeology. Theories Methods and Practice.* London: British Museum Press.

Richardson, P. D. 1968. The generation of scour marks near obstacles. *Journal of Sedimentary Petrology.* 38: 965–970.

Rieck, F. 1994. The Iron Age Boats from Hjortspring and Nydam – New Investigations. In C. Westerdahl (ed.) *Crossroads in Ancient Shipbuilding*: 45–54. IBSA 6. Oxbow Monograph 40. Oxford: Oxbow Books.

Rieck, F. 1995. Ships and Boats in the Bog Finds of Scandinavia. In O. Crumlin-Pedersen and B. M. Thye (eds). *The Ship as Symbol in Prehistoric and Medieval Scandinavia*: 125–130. Copenhagen: National Museum of denmark.

Rieck, F. and Crumlin-Pedersen, O. 1988. *Både fra Danmarks Oldtid*. Roskilde.

Rieth, E. 1988. Remarque sur une série d'illustrations de l'Ars nautica (1570) de Fernando Oliveira. *Neptunia* 169: 36–43.

Rieth, E. 1996. *Le maître-gabarit, la tablette et le trébuchet : essai sur la conception non-graphique des car'enes du Moyen Âge au Xxe si'ecle*. Paris: Éditions du CTHS.

Rieth, E. 2000. The Mediaeval Wreck from Port Berteau II (Charente Maritime), France). In J. Litwin (ed.) *Down the River to the Sea. Eighth International Symposium on Ship and Boat Archaeology, Gdansk 1997*. Gdansk: Polish Maritime Museum.

Rival, M. 1991. *La Charpenterie Navale Romaine*. CNRS Paris.

Roberts, M. 1968. *The Early Vasas. A History of Sweden, 1523–1611*. Cambridge: Cambridge University Press.

Roberts, O. T. P. 1998. An exercise in hull reconstruction arising from the Alderney Elizabethan wreck. *IJNA* 27.1: 32–42.

Roberts, O. T. P. 2004. Llong Casnewydd: The Newport Ship – a Personal View. *IJNA* 33.1: 158–163.

Roberts, R. G., Flannery, T. F., Ayliffe, L. K., Yoshida, H., Olley, J. M., Prideaux, G. J., Laslett, G. M., Baynes, A., Smith, M. A., Jones, R. and Smith, B. L. 2001. New Ages for the Last Australian Megafauna: Continent-Wide Extinction About 46,000 Years Ago. *Science* 292: 1888–1892.

Robert, P. and Trow, S. 2002. *Taking to the Water: English Heritage's Initial Policy for the Management of Maritime Sites in England*. London: English Heritage.

Rodger, N. A. M. 1996. The Development of Broadside Gunnery 1450–1650. *MM* 82. 3: 301–324.

Rogers, E. M. 1962. *Diffusion and innovations*. New York: Free Press.

Rose, S. (ed.) 1982. *The Navy of the Lancastrian Kings. Accounts and Inventories of William Soper, Keeper of the King's Ships, 1422–1427*. Navy Records Society Vol. 132. London: George Allen & Unwin.

Rose, S. 2002. *Medieval Naval Warfare 1000–1500*. London: Routledge.

Rule, M. and Monaghan, J. 1993. *A Gallo-Roman Trading Vessel from Guernsey. The Excavation and Recovery of a Third Century Shipwreck*. Guernsey Museum Monograph 5. Guernsey: Guernsey Museums and Galleries.

Rule, M. 1982. *The Mary Rose*. London: Conway Maritime Press.

Rule. N. 1989. Direct Survey Method and its Application Underwater. *IJNA* 18.2: 157–162.

Ruoff, U. 1972. Palafittes and Underwater Archaeology. In UNESCO *Underwater Archaeology; a nascent discipline*. Paris.

Rönnby, J. 1995. *Bålverket. Om samhällsförändring och motstånd med utgångspunkt från det tidigmedeltida Bulverket i Tingstäde Träsk på Gotland*. Stockholm: Riksantikvarieämbetet.

Rönnby, J. 2007. Maritime Durées. Long-Term Structures in a Coastal Landscape. *JMA*. 2.2: 65–82.

Rönnby, J. and Adams. J. 1994. *Östersjöns Sjunkna Skepp: En marinarkeolisk tidresa*. Stockholm: Tiden.

Rönnby, J. and Adams. J. 2006. Identity, threat and defiance: interpreting the 'bulwark', a 12th Century Lake Building on Gotland, Sweden. *Journal of Maritime Archaeology* 1. 2: 170–190.

Salisbury, W. 1954. The Framing of Models. *MM* 40. 2: 156–159.

Salisbury, W. 1961. The Woolwich Ship. *MM* 47. 2: 81–90.

Salisbury, W. 1961. A Draught of a Jacobean Three Decker. The *Prince Royal? MM* 47. 3: 170–177.

Salisbury, W. 1966. Early Tonnage Measurement in England. *MM* 52.1: 41 – 51.

Salisbury, W. and Anderson, R. C. (eds) 1958. *A treatise on shipbuilding and a treatise on rigging written* c. *1620–1625*. Society of Nautical Research Occasional Publication No. 6. London: Society for Nautical Research.

Sandahl, K. O. B. 1982. *Middle English Sea Terms* (3 volumes). Uppsala.

Sandler, S. 1973. 'In deference to public opinion.' The loss of HMS *Captain*. *MM* 59.1: 57–66.

Sarsfield, J. P. 1984. Mediterranean Whole Moulding. *MM* 70.1: 86–8.

Sarsfield, J. P. 1985a. From the brink of extinction. *Wooden Boat*, 66: 84–9.

Sarsfield, J. P. 1985b. Survival of pre-16th century Mediterranean lofting techniques in Bahia, Brazil. Proceedings of the Fourth Meeting of the International Symposium on Boat and Ship Archaeology. Porto.

Sarsfield, J. P. 1991. Master Frame and Ribbands. A Brazilian case study with an overview of this widespread traditional carvel design and building system. In R. Reinders and K. Paul (eds) *Carvel Construction Technique*: 137–145. Oxbow Monograph 12. Oxford: Oxbow Books.

Scammel, G. V. 1981. *The World Encompassed: The First European Maritime Empires*, c. *800–1650*. New York: Methuen.

Schiffer, M. B. 1976. *Behavioural Archaeology*. New York: Academic Press.

Schiffer, M. B. 1987. *Formation processes of the*

archaeological record. Albuquerque: University of New Mexico Press.

Seppings, Sir R. On a new Principle of Constructing Ships in the Mercantile Navy. *Philosophical Transactions for the Year 1820.* London: Royal Society.

Shanks, M. B. 1995. Archaeology and the form of History. In I. Hodder et al. (eds) *Interpreting Archaeology*: 169–174. Cambridge: Cambridge University Press.

Shanks, M. B. and Tilley, C. 1987. (1992). *Re-Constructing Archaeology: Theory and Practice.* London: Routledge.

Shennan, S. J. 1989. Introduction: archaeological approaches to cultural identity. In S. Shennan (ed.) *Archaeological approaches to cultural identity*: 1–32. One World Archaeology 10. London: Unwin Hyman.

Shennan, S. J. 1989. Cultural transmission and cultural change. In S. Van der Leeuw, and R. Torrence (eds) *What's New? A Closer Look at the Process of Innovation.* One World Archaeology 14. London: Unwin Hyman.

Shennan, S. J. 2000. Population, Culture History and the Dynamics of Culture Change. *Current Anthropology* 4.5: 811–835.

Shennan, S. J. (2011). Descent with modification and the archaeological record. *Phil. Trans. R. Soc. B* 366: 1070–1079.

Skaarup, J. 1995. Stone-Age Burials in Boats. In O. Crumlin-Pedersen and B. Thye (eds). *The Ship as Symbol in Prehistoric and Medieval Scandinavia*: 51–58. Copenhagen: National Museum of Denmark.

Skinner, Q. and Price, R. (eds) 1988. *The Prince. Machiavelli.* Cambridge: Cambridge University Press.

Sleeswyk, A. W. 1990, The Engraver Willem A. Cruce and the Development of the Chain-Wale. *Mariner's Mirror* 76: 345–61

Sleeswyk, A. W. 1998. Carvel-Planking and carvel Ships in the North of Europe. *Archaeonautica* 14: 223–228.

Smiles, S. and Moser, S. (eds) 2005. *Evisioning the past: archaeology and the image.* New Interventions in Art History. Oxford: Blackwell.

Smith, Capt. John. 1627. *A Sea Grammar.* London. Reprinted 1970. London: Michael Joseph.

Smith, M. R. and Marx, L. (eds) 1994. *Does Technology Drive History? The Dilemma of Technological Determinism.* Cambridge: MIT Press.

Smith, R. 1993. Port Pieces: The Use of Wrought Iron Ordnance in the 16th Century. *Journal of the Ordnance Society* 5: 5–16.

Soop, H. 1992. *The Power and the Glory.* Stockholm: Vitterhets Historie och Antikvitets Akademien.

Sorrel, A. 1978. *Reconstructing the Past.* London: Batsford.

Sørensen, M. L. S. 1989. Ignoring Innovation – denying change: the role of iron and the impact of external influences on the transformation of Scandinavian societies 800–500 BC. In S. van der Leeuw and R. Torrence (eds) *What's New? A Closer Look at the Process of Innovation*: 182–202. One World Archaeology 14. London: Unwin Hyman.

Sørensen, M. L. S. 1997. Material Culture and Typology. *Current Swedish Archaeology* 5: 179–192.

Staniforth, M. 1997. The Archaeology of the Event – The Annales School and Maritime Archaeology, in Lakey, (ed.), *Underwater Archaeology*: 17–21. Society for Historical Archaeology.

Staniforth, M. and Nash, M. 1998. 'Chinese export porcelain from the wreck of the *Sidney Cove* (1797)'. Australian Institute for Maritime Archaeology. Special Publication No. 12

Stark, S. 1996. *Female Tars: Women Aboard Ships in the Age of Sail.* London: Constable.

Steel, D. 1805. (reprinted 1822) *The Elements and Practice of Naval Architecture.* London. (limited edition reprint).

Steffy, J. R. 1982. The reconstruction of the 11th century Serçe Liman vessel: A preliminary report. *IJNA* 11.1: 13–34.

Steffy, J. R. 1991. The Mediterranean Shell to Skeleton Transition: A Northwestern European Parallel??. In R. Reinders and K. Paul (eds). *Carvel Construction Technique*: 1–9. Oxbow Monograph 12. Oxford: Oxbow books.

Steffy, J. R. 1994. *Wooden Shipbuilding and the Interpretation of Shipwrecks.* Texas A&M University Press.

Stocker, D. 1992. The Shadow of the General's Armchair. *The Archaeological Journal* 149: 415–420.

Strachey, W. 1610. *A true reportory of the wreck and redemption of Sir Thomas Gates, Knight.* London. (See Wright, L. B. 1964)

Strasser, T. F., Panagopoulou, E., Runnels, C. N., Murray, P. M., Thompson, N., Karkanas, P., McCoy, F. W. and Wegmann, K. W. Stone Age Seafaring in the Mediterranean. Evidence from the Plakias Region for Lower Palaeolithic and Mesolithic Habitation of Crete. *Hesperia* 79: 145–190.

Sturt, F. 2006. Local knowledge is required: a rhythmanalytical approach to the late Mesolithic and early Neolithic of the East Anglian Fenland, UK. *JMA* 1.2: 119–39.

Sumner, H. 1913. *The Ancient Earthworks of Cranbourne Chase.* London: Sutton.

Sutherland, W. 1711. (facsimile edition 1989) *The Shipbuilder's Assistant.* Rochester: Jean Boudriot Publications.

Sutherland, W. 1717. *Britain's Glory: or, Ship-Building Unvail'd.* London.

Svensson, S. 1963. Skeppsbyggeriet. In G. Haldin (ed.) *Svenskt Skepps Byggeri*: 91–108. Malmö: Allhems Förlag.

Svenwall, N. 1994. *Ringaren – Ett 1500 – talsfartyg Med Arbetnamnet.* Stockholm: Stockholm University.

Tailliez, P. 1965. Titan. In J. du P. Taylor (ed.) *Marine Archaeology*: 76–92. London: Hutchinson.

Taylor, J. du P. (ed.) 1965. *Marine Archaeology*. London: Hutchinson.

Thomas, J. 1995. Where are we now?: archaeological theory in the 1990s. In P. Ucko (ed.) *Theory in Archaeology. A world perspective*: 343–362. London: Routledge.

Thomas, J. 1996. *Time, Culture and Identity. An interpretative archaeology*. London: Routledge.

Thompson, P. 1983. *Living the Fishing*. London: Routledge and Kegan Paul.

Thompson, P. 1985. Women in the Fishing: The Roots of Power between the Sexes. *Comparative Studies in Society and History* 27.1: 3–32

Thorne, A., Grün, R., Mortimer, G., Spooner, N. A., Simpson, J. J., McCulloch, M., Taylor, L. and Curnoe, D. 1999. Australia's oldest human remains: age of the Lake Mungo 3 skeleton. *Journal of Human Evolution* 36: 591–612

Throckmorton, P. 1973. The Roman Wreck from Pantano Longarini. *IJNA* 2: 243 – 266.

Throckmorton, P. (ed.) 1987. *History From The Sea: shipwrecks and archaeology from Homer's Odyssey to the Titanic*. London: Mitchell Beazley.

Tideman, B. J. 1861. *Woordenboek van Scheepsbouw*. Vlissingen.

Tilley, C. (ed.) 1990. *Reading Material Culture*. Oxford: Blackwell.

Tilley, C. 1991a. Materialism and an Archaeology of Dissonance. *Scottish Archaeological Review* 8: 14–22.

Tilley, C. 1991b. *Material Culture and Text: the Art of Ambiguity*. London: Routledge.

Tilley, C. (ed.) 1993. *Interpretative Archaeology*. London: Berg.

Tomalin, D., Simpson, P. and Bingeman, J. M. 2000. Excavation versus sustainability *in situ*: a conclusion on 25 years of archaeological investigations at Goose Rock, a designated historic wreck-site at the Needles, Isle of Wight, England. *IJNA* 29.1: 3–42.

Trigger, B. 1989. *A History of Archaeological Thought*. Cambridge: Cambridge University Press.

Tyres, I. 1996. Wood Identifications. In P. Marsden. *Ships of the Port of London. Twelfth to seventeenth centuries AD*. English Heritage Archaeological Report 5. London: English Heritage.

Ucko, P. J. 1989. Forward. In S. van der Leeuw and R. Torrence (eds) *What's New?*: ix–xiv. London: Unwin Hyman.

Ucko, P. J. (ed.) 1995. *Theory in Archaeology. A world perspective*. London: Routledge.

UK Government records: Hansard HC Deb, Vol 483, 26 Nov 2008: Column 2170W

Unger, R. W. (ed.) 1994. *Cogs, Caravels and Galleons*. London: Conway Maritime Press.

Unger, R. W. 1978. *Dutch Shipbuilding before 1800: ships and guilds*. Amsterdam: Van Gorcum.

Unger, R. W. 1980. *The Ship in the Medieval Economy 600–1600*. London: Croom Helm.

Unger, R. W. 1985. Dutch design specialization and building methods in the seventeenth century. In C. O. Cederlund (ed.) *Postmedieval Boat and Ship Archaeology*: 153–164. BAR S256. Oxford: BAR

Unger, R. W. 1991. Grain, beer and shipping in the North and Baltic seas. In C. Villain-Gandossi et al. (eds) *Medieval ships and the birth of technological society*. Vol. 1: 193–202. Malta: Foundation for International Studies.

Unwin, R. 1961. *The Defeat of John Hawkins*. London: Allen & Unwin.

United States Department of Labor. 2005. http://www.bls.gov/iif/oshwc/cfoi/cfnr0012.pdf (9/9/097).

van der Merwe, P. 1983. Towards a three-masted ship. In Conference Proceedings, 4th International Congress of Maritime Museums: 121–129 Paris: ICMM.

Van de Moortel, A. 1991. *A cog-like vessel from the Netherlands*. Excavation Report 14. Flevobericht 323. Lelystad.

Van de Moortel, A. 2000. The Utrecht ship – was the log boat base expanded? *Maritime Archaeology Newsletter from Roskilde, Denmark* 14: 36–39.

Van de Moortel, A. 2003. A New Look at the Utrecht Ship. In C. Beltrame (ed.) *Boats, Ships and Shipyards. Ninth International Symposium on Boat and Ship Archaeology, Venice, 2000*: 183–189. Oxford: Oxbow Books.

Van de Moortel, A. 2009. The Utrecht Ship Type: A Progress report. *Maritime Archaeology Newsletter from Roskilde, Denmark* 24: 11–13..

Van de Noort, R., Middleton, R., Foxon, A. and Bayliss, B. 1999. The 'Kilnsea-boat', and some implications from the discovery of England's oldest plank boat remains. *Antiquity* 73. 279: 131–135.

Van de Noort, R. 2004a. Ancient Seascapes: the social context of seafaring in the Bronze Age. *World Archaeology* 35 (3): 404–415.

Van de Noort, R. 2004b. The Humber, its sewn-plank boats, their context and the significance of it all. In. P. Clark (ed.) *The Dover Bronze Age Boat in Context: Society and Water Transport in Prehistoric Europe* Oxford: Oxbow books: 90–98.

Van de Noort, R. 2006. Argonauts of the North Sea – a Social Maritime Archaeology for the 2nd Millennium BC. *Proceedings of the Prehistoric Society* 72: 267–288

Van de Noort, R. 2011. *North Sea Archaeologies: A Maritime Biography, 10,000 BC–AD 1500*. Oxford: Oxford University press.

Van Yk, C. 1697. *De Nederlandsche Scheeps-Bouw-Konst*. Amsterdam.

Varenius, B. 1992. *Det Nordiska Skeppet. Teknologi och Samhällsstrategi i Vikingtid och Medeltid*. Stockholm Studies in Archaeology 10. Stockholm: Stockholm University.

Varenius, B. 1995. Metaphorical Ships in Iron-Age Contexts. In O. Crumlin-Pedersen and B. Thye (eds). *The Ship as Symbol in Prehistoric and Medieval Scandinavia*. Copenhagen.

Veit, U. 1989. Ethnic concepts in German prehistory: a case study on the relationship between cultural identity and archaeological objectivity. In S. Shennan (ed.) *Archaeological approaches to cultural identity*: 35–56. One World Archaeology – 10. London: Unwin Hyman.

Villain-Gandossi, C. 1985. *Le Navaire Médiéval à Travers les Miniatures*. Paris: CNRS.

Villain-Gandossi, C. 1995. Illustration of Ships : Iconography and Interpretation. In R. Unger (ed.) *Cogs caravels and Galleons*. London: Conway Maritime Press.

Villain-Gandossi, C., Busuttil, S. and Adam, P. (eds). 1991. *Medieval ships and the Birth of Technological Societies. Volume 1: Northern Europe*. Malta: Foundation for International Studies.

Vlek, R. 1987. *The Medieval Utrecht Boat*. BAR International series 382. Oxford: BAR

Waters, D. W. 1949. The Elizabethan Navy and the Armada Campaign. *MM* 35.2: 90–138.

Waters, D. W. 1958. *Art of Navigation in England in Elizabethan & Early Stuart Times*. London. Hollis and Carter.

Wallerstein, I. 1993. Annales School. In W. Outhwaite, and T. Bottomore (eds) *The Blackwell Dictionary of Social Thought*: 16–18. Oxford: Blackwell.

Wachsmann, S. 1995. Early Mediterranean Seafaring. In J. Morrison (ed.) *The Age of the Galley. Mediterranean Oared vessels since pre-classical Times*. London: Conway Maritime Press.

Wachsmann, S. 1996. Technology Before its Time: A Byzantine Shipwreck from Tantura Lagoon. *The Explorers Journal* 74.1: 19–23.

Ward, C. A. 2000. *Sacred and Secular: Ancient Egyptian Ships and Boats*. Archaeological Institute of America Monograph New Series No. 5. Philadelphia: University of Pennsylvania.

Ward, C. A. 2003. Sewn Planked Boats from Early Dynastic Abydos, Egypt. In C. Beltrame (ed.) *Boats, Ships and Shipyards*. Proceedings of the Ninth International Symposium on Boat and Ship Archaeology. Oxford: Oxbow Books.

Ward, C. A. and Zazzaro, C. 2010. Evidence for Pharaonic Seagoing Ships at Mersa/Wadi Gawasis, Egypt. IJNA 39.1: 27–43.

Warmind, M. L. 1995. Ibn Fadlan in the Context of his Age. In O. Crumlin-Pedersen and B. M. Thye (eds). *The Ship as Symbol in Prehistoric and Medieval Scandinavia*: 131–138. Copenhagen: Danish National Museum.

Waskönig, D. 1969. Bildliche Darstellungen des Kolk im 15. Und 16. Jahrhundert. Zur Typologie von Schiffen der Hansezeit. Hamburg. Altonaer Museum.

Watson, PJ. 1983. Method and Theory in Shipwreck Anthropology. In R. Gould (ed.) *Shipwreck Anthropology*: 23–36. Albuquerque: University of New Mexico.

Watson, PJ. 1999. Archaeology in Marginal Environments. http//web.mit.edu/deeparch/www/events/1999conference (20-02-2002)

Watson, PJ., Redman, S. A. and Le Blanc, C. L. 1971. *Explanation in archeology: an explicitly scientific approach*. New York: Columbia University.

Weerd, M. D. de. 1988. *Schepen voor Zwammerdam*. Haarlem: IPP.

Weerd, M. D. de, 1991. Gallo-Roman Plank Boats: Shell-first building procedures between 'sewn' and 'cog'. In R. Reinders and K. Paul (eds) 1991. *Carvel Construction Technique* : 28–31. Oxbow Monograph 12. Oxford: Oxbow Books.

Weibust, K. 1969. *Deep Sea Sailors: A Study in Maritime Ethnology*. Stockholm: Nordiska Museum.

Weski, T. 1999. The IJsselmeer type: some thoughts on Hanseatic cogs. *IJNA* 28.4: 360–379.

Westerdahl, C. 1987. *"Et sätt som liknar them uti theras öfriga lefnadsart." Om äldre samiskt båtbygge och Samisk båthantering*. Umeå: Umeå University.

Westerdahl, C. 1992. The maritime cultural landscape. *IJNA* 21.1: 5–14.

Westerdahl, C. (ed.) 1994. *Crossroads in Ancient Shipbuilding* IBSA 6. Oxbow Monograph 40. Oxford: Oxbow Books.

Westerdahl, C. 1994. Maritime cultures and ship types: brief comments on the significance of maritime archaeology. *IJNA* 23.4: 265–270.

Westerdahl, C. 1995. Society and Sail. On symbols as specific social values and ships as catalysts of social units. In O. Crumlin-Pedersen, and B. Thye (eds) *The Ship as Symbol in Prehistoric and Medieval Scandinavia*: 41–50. Copenhagen: National Museum of Denmark.

Westley, K. and Dix, J. K. 2006. Coastal Environments and their Role in Prehistoric Migrations. *JMA* 1.1: 9–28.

White, L. 1962. *Medieval Technology and Social Change*. Oxford: Oxford University Press.

Whitewright, J. 2008. *Technological Change in the Ancient World: The invention of the lateen sail*. PhD thesis. University of Southampton.

Whitewright, J. 2009. The Mediterranean Lateen Sail in Late Antiquity, *IJNA* 38.1: 97–104.

Williams, J. and Brown, N. 1999. *An Archaeological Research Framework for the Greater Thames Estuary*. Chelmsford: English Heritage, Kent CC., Essex CC. and Thames Estuary Partnership.

Williamson, J. A. 1941. *Sir John Hawkins*. Oxford: Oxford University Press.

Wingood, A. J. 1982. Sea Venture. An interim report on an early 17th century shipwreck lost in 1609. *IJNA* 11.4: 333–347.

Wingood, A. J. 1986. Sea Venture Second interim report – Part 2: the artefacts. *IJNA* 15.2: 149–159.

Wingood, A. J., Wingood, M. and Adams, J. 1986. *Sea Venture: The Tempest Wreck*. Hamilton: Island Press.

Witsen, N. 1690. *Architectura Navalis et Regimen Nauticum. Ofte Aaloude en Hedendaagsche Scheepsbouw en bestier*. Amsterdam.

Wright, E. 1990. *The Ferriby Boats. Seacraft of the Bronze Age*. London: Routledge.

Wright, L. B. 1964. *A voyage to Virginia in 1609*. Charlottesville: University Press of Virginia.

Wylie, A. 1989. Matters of fact and matters of interest. In S. Shennan (ed.) *Archaeological approaches to cultural identity*. One World Archaeology – 10. London: Unwin Hyman.

Zettersten, A. 1890. *Svenska Flottans Historia I*, 1522–1634. Stockholm. (Revised 1942. Malmö: Allhems Förlag)

Åkerlund, H. 1951. *Fartygsfynden i den Forna Hamnen i Kalmar*. Stockholm: Sjöhistoriska Samfundet.

Manuscript sources

Anthony Anthony. 1546. *The Anthony Roll*. Pepysian Library MS 2991, Magdalene College, Cambridge.

Anon. *c.* 1600. '*Newton manuscript*' Cambridge University Library MSS Add 4005 Part 12. (see Barker, R. 1994).

Anon. *c.* 1625? Scott Collection MS 798. Royal Institute of Naval Architects. London.

Anon. *c.* 1620. (John Wells?). Admiralty Library MSS 9. London. (see Salisbury and Anderson 1958).

Baker, Mathew. *Fragments of Ancient English Shipwrightry*. Pepysian Library MS 2820. Magdalene College, Cambridge. (see Barker, R. 1986).

Borough, William. C. 1600. *Of proportions in building of Shipping*. PRO State Papers 12-243-285.

Deane, Sir Anthony. 1670. '*Doctrine*'. Pepysian Library MS 2910. Magdalene College, Cambridge. See also Lavery 1981.

Renzel, Clemens. *Berättilse om Konung Göstaffz Historia*. Royal Library, Stockholm.

Swart, Peder. 1562. *Konung Gustaf I's krönika*. Royal Library, Stockholm.

Timbotta (Georgio Timbotta de Modon) *c.* 1445. *Libro*. British Library, Cotton MS Titus A 26 (See: Anderson, R. C. 1925).

Index

Page numbers in *italics* denote illustrations. The letter n after a page number indicates that the reference will be found in a note.